W9-DIS-757

Reinventing
the Business

THE FREE PRESS
New York   London   Toronto   Sydney   Tokyo   Singapore

Reinventing the Business

Preparing Today's Enterprise for Tomorrow's Technology

ROY L. HARMON

Foreword by Leroy D. Peterson

THE FREE PRESS
A Division of Simon & Schuster Inc.
1230 Avenue of the Americas
New York, NY 10020

Designed by Carla Bolte

Manufactured in the United States of America

10 9 8 7 6 5 4 3 2 1

Library of Congress Cataloging-in-Publication Data

Harmon, Roy L.
    Reinventing the business: preparing today's enterprise for
tomorrow's technology/Roy L. Harmon: foreword by Leroy D.
Peterson
        p.   cm.
    Includes bibliographical references and index.
    ISBN 0–684–82301–2
    1. Reengineering (Management)   2. Organizational change—
Management.   I. Title.
    HD58.87.H37   1996
    658.4′063—dc20   95–40874
                                            CIP

ISBN   0–684–82301–2

Dedicated, with love, to my wife Margarete—
the light of my life—
and to Rita, Diane, Roy III, and Ann, with love
and regrets for all the time lost to business.

CONTENTS

FOREWORD

Opportunities for enterprises to make significant improvements in productivity, customer service, and quality have never been better. Computer, telecommunication, electronic, and automation technologies are advancing faster than our abilities to keep pace, challenging every organization to cast off outdated methods of operations, outmoded products, and old-fashioned services by bold new initiatives that will transform their companies and even entire industries. Progress need no longer be hampered by the natural resistance to change that occurs at all levels of our organizations. Our change management specialists better understand the science of winning the enthusiastic participation of people whose natural resistance to change can be overcome by careful attention to the crafting of people-oriented processes in new organization structures designed to empower them to achieve outstanding performance. Thus, by linking modern technology, creative reinvention agents, and empowered people working in reengineered processes connected to our customers and our suppliers, previously unimaginable goals can now be attained.

The author and I, who share experiences over almost three decades, have experienced few of the reengineering failures that are commonly the subject of innumerable books and articles. We bring to every project a simple but powerful commitment to identify the 10 percent of the processes that, when reinvented, will produce 90 percent of the potential for improvement. Thus, progress is usually funded by reduced costs and revenue gains on a pay-as-you-go basis. This belies the widely held view that significant investment must be made—thereby reducing short-term profitability—in order to fund long-term improvements. We share a commitment to our clients to focus on fast-moving, hard-hitting initiatives that produce early results.

However, the completion of a reinvention project has never yet signaled the end of the process of transformation and the achievement of perfection. In fact, failure to recognize that improvement is always possible is one of the reasons that those too close to a process often become incapable of seeing new opportunities. A 1995 Andersen Consulting study of lean manufacturing practices in seventy-one automotive component factories in nine countries found thirteen that were clearly world class on the basis of both outstanding quality and productivity achievements. Plants in the United Kingdom were initially quite pleased to have raised their productivity 30 percent from the level reported in an earlier, 1992 study. The gain was achieved by a concentration on reengineering coupled with a 25 percent increase in sales volume. As a result, the plants' managements were sure they had closed the gap with Japanese competitors who had far higher productivity in the 1992 study. What a shock for the United Kingdom factories—and those in other countries—to learn that their Japanese competitors had attained a 38 percent productivity increase in the same period, during which their production volume plunged 18 percent! The international quality and productivity war of competition will never see an armistice, although there is a danger that producers in some countries or regions will be forced to surrender if they fail to arm themselves for continuous warfare. The armaments needed, globally, are the tried and tested factors behind every reinvention or reengineering success story.

Successful major improvement initiatives share the common characteristics of personnel commitment and improvement methodology. First and foremost, leading-edge enterprises all share one common trait. They are managed at the top by bold and imaginative leaders who are committed to keeping their operations in the forefront of their industry. Importantly, they convey a sense of urgency—a need for change—to their organizations. They set specific, measurable improvement goals of almost unimaginable magnitude. And they insist on tracking performance against those goals, expecting their personnel to stretch themselves to attain even better results. Chief among these goals is a new, revitalized emphasis on the customer as king. For unless the enterprise's service and product are superior and win the customer's loyalty, all other measures of improvement will be of little avail.

Next to its customers, the enterprise's own people are its most important asset. Every writer and consultant must, by rote, admonish executives to focus on and improve their own core competencies. To give the concept teeth, however, executives must place far more emphasis on the career-long betterment of the core skills of their *people* through education and training. We have found that the power of ongoing cross-training of personnel in multiple business functions produces the most valuable employees, and that multifunctional process design is the reengineering principle that automatically supports personnel in attaining cross-functional skills.

Today's business rage, benchmarking, idealizes the identification of "best practices." And, indeed, many executives with whom we work ask us to compare their companies with other enterprises, including those of their competitors. In fact, the executives of our most successful clients already possess expert knowledge of their industry. For years they have studied information available through industry trade associations and obtained from mutual customers and financial reports, to name a few readily available sources. However, to set goals and to strive to adopt the same "best practices" as competitors, or even those of other industries with even better processes, may be a formula for failure. Those who merely copy today's "best" will risk losing ground to competitors wise enough to realize that the "best practice" enterprises must now be working on even "better practices." Thus, bold, imaginative executives must demand of their business advisors and staffs that their business be the one to leapfrog beyond the goals of yesterday to the strategies of tomorrow. To do so requires discarding conventional wisdom, amassed in career-long experience in a single company or industry, and the opportunity-recognition blindness caused by the success of being the industry leader. For example, German companies reacted quite negatively and defensively to the automotive study mentioned above. They found it offensive that the study identified three world-class component plants in France, two in Spain, and none in Germany. It seemed inconceivable to them that they could have been surpassed by competitors whose productivity and quality had previously always been inferior to theirs. They had to recognize the urgent need to cast aside their complacency and go to work on aggressive new reengineering or transformation initiatives! History is no guarantee of success in today's market. Many second-tier companies are those working hardest to overtake their industry's leaders. In far too many of the "best" companies managements and employees are satisfied with the status quo, making them the most difficult to work with on projects involving process reengineering. Every enterprise's management need to keep in mind, when comparing their business to their competition, that the race never ends, and today's winners are far too often tomorrow's losers.

The author and I share recognition of the most prevalent problem in industry—failure of enterprises to implement sound, well-defined strategies. Most are too timid to change from outmoded, functional departments to the modern cross-functional customer- or product-oriented organizations that epitomize the best of smaller, less bureaucratic, highly service-oriented businesses-in-a-business. Far too many companies are clinging to conventional big-company practices, and continue to build centralized and functional organizations with the incredibly complex systems and policies they engender. What companies need, more than anything, are simpler, more agile organizations and processes. Establishing them also permits their support systems and operating procedures to become radically simpler, lower-cost, and higher-quality performers.

We hope that readers will look beyond their own industries. They will discover opportunities for reinvention that are not yet commonly recognized within their own fields. One important aspect of business today, a topic discussed in this book, is the need for strategic partnering of companies in diverse industries. Such partnering makes possible the sharing of uncommon core competencies in order to achieve results of magnificent scope and technological complexity that no single partner could finance or master. Some chapters of this book will give readers some basic understanding of other industries and their future potentials. Readers involved in product industries, including retailing, manufacturing, and distribution, should readily recognize the need to partner with their pipelines of suppliers and customers. They will find that chapters 1 through 4 address issues related to these potential partners. Cutting the time required to flow products through the pipeline, lowering every partner's operating costs, and increasing quality will be vital to the success and ultimate survival of all of the partners!

Underlying the future of all other business processes, services, and products is the need to productively utilize state-of-the-art computer and telecommunications technology. This technology has been evolving much more rapidly than any other and much faster than the reinvention of business processes. Enterprises must take care to avoid the application of the latest technology to outmoded business processes and organization structure. To do so will waste development and operating costs at an even faster rate than in the past. On the other hand, new technology will create opportunities for significant new business processes not possible with present technology. Management must aggressively search for these breakthrough technologies that will move their companies to the next level.

Those looking for magic bullets to solve their business problems or to create new business strategies will be disappointed to find that the author offers no simplistic solutions. The real keys to success have always been hard work, dedication, and inventiveness, and they will continue to be in the future. Good luck on your journey on the road to reinventing your business.

—Leroy "Pete" Peterson
Managing Partner—Products Industry
Andersen Consulting

PREFACE

Not a single enterprise's executives should fail to view its future as anything less than one filled with revolutionary change. The challenge for executives and their managers is not only to be the change agents responsible for revolutionary improvements in products, processes, quality, and service—improvements made by reengineering existing operations and organizations, a major theme of this book. They must also ensure that their businesses survive and flourish in the longer term. In many instances their operations are on the brink of either cataclysmic revision and growth, or extinction. Recognition of the tides of current change, recent trends, and emerging technologies is not enough to predict the outcome. Visions of the future, incorporating imaginative assumptions concerning inventions not yet conceived, are needed. Developing these predictions is not only practical but can also immediately set the stage for initiating business changes to improve current operating results while laying the groundwork for exciting new and reengineered operations.

HOW TO USE THE BOOK

This book is structured to serve the purposes of various individuals in various industries and functions. Therefore, chapters are organized primarily by industry, as follows.

Chapter

Those more interested in specific topics such as products or industry segments ("telephone" or "hospitals") or references to specific companies are encouraged to use the book's extensive index. However, those who limit their reading to their own industry may be making a mistake. More and more enterprises are finding that other companies in their own industry are *not* the best in certain processes. A hospital, for example, might find that the accounts receivable practices in the hotel business are among the best of all industries. Further, executives are finding more and more reasons to form strategic alliances across industry lines. For these reasons, many readers will benefit from understanding some of the present and future opportunities of a variety of industries.

Some chapters contain topics of broad interest to several industries. For example, purchasing transformation is discussed extensively in chapter 4, "Reinventing Production and Logistics," while modern payment methods are covered in chapter 7, "Reinventing Financial Services." Cooperative intra- and interindustry business ventures are another topic which should be of interest across industries. They are discussed in chapter 4, under the heading "Strategic Alliances: Buy Talent, Spread Risk." These general topics should not be overlooked by any executive, regardless of industry affiliation.

Some chapters address subjects of interest to multiple industries, although examples cited may relate to one specific business. Recent and future reengineering and transformational advances in some industries will lead to corresponding changes in others, both private and public. For example, offices are beginning to undergo both evolutionary and revolutionary transformation to catch up to modern technology. Therefore, every executive and manager should find chapter 3, "Reinventing the Office: Layout, Organization, and Location," of great value. Thus, although readers may choose to start by reading a chapter pertaining to the industry most closely related to their own, ultimately they will find it rewarding to ultimately read all. Chapters in which some sections have general applicability across industries include the following.

Chapter

1   Management Perspective: Strategies and Visions
3   Reinventing the Office: Layout, Organization, and Location
5   Reinventing Computing: Will Big Brother Be Watching You?
8   Reinventing Education: The School at Home
10 Strategic Fundamentals
11 Reinventing the World: Distant Visions
12 Conclusion

I have evaluated and ranked the contents of the book according to my perception of their general importance, in terms of understanding both the immediate tactics and strategies which enterprises should consider as well as their probable futures. Chapter 2 deals with the retail business, the industry that delivers the single largest volume of tangible products to consumers and is supplied by manufacturing, the largest employer in the economically developed nations, after government and the service industry. Chapter 4, "Reinventing Production and Distribution," with its extremely important messages related to procurement and strategic alliances, should also be of high priority. Chapter 5 focuses on present computer technological issues that many will be able to easily accept, because most businesspeople already see the computer technology as the dawning of a new age in which they will witness the transformation of their operations.

The author anticipates that some computer technology topics and predictions will be less readily acceptable to many. For example, chapter 5 plunges into more controversial areas such as "big brother" computer data bases. The inevitable disappearance of printed paper from every aspect of business and private life is a controversial theme. However, there is logical reason to expect this revolution to take place because "electronic paper" is already helping to slash operating costs and streamline the delivery of goods and services. (The chapter's subsection, "Electronic Paper: A Step Toward the Paperless Future," expands upon this topic.)

Education and training, both in the formative years and throughout one's lifetime are also on the verge of transformation. Quantum improvements in the quality of education will vastly improve the value of employees to their enterprises (see chapter 8's subsection, "Reinventing Training: Virtual Workplace Reality"). Enterprises must, however, utilize new training technology for their own product- and process-specific jobs. To do so will have immense benefits, not only in lowering the cost of job-specific training, but also in gaining a flexible work force trained in a variety of the enterprise's processes. These cross-trained individuals will be able to move easily from one work assignment to another as work peaks in one area and declines in another.

Strategic fundamentals of short-term business reinvention and longer-term enterprise visioning, common to all enterprises, are the topics of chapter 10. The basics of reengineered operations, such as the extremely important reorganization of any enterprise into small businesses-within-a-business are discussed in part of this chapter 10's subsection, "Focus: Small Business Is Best." Revolutionary futuristic practices, such as those that will ultimately level demand peaks and valleys are also proposed in the subsection "Seasonal and Day-of-the-Week Demand Peaks: Level Them." Some of these topics are covered in greater detail in my previous books, while others are long-term changes which executives may find interesting but for which they will see no practical application in the foreseeable future. Appendix 3, which lists the subheadings for all chapters, might also be helpful in facilitating the identification of subjects with cross-industry interest.

Executives should be sure to read the executive ("zinger") checklists, near the beginning of most chapters. Each of these zinger lists highlights the most important messages detailed later in the chapter. The zingers are intended as management checklists, pinpointing some of the vital weapons in the arsenals with which superior enterprises, including public operations, can win competitive advantage in the twenty-first century.

Many executives and managers want testimony that the techniques described in this and other books have worked in their industries and countries. My previous books included appendices, "The Achievers" and "The New Achievers," that identified numerous companies internationally in which Andersen Consulting—the firm to which I am an exclusive consultant—played a major role in achieving results. Their achievements, expressed in percentages of improvement, are documented in the appendices. This book is a similar "Achievers" appendix which contains sections for various industries such as health care, financial services, manufacturing, and retailing.

The subjects of chapter 11 are pretty "far out," in terms of their potential for short-term business improvement. My predictions about life as far as one hundred years in the future may be extremely controversial. Leroy Peterson, for example, labels as science fiction the concept of domed communities and the decline of the automobile and growth of neighborhood and intercity mass transit (see the subsection "Automotive Transportation: Going the Way of the Horse and Buggy"). Nevertheless, even the prospect of domed communities (whether or not they ultimately become commonplace) has short-term messages to some industries. For example, I expect that a dome material, whether clear or translucent, will be fabricated from a photovoltaic material. Such a material is likely to be economically feasible in the next few years, thus will soon be available for sheathing homes and business and government buildings, providing them a source of most of their energy requirements. This development will soon begin to transform the utility industries and the photovoltaic material manufacturing business will be a huge new growth industry (see chapter 11's subsection "Home Power Generation: Precursor of the Domed City"). Executives with no interest in visions of the "far-out" future and possible bridges back to shorter-term strategies that may be suggested by these visions might choose to omit reading the chapter. Others interested in far-out visions but with their own strong opinions (such as Leroy Peterson's prediction that mass transportation will disappear and automobiles will be replaced by personal airmobiles) might find my own conflicting forecasts offensive. I recommend that these readers spend only a limited amount of time on far-out visioning—the primary purpose of which is to free their mind-sets from the shackles of their own and their enterprise's experience. It is then a bonus if their vision leads to transformational changes in their strategies.

My previous books, *Reinventing the Factory, Reinventing the Factory II,* and *Reinventing the Warehouse,* are frequently footnoted in *this* book and are sources of definitions and background for subject matter not covered or detailed here. Appendix 2 minimizes the clutter that numerous detailed footnote references to these sources might cause by centralizing the cross references. Those reading only a few chapters of *this* book may wish to first read related portions of the prior books for important background material, and appendix 2 is organized to facilitate cross-referencing between the books.

The remainder of this preface addresses six topics. First, I take special pleasure in "kicking sacred cows"—identifying weaknesses in "conventional wisdom" and arguing an opposing view. Second, many such impatient, well-meaning, action-oriented businessmen whipsaw their organizations from one initiative to another in reaction to the latest "fad of the month." Companies need far-reaching, visionary strategies which they can pursue to their conclusion, modifying their initiatives only when their long-term objectives change. The pay-as-you go approach, which demands fast payback for the investment in improvement is the enabling feature of projects that ensures continuous progress, even while the business weathers periodic business downturns.

Visions and strategies are the third important subject because, in almost four decades of work all around the globe, I have found the almost universal lack of longer-range business foresight to be one of the strategic elements most lacking and the cause of most business failures and market share losses. Therefore, this overview subject should be of vital interest.

My fourth and fifth messages address two essential elements of enterprise initiatives that have achieved resounding success. It is no secret, when groups of executives meet and discuss their experiences, that many have two problems in common. First, although they themselves are strong supporters of new ways of operating, individuals in their organizations *resist change*. As I have written previously, if this is permitted to hamper progress, the fault lies with management, not with resistant individuals. Thus, it is the responsibility of executives to overcome resistance! Next, all too many company executives find that people in their organizations seem to be incapable of accepting or developing revolutionary or transformational ideas for their operations or products. One of their most basic mistakes is failure to realize that people involved in an operation will be the last to see that past assumptions can be discarded. Therefore, the best companies often turn to *outside agents of change* to provide the independent, unbiased, experienced personnel needed to bring imaginative but realistic creativity to the process.

The final preface topic, client-server (computer) technology, high-lights one of my major concerns: technicians who speak a unique language—technobabble! The world of the future will be centered on the use of computers in every imaginable aspect of business, public, and private life. Therefore, executives and managers must understand and apply computerization to their products and processes. To do so, technicians will need to learn standard business language, not force executives and others to learn their technobabble.

KICKING SACRED COWS

I want to forewarn readers that I find pundits who blindly accept the latest popular dogma and fail to challenge their audience on the basis of clear logic to be pathetic. One example of fuzzy but popular dogma holds that modern companies must export globally in order to survive. For example, Frederick Webster, in his excellent book, has written, "The *new* marketing concept is required for today's global customer who can choose among a much larger variety of products and services from producers located throughout the world."[1] For the governments of the world to accept the premise that their companies must perpetually chase cheap foreign labor by producing in and exporting from developing nations would be to doom the industrially developed economies to sink to the levels of deprived nations, while perpetuating unjust economic conditions in disadvantaged countries. I believe that the *hours* (thus real value) required to provide goods and services can be improved to rough parity in every country. Developing nations can and must improve their infrastructures, a critical element that will enable them to move into the ranks of industrially developed countries. Further, all citizens of the world will have access to the best educational programs available worldwide through national and international educational superhighways (see chapter 8, "Reinventing Education: The School at Home"), thus removing inadequate education as a barrier to industrial progress. As soon as any nation is able to function as an industrially developed country it would be nonsensical for it to import goods and services. The transportation and communi-

---

1. Frederick E. Webster, Jr. *Market-Driven Management: Using the New Marketing Concept to Create a Customer-Oriented Company* (New York: Wiley, 1994), p. 249.

cations required to do so would cause their costs to be greater than that of a local provider.

International companies must pursue long-range visions and strategies of local clusters of producers and services, while executing short-term tactics to survive vis-à-vis competitors by chasing low-cost foreign production. Truly global companies, therefore, may ultimately produce and sell in foreign markets. But they will lose out to competitors who produce and sell locally if they are dependent on remote production facilities and must bear the higher costs of transport. Because individual countries, or regional groups of small countries, will be able to most economically produce and distribute the manufactured items they consume, international trade will eventually shrink to consist of raw materials, agricultural products, and energy (as long as raw material and nonreplenishable energy last or until competitive new, replenishable alternatives are found). For resource-poor countries, this leaves only one potential export product possibility—brain products. (In 1987, I visited Sony and discussed the future dilemma that Japan would face in this regard. I was bemused by Sony's coincidental acquisition of Columbia Pictures the following year—egotistically but unrealistically imagining that my presentation might have triggered the event. Sadly, the acquisition proved to be a disaster, probably due in large part to the lack of English fluency on the part of Sony's executives which made it impossible for them to take direct control of the operation.[2] Another of my "far-out" predictions is that the Japanese are likely to be the first non-English-speaking nation to convert their national language to English, solving this weakness (see chapter 10, "Strategic Fundamentals," subsection "Universal Business Language: New English"). And even if such a prediction has little chance of coming about in the lifetimes of our children, the fact remains that *better* English language training is a high-priority need for Japan, one that will make the language education industry one of *its* most important growth areas.

Brain products such as manuscripts, movies, computer software, and new product designs are examples of another form of manufactured products. And with the advent of the radically reduced average

---

2. Laura Landro, David P. Hamilton, and Michael Williams, "Sony Finally Admits Billion-Dollar Mistake: Its Messed-Up Studio," *Wall Street Journal,* November 18, 1994.

work year of the twenty-first century, every country will have more than enough resources to meet their own need. Thus, resource poor nations will undoubtedly see giant new waves of emigration into the countries blessed with abundant raw materials and agriculture.

Another sacred cow that cries out for kicking is the naive notion that every producer should slavishly pursue product customization (chapter 4, "Reinventing Production and Logistics," subsection "Standard or Custom: What Is the Cost?" elaborates on this subject). Webster, for one, has written, "We have moved from the age of mass production to mass customization, made possible by the impact of information technology on order entry, product design, production scheduling, manufacturing, inventory management, product delivery and distribution, and customer feedback."[3] However, even cursory review of this list of areas in which customization effort is required quite clearly reveals that no amount of information technology will eliminate the operations added when a decision is made to change from production of a standard product to a customized one. Proponents of customized products have some rational basis for their belief. Customers *do* want choices, especially when these choices affect styling (furniture) and affordability (bare-bones automobiles for new graduates and newlyweds). Nevertheless, the cost of custom production will never be as low as that of mass production. Supplied with a cookie-cutter, for example, anyone can produce dozens of gingerbread men in minutes. Take away the cookie cutter and impose rules that require a unique design be created for each cookie. This would require a unique cutter to be made, probably by creating a unique computer program to control a free-form cutting machine used to cut out each unique shape, or cookie production would require armies of artisans to manually shape each unique cookie. Either way, hundreds of dollars and hours of labor will be added to the costs of design, tooling, and production.

A more elaborate case, the automobile color option, is just one of numerous custom specifications the customer can order. Automobile manufacturers have the equipment required to provide a *finite* number of colors, but as any of them will tell us, the investment required and operating costs of facilities capable of supplying multiple colors,

---

3. Webster, *Market-Driven Management,* pp. 258–59.

while not major when spread over thousands of cars, are more than they would be if all cars were painted black. And if even more colors than currently available were to be offered, the average costs of painting each color would rise.

Clearly, the vast majority of the earth's population will not begin to match the quality of life of the industrially developed nations by developing facilities designed for custom products. The hope of less-developed nations for the better life rests on beginning a new industrial age in which low-cost, standard products will be affordable for the masses. Eventually, when standards of living have risen to levels much closer to those of the highly industrialized nations, it will begin to make sense to expand the number of products and options available.

FADS OF THE MONTH

It is my fervent (but undoubtedly vain) wish that the latest buzz-words-of-the-month, "reengineering" or "business process reengineering," will disappear from routine business conversation—just as their hundreds of faddish predecessors have—and that they will not be replaced by new and equally short-lived crazes. In the past two decades, an explosion of books with "Just-in-Time" in the title was fueled by Japanese manufacturers' remarkable achievements. Today, "reengineering" is putting a new face on most of the methods and organization forms that the best Japanese and Western counterparts companies have already practiced for one or more decades.[4]

We consultants and authors are guilty of perpetuating the largely nonsensical buzzword creation, with good reason. If that which one writes about, and coins a description for, happens to catch the businessman's imagination, book sales and consulting engagements skyrocket. Unfortunately, there is little in the world that is really new. (I gleefully challenge the authors of all of the recently popular catchphrases to point out any single aspect of their works that has not pre-

---

4. Three examples of recent, valuable books with "reengineering" in the title are Daniel Morris and Joel Brandon, *Re-engineering Your Business* (New York: McGraw-Hill, 1993); Michael Hammer and James Champy, *Re-engineering the Corporation: A Manifesto for Business Revolution* (New York: Harper Business, 1993); and Henry J. Johansson et al., *Business Process Reengineering: Breakpoint Strategies for Market Dominance* (New York: Wiley, 1993).

viously been an integral part of some earlier work. In fact, most "new" publications, valuable as they may be, incorporate virtually all of the best of their predecessors.) Nevertheless, quantum improvements are being achieved through the application of established methods, and implementation of these tried and proven techniques should be the ongoing goal of every organization and all of its personnel. The continuous creation of new fads and buzzwords detracts from the most important message to business and government—99 percent of success comes from hard, routine work on improving *every* aspect of operations and adopting radically different methods that have long been used by someone else, and only 1 percent comes from inventing entirely new practices.

VISIONS AND STRATEGIES

My visions of the future, like any prophecy, cannot anticipate all of the enabling future inventions that are bound to change the very essence of mankind. It seems inevitable to me that new sources of boundless energy will be found, that disease will be conquered, and poverty and despotism eliminated. Unimaginable inventions should be imaginable, but I am no more prepared to anticipate truly inconceivable developments (beam me up to the spaceship, Scottie) than the average reader. Therefore, the visions of this book are almost all bounded by present or currently emerging technology and unshakable blind faith in the ability of mankind to apply its existing intelligence to the solution of relatively simple (except for their political nature) social problems such as unemployment and crime—subjects included in chapter 9, "Reinventing Government: Modern, Simpler, and Better."

It would be a mistake for any private or government enterprise to delay the development of its vision. The pace of sweeping change is now and, in recent centuries, has always been fast-paced. Revolutionary changes occur no less frequently than every ten to twenty years. The first future changes to occur, such as the predictable obsolescence of the use of paper, are imminent and will affect every aspect of business. However, to focus solely on the future would endanger current enterprise operations. The predominant business purpose must continue to be to operate for maximum cost effectiveness and highest quality and customer service *this fiscal year.*

Examination of a future vision would be a waste of valuable management time if it were to be undertaken without planning to use the results of the effort to launch initiatives of immediate payback. Thus, industry and government need a combination of visionary and hardheaded businessmen. The development of business skills is a well-defined field of tangible science and more abstract interpersonal skills. The less well-defined, nonscientific practice of visioning can be organized and executed methodically, with imagination an important ingredient. The inventors among us, given an improved business vision, can then liberate their unique talents from the shackles of unimaginative business restraints and thus accelerate the pace of progress. In doing so, in their lifetimes, our descendants will witness even greater transformation of mankind than our grandparents and parents.

Many will find any visionary technological advance and sociological change to be inconceivable, based on their natural, understandable inability to cast off the shackles of experience in the world of today. In particular I expect some readers to find the notion of the decline of retail establishments and middlemen and the rise of electronic home shopping to be inconceivable (see chapter 2, "Reinventing Retailing: The Living Room Store," subsection "Virtually Real Home Shopping"). Understanding the probability of this change occurring relies on accepting several other premises such as the virtual reality computer technology that will be able to put the shopper (and the shopper's companion) in a "virtually real" retail environment, without leaving the future's home system module. Home delivery improvement, such as the controversial pneumatic or magnetic levitation home-delivery tube systems that deliver purchases at nominal delivery cost within minutes, is another such premise (see chapter 11, "Reinventing the World: Distant Visions," subsection "The Utility and Delivery Conduit"). Among readers who view the futuristic delivery conduit as too improbable or too "far-out," few will argue that the home delivery business, currently dominated by UPS, is one of explosive growth. Furthermore, as the volume of such deliveries increases, the cost of the delivery service will decrease because the length of delivery routes will become shorter as the density of deliveries in each area becomes greater. As a result, low-cost, convenient, and frequent home delivery will become continuously more practical.

I recommend that skeptics place themselves in the role of a late-nineteenth-century citizen to whom the suggestion is made that the horse will virtually disappear from everyday life and that the automobile and other gas-fueled machines will replace it. Following are what could have been the citizen's natural experience-bound reactions.

1. Horses eat hay, corn, and grass, all of which are in abundant supply, and are virtually free to farmers. New gasoline-fueled machines would require paying for fuel, raising the cost of transport and farm produce. Further, there are very few oil wells, nowhere near enough to fuel enough machines to replace the horse. Nor has anyone found enough petroleum to justify developing new wells. And even if they did, the wells would soon be pumped dry, requiring a return to the horse.
2. Gasoline is highly flammable, thus extremely dangerous. And the smell and smoke of the machines is intolerable, as is the incredible noise. It is impossible to conceive of any devices that would muffle the noise and reduce emissions.
3. Horses pull our buggies and sleighs over muddy and snow-covered roads with comparative ease, while the gas-powered machines become mired after the least amount of rain or snow. Those who envision the paving of streets and roads are just impractical dreamers. The expense would be far too great, so we'll just have to continue to live with the inconvenience of dust and mud.
4. Riding horses can be thrilling. The joy of racing at top speed through field and forest atop a horse could never be duplicated by machines that are only practical when operated on level streets and roads. Those who prate of two-wheel bicycles driven by gas engines and rough terrain vehicles are unrealistic visionaries.

The purpose of this example is simply to encourage readers to cast off the mind-shackling bonds of experience and observation, and to free their intelligence-based imaginations to develop practical future scenarios and to then project backward to develop strategies for reinventing today's business processes and tactics for immediate business operations improvement. For, as Herman Maynard and Susan Mehrtens eloquently wrote, "our society, facing momentous challenges in the closing years of the twentieth century, needs visions of the future so attractive, inspiring, and compelling that people will shift from their current mind-set of focusing on immediate crises to one of eagerly anticipating the future—a future where the health and well-being of the earth and its inhabitants is secure."[5]

I hope, in some small way, to lay the foundation for one of several possible visions. However, it would surprise me if the visions of others would not emerge as much more imaginative and, above all, be eventually proven in the only way possible, by comparison to actual future developments. Thus, the real intent of the future-vision portions of this book is not to accurately foretell the future, but to spur those more capable of doing so to begin, and to motivate the movers and shakers in industry and government to apply the lessons of these visions to achieve immediate results.

OVERCOMING CHANGE RESISTANCE: DO IT RIGHT!

I had some pretty shocking ideas about overcoming change resistance in my previous book.[6] For example, I wrote that middle managers, not their employees, were the only ones that usually resist change. And that executive management too often fails its responsibility to move implacable change resisters to other positions, and even out the door! Those who abhor the thought of such cruel treatment might be comforted to know that the I suggest humane ways to accomplish what is best for the enterprise's success only after an exhaustive attempt to convert the resister. Further, I ardently believe and operate on the principle of working with everyone involved and winning their buy-in to the new system by incorporating every good idea that comes from the intense involvement by all concerned.

Perhaps I overlooked another category of change resister in my previous book. Charles Winslow and William Bramer identified this category when they recounted the following response to a U.S. bank's reengineering project. The bank's team had as its goal the improvement of trust fund correspondence management. They achieved this by electronically scanning and filing correspondence, thus enabling customer service representatives to have fast, easy computer access to past mail. "In the initial phase of the project, designers noticed a (for

---

5. Herman Bryant Maynard, Jr., and Susan E. Mehrtens, *The Fourth Wave: Business in the 21st Century* (San Francisco: Berrett-Koehler, 1993), p. 1.

6. For reference to more about overcoming resistance to change, see appendix 2.

them) strange phenomenon. Workers were calling up the scanned image of letters on their computers, printing out a paper copy on their printers, and storing the copy in their desks."[7]

Time and time again, I have noted these types of "change resistance" but have almost always found that the fault is not that of the system's users, but a flaw in the system design, in this case making it more productive for the worker to store the paper copy than to spend valuable time trying to access it on the computer and then waste more time trying to find specific words, because the small monitor screen didn't enable the user to scan an entire page at once or riff through dozens of pages in a second. System users almost always do what makes sense, in order to do their jobs with the least amount of waste effort. Unfortunately, computer system designers virtually never study, from a time and motion standpoint, both the old and new systems operations in order to ensure that the new one in fact reduces the work required and makes it simpler! Technicians, all to often, deem their efforts to be successful when the *computer* operates as designed, and pay far too little attention to the results in terms of the system user's productivity. Subjecting every new system to this user satisfaction test would ensure its almost automatic acceptance and avoid erroneous labeling of user dissatisfaction as change resistance.

OUTSIDERS: THE BEST AGENTS OF CHANGE

The best executives will turn to outside agents of change for help in developing their visions and strategies, even though they and their executive team are outstanding experts *in their own industries.* Nor will they choose outside experts only from their own industry for the key visioning assistance role, because entire industries, such as health care (chapter 6, "Reinventing Health Care: Cure the Cause, Not the Symptom"), suffer from the inbred inability to recognize the insanity of continuing nonsensical practices based on the fuzzy, faulty logic evolved in the industry over decades or even centuries. Specialists in every industry usually value only the advice of other specialists in their own fields, although these specialists rarely invent revolutionary

---

7. Charles D. Winslow and William L. Bramer, *Future Work: Putting Knowledge to Work in the Knowledge Economy* (New York: Free Press, 1994), p. 99.

change to fundamental practices. *Industry specialists are experts in present practices and are too often among the fiercest resisters of change!* In fact, in the medical field, which is largely considered to be predominantly one of science, black art (such as the overzealous radical mastectomy practices of the past, and continuing widespread caesarian delivery of doubtful necessity) all too often seems rife.

For almost two decades I have chided Western enterprises for beginning their pursuit of competitive practices with W. Edwards Deming's advice to the Japanese, generally believed to be primarily related to statistical quality control. What fools, to start where the Japanese started more than forty years ago—rather than to leap over four decades to where state-of-the-art product and process are today! However, to base an enterprise's goals on other companies' "best practices" or "benchmarks" of today is a formula for long-term failure. Today's industry leaders are pursuing earthshaking strategies based on visions that will transform their industries and will leave shortsighted competitors eating their dust (if the competitors even survive). For example, James Collins's and Jerry Porras's review of successful, visionary companies revealed that they all pursued "Big Hairy Audacious Goals."[8]

The slowness of Western industry to leapfrog over Japanese practices of the 1970s and 1980s is not only due to the mistaken belief that the starting point and ensuing step-by-step improvement methods would need to duplicate the Japanese pathway. Bullheaded Western executives and managers for too long resisted the belief that their industries' lifetime practices could conceivably be wrong or outmoded. For example, Gary Hamel and C. K. Prahalad very effectively describe the slowness of the automotive industry to adopt "lean production" because "those principles challenged every assumption and bias of U.S. auto executives."[9] I have found that the most dramatically successful agents of change are individuals with highly honed skills in other industries and technical fields of expertise, whose minds are uncluttered with the useless baggage of erroneous conclusions and misguided practices of past generations of "authorities." Fortunately, ex-

---

8. James C. Collins and Jerry I. Porras, *Built to Last: Successful Habits of Visionary Companies* (New York: Harper Business, 1994), p. 93.

9. Gary Hamel and C. K. Prahalad, *Competing for the Future* (New Canaan, CT: Harvard Press, 1994), p. 12.

ecutives and their independent advisors need not rely solely on rein- venting their own businesses. Rather, a wealth of information is avail- able from those enterprises which have already "reengineered" their processes, introducing radical changes to successfully revolutionize their organizations, products, and services.

CLIENT-SERVER TECHNOLOGY: CLARIFYING TECHNOBABBLE

Enterprise executives, unfortunately, need to understand the relatively new world of client-server computer technology, since it holds the key to finally enabling them to unlock the fantastic productivity potential of the information superhighway. For example, William Cook details incredibly important client-server savings by Avis, the car rental com- pany. Avis cut the average car rental reservation conversation by five seconds, for a savings of one-half million dollars per year and a 50 percent reduction of the time required to train 250 new employees an- nually.[10] (Chapter 5, "Reinventing Computing: Will Big Brother Be Watching You?" explains some present and future technological ad- vances that enable companies that are reinventing processes to achieve improvements of this magnitude.)

To the information technology professional, the following overview explanation of networks may seem unprofessional, because it lacks a plethora of mystifying acronyms and "generally accepted" popular buzzwords. Few lay people, for example, will miss seeing re- peated use of "client-server," a buzzword that has cluttered almost every technical writer's output since the late 1980s or early 1990s. Exhibit P-1 may help to define the terms "network," "servers," and "clients." On the other hand, it may not.

In computerese, the word "network" refers to links between small computing and computer accessing devices and other, larger comput- ers and/or devices. These links can be intracompany as well as global. John Barry may well be the first to formally define "networked com- puting" as "meaning that computing resources can be routed around

---

10. William J. Cook, "Serving Up a New Era in Computing," *U.S. News & World Report,* Octo- ber 17, 1994.

EXHIBIT P–1
Technobabble Buzzwords

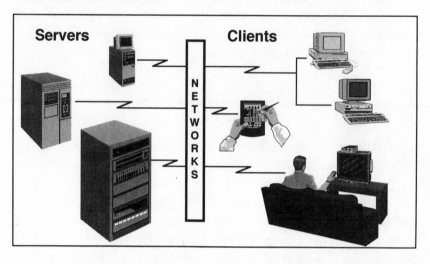

the network wherever they are needed."[11] Barry's book is an excellent source for gaining insight into the nebulous, fast-changing world of computer professionals and users and the unique technical language they use. Almost every term is subject to different interpretations, thus helping to explain why he calls this new language "Technobabble." Many, if not all, technical words bear almost no relationship to their definitions in Webster's dictionary. Further, even Barry's explanations may be difficult for the nontechnician to understand unless familiar with an array of computer manufacturer's equipment (Apollo and DEC), specialized technical terms (32 bit, networked, multi-tasking) and software (UNIX and WINDOW) as used in the following quotations. Barry explains that "certain protocol users of, for example, Apollo workstations can gain access to files on a DEC minicomputer and manipulate them as if they were running on the Apollo machines." Minicomputer is a term likely to be understood by most readers, as it generally refers to a small computer. Workstation may have less common understanding, for, as Barry writes, "Although the distinctions between 'workstation' and 'networked' high-end PCs (personal computers) is blurring, a workstation is generally consid-

---

11. John A. Barry, *Technobabble* (Cambridge, MA: MIT Press, 1991), pp. 10–11.

ered . . . to be a high performance, 32-bit, networked, multi-tasking computer system running UNIX and having a WINDOW system."

The definition of the word "server" is also ambivalent, although it generally refers to a computer at which resident data base information can be accessed and manipulated by various "client" devices. The ambivalence arises with respect to the size of the server and the fact that some of the "clients" are, themselves, computers or computing devices. Examples of "clients" in exhibit P–1 are (1) the box on the home television that enables its owner to communicate interactively with one or more "servers," (2) personal computers, and (3) hand-held personal digital assistants (PDAs).

These definitions are intended to help executives cut through the ludicrous imposition of virtually incomprehensible technical jargon to get to the meat of the important characteristics of the hardware and software that will enable enterprises to transform their processes and businesses into the futuristic operations described in this book. However, it is important to understand that although information technology is often vitally important to improving a company's processes, it is the business, not the technology, that must be the determining factor. For, as Daniel Morris and Joel Brandon wrote, "The links between re-engineering and information services may lead to the erroneous conclusion that Positioning and Re-engineering are information technology methodologies. In fact, both are business activities."[12] They go on, "Separating the concepts of computing and re-engineering is important because re-engineering projects should be the responsibility of line and executive managers, not the company's information services department." Nevertheless, almost every improved process will be computer based. Thus, computer technicians will be a critically important resource on every reinvention project team. Let us hope they go to language school and learn to speak English!

ACKNOWLEDGMENTS

In my nearly four-decade career, I have focused primarily on the front end of the logistics network (producers and their vendors), with lesser

---

12. Daniel Morris and Joel Brandon, *Re-engineering Your Business* (New York: McGraw-Hill, 1993), p. 189.

(although significant) involvement in the tail end (product warehousing and distribution). Accordingly, and in line with my belief that writers and consultants need to walk several miles in the shoes of their readers and clients, I have been heavily dependent on my colleagues' contributions to the chapters and subjects in the manuscript dealing with other industries and government. Leroy D. Peterson, my longtime colleague and friend, wrote the book's foreword and also reviewed the manuscript, contributing substantive commentary and ideas.

Carolyn Nolte, my executive assistant at Andersen Consulting's Chicago world headquarters provided every form of support in the book development, while Gregory A. Lee, previously a graphic artist in Andersen Consulting's Chicago office, coordinated the preparation of most of the book's exhibits. Greg also worked on this book's predecessors in the "Reinventing" series, helping me demonstrate an important business communication truism—that a picture is worth (at least) a thousand words.

Longtime practitioners and pioneers in designing operations and systems of the new, superior ilk are among the most important contributors. Their successful implementation of some of my wildest sounding ideas has proven, over and over, that these things work! A list of contributing colleagues, if one were included, would be extensive. However, practical space considerations dictate general recognition and thanks. Those who have contributed know who they are and that they will always live in my mind and heart.

I fervently hope the reader will find this book stimulating and even entertaining. Far more important, if I have met my objectives, readers will find at least one idea with immediate applicability to improvement of their own enterprises and one other that will completely change their industry sometime in the next century. It is of equal importance that readers consider alternatives to age-long business practices and operations as a prerequisite for discovering their own visions of the future. Undoubtedly, others will have more exciting visionary contributions, and I would enjoy hearing these ideas (via the Andersen Consulting Chicago office).

Good luck on your journey into the world of the twenty-first century!

—Roy L. Harmon

1
MANAGEMENT PERSPECTIVE
Strategies and Visions

Despite recent economic appearances to the contrary, the world is on the threshold of an exciting new era of prosperity and vastly improved quality of life. All industries as we now know them are poised on a critical fulcrum. A lean to one side will doom an enterprise to extinction, while a tilt in the opposite direction will set it in the direction necessary for its future success. Executives in threatened enterprises must, first and foremost, channel almost all of their energy into activities for improving *existing* operations. Fierce competition demands constant improvement—just to achieve short-term survival. And dividend-conscious stockholders rightly demand continuous profitability. This book is intended to provide ideas for the majority of executives whose enterprises need to focus on immediate survival and current profitability tactics. However, even companies that have far exceeded the achievement of others should not be content solely to maximize short-term operating results. As James Collins and Jerry Porras point out in their book describing some of these outstanding visionary companies, "Managers at visionary companies simply do not accept the proposition that they must choose between short-term performance or long-term success. They build first and foremost for the long term while *simultaneously* holding themselves to highly demanding short-term standards".[1] I also believe that every project initiative can be and should be structured to begin to achieve its benefits in the short term, putting development on a pay-as-you-go basis. Thus, to look upon long-term programs as drains on profitability is wrong-thinking.

Recent business and political history have amply proved, and are continuing to confirm, that monumental reinvention of office, factory, and distribution processes is a practical key with which to unlock the secret of seven-league strides towards improved quality, service, and cost. The continuous reinvention of entire process networks, starting with suppliers and ending with delivery to the ultimate consumers of goods and services is the scope of necessary initiatives if the objective is to deliver the best performance to both customers and shareholders. Further, every business, every institution, needs a new mind-set—one that accepts and even embraces radical change as a prerequisite for breakthrough improvements in operations. Timid goals and incremental improvements no longer suffice to maintain the torrid pace of competitive pressures. Companies forced to "restructure"—a fancy term meaning the cutting of conscientious armies of hard-working employees (who busily perform unnecessary work) from the payroll—have learned that the cutbacks they considered draconian were practical, achievable, and far less than the level of reduction needed. The most encouraging aspect of the recent, massive business restructurings is that the creme-de-la-creme of companies, still the best in the world, are making their own draconian changes even though many of them are still at the acme of their competitiveness. This determination to continue to excel will ensure that their competitive dominance will be sustained during the exciting last decade of the twentieth century and into the first decade of the twenty-first.

Private and public enterprises have the opportunity to make gargantuan further strides toward lowering their operations' costs and increasing the utility and value of their products while at the same time providing their customers with unheard of levels of service and quality. For almost two decades, my colleagues and I have been immersed

---

1. James C. Collins and Jerry I. Porras. *Built to Last: Successful Habits of Visionary Companies* (New York: Harper Business, 1994), p. 192.

in the process of *reinvention,* helping companies around the globe to achieve fantastically better performance. In recent years, others have given many new fad names to the process of reinvention—just-in-time, business process reengineering, total quality control, and time-based competition, to name just a few. Leading-edge companies are amazed to learn that their accomplishments of ten or twenty years ago are the same as those described by the latest catchy buzzword. Worse yet, enterprises now pursuing the same objectives will only be playing catch-up, just to find that their leading-edge competitors have again left them in their dust by virtue of having set new, higher improvement goals.

A fundamental key to successful implementation of new processes, products, and services has been our insistence that companies stretch their creativeness to limits never before imagined. Every project must start with setting goals far higher than ever before. Ambitious goals, not merely targeting achievements equal to those of other enterprises ("best practices"), are the drivers that lead superior enterprises to excel. High goals force company personnel to invent new ways of doing business and new products and services—a process that demands bringing new, unique imagination and creativity to bear. A few of the *typical* (not exceptional) ranges of goals that companies have set, and have subsequently achieved, include the following percentages of improvement.

Percent		*Percent*	
50–80	Space reduction	75–80	Changeover cost
75–95	Inventory investment	15–55	Productivity
75–95	Process time	75–80	Quality defects
50–90	Improved service	75–95	Customer response time

With this book, I intend to provide incentive to those in every conceivable industry and public enterprise to begin or continue the process of reinvention in their own operations. Examples of the recent achievements of various enterprises in several industries are chronicled in appendix 1, "The Achievers." Following are some of the outstanding, recent achievements in selected industries and enterprises.

Retailing: 59 percent reduction of stockouts, 60 percent less time required to train new employees.

Construction: 75 percent reduction in the time required for the monthly financial closing, 90 percent faster payables processing.

Government: 140 percent personnel productivity improvement, 42 percent improvement of managerial span of control.

Financial services: 100 percent improvement in data accuracy, 250 percent improvement of teller productivity, and 89 percent faster entry of new customers.

Utility: 95 percent warehouse space reduction, personnel productivity improvement, 200 percent.

Health care: 62 percent improvement of the quality of care provided, 32 percent reduction of nursing directors, 40 percent lower peak period workloads.

Distribution: 66 percent reduction of supervisory time, 50 percent warehouse space.

Manufacturing: 75 percent reduction of computer costs, 135 percent improved productivity, 60 percent gain in market share.

However, winners of many battles often lose the war. Therefore, I hope to ignite executives', managers', and associates' imaginations and inventiveness and to kindle their enthusiasm for new universes of operating strategies. Practical short- to mid-term strategies will only prove their merit after they have been subjected to the longer-term test of time. Unimaginative, shortsighted strategies are likely to fail the trial. By contrast, strategies founded on the most realistic future visions will guide bold enterprises into the winner's circle of tomorrow's industry.

THE FOUR CORNERSTONES:
A FOUNDATION FOR SUCCESS

Far too few enterprises are transforming their operations as speedily, thoroughly, and creatively as they should—if they intend to attain or maintain a position on the leading edge. A major cause of their failure to begin the transformation is that few companies' initiatives bring vital expertise to their projects in all four of the areas that must be mastered to achieve the best results. The three-pronged approach to enterprise transformation, illustrated by the trident in exhibit 1–1, identifies these four elements. The first and foremost driving force behind reinvention is that of process improvement—reinvention of the enterprise's processes (operations) and even those of its customers and suppliers. A wise blend of full-time project personnel with specific industry experience and those skilled in the reinvention of processes in *any* industry is a guarantee that the initiative will not be inhibited by people blind to improvement opportunities, based on their career-long exposure to traditional industry practices.

In office, factory, retail store, and warehouse, the most important method for reinventing processes is the reorganization of functionally organized operations into "work cells" inside smaller businesses-within-the-business. Breaking traditional functional departments apart and putting operations from several departments' (all of which work on a common process, product, or class of customers) into a single new entity—the work cell—causes quantum improvements in the elapsed time between completion of first and last operations. Typically, the time required is reduced from days and weeks down to hours or minutes. For example, the team in one work cell might enter a customer's order, configure it, check the customer's credit-worthiness, issue shipping paperwork, and ship the order all within the same day. And by operating as a small, entrepreneurial business, mountains of bureaucratic and "turf war" inefficiencies are eliminated, reducing operating costs. In fact, the ultimate form of process transformation is the complete elimination of a process. For example, matching sup-

EXHIBIT 1–1
Enterprise Transformation

plier invoices to receiving reports was a costly purchasing and accounting process that I recommended Harley-Davidson eliminate—only one of several key differences in the efficiency between Harley-Davidson and my other motorcycle client, Yamaha Motors. Closing performance gaps between it and its Japanese competitors has been instrumental in helping Harley-Davidson recapture a dominant share of its motorcycle market.

The second prong of the enterprise transformation approach illustrated on the trident is the application of the latest technology to the reengineered processes developed on the first prong. The preeminent technological expertise that must be brought to bear is computer and telecommunications know-how. The problem most enterprises face in successfully applying their technological expertise to reinvented operations is the vast morass of decades-old computer systems which have been continuously modified (patched) to incorporate new technology—without ever completely revising the process itself. As a result, most of the enterprise's technical personnel must spend the majority of their time keeping their complex, bug-prone systems operating—with little time to devote to transforming the process and replacing the computer systems. Further, the speed with which technology is advancing is so great that when systems are reinvented to take advantage of the latest hardware and software capabilities many are already out of date by the time they are put into operation. Additionally, in coming years, the speed with which existing computer systems become obsolete will only increase. Therefore, those enterprises that succeed in keeping pace with technology *and* process reinvention will need to drive their initiatives with vision-based strategies of far-reaching imagination and creativity, as illustrated by the handle of the enterprise transformation trident.

The third trident prong, people, is an equally important element of the successful approach to enterprise transformation. As John Whiteside writes, "Workplace transformation requires participants committed to action. The future does not exist as foreordained. It is created."[2] However, too many companies undertake initiatives which naively focus almost exclusively on people issues and company-wide, people-

---

2. John Whiteside, *The Phoenix Agenda: Power to Transform Your Workplace* (Essex Junction, VT: Wight, 1993), p. 292.

empowerment programs. My colleague, Leroy Peterson, calls some empowerment programs "happiness programs" and has seen them add to bloated overhead costs, thus becoming one of the major causes for the decline of many past industry leaders. This occurs because the companies, and the professional firms they engage to help them, rarely have in-depth experience in all four of the vital ingredients. Those fortunate companies with the will to excel and the internal staff and external consultants equipped to meet all four critical skills will lead their industries into the new world, but will do so mindful of maintaining profitability and limiting costs by undertaking projects of reasonable magnitude and scope. Finally, however, it continues to be an important truth that people are the most important asset a company has. Therefore, failure to include the people element in an enterprise's initiatives might well waste resources spent in pursuing new strategies and employing upgraded technology in reengineered processes.

MAGNITUDE AND SCOPE OF ALTERNATIVE INITIATIVES

Far too many executives have fallen under the spell of the siren song of too-good-to-be-true employee empowerment programs that promise to streamline, reengineer, and even transform an entire organization and its operations. It is naive to expect individual employee teams to have the expertise necessary to make changes as broad in scope as reengineering an entire process or transforming a complete business. Exhibit 1–2 illustrates the various alternative improvement initiatives a management might consider launching, and it shows the range of different project scopes. For example, one type of improvement initiative might cover a single business function, such as an accounts payable department, and would simply involve streamlining its operations to improve its speed and productivity. An initiative of greater complexity, broader scope, and significantly higher potential benefit might encompass all functions of the procurement process. For example, exhibit 1–2 depicts a project that encompasses inventory management, purchasing, stores, and payables functions, all of which are involved in the procurement process. However, even on a project of this scope, an enterprise's objectives might be too timid, intended merely to streamline the process across existing functions. Companies expecting to achieve quantum improvements would undertake the reengineering of the entire process and its organization structure. This could be done in copycat mode, by targeting another company's "best practices" as the goal. Copying another company's processes, a slightly bolder objective than streamlining, is an approach doomed to make the company second best to those companies already preparing to pioneer an entirely new and superior process method.

The increasingly broader improvement initiatives of many projects include bringing suppliers and even multiple tiers of suppliers and customers (including retail outlets) under the blanket of a more massive undertaking—illustrated by the network of factories on exhibit 1–2. Because of the extremely broad scope of such an undertaking, merely streamlining operations would have comparatively little beneficial impact on results, compared to the more aggressive reengineering objective. Thus, companies with the will to undertake sweeping initiatives in their networks of suppliers and customers are usually wise enough to pursue reengineering approaches but are often still far too timid to pioneer new practices. Only a handful of companies have the courage to define visionary goals that subsequently transform their businesses and even entire industries. It is little wonder that these companies are among the most highly respected and have the longest

EXHIBIT 1–2

Streamline—Reengineer—Transform

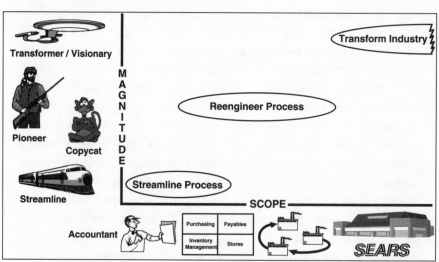

consistent record of industry leadership. Sears Canada's project, described in chapter 2, is an example of a reengineering initiative with at least one element bordering on transformation.

THE COMING COTTAGE INDUSTRY EXPLOSION

All enterprises share a common need to maintain an office force, thus office processes are one of the great frontiers on which improved services, costs, and quality can be developed by every business and public entity. A synopsis of the all-important movement to transferring office work into employees' homes is presented here and further elaborated in chapter 3, "Reinventing the Office: Layout and Organization."

Technology already available enables modern industry to disburse work from expensive offices, far from employee's homes, into locations near or even in their homes. Most modern offices feature seas of workstations equipped with telephone and fax communications to customers (or clients), suppliers, and other functional departments of the company. Virtually every business transaction is entered or altered on the workstation computer and, indeed, many transactions are communicated between customers and suppliers via telecommunication links between computers, eliminating the need for manual transaction processing. Telecommunication networks can, just as readily, link individual computer workstations in employees' homes to central processors as to workstations in the large office. Thus, the office building of the future, for many companies, may be no building at all! Various other types of work have the same potential for movement out of company-owned buildings and into homes and other places.

Further, elimination of company-owned facilities need not be restricted to offices. Northwest Water, a utility in the United Kingdom, for example, eliminated forty-five depots which were home base to work gangs that repaired and installed water and sewage equipment in the purview of the company's operations. Now, the gangs work from their repair vehicles, receiving assignments and reporting their completion from computer terminals in their vans. The work gangs are no longer employees, but rather contractors to the company. Thus, the bureaucratic personnel and supervisory organization structure required for the management of the work gangs has been eliminated. Northwest Water's experience need not be an exception. Hundreds of thousands of nonmanufacturing jobs can now be performed any-where. Modern telecommunications, in combination with low-cost personal computers, personal copiers, and fax machines are tools that enable companies to shift the workplace to the home. The costs of these tools have plummeted and will continue to drop, making the home workstation less and less expensive. Home workstations will help to reduce operating costs. With less office space, all of the costs of the resulting smaller corporate building, which will house mainly executives, will be a small fraction of the costs of the traditional big office. Most workers will easily fit today's personal office equipment into a corner of their bedroom or den.

The customer service possibilities for workshops and offices on wheels are also virtually endless. For example, Scott Gordon, owner of SBBS Software and Consulting, Inc., credits his office on wheels with bringing in twice as much business as otherwise possible.[3] As a consultant, I know that a routine problem—finding suitable working space in a client's factory or office—can be solved by driving my office van to the client site and parking it adjacent to the office or shop where the work is to be performed. And though few clients have spare offices equipped with the latest high-tech computer, telecommunications, and audio/visual tools needed by fast-moving, hard-hitting projects, a project team van would also be equipped to answer this problem.

When they begin to work in the home, employees' lives will be incredibly enriched. Workers-at-home may sometimes gain hours, by eliminating commuting, and will be able to bank the cost thereof. However, avoidance of wasteful costs and travel time is only a minor part of the benefits available when the workplace is shifted from giant city skyscrapers into the suburban and urban employees' homes. An office in the home can be readily accessible to spouse and children, bringing back a sorely lacking family bond that has arisen since both parents of many families have become part of the working, commuting force. On the negative side, some studies have shown that those working in the home miss human interaction with colleagues. However, as explained in chapter 5, video-telecommunication and virtual

---

3. Sue Ellen Christian, "For Office on Wheels, Superhighway Is Here," *Chicago Tribune,* July 12, 1994.

reality will provide as much human interaction as is required to ensure this element of work satisfaction.

Because almost all white-collar work is now done on computers, employers might worry that home workers might not actually work as much as they should. However, it is easy to see that performance and work hours can be managed via the computer network and work-monitoring programs. Enlightened employers understand that happy employees are the best workers, and no employee will be more rested, more motivated than tomorrow's home worker.

COMPUTER: BUSINESS, PUBLIC AND HOME CENTRAL

Advances in computer and telecommunications technology are central to every aspect of future work and home life. The application of computer technology to radically reengineered processes such as catalog order taking (see chapter 2, "Reinventing Retailing: The Living Room Store") has already decreased the number of employees needed to enter orders and cut the customers' wait for assistance. Soon, even more advanced computer software will enable voice communication to be used between the computer and customers and between various other people who communicate with computers. Interactive computer voice systems will completely eliminate dozens of occupations including those who type or key enter data—airline reservationists, travel agents, bank and broker "back room" personnel, and law clerks, to name a few. Every executive and manager must understand the new available hardware and software capabilities and how they can change in very fundamental ways how transactions are processed. The speed with which these technologies have progressed has far outraced the pace with which they have been applied. Therefore, if enterprises are ever to catch up to available technology, executives and managers must better anticipate its future capabilities and begin to lay the groundwork for its application to their processes.

Nor is the need to apply emerging technology limited to business processes. A whole range of occupations is subject to elimination through product improvements that will replace factory workers. For example, drivers of highway, industrial, and farming equipment will be replaced by vastly improved automatons that are guided by satellite communications and location guidance and control computers. Such inventions are discussed further in chapter 11, "Reinventing the World: Distant Visions." In general, that chapter is likely to be of little interest to readers whose interests are primarily concerned with immediate improvement initiatives. It is my vision of the longest-term future, and is meant as a foundation for "visioning" by breaking the confining bonds of today's realities. In my experience, executives and managers who free themselves from the limiting parameters of today's world will inevitably begin rapidly to work backward from their future vision to tomorrow's practical strategies.

Private and public enterprises have poured untold billions into the development of computer systems uniquely customized for their own use, and the rate of spending is increasing, as seen on exhibit 1–3. Although software companies have had some success developing standard systems for some applications (i.e., purchasing and order entry), their use is not yet universal because potential users have designed and operated their own processes in ways incompatible with the standard system. (Just imagine how many fewer computer systems would be required by both government and individuals, for example, if every state had a common income tax.) Such unique custom processes cry out for reengineering, in order to benefit from the low cost and efficient processing of standard computer software. And the recent trend

EXHIBIT 1–3

Corporate Info Technology Spending

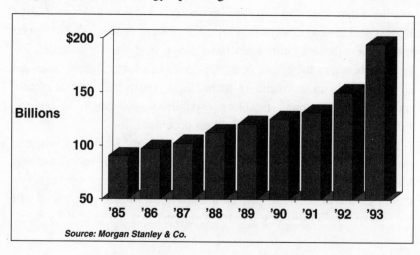

Source: Morgan Stanley & Co.

to the use of "client" and "server" computers (small personal computers and large central processors) has just begun. As the number of
"clients" continues its soaring growth, computer utilities networks
and related telecommunications will also grow, as will the use of their
continuously improved common software systems. Eventually, every
community will be served by a (perhaps public) computer utility
linked with every other community computer in a worldwide network.
These utilities, which will process every conceivable business, public,
and private transaction, are an important subject in chapter 5, "Reinventing Computing: Will Big Brother Be Watching You?" and elaborated in several other chapters as they relate to future education, financial services, retailing, health care, production, distribution, and
government.

VISIONS AND STRATEGIES: VITAL EXECUTIVE FORTE

Today's executives must make another giant leap forward. They must
empower people in newly restructured business-within-a-business organizations.[4] Thus, instead of being completely embroiled in daily operations and in the development of solutions to myriad problems that
repeat time after time, the executive's time will be liberated and available for more productive activity. Now, enlightened executives, those
whose organization structure puts authority and responsibility for ongoing operations in the hands of managers and empowered work
teams, can begin to focus on the most important and most exciting
management facet—molding and overseeing the execution of their
companies' new, vision-based strategies.

The world of the next century will be so radically different as to
make it almost impossible for many executives to fathom, thus most
companies' "visions" will merely be extensions of present and developing trends. However, without an imaginative but realistic and practical long-range vision, businesspeople will find themselves stumbling
into future market and product advances and declines and continuously missing out on the golden opportunity to be industry leaders
and innovators rather than followers and imitators. As Henry

---

4. See appendix 2 for reference to my previous works on empowerment and focused businesses-
within-a-business.

Mintzberg wrote, "with the disappearance of the visionary approach goes vision itself, as broad, integrated strategic perspectives get reduced to narrow, decomposed strategic positions."[5] The entry into the twenty-first century will not be a gradual, inch-by-inch crawl, but a series of rapid seven-league steps. If the pace of invention seems deceptively slow, it is because hindsight is restricted to only a few recent years. The pace can be recognized to be lightning-fast when viewed with a perspective based on past decades and centuries. For example, who would have dreamed, in 1784, of transport between cities ten or more times faster than by the then state-of-the-art horse drawn coach. Yet Watt's 1785 steam engine laid the foundation for the development of the locomotive and steamboat within the next two decades, as shown on exhibit 1–4.[6] In 1834 the fastest long-distance communications took days, weeks, and months. No one dreamed, when the telegraph was invented in 1835, that overseas communications would be inaugurated in less than two decades, or that the invention of the radio would enable sound to travel around the world with the speed of light—as pictures would just a few years later. The relative speed of future invention is likely to be even faster than that of the past. Nor will future inventions be limited to private industry's products, services, and infrastructure. The reinvention of government holds the promise of being one of the most exciting avenues for increasing the value of life, by eliminating vast waste and corruption and transforming government into a true democracy of the purest form—direct participation by every voting-age citizen.

However, developing a vision first requires defining what visions and strategies are and are not. I have previously defined a process in which visions of the coming *century* are the basis for launching strategies for the next *decade* which, in turn, are the foundation for the tactics employed in operations during the current *year.*[7] Incidentally, my most valued colleague, Leroy Peterson, doubts that any executive will be interested in visions as far as a hundred years in the future. He believes, and I concur, that businesspeople want visions spanning twenty years and strategies for the next five or ten. And although I

---

5. Henry Mintzberg, *The Rise and Fall of Strategic Planning* (New York: Free Press, 1994), p. 209.

6. H.G. Wells, *The Outline of History* (Garden City, NY: Doubleday, 1956).

7. For reference to a more complete description of visions, strategies and tactics, see appendix 2.

EXHIBIT 1–4

Major Inventions—18th & 19th Centuries*

1728	Rolled Sheet Iron	1783	Rolled Rods & Bars
1785	Watt's Steam Engine	1802	Steamboat
1804	Locomotive	1825	Railroad
1835	Telegraph	1839	Steam Hammer
1851	Undersea Cable	1856	Bessemer Steel
1864	Open Hearth Furnace		

* Wells, *The Outline of History.*

agree with this, I nevertheless continue to believe that a very long-range vision (to which a balanced amount of time is devoted to both immediate operations and long-term initiatives) will either prove to be a valueless activity or will, in at least a few cases, serve to trigger shorter-term visions and strategies that would otherwise not emerge. We both agree that many companies need more long-range vision than they currently possess.

Until reading a definition advanced by Paul Schumann and colleagues, I had some difficulty in succinctly explaining a vision, either long-term or very long-term. One element of that definition stands out as especially important and descriptive: A vision "depicts a future state that does not exist and never existed before."[8] What makes such a vision unique is that it intelligently and imaginatively *predicts* the future, and does not merely describe an extension of current trends. However, I hold that executive visioning cannot simply end with a fuzzy outline of the future world and the company's prospective role in it. The vision *must* be translated into practical action strategies and

8. Paul Schumann, Donna Prestwood, Alvin Tong, and John Vanston, *Innovate! Straight Path to Quality, Customer Delight, and Competitive Advantage* (New York: McGraw-Hill, 1994), pp. 74–77.

tangible, quantified improvement targets. (Mintzberg puts it this way: "Vision sets the broad outlines of a strategy, while leaving the specific details to be worked out.")[9] These visions and strategies will become commonplace in the enterprises that intend to dominate public and private commerce and government in coming decades. Craig Erhorn and John Stark expressed the same thought regarding the practical use of a vision: "After describing the overall . . . in mainly qualitative terms, the vision must define some clearly expressed quantitative targets. Because the vision describes a hazy view of the company in the future, top management needs to translate the vision into clear, reasonable and achievable targets that can be expressed in business terms."[10] However, Erhorn and Stark's definition of vision corresponds more closely to my definition of relatively short-term strategy than of longer-term vision. Despite some differences, we are *all* in accord with the need for concrete, businesslike plans for achieving tangible results over the next few years. One such plan would be to reorganize the office workplace into slimmer, more productive facilities and even to move jobs from offices to homes!

FUTURE WORK: HOURS PER YEAR

The most earthshaking economic and social development of the twenty-first century will be the near-disappearance of work. For, as Jeremy Rifkin wrote, "Today the century-old dream of a future techno-paradise is within sight. The technologies of information and communication revolution hold out the long anticipated promise of a near-workerless world in the coming century."[11] At first, simple, repetitive tasks will be automated and then more complex jobs will be surrendered to fantastically better robots and computer programs that are capable of near-human intelligence, vision, and speech but are vastly faster than humans. Nor will job disappearance be solely linked to improved automation and computerization—much better govern-

---

9. Mintzberg, *The Rise and Fall of Strategic Planning*, p. 209.

10. Craig Erhorn and John Stark, *Competing by Design: Creating Value and Market Advantage in New Product Development* (Essex Junction, VT: Oliver Wight, 1994), p. 161.

11. Jeremy Rifkin, *The End of Work: The Decline of the Global Labor Force and the Dawn of the Post-Market Era* (New York: Jeremy Larcher, 1995), p. 56.

ment, products, health solutions, and infrastructure change will contribute to further work reduction. However, it is human nature to need
to be productively busy. As Michael Zey has written, "When we assume that the basic motivating force of human behavior is leisure, or
the absence of work, we misread fundamental human needs. Although
they value free time, people get their primary satisfaction from participating in and contributing to the common good."[12] As result of di-
minishing work and human need for activity, industries and occupations that can be expected to undergo rapid growth are those that will
fill the void. Examples include entertainment, recreation, educational,
and hobby industries such as woodworking and gardening.

Predictions of changes in products, infrastructure, and public institutions are best summarized in terms of the industries and occupations
that will grow and those that will wane or die out. For example, the
age of "electronic paper" will result in massive elimination of occupations, starting in the forests with lumberjacks who cut the trees from
which paper is made, through the pulp and paper mills, back to the
manufacturers of the equipment used by the mills, and forward into
printing companies and the manufacturers of printing presses. Various
occupations and industries that have paper processing at their core
will also suffer. Publishers, postal services, manufacturers of computer printers, copiers, and filing equipment are additional examples
of enterprises that must undergo radical transformation. They should
already be initiating strategic changes to bridge the transition from
paper to electronic images. (See chapter 5's subsection, "Electronic
Paper: A Step Toward the Paperless Future" for a lengthier explanation of this subject.)

Most chapters summarize the predicted industry and occupation
changes, because these best indicate where managements should chart
the future courses of their enterprises. In some chapters, I have segregated the predicted changes into those expected to occur soon and
those that will take decades to come to pass. Individual companies
should come to their own decisions as to the probability and timing of
these changes. Should their vision be different from and superior to

---

12. Michael G. Zey, *Seizing the Future: How the Coming Revolution in Science, Technology, and Industry Will Expand the Frontiers of Human Potential and Reshape the Planet* (New York: Simon & Schuster, 1994), p. 343.

mine, so be it. The need is not to agree or disagree, but rather to begin the process of visioning and linking visions to enterprise strategies and tactics.

Some readers might view the accelerating trend of the disappearance of work and of selected industries as frightening and threatening. Indeed, in the short term society faces the need for monumental changes to accommodate this continuing shrinking of the work required to sustain high life-style standards. I am confident that the most important of the changes—shortened workweeks—will prevail, and those preferring retirement will be encouraged to do so. Further, the additional "leisure" hours will provide wonderful opportunities for enhancing the quality of life. Those who enjoy invention, research, and authorship will fill their days with these occupations, while sports enthusiasts, travelers, lifetime students, and hobbyists will have unprecedented time available to pursue those activities. And incorrigible workaholics, whose only interest is to excel in enterprise management, are likely to be those for whom there will still be continuing full-time need as business and government professional executives.

SUMMARY

To date, I have never visited and reviewed any enterprise, anywhere in the world, in which I was unable to see opportunities for quantum improvements in productivity, customer service, and quality. The path companies must follow varies depending on the current state of their processes. Most companies that choose to streamline their operations will lose ground to their competitors who have already or will soon undertake projects to "reengineer" their processes. The leaders, however, will be those with the foresight to begin a systematic transformation, guided by their overall vision-based strategies. Nor is it necessary for any company to conclude that it must proceed, step-by-step, through a process of streamlining followed by reengineering and then by transformation. The best success will come to those with the courage and will to leapfrog directly to their ultimate goals. In the meantime, there is no reason to delay beginning to work to achieve the giant benefits attained by setting new, short-term, higher "stretch" goals that challenge an organization to improve performance to levels unimaginable in the past. Savvy executives understand that they will achieve the biggest benefits by focusing improvement efforts on the 10 percent of their processes that offer 80 percent of the improvement potential. Thus, they avoid the danger of undertaking efforts of such a broad scope that it becomes impossible to accomplish anything. The same executives understand that success depends on bringing expertise to bear in every one of the critical resource areas:

Process reinvention
Technology
People issues
Vision and strategy

By doing so, success is virtually guaranteed.

Beyond each enterprise's short-term initiatives, future vision is a vital necessity for long-term survival, because sometime during the next century earthshaking changes will occur. The ways consumer products are designed, manufactured, distributed, and sold will undergo revolutionary change. Some products and industries (paper, for example, as previously noted) will virtually cease to be used, while other entirely new products will proliferate. By the end of the twenty-first century, the consumer's entire lifestyle (recreation and work) and community infrastructure and government will undergo unimaginable metamorphosis. For example, technology will drastically reduce the amount of human work needed while, at the same time it increases life expectancy and eradicates most human diseases. As it becomes increasingly obvious that society needs very little labor to provide mankind's requirements for goods and services, massive amounts of work can be devoted to improving the public infrastructure—to the point that the mass transportation systems and vehicles of the future will bear no resemblance to today's clogged, exhaust-polluted streets and highways and the automobiles that they will replace.

Further, in the far-out future, new self-sufficient (perhaps domed) communities will be located throughout the land. The urban plagues of crime and poverty will be defeated by moving ever more population from giant city ghettos to smaller communities in which family and neighbors will be reestablished as the bedrock foundation of moral life. For all of these reasons, no giant private or public enterprise and no smaller entrepreneurial business can afford to be satisfied with the recently developed but now routine continuous "reengineering" process. What the future demands is that companies and federal and local governments develop and continuously expand their visions of the future. Then they must launch strategic initiatives not only to prepare for the inevitable world of the future but also to accelerate the pace of progress towards achieving its promise.

2

REINVENTING
RETAILING

The Living Room Store

The retail industry began to be transformed during the 1980s. Wal-Mart led the industry by pioneering practices similar to those of the Japanese "just-in-time" delivery systems. These systems routinely deliver goods in the exact time required and in the precise amount needed. Recently, Sears Canada has taken these practices a giant step forward by forming cross-functional procurement teams, tremendously simplifying the processes for ordering, receiving, and paying for purchases and radically reducing the cycle time between ordering and receipt. To date, these innovations have lowered inventory 27 percent (projected to improve to 50 percent by the end of 1995). Further, Sears has simultaneously cut stockouts by 59 percent. The simultaneity of lowering inventory while increasing customer service flies directly in the face of conventional retailing "wisdom," which holds that big inventories are necessary to avoid disappointing customers due to stockouts or inability to make timely delivery. No wonder Donald Shaffer, Sears Canada chief executive officer, has said, "This endeavor is the most significant reshaping of methods and procedures in the company's history."

Low-cost, fast implementation of simple, standard electronic data interchange is one of the keys to lightning-fast ordering and quick

supplier reaction. Sears proved it was possible to put simple but effective systems into operation in weeks (groups of suppliers, at different
times, were allowed ninety days to conform to the Sears requirement),
whereas many traditionalists argued that it would take years, perhaps
decades, to achieve the compliance of all suppliers to this already routine method of data transmission. Vastly simpler, lower-cost, and capi-
tal-freeing inventory management processes are short-term initiatives
that promise to help retail enterprises (those with the will to boldly
break with tradition) leap into an exciting new era. This will enable
them not only to survive, but also to vault beyond the outmoded practices and resulting higher-than-necessary prices and poor service of
their competitors.

The most remarkable recent retailing growth sector is that of home
shopping. Most consumers have experienced an explosion in the number of catalogs that arrive in their mailboxes. The companies that send
them are in fierce competition with both retail stores and catalog sales
competitors. In order to beat their competition they must offer no less
than competitive value but must excel in providing customer service
better than that of their rivals. The Customer Service Direct system
recently installed in catalog sales giant Damark International's telephone center is an interactive computer tool which is of major importance in meeting these needs.[1] It permits the customer service representative to quickly and efficiently respond to the customer's need in
a sequence driven by listening to what the customer says and then acting on the shopper's specific input (versus insisting on a rote taking of
information in an inflexible, computer-dictated sequence). The system
reduces the number of times customers call back to request order status, by instantly and accurately advising the buyer of important information such as credit approval, the projected arrival day, and the delivery carrier's name. Lowering order entry and order inquiry costs
has helped Damark to increase the value of their goods and services.
For example, like every other catalog retailer, Damark has a monstrous Christmas demand peak that requires hiring part-time personnel. Some competitors need up to two weeks of training to bring their
seasonal workers to basic competence in using the order entry computer system. Damark has reduced the time required to four hours.

---

1. Customer Service Direct is an Andersen Consulting trademark.

And the Customer Service Direct system provides different levels of automatic guidance for different levels of system mastery as employees continuously improve their skills through on-the-job experience.

The Sears and Damark case examples described here and in the Sears case in chapter 4 will demonstrate that these opportunities are not only feasible, but achievable in the relatively short term. Another purpose of this chapter is to introduce one important aspect of my future vision—the new home system module. This new "appliance" will revolutionize retailing and distribution by bringing the retail store and grocery into the home. It will be connected with other local, national, and international businesses via information streets and superhighways.

EXECUTIVE CHECKLIST: RETAILING ZINGERS

The following checklist is intended to summarize the most important messages of the chapter, allowing executives, managers, and every associate to compare their enterprise's and personal tactical and strategic plans and long-range visions.

Short-Term Tactics and Strategies

1. Retailers and their supply chains have far too much invested in inventory but still experience high levels of stockout. Drastic reductions of inventory can be achieved while simultaneously increasing customer service.
2. Electronic data interchange should be used to replace purchase orders, invoices, and all other forms of paperwork between retailers and their suppliers. Doing so will greatly reduce the cycle time between ordering decisions and receipt of merchandise. It will also reduce tremendously the number of personnel required to process paperwork.
3. Dramatically increased use of interactive computer telephone response systems can provide major improvements in fast, courteous response to customer calls while slashing personnel costs. Improving technology can be expected to continuously increase the amount of customer calls handled by computer, or with minimal human effort.
4. Paper will virtually disappear in the next decade or two. Therefore, enterprises already making electronic product offerings and order-

ing services available via today's state-of-the-art hardware, software, and telecommunications will lead the way onto the information superhighway. Development of such systems for the customer's convenience and ease is vital to short-term competitiveness.

5. Home delivery service will continue to grow. Companies like UPS, as a result, will have much shorter and denser delivery routes, cutting their operating costs for the volume delivered.

Future Visions

1. Forward-looking executives will ensure the survival of their enterprises in the twenty-first century by creating and continuously updating visions of future business and systems, and launching strategies that will lead their industry into the future—starting tomorrow.
2. The interactive virtual-reality voice-response telecommunication home system of the future will dramatically shift the process of shopping from retail establishments into the home. Home shopping will give the buyer access to *every* available product and service and the ability to see and to compare prices, which is now impossible except by visiting hundreds of different establishments or reviewing dozens of catalogs.
3. Enterprises best prepared to "deliver" their catalog offerings and process orders on the information streets and highways will lead the pack when it comes to establishing market share.
4. Radically improved distribution methods, including pneumatic or magnetic tubes, will rush deliveries from local suppliers to individuals and businesses with incredibly short delivery time. Very few products will take long to deliver due to being supplied from distant locations. In the near term, suppliers with the fastest delivery will increase their market share.

RETAIL JUST-IN-TIME: KEY TO BETTER, LOWER-COST SERVICE

Suppliers to Sears Canada have recently been required to adopt the use of electronic data interchange to facilitate the speedy, low-cost exchange of order and shipment information. Exhibit 2–1 is a simplified illustration of the process. The process starts with the recording of sales at the point-of-sale cash register (1). Sales from all Sears stores and cat-

EXHIBIT 2–1
Electronic Data Interchange

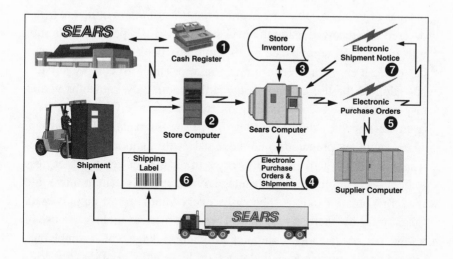

alog outlets are transmitted electronically from the store computer (2) to the Sears central computer. The store inventory balance (3) is then updated, and replenishment orders, if necessary, are generated, added to the electronic purchase order file (4), and electronically transmitted (5) to the supplier's computer system. Upon receipt of the electronic purchase order, the supplier's system produces the bar-coded shipping label (6) which accompanies the shipment of the ordered item(s) to the Sears store. At the time of shipment, the electronic shipping notice (7) is transmitted to the Sears computer where it is matched to the authorizing purchase order, priced, and payment is authorized. Upon receipt on the store dock, the bar-coded label is scanned and the receipt information is fed to the Sears computer to add to the store inventory. (The electronic shipping notice identifies the package number, and the "structure" of its contents, in terms of order numbers, item numbers, and quantities of the packages within the overpack). This process—which eliminates the need for printed supplier invoices, packing lists, and receiving reports—has long been practiced by the best Japanese manufacturers. It was pioneered by the Toyota Motor Company and then on the author's project at Yamaha, both in the 1970s. (Those familiar with the famous Japanese *kanban* system will note that the Sears system is essentially the same except that kanban cards have been replaced by *electronic kanban,* an innovation I started to help my non-Japanese clients implement in the 1980s.)[2]

Contrary to the almost universal skepticism in the industry, over 80 percent of goods received by Sears at the time of this writing are being ordered and received using the new system, and 100 percent of its suppliers will be in compliance by the time this book is published. Sears has made it easy for every supplier, large or small, to comply. First, it has adopted the use of format standards (commonly known as voluntary inter-industry communications standards, or VICS) which have been developed by the Retail Electronic Data Interchange Users group. Thus, suppliers prepared to communicate with Sears on modern electronic highways will be able to offer the same service to other customers—a big competitive advantage over rivals reluctant to move into modern communications. Secondly, every supplier can comply with Sears' need by alternative means. These alternatives include the use of a low-cost, ready-to-use computer software package which can be purchased for a few thousand dollars or leased for considerably less. Other suppliers can elect to create their own unique computer programs to interface with Sears while still others can use service bureaus to convert Sears' electronic orders and their own shipping notifications to and from whatever format (paper or electronic) they chose.

Naysayers, including only a small number of Sears' suppliers, object that small manufacturers will suffer from the requirement to receive electronic orders (versus paper orders which must be processed by clerks into electronic form) and transmit electronic shipping notices to Sears (versus using their electronic data to print invoices). Tudor Negrea, a retail information specialist at one of the Big Eight accounting firms, had a reaction typical of the uninformed who favor the status quo over progress. He was quoted as saying, "Retailers benefit more than suppliers from EDI (Electronic Data Interchange). The small [suppliers] have particular problems. They generally in their administrative processes are less computerized."[3] Such shortsighted re-

---

2. For reference to more about *kanban* and *electronic kanban,* see appendix 2.

3. Paul Brent, "Store Chains Put the Squeeze on Suppliers: Pressure to Adopt New Technology, Accept Concessions Puts Heat on Small Suppliers," *The Financial Post* (Toronto), November 26, 1994.

actions overlook the potential for cost reduction and competitive advantage for *every* supplier, including the small ones. Further, in the information age, no rational reason exists for small companies to be any less modern in the application of data processing to their businesses, especially in light of the availability of low-cost software, computers, and telecommunication equipment. In fact, I usually find modernization projects in aggressively managed small businesses are much faster and lower cost than those of large institutions. The difference usually stems from the speed with which changes can be made when no giant bureaucracy exists to fight for the status quo.

FOCUSED WORK TEAMS: BREAKING DOWN COMMUNICATION BARRIERS

Functionally organized enterprises are automatically suspect, as the functional and physical segregation of various people having roles in a common business process causes unnecessary delays in the process and erects barriers to fluid communication and cooperation between the functions. For example, when the Sears Canada procurement process flow was analyzed, the various functional organizations were scattered over the nine-story building illustrated on Exhibit 2–2. The

EXHIBIT 2–2
Process Flow Barriers

sheer number of functions and the distances between them permitted a growth of bureaucratic procedures and inhibited routine productive communication. As transactions were sent from one group to another, delays in processing were the rule, not the exception. One of the worst aspects of any functional organization is that no single function is empowered to completely control and therefore be measured by the financial and service level success of the entire process.

As one of the important "Sears Way" project initiatives, large portions of the functional organization were torn apart and people were reorganized into fast-moving, hard-hitting business-within-the-business teams equivalent to the factories-within-factories that the author has advocated since the 1980s. Exhibit 2–3 is an illustration of one such thirty-person team, for the bed and bath product line. For various components of this line, roughly eight-person, cross-functional subteams consisting of buyers, merchandise flow analysts, and process enablers work as a close-knit group, empowered to completely control the performance of their products, in terms of inventory investment, financial results, and customer service. All of the teams in this example, and their business manager, are supported by a financial analyst and marketing managers and analysts.

EXHIBIT 2–3
Sears Process Teams

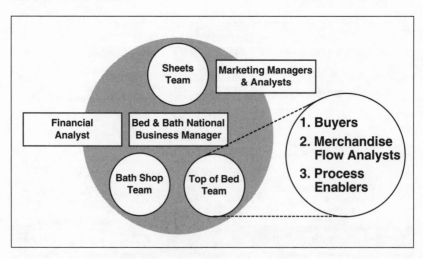

CUSTOMER SERVICE DIRECT: PRECURSOR OF FUTURE SHOPPING MODES

All direct delivery retailers (and retail stores, for that matter) need systems that will help to guarantee their continued business viability in an age where consumer shopping is already beginning a metamorphosis that will increasingly separate the place where goods are available—retail stores—from the place where customers select and order their purchases. For example, no department store chain will ever be able to locate full-service stores in every neighborhood, although the convenience of a nearby store is a powerful tool for winning customers from other chains with no stores in the area. Modern technology, however, is now capable of bringing the full-service store into any neighborhood, in the form of an interactive video system, housed in a kiosk.

In fact, the catalog already brings shopping closer to home than will ever be possible with neighborhood kiosks. People can browse through catalogs in the comfort of their homes. For this reason, an informed retailer could not fail to anticipate a boom in interactive television retailing by no later than the first decade of the twenty-first century. With that in mind, retailers modernizing their systems must not only adopt computer techniques which use the best of today's technology to maximize the efficiency and customer service of reengineered processes such as customer order entry and fulfillment. They must also use design techniques that will extend their systems' useful lives into the interactive age. To fail to do so risks seeing competitors capturing such a significant lead in the new home sales retail arena that they may never be able to overtake them. The Customer Service Direct computer tool is a flexible system designed to provide the best direct customer delivery today and in the future.[4] It reduces the time taken to enter a customer's order, puts the same catalog a customer is reading on the order taker's screen, eliminating the awkward search in a stack of catalogs, prompts the order taker to sell substitute products when an item is out of stock and to suggest related items. Above all, it

---

4. Customer Service Direct is a registered trademark. A demonstration of the system can be seen at Andersen Consulting's "Retail Place" in Chicago.

shortens the time required to train the armies of temporary order takers hired in peak sales seasons such as Christmas.

One leading direct mail catalog retailer recently adapted such a computer tool to allow the customer service agent (order taker) to enter the order information in the sequence that the customer prefers. For example, if the customer states she wishes to place and order and asks what information is needed, the agent will ask for the information in the most efficient sequence. Customer service computer displays, of which exhibit 2–4 is the home base, guide the information input and are purposely designed in almost exactly the same format as the mail-in order form in the catalog. (The manual back-up form shown in exhibit 2–5, used by order takers during brief periods when the computer is down, is also the same format.) Thus, if the customer has entered his order information on the form in preparation for ordering by telephone, the sequence in which information will be asked for will match the form the customer is looking at. The "click-on" buttons across the top of the customer service screen best illustrate the versatility of the system. By "touching" the button, the following displays can be instantly accessed in the sequence most natural to the customer, or in a standard sequence if the customer has no preference.

EXHIBIT 2–4
Customer Service Screen

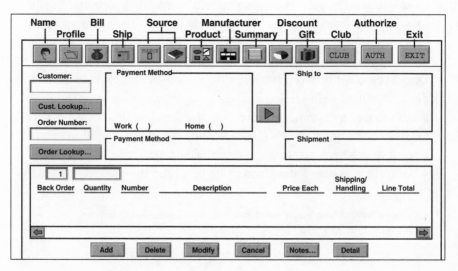

EXHIBIT 2–5
Manual Order Form

MANUAL ORDER FORM

MAIL TO:

NAME: _____

ADDRESS: _____

CITY: _____

STATE: _____

POSTAL CODE: _____

PHONE: _____

SHIP TO:

NAME: _____

ADDRESS: _____

CITY: _____

STATE: _____

POSTAL CODE: _____

PHONE: _____

BILLING:

____VISA   ____MASTERCARD   ____ DISCOVER   ____ AMEX

CREDIT CARD #: _____   EXP. DATE: _____

RESERVATION #: _____   DOB:#: _____

Name: This choice returns a screen for entering customer information (such as name and address) for first-time customers. Every name entered is checked against the data base to avoid unnecessary reentry of the information. However, most catalog recipients have been assigned customer numbers and, if the customer is able to supply this number, the customer information is automatically retrieved and can then be verified with the customer.

Profile: A profile of the customer's shopping history is helpful in answering questions regarding recent orders and useful for other customer service functions.

Billing: The customer's billing address.

Shipping: The address to which to ship an order, if different than the billing address.

Source: Screens used to access catalogs.

Product: Screens used to look up offerings for products, generically, when product numbers are not known.

Manufacturer: Used to look up the products of specific manufacturers.

Summary: Upon completion of the order entry, the entire order is displayed for final review before authorizing it to be entered.

Discounts: An item may have been listed in more than one catalog, with different prices. This display identifies the various price offers for an item.

Gift: The customer may use gift cards or coupons and these screens support fast entry of this special information.

Club: Club members who receive discounts are guaranteed to recoup the membership fee in the first year or receive a refund. If a caller is not a club member, the customer service representative will be automatically cued to promote membership.

Authorize: After an entire order has been entered and verified, it is authorized by "touching" this button.

Exit: If it becomes necessary to abandon an order being processed without authorizing its entry, this button is used. (For example, if the telephone connection with a caller is broken in the middle of the process.)

The first *standard* item the order taker would ask for would be the caller's customer number. This previously assigned number would enable the computer to retrieve name and address information for use with the new order. First-time callers would be asked credit card information. Early entry of this information permits the computer to check the credit card company's computer to make the earliest possible determination that the caller's credit is acceptable. This is a far superior procedure to one that requires a later callback if the order charge is not accepted by the card company.

If a caller, instead of asking what information to supply, starts by giving the order taker the catalog item number, the order taker can "touch" the applicable button and instantly begin entering the item(s) ordered. And should the customer then proceed to give a "ship to" address other than her own address, it is equally fast and simple for the order taker to switch the process to take that information next.

This type of computer system is also useful when the customer starts the conversation with a question concerning a specific catalog page. In the past, each order taker needed a supply of all currently valid catalogs, and would have to find the relevant catalog and riff through it in order to respond to questions. Now, the system stores images of every catalog and every page. In just seconds, the order taker can retrieve the catalog page and display it on the screen (see exhibit

EXHIBIT 2–6

Catalog Page Overview

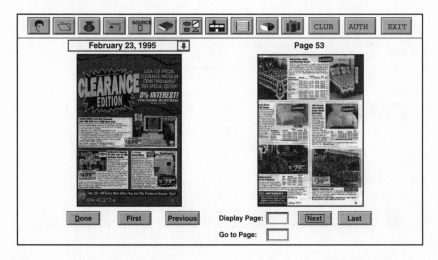

2–6). After determining which item the caller wants, a more detailed display of that item (see exhibit 2–7), can be retrieved almost instantaneously. The desired item can then be "touched" to select and insert it in the order being developed.

EXHIBIT 2–7

Catalog Item Display

EXHIBIT 2–8
Catalog Item Specifications

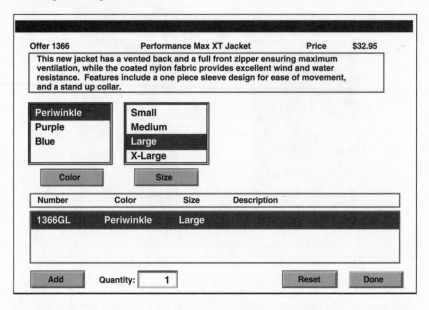

| Offer 1366 | Performance Max XT Jacket | Price | $32.95 |

This new jacket has a vented back and a full front zipper ensuring maximum ventilation, while the coated nylon fabric provides excellent wind and water resistance. Features include a one piece sleeve design for ease of movement, and a stand up collar.

Periwinkle
Purple
Blue

Small
Medium
Large
X-Large

Color   Size

Number	Color	Size	Description
1366GL	Periwinkle	Large	

Add   Quantity: 1   Reset   Done

If the caller wants to order a jacket next, she might ask about the availability of various color/size combinations. The order taker will then use the item specifications display shown in exhibit 2–8.

Another advantage of this type computer system is the automatic "sell-up" built into each order and selected order items. For example, the buyer may be offered the option of selecting a faster delivery mode, such as overnight air express, at an additional cost. Or she may be offered service contracts on an electronic or electrical appliance. The purchaser of a camera might be prompted to consider the need for film and carrying case. Exhibit 2–9, an order taker prompting screen for the third item the caller wants to order, sunglasses, shows the script that is read to the customer. This formalized script—a professional writer's best, briefest, and most appealing message—is uniformly that which every potential sell-up customer hears. If it piques the caller's interest, specific options can be retrieved and used to further explain what is available and to enter the customer's order (see exhibit 2–10).

EXHIBIT 2–9

Sunglasses "Sell-up" Script

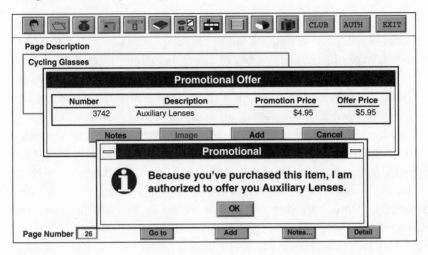

EXHIBIT 2–10

Sunglasses "Sell-up" Options

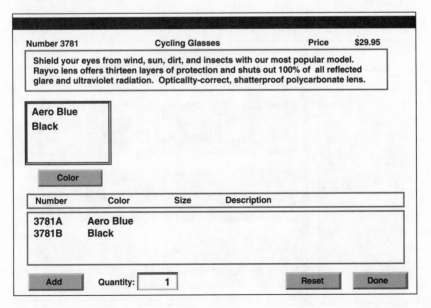

ELECTRONIC SHOPPING KIOSK: MOVING STORES TO CUSTOMERS

Chain store retailers must all consider ways to expand their market share—especially in light of the dynamic growth of catalog retailers and an explosion in the number of stores being constructed. One way for chains to increase market share, in locations where potential sales volume is not enough to support the massive capital investment required to open a full-service store, is to put small, low-cost, shopper-friendly, electronic shopping kiosks in locations convenient to small-town shoppers and local neighborhoods. These kiosks, equipped with touch-screen computer monitors and credit card readers will make it fast and simple for a shopper to browse through an entire major "department store," arriving in seconds at the department in which he wishes to closely examine the wares available.

The shopping tour starts when the customer touches the name of the department in which the wares of interest are located. (The screen shows examples of items sold in each department in case the department name is unfamiliar to the shopper.) On exhibit 2–11, the department on the touch-screen which is the subject of the shopping "trip" is

EXHIBIT 2–11
Kiosk Departments

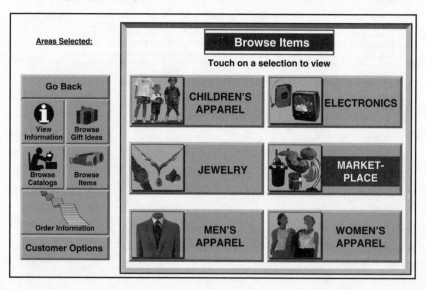

EXHIBIT 2–12
Select Category

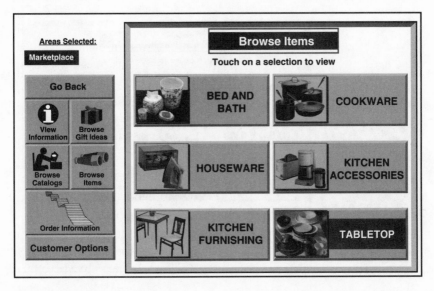

"marketplace." Instantly, a more detailed selection of the goods sold in the marketplace appears on the screen (exhibit 2–12). The choices available include bed and bath, housewares, kitchen furnishings, cookery, kitchen accessories, and tabletop. Since these titles may not be clear to the shopper, the display includes pictures of some items in each category. Since the shopper's interest is fine china, he touches the tabletop image on the screen, and a screen immediately asks which price category is the customer's primary interest. In this case, he selects the "up to $200" price category (exhibit 2–13).

Next, the names of the various china manufacturers are displayed and one is chosen. The shopper is able to see images of the china, and can ask to see specific items (e.g., the cup and saucer only) closer up (exhibit 2–14).

After viewing several china patterns from several manufacturers, the shopper might decide to make a purchase. Touching appropriate screen items and quantities would construct an order record to which his credit card information would be added when he passes his card through a magnetic stripe card reader. Next, his name and address, "ship to" address, and any other special information would be added

EXHIBIT 2–13
Price Category Selection

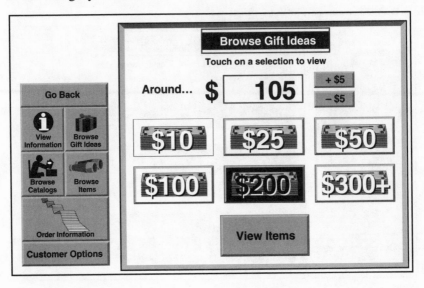

EXHIBIT 2–14
China Images & Prices

to the order record, electronically, by one of several alternative methods. One such method would use a keyboard or a touch-screen keyboard; another might record voice information for later key entry by computer center order processing personnel. Customers previously assigned identification numbers would need only the number, since the computer could use the number to retrieve the information.

The user-friendly aspects of this example of kiosk shopping are equally important to systems developed for short-term order-taker processing methods and for the ultimate home shopping process of the future.

DIRECT DELIVERY: BIGGEST THREAT TO RETAILERS

The costs and profits of distributors, wholesalers, and retailers greatly inflate consumer prices compared to the producers' prices at the beginning of the pipeline. Producers are increasingly recognizing the tremendous benefits of direct factory-to-consumer sales and delivery. These include substantial reductions in the prices they are able to charge for their products vis-à-vis competitors not yet able to offer a similar service. Lower prices usually lead to increases in market share. Ensuing improved economies of scale may then further increase the industry leader's cost/price advantage.

My previous book discussed the shrinking role of middlemen, primarily between producers and retailers.[5] Obviously, the producers with the greatest potential for direct consumer sales and delivery are those producing the largest, most expensive products. Automobiles and appliances are two categories that come to mind most immediately. However, innovative producers of small, less expensive products are also taking advantage of direct sales and delivery and enjoying the same benefits. The subsection "The Disappearing Middleman" in chapter 7 identifies a producer of soft, disposable contact lenses as an example of one recently organized direct sales initiative.

Every retailer must systematically review its vulnerability to direct producer sales and develop a strategy for delaying the complete loss of revenues that might result from these sales. One such strategy

---

5. For reference to additional information about shrinking middlemen, see appendix 2.

would be to provide consumer ordering services that would, at minimal cost, capture customer orders and forward them to the producer electronically. The retailers' regional warehouse operations and systems should be prepared to most economically supply producers with these warehousing and distribution services as an alternative to the producer developing its own. By continuously reengineering their systems and operations, thus reducing their costs, retailers should be able to delay the advent of complete loss of direct sales and delivery.

Every producer with the practical potential for direct sales, however, should also have a strategy for systematically beginning to develop the order-capture systems and distribution and order-filling facilities to eventually do so.

PERPETUALLY PLEASANT "PEOPLE": THE SYSTEM'S REPRESENTATIVES

Some of the most exciting emerging trends are at the end of the supply, production, and distribution pipeline in links between retailers and customers. One of the most important trends is the preliminary (albeit tentative) movement towards interactive home teleshopping. The linkage between interactive home shopping and vastly improved customer service holds the promise of unimaginably better customer relations. And history will likely record the 1990s as the decade of the customer, based on the renewed emphasis on the customer as king. Sales and marketing organizations and executives have never failed to understand the importance of *every* customer, and the vital necessity of rapidly providing high-quality goods and services at the lowest possible cost consistent with reasonable profitability. Never, however, has this awareness been driven home to the rest of every enterprise as effectively as during this decade. This new awareness has led many businesses to reorganize their operations along customer lines, in order that all or most business functions serve a single customer or class of customers. Nor should the drive for ever-improved customer service be allowed to decelerate. Until customer needs are almost instantly met—whether processing customer orders, delivering goods and services, or answering inquiries and solving problems to all customers' satisfaction with businesslike courtesy and friendliness at the lowest possible cost—the job will not have been completed.

Continuous technological improvements promise to support achieving ideal customer service objectives. Leading retailing thinkers now have some entirely new visions of customer service. For example, Thomas Gunn quotes Peter Drucker: "For traditional merchants, service means salespeople who personally take care of an individual customer. But the new retailers employ very few salespeople. Service to them means that customers *do not need a salesperson,* do not spend time trying to find one, do not have to ask, do not have to wait."[6] Thus, retailers are already taking steps to eliminate the necessity for interpersonal contact. Customer/computer interaction is one of the key characteristics of the home (computer) system module era that will make the electronic "salesperson" a retailer's dream representative. However, even in the short term, designing stores and information systems toward the end of no longer needing salespeople to assist in stores or on the telephone can be of significant value in a retailer's drive to squeeze costs, increase customers' satisfaction, and improve or maintain profitability.

Customers must always be treated with respect, dignity, and friendliness—a universally accepted business principle. However, people capable of maintaining the proper decorum when faced with unreasonable, unfriendly, angry, or offensive customers are hard to find. Worse, an enterprise's own representatives may occasionally, because of illness or domestic or business problems, themselves become unreasonable, unfriendly, angry, or offensive. Worst of all, some human beings (enterprise representatives *and* customers) are just naturally nasty or are products of a bureaucracy that permits some individuals to get by with offensive behavior and with refusing to provide the timely, courteous service customers deserve. (A few government bureaucrats, secure in their lifetime employment and the virtually discipline-free protection of civil service regulations, are responsible for *all* civil servants being unfairly viewed unfavorably. Others, like the

---

6. Thomas G. Gunn, *In the Age of the Real-Time Enterprise: Managing for Winning Business Performance with Enterprise Logistics Management* (Essex Junction, VT: Oliver Wight, 1994), p. 127.

clerks in my local post office, are models of customer service providers). Little can be done to change the customer's nature or condition, but a way to provide perpetually perfect "people" to interact with the public is already at hand.

The solution is simple: Replace real people with "virtually real" representatives. Tens of thousands of enterprises are finding they are able to eliminate armies of personnel who handle routine customer phone conversations, replacing them with modern computer-based interactive "people" whose demeanor is *always* ideally businesslike, friendly, and helpful. In the forefront of such applications are institutions such as telephone companies, banks, credit card companies, mutual funds and airline mileage-plus operations. These companies use automated phone handling systems which interactively offer optional services that the customer can respond to using a touch-tone telephone.

For example, modern telephone companies' interactive collect- calling systems no longer require long distance operators. They lead the caller through the process of identifying himself by voice recording, then ask the call recipient to approve the call after listening to the caller's recorded name. In this case, the recipient's *yes* response is "heard" by simple voice recognition systems which then connect the call or advise the caller that the recipient refuses to accept the charges. Ameritech, a pioneer in the field, is planning to expand the voice recognition service to encompass eleven-digit calls. It expects to inaugurate this enhanced system in the Chicago area by early 1996.[7] Banks and credit card companies, using similar systems, respond to customers' requests for account balance information, recent charges, current savings and debt interest rates, and available credit. Mutual fund companies also provide account information and current prices and earnings information for the funds managed. Airline mileage-plus systems provide interactive account balances and recent flights recorded.

Many enterprises have found they are able to enhance customer service by simply recording the customer's inquiry, complaint, or problem with interactive systems that capture the customer's identifying information (order number, customer number, product number,

---

7. Jon Van, "Voice-activated Phoning in Pipeline for Callers Wary About 11-digit Dialing," *Chicago Tribune,* February 20, 1995.

etc.), and promising a representative will call with a response as soon as possible. Such systems improve customer service in the following ways. First, the system (on line twenty-four hours per day, seven days per week) responds almost instantly to all calls—a big advantage to customers who work and are unable to call during normal working hours and those calling from other time zones. A second helpful feature is that customers need not be put on hold for seemingly endless periods because "all customer service representatives are busy," a frequent and distressing occurrence during the times most callers wish to communicate (i.e., lunch hour). Third, few enterprises are able to man human answering systems at the variable staffing levels necessary to avoid both wasting labor and offending customers. The automated system permits recording of messages as they occur, to be answered as soon as possible, but always within a reasonable amount of time. This permits leveling of the work force while still taking each caller's call immediately. For callers with unique, urgent need for even faster response, the system can channel the call to a limited staff dedicated to immediately servicing the customer's need.

My own primary client, Andersen Consulting, has been on the leading edge of enterprises that have adopted the use of voice mail and electronic mail over the past several years. An added advantage these systems offer is a radical improvement in the communication efficiency of both the firm and its clients. Telecommunication charges have been lowered as a result of the conversations naturally becoming more abbreviated when they are recorded rather than live. Without the small talk and time spent thinking through answers while both parties are on the line, messages are brief. Responses are similarly brief, usually recorded only after the call recipient has thoughtfully formulated an effective, to-the-point answer. Thus, the average telecommunication length is far shorter, and there are fewer communications as a result of eliminating telephone tag, a common phenomenon in communications between managers and executives. For example, you call him, but he is in conference, so you leave a message to have him return your call. He then becomes available and returns your call, but now *you* are in conference, so he leaves you a message to call again. The process can continue for days. Andersen Consulting has found that its national and international voice mail communications between its far-flung offices require far less connection time, as high-speed batches of electronically digitized voice messages are transmitted in a fraction of the time required by conventional, two-way conversations.

It is clear that ongoing improvements in telecommunications and computer technologies will broaden the scope of electronic customer inquiry applications continuously. As computers are taught to understand speech better and to respond with intelligence, the range of automated services will grow. Ultimately, interactive computer voice communications will virtually replace human enterprise representatives. Airline reservations personnel, bank tellers, travel agents, hospital admittance staff, and order-entry clerks, to name a few, will no longer be required. The reduced costs of transaction processing and fewer personnel will help to enhance the quality of life. Further, the present purveyors of these services will eventually become the contract managers of the community computer utilities and software writers who will continuously improve the variety and efficiency of the utilities' processes. This development will also contribute significantly to lowering the services' cost.

One of the author's most important messages to executives is that he has seen, read, or heard of few enterprises with coherent, long-range visions of the world and of their place within that future world. In the realm of customer service, it should be clear that the tide of the future for customer relations will be electronic communications. However, right now countless private and public enterprises are doing a terrible job in terms of taking measures to improve customer service. The first step in improving the process must be the development of a vision. The author is in wholehearted accord with David Freemantle in seeing little possibility that any conceivable vision can fail to suggest tactics for immediate implementation and strategies for the medium term. Freemantle wrote, "Incredible service can only be achieved with a clear vision of what it means to your organization in the long term and a clear strategy to achieve this." He added, "The key thing about a vision is that you can make substantial progress toward achieving it."[8]

---

8. David Freemantle, *Incredible Customer Service: The Final Test* (London: McGraw-Hill, 1993), p. 69.

CUSTOMER CHARACTERISTICS AND
CATALOG PREFERENCES

The author receives several pounds of catalogs and other product and service offerings in the mail each week. The author's mail processing procedure starts with a trip to the roadside mailbox and a stop at the author's waste recycling center in the garage. The majority of the commercial items in each day's mail are not offerings for products and services in which the author or his wife are interested and go immediately into the recycling container. Similarly, when two or more identical catalogs arrive, a frequent occurrence, the duplicates are instantly discarded. The same applies to material of an offensive nature, such as advertisements and catalogs for sexually explicit books and video tapes. Some of the items, such as those related to gardening and plants, are of special interest to the author's wife, and are sorted into a pile for her review. Catalogs of interest to the author—hand and power tools, computer and office hardware, and business books—are sorted for careful review at the author's earliest convenience. Far more of these catalogs of interest arrive than any other type, because the suppliers have noted our frequency of purchase or have obtained our name and address from any one of several companies (such as credit card companies) that have solicited the author's family's specific interests. The author always responds to these surveys because, by specifying highest interest areas, he is assured of receiving as many related catalogs and service offerings as is possible. (That there is significant duplication of this information is obvious since two or more of the same catalogs are often received at the same time.) Still other catalogs of *compulsive* interest might be riffed through and either sorted into a discard pile or saved for further review. After reviewing the selected catalogs at a convenient time, most are discarded while a few are filed for possible future use. Five or six catalogs per month (less than 5 percent of all of those received) trigger ordering. Further, once or twice per month a need arises for items for which catalogs have been retained. It is then necessary to review competitors' catalogs to compare specifications and prices, and select and order the products with the highest value for the price. It seems obvious that this system, in which over 90 percent of all catalogs are discarded without even being read, is unnecessarily costly for the catalog suppliers. Moreover, customers must ultimately pay more for the products they purchase to cover this exorbitant catalog printing and mailing cost. Further, we, as consumers, are frustrated by the time wasted in culling out items of little or no interest. Even worse, we know we receive only a small fraction catalogs from suppliers in which we would always be interested and no catalogs at all for other items in which a need sometimes arises. Finally, some of us are offended by the unnecessary damage to the ecology arising from the vast amounts of paper the catalogs require.

INTERACTIVE HOME GROCERY SHOPPING

Grocery costs, one of the largest components of the average family's budget, are far higher than necessary, because self-service in grocery stores adds to the consumer's cost in both travel expense and hours spent in travel and shopping. The excessive costs of the stores' wares arise from the labor-intensive store and distribution operations and the huge amounts of inventory in the pipeline between producers and the ultimate customer. Retail chains like Aldi and Sav A Lot, which eliminate frills, also eliminate most of the labor that conventional stores expend on stocking shelves and bagging groceries. They save on administrative costs by carrying a limited range of items—choosing not to carry multiple, competing brands. As a result, Judith Schoolman, reporting on no-frill chains, found in a shopping-basket comparison of 301 items that Aldi's composite prices were 31 percent lower than similar items purchased from Sam's Club, another chain.[9] Nor are these avenues of cost reduction the only potential improvements. *Fortune* cites a study that concludes that streamlining logistics would save the industry $30 billion dollars in annual operating cost and interest expense.[10] And these cost savings, when realized, would accrue mainly to consumers, in the form of price reductions. However, prices could be still lower and variety higher. Home shopping, from a neighborhood grocery distribution center is the key.

9. Judith Schoolman, "Big Savings Are in the Bag at These Food Stores," *Chicago Tribune,* November 7, 1994.

10. Ronald Henkoff, "Delivering the Goods," *Fortune,* November 28, 1994, pp. 64–78.

Future interactive home shopping systems will not be limited to hard goods and soft goods, but will also be applied to groceries. Indeed, *The Economist* article quoted my London office colleague, John Hollis, as thinking "the biggest potential for interactivity lies in basic, regular food retailing."[11] And although John foresees greater potential for canned and packaged products than for gourmet food and fresh produce, I believe there is no reason not to expect the purchase and delivery of the latter items to be as appropriate for the home shopping system as the former. Small wonder that grocery shopping is one area in which home shopping is expected to flourish. For, as Andersen Consulting's Glen Terbeek is fond of saying, "Surveys by some grocery organizations show that most people rank the dislike of grocery shopping about the same as going to the dentist. When customers don't like you, you are a prime candidate for reinvention."

When home grocery delivery comes to pass, the cycle will have come full circle. In my youth I worked as an assistant on a delivery truck for a grocery store that took telephone orders and delivered both fresh and packaged groceries to its customers, the same day. The widespread ownership of the automobile and fierce price competition with supermarkets (which did not deliver) eventually killed the service. However, new modes of transportation and the future growth of production and distribution clusters (see chapter 7, subsection "Production and Distribution Clusters") in combination with an explosion of vastly improved, lower-cost home delivery services will be important advances underlying the rebirth of home grocery shopping and the death of many supermarkets. *The Economist* notes two such pioneering home shopper services, Shopper Vision—in conjunction with Time Warner's trial in Orlando—and Peapod in affluent sections of Chicago and San Francisco.[12]

The "electronic shopping mall," an Andersen Consulting research prototype described by Charles Winslow and William Bramer, contains not only the electronic grocery store and its generic offerings of basic foodstuffs, but also features shopping "solutions" to help the meal and party planner make menu decisions by recommending dishes and bev-

11. Uncredited. "The Interactive Bazaar Opens," *The Economist,* August 20, 1994, pp. 49–51.

12. Ibid.

erages that complement the main entree.[13] This is one of the vast array of possibilities for utilizing future technology in ways comprehensible to *today's* retailers and their customers. However, systems for even better menu decisions for guest entertainment are on the far distant horizon. For example, the host of the future will have access to the menu preference portion of each guest's data base. Therefore, the host can plan to incorporate guests' culinary likes and dislikes into the plan, perhaps customizing a menu for each guest. Certainly this will someday be a far superior way to insure the ultimate in hospitality.

Today's chain grocery operations face a future in which customers will easily order the lowest-cost supplier's items from a neighborhood distribution facility through the home shopping computer utility. Thus, grocery store traffic will start to disappear, and eventually the sole remaining role of any grocery chain will be the ordering and delivery of products to the distribution point (it will not make economic sense for several different competing distribution points to exist, each carrying largely duplicate or similar products). The chains will likely compete with one another on their ability to deliver products to the various neighborhood distribution facilities competitively, probably submitting an annual contract bid to each facility. Therefore, the chain with the fastest, most efficient inventory and purchasing management system, delivery capability, and lowest-cost operations in each region is likely to dominate the region's industry.

SPEEDY HOME DELIVERY

Logistic companies that establish or expand local delivery services and retail establishments that take advantage of these services to enter or expand the home delivery business will soon be riding on a crest of explosive growth that will continue over the next two or three decades and eventually decimate the number of in-store shopping businesses. Discount stores, grocery stores, and every other imaginable type of retail establishment are blossoming across the landscape of the industrialized world on the very eve of an important new era—the era of home shopping and speedy, low-cost home delivery. It is obvious that,

---

13. Charles D. Winslow and William L. Bramer, *Future Work: Putting Knowledge to Work in the Knowledge Economy* (New York: Free Press, 1994), pp. 258–262.

like the real estate boom and bust of the recent past, the supply of retail establishments is outstripping the demand. Further, the number of mail order businesses is burgeoning, evidence that growing numbers of consumers are sick and tired of the hassle of driving on traffic-clogged roads only to find parking spaces hundreds of yards from the shopping mall or grocery store entrance, and elbow-to-elbow hordes of shoppers filling the aisles. The time is ripe for many retail establishments, threatened by overbuilding of their own stores and those of their competitors and by the growing mail order industry to launch initiatives to enter one of the home delivery markets: mail order, store delivery, and interactive home ordering systems.

The winners in this explosive new market will be those who master the science of fastest possible delivery at the lowest possible cost. None of the individual companies, with the possible exception of the very largest chains, will initially have the high volume of home delivery to support low-cost, fast delivery. Thus, new and fast-growing logistics companies will provide this new service. Eventually, the volume of home deliveries will increase to the point that the largest chains will integrate their retail operations with their own logistics ventures. As always, the fastest, lowest-cost service providers will dominate the market.

HOME GROCERY DELIVERY: EXPLOSIVE NEW INDUSTRY

Grocery retailers (and all other retailers) intending to retain the lion's share of their present business must excel in reinventing their processes. Those who are most aggressive will start to enter the home delivery market. The company that first organizes for efficient residential delivery will be one that delivers *everything* from all suppliers in a community to all of its consumers. It will preclude competition from entering its territory because the high density of its deliveries will yield the lowest possible cost per delivery. Grocery retailers are in the envious position of having customers with daily delivery frequency and volume potential higher than any other industry. Thus, eventually they could win the business of delivering all other products. And the first to offer the service in any neighborhood is likely to forever dominate delivery *and product sales* in that area.

Before the rebirth of home delivery, revolutions in grocery shopping will continue to make shopping more user friendly. For those addicted to buying with coupons, but fed up with their clipping, filing, and use prior to the expiration date, relief is in sight. Major chains are already using point-of-sales coupon dispensers with which the retailer and the supplier can produce coupons (at the cash register) targeted to the individual consumer's latest purchase or purchase history.[14] In the relatively short-term future, the physical coupon will be replaced by electronic coupons which chains and manufacturers will advertise. But the price discount will be automatically computer-applied at the cash register. (Most producers are loath to end the use of coupons, since they are useful tools for forcing stores to anticipate the sales surge generated.) Innovations of this ilk, the number of which has recently exploded in the grocery industry, are some of the most important examples of the opportunities for reinventing products and processes, enabled by the lightning-fast improvement of computers and software. Agility in implementing the very latest innovations and inventing even better mutations will be critical to successful competitiveness in both short-term and long-term operations.

COMMUNITY COMPUTER UTILITY: HOME SHOPPING CENTRAL

Catalog suppliers would benefit significantly by improving their existing systems for soliciting customer responses regarding their interest in the suppliers' catalogs. Catalog retailers should also develop automated, rapid response systems for fast delivery of requested catalogs when a customer need arises. For any company that now solicits sales or *should* do so, it is inexcusably unprofessional not to organize superbly efficient systems for capturing high-potential customer mailing list information, for acquiring it from existing sources, and for soliciting it from potential customers.

In the longer term, the future's computer utility will permit the cus-

---

14. Frank Feather, *The Future Consumer: Predictable Developments in Personal Shopping and Customer-Centered Marketing on the Information Superhighway* (Los Angeles: Warwick, 1994), pp. 170–175.

tomer himself to maintain portions of the sole, unduplicated record of his product and service preferences (see chapter 5, "Reinventing Computing: Will Big Brother Be Watching You?"). Additionally, the computer utility, which will eventually process every purchase transaction, will use transaction history to build a buyer purchase profile, useful for "putting" suppliers' electronic catalogs in the "riff-through" electronic mailboxes of individuals with the highest purchase potential. Catalogs of high interest to the individual could be "put" in a separate electronic "in depth" review mailbox. Still other catalog items could be electronically accessed by the customer as a need or an impulse occurs.

These future systems will still provide catalogers with the option to advertise their wares and generate sales through the periodic distribution of electronic catalogs with vastly better, targeted "mailings." They will deliver catalogs electronically, at a small fraction of the cost of delivering printed matter, and do so more rapidly. The customer will control which material is placed in his various "mailboxes" and will be able to ban certain types of offensive offerings. Most important of all, the customer will have ready access to the offerings of all suppliers of a desired item at the time the need or the impulse arises. Thus, with the future's virtually real shopping system and targeted catalog delivery suppliers will be delivering the penultimate in customer service.

VIRTUALLY REAL HOME SHOPPING

Most printed products will inevitably go the way of books, newspapers, and magazines, replaced by electronic versions delivered on the information superhighway. In previous works, for example, I predicted the demise of printed catalogs as a result of new, interactive home video catalog and shopping systems.[15] My colleagues and I have widely diverse opinions as to when such systems will come into use, but I expect the earliest, crudest systems in the next ten years with the most sophisticated systems following within twenty years. Kenneth Stone, for one, agrees with the relative speed with which in-

---

15. For reference to more information about interactive home shopping, see appendix 2.

teractive home shopping will burst upon the scene: "It appears that interactive electronic mail order will be a reality within a few years. By using a computer or an interactive cable TV system, consumers will be able to call up a type of merchandise they are interested in and see comparisons of benefits, features and prices."[16] At the other extreme, some expect it will be decades before such systems are widely used.

The future's systems will be radically different than present and planned "home shopping" television, which typically features a single supplier and a limited number of that supplier's products. Suppliers of the future will pay nominal fees to put their electronic catalogs into the consumer's electronic "mailbox" through the community computer utility network. National and international companies will be able to put three-dimensional pictures and voice and written specifications into their catalog data bases and broadcast them over the information highways to all (or to selected) community utilities. Further, by specifying the characteristics of buyers to whom their products would appeal, electronic catalogs could be "put into" the electronic mailboxes of only those consumers most likely to purchase their offerings. The recipient could then, at her convenience, browse through her mailbox electronically, deleting catalogs of no interest and notifying the system to remove the product line or supplier's catalogs from *her* approved list. Upon deciding to order, she can interactively place the order and authorize an automatic funds transfer payment from her "bank account" to that of the supplier. (See chapter 7, "Reinventing Financial Services: Bankerless Banking," for visions of future "wealth accounts".)

The home system module of the not too distant future (exhibit 2–15) will permit the home shopper to browse through electronic catalogs of numerous suppliers of a wide variety of products. The system's voice synthesizer and voice communications features will allow the user to talk, interactively, with the electronic "salesperson," to define the types of products in which the buyer has an interest. Recent and projected voice recognition revenues (exhibit 2–16) show that growth can be expected to fuel ever-increasing research and develop-

16. Kenneth E. Stone, *Competing with the Retail Giants: How to Survive in the New Retail Landscape* (New York: Wiley, 1995), p. 39.

EXHIBIT 2–15
Home System Module

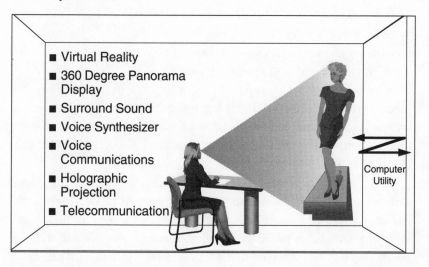

ment budgets which will lead to vastly improved interactive speech capabilities. However, the onslaught of voice systems is already underway. Though practical man/computer interactive speech has not yet arrived, "voice control that uses few words but is very powerful"

EXHIBIT 2–16
Speech Recognition Revenue

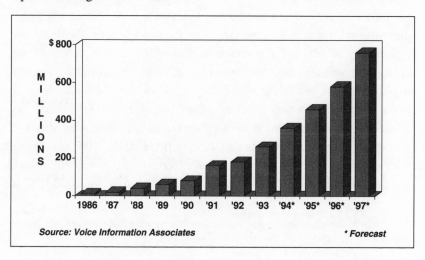

already exists, according to William Meisel, editor of *Speech Recognition Update.*[17]

In the case of garments, an interactive shopper will give the home system module's three-dimensional, life-size, electronic "salesperson" the specifications (style, color, and target cost range, for example) of the garments he wants to see and "try on." The electronic browser will then be able to see *all* available products (from every supplier) that meet his specifications. Without leaving the comfort of home, he can browse through the equivalent of dozens of retail stores, viewing a much larger variety of garments than would be possible if it were necessary to travel to them.

Initial efforts to market electronically to home shoppers are bound to have mixed success, due to the inadequacy of pioneering efforts. For example, J.C. Penney's aborted first attempt to sell through home shopping television probably failed because of the limited array of goods that can be displayed in the time viewers tune in. Further, many people find garments look different and fit poorly once they don them, thus the rate of returned goods is shockingly high. Purchases made through the home system module will seldom be returned because the browser will be able to put clothing on a three-dimensional, holographic model of his own measurements and facial and body appearance. Then the home shopper will use virtual reality system features to rotate his lifelike figure, viewing the garment on "himself" from every conceivable angle. (Modern computer assisted design [CAD] systems already contain the basic capabilities to support such three-dimensional, rotational viewing). Thus the browser can check the appearance and fit of the garment without the inconvenience of the changing room and the time consumed in changing from one garment to another. As a result, the likelihood of the shopper being dissatisfied and returning the item is lessened. Many browsers will love the ability to electronically "try on" dozens of outfits in the same time it would otherwise take to change into a single outfit. Finally, after comparing various suppliers' similar or identical offerings and prices and selecting her purchases, the browser will tell the electronic "salesperson" to

---

17. William M. Bulkeley, "Speech Recognition Gets Cheaper and Smarter," *Wall Street Journal,* June 6, 1994.

have the items delivered. Payment will be instantaneous and automatic because the computer utility will transfer wealth from the buyer's account to that of the supplier.

Crude interactive home shopping systems are already becoming the pioneering precedents of the ultimate home system module. Time Warner, in a test involving four thousand homes in Florida, and Viacom and AT&T in one thousand households in a suburb of San Francisco were two of the earliest to blaze the trail. Whether these tests are successful or not (depending on how well they are conceived and executed) they will nevertheless form an experience base on which all subsequent systems will be founded. As *The Economist* puts it, "the real argument is now not about whether interactivity will transform retailing, but when."[18] Walter Forbes, chairman of CUC International, a fast-growing pioneer in interactive retailing, predicts in the *Economist* article that interactive retailing will capture "between 5 percent to 15 percent of America's retail sales ($2.1 trillion) in ten years." I deem this estimate to be conservative, and envision massive conversion of retail outlets into distribution facilities designed to rapidly fill and deliver orders to the neighboring community in the coming two to three decades. CUC's service offers "electronic catalogs" through which subscribers can browse containing one-quarter million products from hundreds of manufacturers. CUC processes orders both electronically and by telephone and then forwards them to the manufacturer for shipment to the customer, allowing it to cut product prices to its members by up to 50 percent.

Present home-shopping cable television services are another crude movement towards interactive purchasing in the home but, predictably, it has not been an outstanding success. Although the industry generates over two billion dollars in annual revenue, it suffers from offering the viewer no choice as to which commodities to view and the product variety is limited. As Mark Robichaux points out, for example, more than 40 percent of revenues come from jewelry sales. Pricier products of higher quality might also have a better chance of winning customer loyalty. For example, Douglas S. Briggs, president

---

18. "The Interactive Bazaar Opens," *The Economist*, August 20, 1994, pp. 49–51.

of QVC electronic, is cited as suggesting, ". . . the answer to expanding beyond its traditional audience may be mainstream products of higher quality than those typically associated with home shopping."[19]

Marketing executives are fast to point out the social value of the shopping experience (the age-old expedition of two or more friends getting together for a shopping trip). However, it would be naive to think that all (or even most) shoppers would view the ordeal of traffic and the crush of shoppers in the retail stores as a pleasant diversion. Future social meetings are more likely to be sociable events in the home or in new "shopping restaurants." My Korean colleague, B. C. Cho, however, helped me understand the difficulty of converting some inveterate shoppers to interactive home shopping systems. His wife's comment, upon seeing an early draft of the home shopping module shown in exhibit 2–15, was "I hate it!" She is one of the world's home-keepers fortunate enough not to work outside the home, and thus enjoys spending time on shopping expeditions accompanied by her friends. It would have been advisable to have depicted not only the shopper but also *her friends,* in the exhibit, to have better answered objections of the important category of shoppers who view the experience of shopping in retail stores as a pleasant social outing.

Perhaps every great innovation, at its inception, has its host of pessimistic naysayers. The home system module on the information superhighway is no exception. Objectors find valid reasons to point to the probable delay and even failure of this vision to become a reality.[20] One such reason is the relative slowness with which many new products such as the home system module win a place in a majority of households. For example, color televisions and video recorders each took fifteen years to enter 50 percent of all households in the United States, as seen on exhibit 2–17. However, some analysts make a mistake by interpreting this fact negatively. They sometimes conveniently overlook an important reality—that the approximately four million households that purchased these products in the first six years were a large enough base on which manufacturers could justify product and process improvement expenditures that ultimately brought prices

19. Mark Robichaux, "TV Shopping Losing Its Shine for Retailers," *Wall Street Journal,* November 22, 1994.

20. Jon Van, "Interactive TV May Get Muted Reception," *Chicago Tribune,* June 13, 1994.

EXHIBIT 2–17
New Product Acceptance

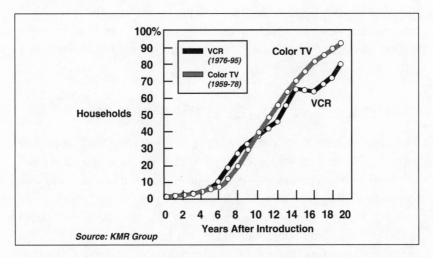

Source: KMR Group

down to an almost universally affordable level. Today even the poorest slum tenements have long been festooned with forests of television antennas.

Not all companies are reluctant to begin the trek into the future of interactive home shopping. For example, Microsoft and Visa International made an exciting announcement in November, 1994,[21] with a plan to launch sales of interactive home shopping software to owners of personal computers and to retail merchants in 1995. Use of this tremendous new applied technology, although an important stride towards the ideal twenty-first century system, is undoubtedly going to be limited to computer literate people willing to struggle with the complexity of processing orders using recently released software, which most users (and I include myself) find increases the complexity of its use and adds to the time it takes to do the same tasks performed using early, less technician-oriented software. I predict that this software will increase the amount of time a computer illiterate will require to riff through the merchant's electronic catalog and place an order, compared to the old-fashioned alternative of riffing through a

---

21. Don Clark, "Microsoft, Visa to Jointly Develop PC Electronic-Shopping Software," *Chicago Tribune,* November 9, 1994.

paper catalog and ordering by telephone. Nevertheless, personal computer windows-genre systems will be a vital interim step—a precursor to future development of the far superior, "user friendly" home system module. And for the computer illiterate and those unschooled in typing, the interim process will range from impossible to extremely difficult.

ENTERTAINMENT CENTER: HOME SYSTEM MODULE

The home system module of the future will incorporate all important aspects of virtual reality, including 360-degree image projection and surround sound. Therefore, separate specialized video and audio systems will no longer be required. It should be possible to "play" music stored at the community computer utility by simply asking the system to do so. Since both audio and video will be stored electronically on the computer utility, the production, distribution, and sales of video and audio tapes and disks will be among the ranks of the twenty-first century's waning industries. Libraries will no longer exist, since every existing title will also be included in the community's computer utility data base.

There are widespread differences of opinions regarding how soon this will come to pass. I believe it can and should be beginning *now* and will come to widespread fruition in the next ten to twenty years, because the savings to consumers can be enormous. My valued colleague Leroy Peterson thinks the hundred-year time frame may be more realistic. Whenever the electronic-telecommunication library system becomes available, the prospective reader will be able to specify the subject about which he is interested, and the electronic "librarian" will suggest a list of possible titles from which to select either brief synopses or make a decision. Since the pages of the electronic book selected will be displayed on the walls of the home system module, the giant print can be easily read by even those with severe optical problems, while electronic voice books will meet the need of the visually impaired.

The trend to electronic cameras will continue, and a single panoramic camera will serve to capture both moving and still images. These images, transferred to the individual's image data base will be accessible for display in the home system module, or on large group viewing screens. Simple cross-referencing will permit rapid access according to the verbal request made to the system. For example, the requestor might ask for all past still pictures of past visits with an aunt and uncle, a feature of great value when the aunt and uncle pay a visit. Or, in a nostalgic moment, she might request all past pictures of Hawaiian vacations.

TELECOMMUNICATION CENTER: HOME SYSTEM MODULE

The "information street" to the community computer utility is likely to replace the personal computer because the telecommunication links ("information highways") between national and international residences and enterprises will permit the consumer to "telephone" friends and businesses from the system module and to access "broadcasts" such as news programs. Thus, the need for local and network radio and video stations will be transformed, and costly, high-powered radio wave transmission equipment is unlikely to be required. Programs will be "delivered" to the community computer utilities via the national and international information highways.

Interactive voice communications will most likely make obsolete the need to publish telephone directories or to maintain individual or enterprise telephone lists. The system should be able to keep track of "numbers" frequently called, and look up those not previously recorded. Obviously, the same information streets and highways that link residences and enterprises through the community computer utilities should be the common carriers of information. Thus, the need for telephone sets in the home would be eliminated by the home system module itself and by video/speaker/microphone outlets linked to the module and strategically placed in several areas of the home. The two-way voice and video communication in every room would not only carry "telephone" signals but also pipe in music and video.

FACILITY CONVERSION: RETAIL TO HOME DELIVERY

As home shopping continues its explosive rate of growth, vacant retail outlets and grocery stores will become common phenomena. The large retail and grocery chains' massive investment in leases and ownership of these properties and the potential for massive new investments in distribution facilities to service home delivery are factors that might seem to inhibit their enthusiasm for conversion to home delivery operations. Indeed, the present seemingly timid pilot endeavors are the only practical way to get started. The pioneers know that when their home delivery pilot facilities start to operate perfectly, the tremendous success will force them and their competitors into dynamic Wal-Mart-like growth of the new-wave home delivery systems and facilities.

The grocery chains that most rapidly establish their home delivery capabilities will find that their retail store buildings are almost ideally suited to become the new neighborhood home delivery distribution centers. They are typically ideally located, in the middle of their customer base, and thus will have short, dense delivery routes. Relatively poor cubic space utilization in the shallow, low display racks of the grocery store will give way to higher-rise storage facilities and order-picking mechanization designed for highly efficient picking and assembly of orders and delivery-route-sequenced loading of small, fast-moving delivery trucks.

Nevertheless, only one of three, four, or more grocery stores in every neighborhood will ultimately be needed to distribute deliveries efficiently to that neighborhood, leaving most buildings unoccupied and the chains that previously operated them out in the cold, with almost no possibility of recapturing the market in that area. The glut of vacated buildings will present both challenge and opportunity, as discussed in chapter 11, in the subsection "Vacant Building Rehabilitation: Growth Industry."

The concluding section of this and following chapters will summarize many of the waning and growth industries highlighted in the chapter.

SUMMARY

Executives' attention should focus on growth opportunities in coming years, not just short-term profitability. Examples abound of major companies that have had long, unbroken successes in terms of past profitability, but that unfortunately have overlooked the need to (1) reinvent their current business processes, and (2) define short-term

EXHIBIT 2–18
Growth Industries & Occupations

Interactive Touch-tone Data Entry	**Neighborhood Retail Distribution Centers**
Targeted Mailing Lists	**Shopper Buying Profiles**
Home Shopping	**Home Shopping Software**
Home Delivery Service	**Electronic Marketing**
Home System Module	**Direct Customer Delivery**
Electronic Catalogs	

strategies and long-term visions to reshape their businesses as the world around them changes.

The first priority of every company must continue to be the pursuit of greater productivity and, thus, lower costs and customer prices. Equally important is the need to improve the quality of goods and services provided. Integration of the operations and systems of retailers, their suppliers, and logistics into a smooth-flowing pipeline of information and goods is the key to quantum short-term reengineering. Home shopping and delivery services may be vital components of the industry's transformation.

This chapter has defined numerous short-term and long-term areas of future growth potential, which are summarized on exhibit 2–18. Companies that are, or should be, directly involved can start actively realigning their operations in order to capitalize on these new opportunities. Others indirectly affected may use these predictions to help define their visions, strategies, and tactics in light of their own analysis. Due to the impending arrival of the home shopping wave, some companies should have shifted into high gear in order to ride the crest. A few examples of areas of need—and therefore of great potential payback—are as follows.

1. Interactive home shopping software, including catalog scanning and order placement
2. Interactive home shopping video interface hardware
3. Home shopping computer utility and customer data base
4. Neighborhood home delivery distribution centers
5. Neighborhood home delivery common carriers
6. Electronic catalog "mailbox" service
7. Home fiber-optics utilities

In summary, interactive home shopping will offer ultimate convenience to consumers. Through virtual reality, should they choose to do so, they will be able to "talk" interactively with "salespersons" in a "retail store," and see the products offered in three dimensions, "trying on" clothing and shoes on their life-size, three-dimensional electronic image. They will have instant access to the wares offered by every supplier, and will be able to compare all of their prices. Thus, because middlemen are eliminated, prices will be lower. Finally, every consumer's time for leisure activities will be expanded, and the environment will be freed from massive traffic and resultant air and noise pollution.

It is important for enterprises and individuals involved in businesses and occupations predicted that are expected to wane and perhaps even die to evaluate the timing of their demise. Those changes evaluated as very long-term developments could logically be ignored, especially by businesses that are fighting to survive, and whose most immediate need is to reinvent their processes. However, those who evaluate changes as short-term to intermediate-term and who are not threatened with competitive extinction would be remiss to ignore the demand for shifting the business to achieve long-term survival, at a minimum, or industry leadership, at best.

For those inclined to feel anxious or offended by the definition of some industries and occupations as waning or dying, there are several important points to keep in mind. These points are repeated briefly in every chapter, because some people will read only selected chapters. First, the change may not occur in the foreseeable future. Second, the future continuous reduction of work will be universal. As a result, society must and will reduce average workweek hours in order to maintain full employment. Third, the era of reduced work and increased

EXHIBIT 2–19
Waning Industries & Occupations

Order Entry Clerks

Customer Service Clerks

Hospital Admittance Clerks

Catalog Printers

Compact Discs (Music)

Radio, Television, Telephone

Accounts Payable Accountants

Airlines Reservation Clerks

Bank Tellers

Retail Stores

leisure time will be one of unprecedented quality of life and affluence. My predictions about which of the industries and occupations mentioned in this chapter will wane are listed on exhibit 2–19. (Similar exhibits are included in the summary section of most chapters.) As the exhibit shows, several customer service occupations, previously provided over the telephone and at airline, travel bureau, and bank counters, will be replaced by the computer-based interactive voice systems, through the home system module and its business counterpart. These and other occupations are already on the wane in the world's leading enterprises—public and private.

3

REINVENTING
THE OFFICE
Layout, Organization, and Location

One purpose of this chapter is to introduce an important aspect of one strategy and vision of the immediate and long-term future—the office at home. However, for companies with massive office staffs and operations too complex to be quickly distributed to offices in the home, quantum improvements in office operating costs and capital investment are still possible through a combination of reengineering the office operations (processes) and relocating the revised office work cells into new layouts that can improve space utilization by 50 percent or more.[1] Operation reengineering, which has the potential for drastically improving productivity and reducing the time from start of process to completion is discussed as part of other chapters dealing with the reinvention of various industries. Office layout, organization, and location are the important subjects of *this* chapter that will apply to *every* industry.

New and emerging technology are vitally important ingredients in making the worker's location completely flexible. After all, notebook computers and cellular phones already enable people to work as effec-

---

1. For reference to more about space utilization in factories and warehouses, see appendix 2.

tively at the beach or in the home as at the office—at least from the technological standpoint. However, when people work in remote locations, the lack of the supervisory function of attendance and work monitoring is a legitimate concern. Won't employees slack off, work fewer hours, and do less while working? The answer is also part of the reason that the office in the home will reduce costs—office supervisors are no longer required. Modern computer systems are now the focus of every routine office function (or should be, where they are not yet). Thus, modern software systems should replace the attendance and work monitoring functions by recording the elapsed time worked and the amount of data processed.

Many enterprises' office operations are already beginning a phase of revolutionary change as workplaces move from office to office-in-the-home. Offices-in-the home are already connected with other local, national, and international private and public businesses via existing telecommunication technology. The far faster and lower-cost information superhighway will further reduce the already practical telecommunication cost and give even more support to the movement to transfer workers into offices in the home. The beneficial impact of this shift is enormous. Businesses will be able to convert millions of square feet of costly office space into more productive use—manufacturers might use the space for production operations, for example. Alternatively, the cost of vacated office space that is rented would easily be eliminated by terminating the lease. If owned, the office space could be sold or leased, shifting assets into cash accounts that could be used for more productive investments.

Employees who work at home will be spared the expense and trauma of a long daily commute and will benefit by gaining time to spend with their families. Or, if they choose to do so, they might add the hours gained to their productive work day. Further, the reduction in numbers of commuters' automobiles will ease the bumper-to-bumper single-passenger traffic that now clogs streets and highways and burns untold millions of gallons of nonreplenishable fossil fuels.

Modern computer technology is already beginning to remove paper from the office. Switching from a business world in which multiple paper copies are created for every transaction, then filed pending action and refiled for just-in-case history to a world of electronic transactions transforms not only the clerical process. It also completely changes the amount of office space required. File cabinets often occupy as much as 30 to 50% of the entire office space. Elimination of paper transactions and files should be part and parcel of every office modernization program.

EXECUTIVE CHECKLIST: FUTURE OFFICE ZINGERS

Every enterprise should begin to look at white-collar employees and their offices in a new light. The processes that involve office personnel should be reengineered to increase efficiency and speed of processing. Next, the office space itself should be reorganized to reduce required facility and equipment costs. Ultimately, however, the ideal enterprise office will be no office at all! The following checklist focuses on the immediate improvements that companies should be making to their present offices, while the list of future visions is mainly a look into the future world of the office in the home.

Short-Term Tactics and Strategies

1. The space utilization of existing offices is usually terrible but correctable. New layouts, in tandem with reengineered operations, can reduce occupancy and equipment costs.
2. The utilization of most equipment in the typical office is shockingly low. Computers, copy machines, and telephones are seldom in continuous use in many offices, thus the investment in equipment is much higher than necessary to supply the required capacity. Reorganized offices should target increased equipment utilization, thus reducing capital investment.
3. Telephone and video-telephone conferencing are already increasing executive and managerial productivity by allowing them to "attend" meetings without leaving their offices. For enterprises with far-flung operations, suppliers, and customers, this can slash travel costs and time.
4. Document-scanning hardware and software are technologies that offer powerful ways to capture, store, and retrieve massive amounts of documentation at far lower cost than clerical alternatives. Fast computer retrieval of such information can put the an-

swer to customer inquiries at the hands of the customer service person with lightning speed, compared to retrieving correspondence from file cabinets.

5. Programmed training aids that lead new employees through the maze of complex operations should almost completely eliminate the training roles of supervisors and significantly reduce the time required to make a new employee productive.

6. A multitude of office jobs can already be performed equally as well in the home as in the office. Moving work to the home can drastically reduce the cost of office facilities and commuting time and cost.

7. Electronic transactions and files should be designed to eliminate paper equivalents. Thus, the labor involved in distributing and filing transactions and the space to store files can be eliminated.

Future Visions

1. Future telecommunication systems can put the manager in direct contact with employees working in the home. Computer virtual reality and telecommunications technology will enable company executives to participate in internal meetings and sessions with external customers and suppliers without leaving their own offices (which may well be in their homes).

2. Virtual reality and video telecommunication technology will eventually enable teleconferencing executives to "sit" at a conference table with other attenders surrounding them without leaving their own office or home system module. Thus, their need for human contact will be satisfied.

3. More and more appliances (integral fax modems, for example) will be merged with continuously improved computers, making obsolete stand-alone appliances such as telephone, television, fax, calculator, radio, clocks, tape player, slide projector, and VCR. The ultimate "home system module" (see chapter 2's subsection "Virtually Real Home Shopping") will be a combination of all of these plus some that have not yet been invented.

4. Computer work-monitoring and performance recording software, which will keep track of productive hours worked and the quantity and quality of work completed, should almost completely eliminate the work-monitoring roles of supervisors.

5. Interactive voice recognition and response systems are fast being perfected. Eventually, these systems will enable all communications between computer users and their systems to be conversational. This
will eliminate the need for typing and data key-entry occupations.

INTERIM OFFICE: FACTORYLIKE EFFICIENCY

While working with an Indonesian/Japanese joint-venture computer
plant in Indonesia, I once visited the factory after a management team
from Japan had visited and reviewed the operation. The Indonesian
managers were dismayed because the Japanese had commented, before leaving, that they found the operation to be very inefficient. This
was perplexing to them, because the *factory* equipment, made in
Japan, was exactly the same as that used by the Japanese factory. Further, the hours per unit produced were roughly the same, while labor
costs were a small fraction of those in Japan. However, the conclusion
of the Japanese that the factory was a high-cost operation was no
mystery to me. The building in which the factory was located also
housed the offices, and the office area was more than twice as large as
the factory! My Japanese compatriots would automatically consider
the large office space (and the people therein) as unnecessary overhead cost, and evaluate the overall operation less than cost effective.

While working in Japan in the late 1970s, I discovered that executives and managers rarely occupied individual offices. At Yamaha, for
example, only one of every five thousand employees were provided
private offices. As exhibit 3–1 shows, almost all executives' and managers' desks were usually in the large room in which their employees
worked, with managers' desks at the head of a block of desks occupied by their employees. This block layout had many advantages for
employees and for their managers and executives. For example, communication among the group members was extraordinarily easy, even
though the noise level was often equally phenomenal. The desks in the
Japanese office are also far less expensive than those used in the West,
requiring less capital investment. Radically reduced drawer space, for
example, was compensated for by space in a common storage block
for personal materials such as work papers currently in process and
working tools (writing instruments, pocket calculators, etc.).

I observed additional operating cost advantages in the Japanese sys-

EXHIBIT 3–1
The Japanese Office

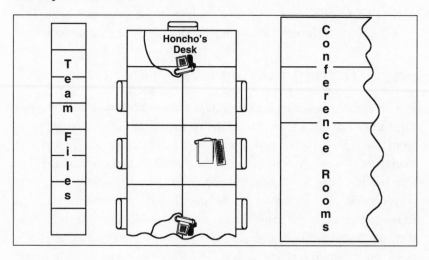

tem, including team files rather than file cabinets for each individual. Instead of making copies of everything for everyone and providing file space for mountains of duplicate material, each working group shared most file documents of common interest. One of the benefits of fewer copies was that far fewer copy machines were needed. In addition, personal computer and telephone equipment costs were lower. As seen in the exhibit, the work group was equipped with the number of computers required to achieve near full-time utilization—one computer for the group, in this example. In many Western offices the number of computers is equal to the number of people, and average utilization is typically much less than full-time. Telephone costs and investments in Japan are also much lower. The number of phones per work group of ten or slightly more people was typically two. Even so, the time the telephones were in use was *far* less than 100 per cent. Western offices, in which it is common to put a telephone on almost every employee's desk, spend inordinately more for telephone communication. And the costs are not merely for telephones, but more importantly for the lines and switching equipment necessary to support them.

At Yamaha, conference rooms of various sizes and levels of comfort were available in which to host meetings with customers, suppliers, and colleagues from other functional areas of the company. Conference rooms were shared by colleagues from several blocks of desks, a fact not illustrated on the simplified exhibit. In the West, virtually every executive's and even manager's office has an area for meetings. Many top executives have their own dedicated conference rooms. These areas are rarely in use because so many meetings involve groups too large for the executive's own meeting area or private conference room. Further, the typical Western conference room is relatively large and there may be several such facilities, though the average occupancy (productive space utilization) of the rooms (as a percent of room capacities) is quite low.

Perhaps it is far too extreme to imagine that all Western executives and managers will accept elimination of private offices. I, for one, shudder at the thought of working an entire career in the fishbowl openness of the Japanese office. Bold companies, however, are already taking steps to revolutionize office design. For example, T.J. Howard reports that the new headquarters for Morningstar, Inc., a financial publishing company, will have only three private offices, although it has five hundred employees.[2] However, it is reasonable to expect that many individuals who want private offices will acknowledge the need to improve the cost effectiveness of the office and to begin to move in the direction of openness.

The short-term future office, exhibit 3–2, will feature fewer, and much more compact individual offices for managers and executives. A good deal of the office space reduction comes from moving meeting facilities from individual offices into conference rooms. In this example, one of numerous plausible variations, the office is divided into smaller, business-within-business groups, along service lines, product lines, or customer groups. Functional departments have been reorganized so that every person involved in a *process* has been moved into a multifunctional, cross-trained team responsible for the entire process. The most modern computer systems already reduce the complexities of learned operations to a series of screens that automatically guide each worker through the maze, thus enabling each person to function as a team of one. These teams of one are then more easily moved, eventually, into offices within the home. The dotted lines sep-

---

2. T.J. Howard, "The Office Shapes Up: Future Workspaces Will Be Open, Friendly—Even with the Boss in the Middle," *Chicago Tribune,* August 22, 1993.

EXHIBIT 3–2

Cost-Effective Office

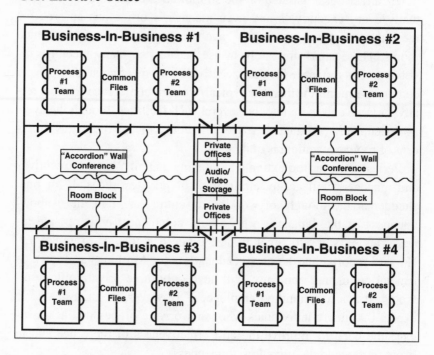

arating the businesses-within-a-business illustrate the openness of the space and the ease of communications and movement between them. Richard Schonberger and Edward Knod note that two important "advantages of open layouts are that they foster better employee communications and provide flexibility for easy re-layout."[3] The use of walls between the businesses not only inhibits these vital functions but also reduces the enterprise's flexibility—teams can not as easily add or reduce members as business volumes fluctuate and as the teams continuously improve their productivity. (In the case of manufacturers, each business-in-a-business office would best be located within its corresponding factory-in-a-factory.[4])

---

3. Richard J. Schonberger and Edward M. Knod, Jr., *Synchro Service! The Innovative Way to Build a Dynasty of Customers* (Burr Ridge, IL: Irwin, 1994), p. 347.

4. For reference to more about factories-within-factories, see appendix 2.

The conference room blocks, the ideal total area of which can be determined by careful analysis of current practices plus projections of need based on new working methods, are accessible and available to all of the businesses-within-the-business. This helps to ensure maximum utilization. They are dividable by soundproof "accordion" partitions, enabling users to create different-sized spaces depending on the number of participants. This also increases the participant/space utilization ratio. The team clusters of desks are separated by banks of common files and storage shelves. Some of these shelves are used for team-size copiers and a team's or business's facsimile machine. Telephones and computers are shared, to increase their utilization. The team members, rather than executives and managers, have the prized locations nearest windows. It is one way in which management proves its recognition of the value of its associates (employees), one that coincidentally contributes to higher productivity, since the brightest workplaces are often the most productive locations. Stephen Frangos, in discussing Kodak's Black and White Film's decision to adopt the open office layout, points out how important the window position is. He quotes himself as having said, "I'll go with an open office but I've got to have a window. It took me 25 years to get one and I'm not about to stare at a wall now!"[5] Nor are the managers and executives and conference attenders robbed of the outside view and light. Partitions that separate the private offices and conference rooms from windows to the outside are glass, with lightproof shades for use when video or projection equipment requires lower light levels. Moreover, executive and manager offices do not really need to be isolated from their organizations and peers by floor-to-ceiling partitions. Alcoa, for one, is planning to use cubicles for their executives and managers.[6] The occupants will be able to talk to colleagues by simply leaning over the short walls, a far superior way to communicate than holding formal meetings. Employees should share common blocks much like

5. Stephen J. Frangos with Steven J. Bennett, *Team Zebra: How 1500 Partners Revitalized Eastman Kodak's Black & White Film-Making Flow* (Essex Junction, VT: Wight, 1993), p. 71.

6. Raje Narisetti, "Executive Suites' Walls Come Tumbling Down," *Wall Street Journal,* June 29, 1994.

their contemporary Japanese counterparts, with short, sound-deadening screens providing at least some privacy and reduced noise level.

In my own firm, a new office layout was adopted for professional partners and managers who often spend most of their working days at client sites. Previously, each manager was assigned an office. Based on a study that indicated offices were used less than ten percent of the time, the new layout provided three larger offices, each of which was shared by ten managers. The manager response was *not* disappointment at losing a traditional status symbol (the private office). According to the partner who described the pilot project to me, the managers, almost as a group, questioned whether they needed an office at all! Their most frequent use of the office was in the early morning or evening to pick up and leave mail, and home delivery and pickup eliminated that reason for an office, and permitted them to spend more time at home and at client sites and less time traveling to the downtown office. The desks in the partner's offices were replaced by tables, making the rooms suitable as small conference rooms in the partners' frequent absences.

Despite the major opportunities for improving the efficiency, communications, and costs of enterprise offices, however, the ultimate office of the future will be the office in the home.

HOME OFFICE: DO AS I SAY

I, for one, practice what I preach! A few years ago, I found myself fast becoming a business anachronism: (1) I commuted up to three hours daily to a traditional large office; (2) I was drafting my book's text, client correspondence, and graphics in longhand; (3) I was communicating inefficiently by direct telephone conversation with colleagues in offices around the world. I was dependent on my executive assistant for word processing, obtaining copies, sending faxes, and maintaining both current working files and noncurrent files which had been transferred to the storage vault. Today, no longer a complete anachronism, I operate over 90 percent of my business from my semi-modern, U-form home office (exhibit 3–3). This office cell is my pride and joy. Its highly compact layout, like those of the factories

---

7. For reference to more about factory U-form cells, see appendix 2.

and warehouses I design for my clients, is extremely efficient in mini-mizing wasteful time and motion.[7] Every element of the cell is within reach without leaving the chair. However, the cell's equipment and software can be better described as simple, low-cost automation than as state-of-the-art (costlier and more complex) automation.

The cell's telephone communications connect me to colleagues around the world and to my executive assistant in the office forty miles away, but with vastly improved productivity. The firm's world-wide voice-mail system has helped to minimize the time waste and frustration of playing two-way telephone tag with others in different time zones. Eventually, after connecting with the person called, old-fashioned conversations were all too often highly inefficient. Both parties generally felt obligated to spend some amount of time in ex-change of nonessential pleasantries and small talk (sports, weather, families, etc.). Many calls involving complex questions and issues tended to embroil both parties in slow, nonproductive brainstorming even though the ultimate answers rarely evolved from these conversa-tions. The voice-mail message system, by contrast, automatically dis-ciplines users to be businesslike. A call to ask a question, raise an issue, or deliver a message is now usually brief and to the point. The answer, formulated with careful thought before responding with a re-

EXHIBIT 3–3
U-Form Home Office

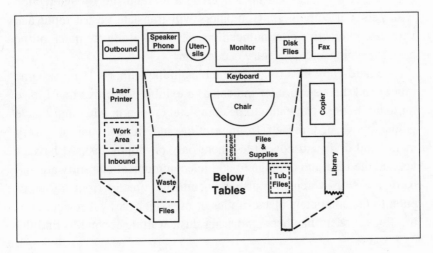

turn message, is similarly concise and is usually more to the point than the outcome of instant brainstorming attempts of the person-to-person conversation of the past.

Modern, low-cost facsimile equipment now enables me to send lengthier messages and report directly to global colleagues and to my executive assistant, eliminating the delay and additional cost of delivery to and return from the old central facsimile service. I have resisted the urge to buy the latest plain-paper facsimile machine, which is not especially expensive. The machine I use, an old-fashioned treated-paper design, was a gift from its inventer, my friend, Makoto Takayanagi, president of TTT Corporation in Hamamatsu, Japan.

For a few years I shied from adopting the use of a personal computer, doubting—among other things—that my typing skills would be adequate. I had not typed seriously for over thirty years. The center of the home office is now my personal computer, on which I produce virtually everything that involves text and numbers by direct keyboard entry, using powerful word processor software. This has eliminated the inefficiency and time loss of handwriting a draft for key entry and proofreading by both the word processing department and me. WordPerfect software catches misspellings that have slipped through *both* (specialist and author) proofreaders in the past. Now it is much easier to proofread, modify, and rearrange my work as I create it, rather than during a separate proofreading cycle. Typing, I learned, is like bicycle riding. Once learned, one never forgets. However, in coming years typing will no longer be a prerequisite for interaction with personal computers. Computers will translate verbal input and verbalize interactive communications. This will eliminate much of the need for typing and data entry occupations.

The hard-copy files (under the tables in the author's U-form home office) and the laser printer indicated in exhibit 3–3 prove that I have far to go before I can claim to be completely modern. Although I have gradually weaned myself from printing and filing copies of every memo and draft and now "file" them only on floppy disks, I haven't yet had the time and courage to add telecommunications software and hardware with which to transmit documents directly from my computer to the computers or facsimiles of my colleagues. (A telecommunications modem has been gathering dust, waiting for me to find the time to learn how to install and use it). But my colleagues, clients, and publisher are almost all still dinosaurs, continuing to send reams of paper documents via fax and mail. This has caused me to perpetuate filing hard copies. The ultimate, not-too-distant direct communication links between the my own and my contacts' computers will serve to queue "documents" electronically for review and disposition in the following ways.

1. Retransmission to another colleague as an assignment to be completed or for information only
2. Erasure of documents of no further interest
3. Suspense of documents pending later disposition according to assigned priority
4. Transfer to an appropriate active or historical "file"

I am considering a fast, simple, low-cost interim alternative to computer-to-computer communication. Scanners are now available with which one can quickly capture electronic document images for pending and history files. (A scanner and related software are also gathering dust, pending available time to study their installation and use.) Complete or partial modernization (doing away with printed copy) will eventually eliminate equipment in the office U-form cell, since the printer, copier, and file cabinets will no longer be needed.

The exhibits in this book have been prepared using a practical combination of low and high technology, as follows. First, I sketch a freehand draft in the work area illustrated on exhibit 3–3. The simple sketches include stick figures for people and crude outlines of other complex figures. I send these to the firm's graphic arts department specialist, who uses powerful graphics software to convert them into professional electronic "drawings" which are printed as artwork for the book's publisher and in multicolor form for my 35mm slide presentations and video tapes. Modern writers and their modern publishers insert electronic graphics into the computer's electronic text, using modern software to edit the manuscript into press-ready plates. At some date, an upgrade of the my own computer hardware and software will put graphic sketching tools into my own tool kit, eliminating the need for the cell's work area. However, the sketches will still be sent to the graphic arts specialist, albeit via electronic transmission, because the specialist's software systems and data base of stored images are far too complex for use by anyone other than a full-time professional.

VIDEO TELECONFERENCE: ATTENDING IN VIRTUAL REALITY

At one time, I had need to attend numerous meetings in different locations in my area and around the globe. These meetings necessitated hundreds of hours of travel and tens of thousand of dollars of expense each year. A few years ago, I began to use the power of today's high-quality speaker phones and facsimiles to allow me to "attend" those meetings within my own home office. Now, whenever I am invited to a meeting, I arrange to "attend" the meeting at home or, when out of town, in an office with a speaker phone and ask the others in the meeting to use the conference room speaker phone or conference call connections. Thus, all attenders can hear and be heard clearly. If hard-copy material or visuals are presented at the main meeting site, I can follow the presentation by viewing copies received via facsimile. Of course, many of the firm's offices and those of clients are now equipped for video-teleconferencing, a technology which, while cur-

EXHIBIT 3-4
Video Telecommunications Cost

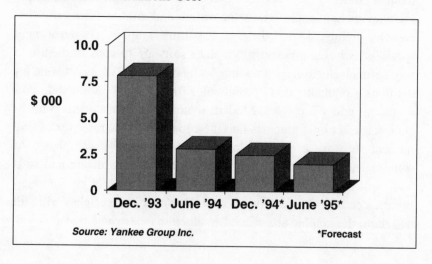

Source: Yankee Group Inc.   *Forecast

rently too expensive for the home office, will become practical in the not-too-distant future.[8] Recently, for example, the costs of desk-top video systems, not including the personal computer, have been falling rather rapidly (exhibit 3–4), as have prices for virtually all electronic/telecommunication devices during the limited time between their inception and replacement by improved products.[9] Booming sales, projected by Researcher Dataquest, Inc., will reach 400,000 by 1997.[10] This explosion of demand, through economies of scale, will help to lower the cost per teleconferencing system to the range of $500, thus enabling even employees of a single company building to "conference" via video-teleconferencing stations in each work cell.

FILING "ELECTRONIC PAPER"

The demise of paper, which I expect to occur in the next decade or two, if not sooner, is already having an impact on the labor and facility costs of stored paper documents. The electronic "filing" of documents, worldwide, will eliminate employment for armies of file clerks and do away with paperwork files filling the equivalent of thousands of buildings. Progressive companies are already finding that massive savings are available by eliminating paper copies of business transactions and other business communications. However, as long as these costly paper documents continue to be in existence, stored and accessed, efficient filing (warehousing) systems can lower the costs of keeping them.

The tub files indicated on exhibit 3–3 are large, portable working files that I use for storing the printed documents involved in large, complex projects in process, such as writing this book. Once the project is completed and no longer actively accessed, the files are transferred to my home/business warehouse in the basement. I am inordinately proud of this facility, a perfect model warehouse in which

---

8. For more on conducting high-productivity meetings via video teleconferencing, see appendix 2.

9. Bart Ziegler, "Video Conference Calls Change Business," *The Wall Street Journal,* October 12, 1994.

10. Jim Carlton and Don Clark, "Video Conferencing Takes Center Stage," *Wall Street Journal,* November 11, 1994.

EXHIBIT 3–5

Home/Business Warehouse

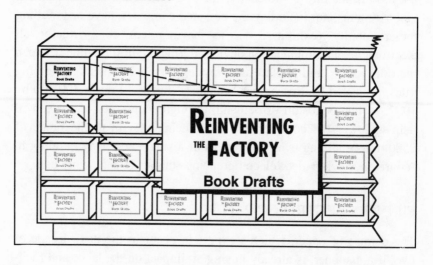

cubic space is as extremely well utilized and stored items are as simply located (without complex location control systems) as in the warehouses designed for my clients.[11] The shelving, used for both business and household storage, was purchased from an industrial warehouse supply company. The adjustable shelves were spaced to almost exactly fit the height of the standard size cardboard cartons used for storage, as seen on exhibit 3–5. Further, the shelf depth is exactly the same as that of the carton, thus the storage space occupied by the cartons is almost perfectly utilized. And, although the system stores almost two hundred large containers, a complex locator system is not required to find any specific box. Large, easy-to-read labels on each box identify its contents (e.g., beach balls, picnic supplies, gift wrap, winter boots). Different zones of the warehouse are used for items of like characteristics. For example, business and personal records are stored in two of the zones. One subsection of the business records zone is dedicated to storing drafts of my first three books (each previous book required three or four boxes of drafts from the various stages of production). Since then, I have learned that these paper

---

11. For reference to more on warehouse design, see appendix 2.

copies are not really necessary and I am relying solely on computer files for the production of *this* book. Finally, one relatively small zone of the home/business warehouse is used for items too large for the standard cartons.

SUMMARY

Every business has office operations. The cost of these operations can be reduced dramatically. There are three initiatives by which every business can make quantum improvements in the office productivity. One of the fastest ways is to relocate process teams in revised office layouts with equipment better matched to the workload of the team. Complete reengineering of the office processes is a second initiative that takes longer and needs someone to bring independence and creativity to the effort if the best results are to be achieved. Part of the process of reengineering involves the application of the latest computer technology to electronic transaction processing that eliminates paper documents and manual files. Systems designed to eliminate paper can slash clerical office costs and contribute 30 to 50 percent reductions in the size of an average office. The third, longer-term office improvement initiative, moving employees' workplaces into their homes, is close to the lowest-cost ideal. Every company should have a plan for eventually achieving this ultimate objective.

Formal offices, with their large numbers of employees who commute to work daily, will continue to exist well into the future. Until the need disappears, if ever, enterprises should drastically improve the economics of their office operations and layout. However, in the end, office work will almost universally be performed by people working in their own home offices, in their ultra-modern home system modules. The home office trend is already spurring the growth of several industries and occupations (exhibit 3–6). For example, a large number of the personal computers sold in recent years have gone to the over 40 million U.S. workers who now work at home. And, home offices need office furniture, especially computer work stations to house the computer, monitor, scanner, and printer. Home work-monitoring software development will be one of the new growth industries, since it will answer the need for "supervising" the attendance and productivity of those who work in the home office. Eventually, interactive voice

EXHIBIT 3–6
Growth Industries & Occupations

<table>
<tr><td>

Home Office

–Computer

–Furniture

**–Monitoring
Software**

</td><td>

**Voice Recognition
& Response**

–Software

–Hardware

Home System Module

</td></tr>
</table>

recognition hardware and software will permit everyone to communi-cate with their computers in the simplest, fastest mode possible, by normal speech. Thus, companies that lead their competitors in devel-opment of hardware and software will have a giant new market.

The manufacturing of home system modules (explained in chapter 2) will be the biggest new industry of all. These will replace several stand-alone devices that are shown on exhibit 3–3 as products (there-fore, industries) and which can be expected to wane or even die in the twenty-first century. For those inclined to feel anxious or offended by the definition of some industries and occupations as waning or dying, there are several important points to keep in mind. (The following points are repeated briefly in every chapter, because some readers may read only selected chapters.) First, the change may not occur in the foreseeable future. Second, the future continuous reduction of work will be universal. As a result, society must and will reduce aver-age work week hours in order to maintain full employment. Third, the era of reduced work and increased leisure time will be one of un-precedented quality of life and affluence. The author's predictions of dying and waning products, some of which are listed on exhibit 3–7, include facsimile machines, computers and computer components (es-

EXHIBIT 3–7
Waning Industries & Occupations

Office Supervisors

Standalone:

- **– Facsimile**   **– TV & VCR**

- **– Calculator**   **– Computer Printer**

- **– Telephone**   **– File Cabinets**

---

pecially printers), television and video tape recorders, telephones, and file cabinets. Electronic storage of "printed" material and displaying it on the walls of the home module will make paper obsolete, therefore will eliminate the need for printers and file cabinets.

4

REINVENTING PRODUCTION AND LOGISTICS

Manufacturing and distribution will be among the most pro-
foundly changed industries during the twenty-first century. Two
factors leading the revolution will be increased factory automation in
manufacturing, and clustering of smaller, more efficient factories in
the regions in which products are sold. The most urgent need for manufacturers, therefore, is to continuously improve the efficiency of their
factories and offices and the cost and quality of their product design.
That quantum improvements are a short-term, achievable objective is
proven by the magnitude of gains in recent years. Typical factory and
warehouse project targets, documented in my previous books, include
the following percentages of improvement.[1]

Percent		*Percent*	
80	Setup/changeover cost	50	Space Utilization
	Inventory investment:	10	Purchase Prices
95	Work-in-Process	80	Quality
75	Materials	80	Down Time
75	Finished Goods	75	Record Accuracy
80	Customer Service		

---

1. For reference to more about targets for improvement see appendix 2.

Reengineering the supplier-customer relationship and processes is probably the area in which business has the greatest potential for improvement. Yet it seems to be one of the slowest to develop, in terms of operating at peak efficiency. Producers' ability to deliver high-value products, when customers need them, is all too often controlled by the production efficiency and quality and speed of delivery of their suppliers. Far too many procurement executives and managers are still enmeshed in yesterday's approach to attaining performance improvements from their suppliers. The outmoded control system is one designed to measure the supplier's performance by capturing delivery and quality information, and perpetuates maintaining adversarial relationships. John Schorr's excellent book on purchasing, for example, combines widely recognized state-of-the-art practices—in terms of just-in-time suppliers capable of perfect quality and delivery at reasonable prices—with prevalent but outmoded methods such as statistical quality control and vendor qualification/certification.[2] These passé methods are precisely the failed techniques that have led to productivity crises.

Price is still far too important a factor in selecting and ending supplier-customer relationships. Although the supplier's competitive price is ultimately one of the most important factors in the success of both customer and supplier, the underlying, more important issue is the supplier's costs. After all, if the relationship is honest and legitimately concerned with the continuing growth and profitability of both "partners in profit," the price should be determined by the supplier's cost, and that cost will be competitive only if all necessary steps are taken to keep it at or below those of other suppliers. The formula for developing more perfect suppliers, at the technical level, is to encourage, and even to help, them embrace and energetically implement *every* new method that, in combination with every other method, converts a so-so producer to a superior supplier. The most important of these *technical* management organization and process methods include reorganization of big factories into many smaller factories-within-a-factory, establishment of flow from operation to operation, process quality fail-safing, and virtual elimination of machine/process

---

2. John E. Schorr, *Purchasing in the 21st Century: A Guide to State-of-the-Art Techniques and Strategies* (Essex Junction, VT: Wight, 1992).

changeover cost—not just moving it off-line, as described by Schorr.[3] (Schorr merely falls into the trap of earlier "experts" who failed to understand that the economics of setup versus inventory costs are unchanged when setup is merely moved off-line. To gain financially, the *cost* of the setup must be reduced.) These and many other *technical* solutions are detailed in my previous books and will not be repeated here. Nor will I dwell on the countless "fads of the month," all variations of ways to achieve these technical solutions, and new buzzwords. A few of these, for example, are quality circles, statistical quality control, total quality control, empowered work teams, and, quite recently, reengineering.

At the top management level, far more important supplier relationship issues, when addressed, can more rapidly move both customer and supplier to weld a bond of partnership that will lead to better performance of each. For example, one of the primary factors behind outstanding supplier performance and dedication to success of both parties has been the interlocking ownership of customer and supplier. Even a minimal interlocking ownership motivates each partner to work cooperatively for their common good—more than any other factor. And establishing cross-ownership is as simple and cost-free as exchanging treasury stock. Once the ownership exchange has taken place, the bottom line of each partner is directly affected by the dividends received from the stock of the other; thus it behooves each to help the other improve or maintain excellent profit levels.

The emerging business information highway, linking the entire chain of a producer—its customers, its suppliers, and their suppliers—is a prerequisite for survival. Scarcely fifteen years have elapsed since a major U.S. automotive producer's executives scoffed at my description of these vital links as a certain future development. The predominant sentiment then was that this would never occur in their lifetime—at least not in this country, even though it was common in Japan at that time. Today, every knowledgeable distributor and producer executive recognizes the inevitability of competitive dominance by the companies best equipped for rapid response to market needs by virtue of the speed with which they can feed information through the supply chain and deliver products.

---

3. Ibid., p. 67.

Further, the recent political clamor for reduced government intrusion and interference will continue and will eventually result in a decrease in the number of regulations that are causing industry to drown in paperwork. While the effect will not be minor, it will have far fewer beneficial results than initiatives addressing the reengineering of white-collar processes and the increased application of automation of repetitive clerical tasks.

Manufacturers' and distributors' formal visions for their industries are almost uniformly nonexistent, thus company strategies are extremely limited in terms of anticipating the future and being in the forefront of companies that cause the future vision to become tomorrow's reality. Far too many enterprises are not even keeping pace with reengineering their own production and office processes and restructuring their organizations using *today's* technology and methods. It is time that every company go to work on both! This chapter will conclude with an explanation of the technological forces that will radically change future production and distribution operations and employment.

EXECUTIVE CHECKLIST: SELECTED PRODUCTION AND INVENTORY ZINGERS

Even the most advanced enterprises and their supplier networks are in the Stone Age of the information systems era, and their facilities and the infrastructure in which they operate are also archaic, relatively speaking. Working in new, closer relationships with suppliers clearly holds the key to radically improved service, quality, and cost. Following is a brief synopsis of the key issues covered in this chapter. Executives should ask themselves if their visions and strategies are aligned with making major gains in these areas. Many of the short-term "zingers" on this list, detailed later in this chapter, will take years to develop, while the longer-range visions may require decades to come into existance. However, many enterprises may find some tactics to be feasible in a much shorter time frame or that preparatory work towards the vision can already be launched. Therefore, executives and their management teams may find this checklist and their own experience useful as tools to update or to cast their visions and strategies.

SHORT-TERM TACTICS AND STRATEGIES

1. Every supplier program should have as its objective permanently using far fewer suppliers—those willing to adopt all of the new-wave operating processes necessary to become superior performers.

2. The focus of customer and supplier cooperative communications should be the supplier's cost, not price. Customer and supplier should share fairly in joint efforts to reduce and eliminate as many unnecessary costs as possible.

3. Radically new price negotiating methods must be used if new, single-supplier relationships are to successfully keep the supplier's prices competitive and if both customer and supplier are to share fairly in the rewards of a successful "partnership in profits."

4. The horrendous processing costs and inventories in the pipeline between producers and suppliers cry out for improvement. The best modern computer/telecommunication technology must be used, in tandem with pipeline simplification, to lower them.

5. Since accurately forecasting demand at the level of individual items is not possible, producers must solve the problem of poor customer service by cutting the time required to produce and distribute products and provide flexible capacity to meet demand peaks.

6. Levels of distribution and retail facilities between a community's consumers and their suppliers will be radically reduced. Therefore, producers will need information and logistics systems capable of managing direct ordering and delivery.

7. Every private and public enterprise must understand that its functions today are more expensive than if performed by a profit-making outside service. Then, the enterprise must decide whether to outsource functions or to reengineer them in-house to perform even better.

8. Product design standardization and highest possible production volume are, and will always continue to be, the basis for the best quality and price. Producers of custom products must invent ways in which to standardize products, product options, or components of products.

9. Customers will continue to demand increased ability to create custom order specifications, but without the odious chore of mas-

tering massive catalog and specification documentation. The best producers will rationalize their product lines and options, simplifying their *modular* specifications to benefit both the customer and their own order processing.

10. The natural process of merger, within existing industries, will continue to reduce the number of competing enterprises, while increasing the economies of scale. However, big companies need to reorganize into smaller, more dynamic companies-within-companies to avoid the enormous dis-economies of scale.

FUTURE VISIONS

1. Future communities will be significantly more self-sufficient, in terms of manufacturing, agricultural, educational, and recreational enterprises. Manufacturing will lead the way by developing "clusters" of producer and supplier factories in the vicinity of the market, thus radically lowering the logistics costs of remote production and long-distance distribution.

2. Community computer utilities' demand planning and inventory replenishment systems, using software of incredibly effective design, will link ultimate customers (individuals and public and private enterprises) through the entire supply, production, and distribution chain.

3. Improved product designs will enable robots and other forms of factory automation to finally replace humans in assembly operations historically performed in spaces unsuitable for nonhuman workers.

4. Factory machine speeds, bearings, control systems, and costs will improve in quantum leaps. Manufacturers must be in the forefront of the visioning, strategizing, and installing of new, but proven, equipment in their factories to survive in the new technological arena.

SUPPLIER PRICE NEGOTIATION: A CHALLENGING NEW ARENA

If customers are to form new long-term relationship with suppliers, dropping other sources of supply, entirely new methods of controlling the suppliers' prices must be employed. However, the need for better controlling prices is not limited to companies that have formed new partnerships in profits.[4] As my colleague Mary Tolan has said, "Too many suppliers have buyers in their pockets—the buyers have more loyalty to the suppliers than to their own companies." Managements have the potential for short-term supplier price improvement if they move to solve this dilemma by instigating new programs to improve the quality of price negotiations. Companies like Sears Canada are bringing logical business arguments to the table to support their insistence on fairer sharing of the benefits of their high-volume purchases. For example, one routine tool used is a graphic presentation of the prices Sears has been able to charge retail customers in recent years compared to the industry average for the same item and compared to the price Sears pays to its supplier of the item. An example, exhibit 4–1, converts all of these prices to percentages of the prices in a starting base year (Sears uses the actual prices—the exhibit is my own creation). In this example of an automatic washing machine, the average price to retail consumers of all brands has been dropping continuously, and Sears has needed to follow industry pricing trends in order to remain competitive. At the end of the three-year period, prices of both Sears and all other brands had dropped between three and four percent. During the same period, the supplier's prices had *increased* almost one percent. By itself, the information is not a completely compelling argument for a price decrease. However, coupled with a systematically developed relationship to other data, such as the supplier's profit increases, cost reductions, and executive pronouncements to the media, it may become clear that the entire industry is benefiting from continuous cost reduction that has occurred as improvements to product design and manufacturing and distribution productivity have been achieved. Then it can become obvious that the supplier in question has not been fairly sharing the fruits of its cost reduction initiatives, and there is solid, rational basis for expecting price improvement.

As in the case of the author's leading-edge clients 3M and Harley Davidson in the early 1980s, Sears Canada's chief executive officer, Donald Schaefer, has played a major role in these negotiations. When the top executives of the customer and supplier meet during negotia-

---

4. For reference to more reading on the subject of "partners in profits" see appendix 2.

EXHIBIT 4–1
Price Negotiation
Automatic Washing Machine

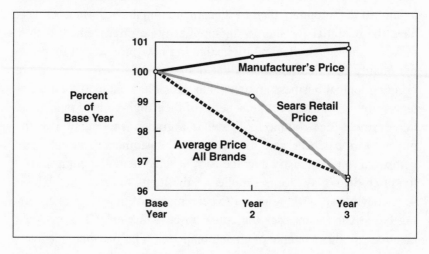

tions, they are far more likely to strike mutually beneficial relation-ship agreements than their buyers and sales representatives. After all, Sear Canada purchases less than two percent of the appliance sup-plier's output, giving it relatively little leverage. However, as I have previously written, even low-volume customers are always much more important to suppliers than they expect. For most suppliers, the last few percentage points of sales are those that contribute most to profitability—by virtue of the fact that all overhead has been absorbed by other sales. The supplier's chief executive officer can readily rec-ognize that if Sears is forced to raise its prices to levels higher than its competitors—in order to maintain reasonable profitability—it will soon start to lose market share, and both Sears and its suppliers will suffer from declining volume.

MULTIPLE SOURCE SUPPLIERS: A STRATEGY FOR DISASTER

Conventional wisdom, in purchasing circles, has always favored for-mally maintaining relationships with several suppliers capable of manufacturing/supplying the same items, and awarding purchase con-tracts, agreements, or orders to the lowest bidder able to meet delivery requirements. But as Charles Poirier and William Houser note, "Awarding business solely on the basis of price does little to enhance reliability, quality, service, or long-term loyalty. The seller may sincerely promise those features, but the seller's supporting system (plant, equipment, distributors, and so on) will lack the dedication to make it a reality."[5] Suppliers have seen some customers switch their business to a competitor overnight when those customers suddenly find a new lower-cost vendor. This leaves the supplier holding the bag for the cost of layoffs and idle capacity. The company that loses the business is especially frustrated when it knows a competitor has low-balled his bid in order to win the business. The competitor, once he wins the business, usually expects to increase his prices the next time competitive bids are sought. Xerox was one of the earliest non-Japanese major corporations to heed the advice to select virtually permanent suppliers for a given part or commodity. As William Davidow and Michael Malone report, Xerox cut the number of their active suppliers by more than 90 percent, from 5,000 to 325.[6] Nor has Xerox been the only major company to recognize the value of reducing the number of active suppliers. Other companies that have sharply reduced the number of active suppliers are listed on exhibit 4–2, summarized from Charles Gevirtz's somewhat more detailed chart. Gevirtz writes that reducing the number of active suppliers yields another major benefit, improved leveraging. As he notes, "This improved leveraging should assure better quality assurance, service, support and sometimes even greater price concessions."[7]

Few suppliers, faced with the possibility of losing a customer's business overnight, would be foolish enough to invest in improvements benefiting that customer (i.e. improved cost, quality, and speed of delivery). Further, the practice of switching periodically from one supplier to another has often had disastrous results in terms of causing

---

5. Charles C. Poirier and William F. Houser, *Business Partnering for Continuous Improvement: Make the Drive for Quality, Productivity and Profit Improvement a Permanent Feature of Your Company* (San Francisco: Berrett-Koehler, 1993), p. 182.

6. William H. Davidow and Michael S. Malone, *The Virtual Corporation: Structuring and Revitalizing the Corporation for the 21st Century* (New York: HarperCollins, 1992), p. 139.

7. Charles Gevirtz, *Developing New Products with TQM* (New York: McGraw-Hill, 1994), p. 156.

EXHIBIT 4–2
Reduction of Suppliers
1991

Company	Percent Reduction
Xerox	90
Motorola	70
Digital Equipment Corporation	67
General Motors	45
Ford Motor Company	44
Texas Instruments	36
Allied-Signal Aerospace	20

Source: *Wall Street Journal*, Revised by Charles Gevirtz

"quality" problems. The usual reason is that customers and suppliers who have worked together over a period of time have found that the supplier's products cause the customer the fewest problems when produced at one end of the acceptable tolerance range—usually a conclusion reached by trial and error and never documented by changing the specifications. If a new supplier's products meet the specifications, but tend to fall in the center or at the other end of that range, they may not function and fit in the customer's application, resulting in rejection, scrap, and rework.

Suppliers who fear a customer will switch to another source as soon as one offers a bid of a few cents less are highly unlikely to dedicate production equipment to that customer's items. The best, lowest-cost service a supplier can render occurs when a customer's demand for a family of similar items is high enough to warrant virtual dedication of a machine, machine cell, or factory-within-a-factory to the customer's products. Not only the manufacturing processes would be dedicated, but also the entire organization of the factory-in-a-factory. Therefore, one of the most important new supplier program practices is systematic review of supplier processes in order to determine if the supplier already has dedicated processes or has the potential for creating them, mainly by rearranging existing equipment. Two factors would defeat this objective. The first would be if the customer gave the supplier only a fraction of its business for some items in a family of like items, causing the demand to be too small to warrant dedicated processes. For this reason, the new practice of placing *all* of the demand with a single supplier is vitally important. The second factor would be if the customer had the practice of switching sources periodically, making the investment in dedicated resources a risky proposition.

Faced with phenomenal Japanese success with their suppliers' quality, Western producers, rather than imitate their underlying practices (namely asking producers to design fail-safe processes and eliminate the costly process of routine or even periodic sampling of quality) have fallen back on an old, bureaucratic practice of certification. I find the resulting Malcolm Baldrige program a ludicrous process, more suitable to twentieth century processes than those of the twenty-first. (Another instance of kicking a sacred cow.) And thinking entrepreneurs have the same reactions. For example, James Cali documents an instance in which a supplier to Motorola's European units decided to forego compliance with its requirement to apply for Baldrige certification.[8] He quotes the company's president as saying, "My total management system is to buy product, inspect it and ship it out on time. How do I refine that to make it better? Say 'Cross my heart and hope to die that I'm shipping you good stuff'?" His decision was based on the high cost of applying for certification. I would prefer clients instead to spend the money on process improvement!

In my work on the Harley-Davidson supplier program in the early 1980s, I was one of the first in the country to recognize that long-term contracts were not the solution for the lack of customer/supplier loyalty and singleness of purpose. The vast and complex Western legal system has been a major cause of confrontational customer/supplier relationships. It is extremely difficult to work together for mutual benefit when the body of laws is designed to formalize methods by which customers and suppliers can penalize each other for failures to perform according to contract conditions. The customer company and its suppliers must be committed to maintaining a mutually rewarding long-term relationship. However, it is not enough for a purchasing executive or even the chief executive officer to espouse this nonbinding

8. James F. Cali, *TQM for Purchasing Management* (New York: McGraw-Hill, 1993), p. 109.

commitment. With the frequent turnover of executives, no less than company-wide commitment—starting with the board of directors—will be enough to start to convince both supplier and user of the sincerity and resolution of each to begin the methodical forging of a new partnership for mutual profitability.

SUPPLIER COST: FOCUS OF THE NEW RELATIONSHIP

Mutual customer/supplier trust and shared profitability will surge when both are committed to lowering supplier cost but maintaining profit margins. Manufacturers must work with their suppliers to lower costs and improve quality in order to, in turn, pass the results on to *their* customers. After all, most manufacturers' purchases make up 50 percent or more of production cost. Therefore, their in-house improvement programs could accomplish far less than a program that also encompasses their suppliers. A company's costs have long been viewed as critically important from a competitive intelligence standpoint. Thus, many companies bar access to cost information fanatically, whether the party interested is potentially a source of information to competitors or a valued customer.

In my work with hundreds of clients, over several decades, I have found the extremist guarding of cost information to be comical, in terms of worrying about possible usefulness to competitors. As a consultant given free access to *all* financial and cost data, I have come to understand that the cost data, by itself, is virtually worthless, even within the company to which it belongs. A wide array of factors contribute to the build-up of cost, and without the underlying detail, the cost figure itself means little. Further, costs vary radically with different levels and mixes of demand. Thus, to imagine such a thing as an "accurate" cost is naive.[9] However, suppliers have different reasons for apprehension when it comes to sharing cost and financial data with a customer. With a long history of adversarial relationships, most suppliers realistically view a customer's primary interest in access to cost data as a prelude to insisting that the supplier's prices be lowered by lowering profitability. For example, a customer might object to one component of the supplier's margin—advertising. In making its case,

---

9. See appendix 2 for reference to more about cost management.

the customer could espouse a position that the supplier, should it become the winner in the long-term relationship bid, would no longer need to advertise in order to win its business. The supplier, taking the opposite tack, would argue that winning additional business *would* benefit the customer, since the increased volume would better absorb fixed overhead, lowering it in the long run. An entirely new world of mutual interest arises when the new business philosophy of both supplier and user focuses on how to *permanently reduce the cost.* Then, the examination of costs becomes an exercise in how to improve them, not how to treat them in determining the supplier's price.

SUPPLY CHAIN MANAGEMENT: MANAGE, DON'T SOLVE THE REAL PROBLEM

A staggering 10.5 percent of the United States' gross domestic product is spent "to wrap, bundle, load, unload, reload and transport goods"—all activities of the product supply chain.[10] As a result, systems and operating improvements to speed the flow, reduce the glut of materials and products flowing through the pipeline, and deliver precisely when needed are the most important activities in which logistics executives and their organizations are currently working. Henkoff explains just how ludicrous present logistics systems are—citing as just one example the three and one-half months a typical cereal box spends in warehouses and on trucks between the time it is produced in a factory and the time it is placed on a supermarket shelf! A large part of the problem is simply lack of modern computer systems and simplified operating processes (a dynamite tandem combination) capable of keeping a uniform flow in perpetual motion throughout the entire supply chain.

There can be no doubt that quantum advances are practical and urgently needed. Nor is there any doubt that seven-league strides are already being made by a handful of industry leaders. However, in the long term, industry will find that another root cause of the difficulty in controlling the supply chain is that it is unnecessarily long and com-

---

10. Ronald Henkoff, "Delivering the Goods: Logistics Has Become a Hot Competitive Advantage as Companies Struggle to Get the Right Stuff to the Right Place at the Right Time," *Fortune,* November 28, 1994, pp. 64–78.

plex, often spanning countries and oceans. Isn't it readily apparent that a single cereal factory with a complex distribution network, serving an entire nation, must inherently be far less controllable than several smaller factories with less complex distribution operations in every regional market area? My views on the misleading theories of economies of scale and different practical, real-world results stemming from dis-economies of scale are detailed in prior works, and will not be duplicated here.[11] Industry is now learning how to downscale to more economical facilities and distribution operations, and the need for complex supply chain management will certainly evaporate for companies and their suppliers who do so. However, this is not to say that systems for scheduling the flow throughout the entire production and distribution pipeline are not or will not be important. Quite the contrary is true. In the 1980s, I pointed to the radical differences between Western and leading Japanese companies in terms of their multiplant systems.[12] Such systems, which replace purchase orders with supplier schedules, are now starting to be used by major Western producers. John Proud, for example, notes that Xerox Corporation is leading the charge into use of electronic data interchange for interplant schedules.[13] Such systems, not only for a company's own factories but also for those of its suppliers and their distribution and even for the retail pipeline, must be a top priority. However, some authorities, while recognizing the importance of the supplier schedule, still discuss it in yesterday's context, rather than that of today's "just-in-time" ideal. Alfred Webber, for example, describes it as one that would typically schedule requirements by *week*.[14] Such grossly imprecise timetables are precisely the reason that companies employing them are incapable of performance comparable to those that schedule in daily (or even hourly) delivery increments.[15]

---

11. For reference to more about focused factories economies of scale, see appendix 2.

12. For reference to more about multiplant systems, see appendix 2.

13. John F. Proud, *Master Scheduling: A Practical Guide to Competitive Manufacturing* (Essex Junction, VT: Oliver Wight, 1994), p. 422.

14. Alfred W. Webber, "Supplier Scheduling: Linking Suppliers with Customers," in *Instant Access Guide: World Class Manufacturing,* Thomas F. Wallace and Steven J. Bennett, editors (Essex Junction, VT: Oliver Wight, 1994), pp. 409–417.

15. For reference to more about supplier schedules, see appendix 2.

BUSINESS FORECASTING:
MANAGEMENT'S ACHILLES' HEEL

Considering the virtually impossible job business and government have when attempting to forecast relatively short-term circumstances, it is little wonder that many will view visioning for their own companies as an even greater impossibility. Niemira and Klein have written the following succinct summary of the challenges of forecasting.

> The task confronting modern entrepreneurs is formidable. To begin with, they must anticipate, with some precision, what the demand for their product will be in the future, and they must try to coordinate the growth in their capacity with the expected growth in that demand. Even more, they must recognize that, among other things, they may be wrong in their estimation of how long it will take to modify their capacity, and they may fail to calculate accurately the technological changes, that can change the capacity-output ratio itself, as well as the length of time required to adjust capacity. Finally they may have been wrong in their original estimate of the growth in demand for their final product, or they could have been correct in that original estimate (they might have correctly interpreted all the factors that were originally available to them in estimating how demand might grow) but the consumer demand could still shift markedly higher or lower, given abrupt changes in aggregate domestic and international economic conditions.

Nevertheless, the authors conclude this passage on a upbeat theme, writing,

> Hence, it is remarkable that the rate of growth of capacity and the final demand are as well coordinated as they are. This highlights one of the marvels of the free enterprise system. The free market allocation mechanism is impressive, even though, at times, it might be strained to maintain stable growth when coordinating thousands of individual investment decisions.[16]

The author has similar views regarding the difficulty of accurately forecasting individual products and even product families. Therefore,

---

16. Michael P. Niemira and Philip A. Klein, *Forecasting Financial and Economic Cycles: How to Understand and Predict Changes in the Stock Market, Interest Rates, Inflation, Industries, Regions, Global Economies* (New York: Wiley, 1994), pp. 447–448.

although I see hundreds of companies with opportunities to improve their *statistical* forecast systems, the ultimate solution lies primarily in becoming more agile, adjusting daily to each day's demand. In the main, this requires that companies be able to reduce the amount of time to process new demand though planning, production, and delivery to the customer.[17]

STRATEGIC ALLIANCES: BUY TALENT, SPREAD RISK

Strategic alliances, as an operational tool, blossomed in the 1980s and continue to bear flower. Such alliances were a natural outgrowth of the earlier explosion of customer-supplier "partners-in-profit" programs and a recognized need for large, bureaucratic companies to find ways to infuse new, innovative product and process designs into their operations. During the period 1988 to 1992, for example, IBM forged "at least 15 strategic alliances, aggregating over $100 million for equity slices ranging from 2 percent to 40 percent."[18] Can there be much doubt that these alliances, small potatoes for IBM, were of the nature of acquiring entrepreneurial talent in order to provide IBM fast, lower-cost access to brainpower that in its own enterprise was partially paralyzed by the bureaucracy? Fortunately, IBM's executives recognized the problem and undertook this speedy route to solve the problem with external resources, giving it time to work on the solution of its internal problems.

In recent years, most strategic alliances in the public spotlight have been much grander in scope. Here, the need is to share the risk and enhance the likelihood of a successful conclusion of the shared goals. Grand visions lie behind much of the profusion of such cooperative undertakings. For example, few challenge the vision of national and international electronic information superhighways. They will be developed, but unprecedented resources will be necessary to be in the competition to become one of the few whose networks will carry the

17. For reference to more of the author's thoughts about forecasting for capacity planning, see appendix 2.

18. A. David Silver, *Strategic Partnering: How to Join Forces with Other Companies to Get: Capital, Research and Development, Marketing, Product Testing, Sales Support* (New York: McGraw-Hill, 1993), p. 1.

new traffic and the software developers whose programs will operate it. And some of the players will pour money into telecommunication designs and operating systems that will fall by the wayside as better alternatives become the ingredients of the twenty-first century networks. Therefore, the risks to each participant are minimized by joint investment in common research and development efforts. Further, international competitors, especially the Japanese, have gained worldwide dominance in certain product lines through these types of joint investments. In today's fiercely competitive global business environment, companies must band with other partners to compete effectively with companies already working with joint venture partners.

Smaller company mover-shaker executives should consider a more practical and speedy way to upgrade their competitive ability, through cooperation and pooling of resources with other manufacturers. Bopaya Bidanda and colleagues have entitled such an undertaking "shared manufacturing" and have defined this as ". . . *different manufacturers with similar needs sharing modern manufacturing technologies, facilities, equipment, and management systems.*"[19] They proceed to point out that foreign competitors are already using new cooperative arrangements, often with government support.

ENTIRELY NEW SOURCES: OUTSOURCING TRADITIONAL FUNCTIONS

One highly successful way in which companies and government have found they are able to "downsize" is to outsource functions traditionally performed by internal departments. The business providing the outsourced service has *always* been able to lower the cost of performing the function, even though the service provider's charges include its profit! The reasons that the outsourced service is less expensive than the internal operations are as follows.

1. The pay rates of the outside source, and its benefit packages, are often less than those of the customer.
2. Even when the customer's employees are transferred to the outside

---

19. Bopaya Bidanda, David I. Cleland, and Shriram R. Dharwadkar, *Shared Manufacturing: A Global Perspective* (New York: McGraw-Hill, 1993), p. 22.

source as part of the agreement, their wages might be the same or even better, since they will become much more efficient. However, the source's accumulated liability for prior pension will often be nil, and their benefits package will most often be less liberal, at least initially.

3. The outside source has a profit motive often too abstract a concept for the departments of a large internal organization to understand. Thus, the independent service provider is always attuned to increasing the efficiency (productivity) of the operations, *even when the operations are performed in exactly the same way,* for example, due to better employee motivations.

4. Most long-established private and public businesses are too liberal when it comes to spending for facilities and equipment. Thus, the space in their expensive facilities is often not productively used and expensive equipment is often underutilized and used wastefully. Outside sources are usually newer, leaner operators paying much more attention to productive use of facilities and equipment. Often, entities outsourcing operations are able to sell or rent vacated facilities and equipment, adding to the one-time financial benefits of outsourcing.

5. In-house operations inevitably grow in bureaucratic waste as well as inefficiency of operations. The lean new service provider pays more attention to eliminating excess layers of management and supervision. Typically, it requires fewer people to perform the same operations faster and more accurately.

6. Managers of in-house operations are usually too close to the forest to see the tree, when it comes to reinventing their operations. By contrast, service providers, highly motivated at the prospect of greater profitability, are more easily able to recognize ways to streamline the process.

7. New service providers find it easy to systematically measure the operation's delivery and quality performance. By simply reporting important performance information to managers and individuals responsible, significant, sustained improvement is inevitably the result.

Advocates of outsourcing point to two major advantages of doing so. First, there are the financial benefits. However, some readers will see that the outsourcer must admit to being somewhat less than com-

pletely competent. The proof of incompetence is that the new outsource service provider provides exactly the same services, albeit
faster and more accurately, and charges less than the previous cost but
still makes a profit. Prideful executives would recognize that they
should be able to reengineer their in-house operation to achieve even
better results, since doing only as well as the outside service provider
would lower the costs still more by eliminating the outsourcer's profit.
However, the second advantage of outsourcing is often an overriding
consideration when weighing the alternatives of reengineering the in-
house process versus farming it out to a service organization. This
outsourcing benefit is that management's time can be freed from responsibility for routine, often clerical, operations and thus they can
concentrate on more important issues of greater tactical and strategic
importance.

One caveat: a very financially rewarding short-term outsourcing
arrangement can lead to long-term disadvantage when the outsourcing
company gives up its proprietary rights to product and process design.
The Pinchots write of one such case, IBM's decision to outsource key
components of its personal computer to Microsoft (operating software) and Intel (central processing unit chip).[20] The initial results
were fantastic, allowing IBM to enter the market competition with
sales that escalated from $10 million average per month in early
stages to $4 billion in the third year. And it brought its new computer
to the market in a fraction of the time its own bureaucratic organization would have required. However, as the companies holding the
technological expertise, Microsoft and Intel became the largest suppliers of software and chips to IBM's competitors and at the cost of
IBM's own potential sales of these products.

I find myself torn between the two major alternatives, outsourcing
versus in-house reengineering. In the long run, I believe that in-house
reengineering, when pursued to its greatest improvement potential,
will yield the best quality and service performance at the most competitive cost. Therefore, only when spectacular tactical and strategic
avenues truly require maximum executive and managerial attention

---

20. Gifford and Elizabeth Pinchot, *The End of Bureaucracy and the Rise of the Intelligent Organization* (San Francisco: Berrett-Koehler, 1993), pp. 169–171.

would I recommend the outsourcing route. The exceptions to this are government functions. I am not alone in believing that government bureaucrats and politicians will always be incapable of achieving high-quality, high-service, efficient operations management comparable to that of private industry. Thus, *every* possible government function, including most of those traditionally the realm of elected officials, should be outsourced or privatized as expeditiously as is feasible.

Fortunately a compromise between outsourcing and in-house reengineering, designed to temporarily but almost immediately lower costs and improve performance, is feasible. Such a compromise would be appropriate when management's immediate attention to tactical and strategic issues needs maximum effort or when the organization is too deeply entrenched in the belief that present business processes are the only feasible way to operate the business. The obvious options are to oursource temporarily until management can afford to spend more time on reengineering or to engage a professional firm to lead the reengineering effort. Executive and management teams with the will and wherewithal to reengineer rather than outsource operations will be well advised to pay attention to the problem of seeing the forest rather than trees. They, and their minions, are unlikely to identify radically different process and organizational alternatives. Therefore, I would recommend that they use the outside service provider to work with them to perform the role of catalyst and even temporarily to assume authority and responsibility for the function's management during the reengineering process. The outside service provider should be given the power to make decisions and implement changes, a vastly important way to overcome an organization's resistance to change.[21]

STANDARD OR CUSTOM: WHAT IS THE COST?

What do customers want? Industry today, more than ever, is striving to answer that question. Many advocate a strategy of moving away

---

21. My colleague, Leroy Peterson, and I have written extensively on overcoming resistance to change and the middle-management roadblock. See appendix 2 for reference to additional material on these subjects.

from standard products to goods produced to the custom specifications of the buyer. One argument favoring such a position suggests that fantastic reductions in the costs of setup (changeover) of machines and assembly lines and the increased use of "flexible machine systems" in recent years should increase producers' "flexibility." These arguments have only slight basis in fact. For example, these systems *do* permit changing production from one item to another with negligible cost penalty. However, the flexibility of "flexible machine systems" is questionable. The proof of relative inflexibility is that the systems are always custom built for the machining application and virtually no two identical systems have been produced. For these reasons, the advice of extremists who preach a strategy of custom design should be regarded with healthy skepticism. William Pasmore, for one, is among the thinking skeptics. He writes, "How flexible can your technology be before it becomes inefficient? Should we be producing a different automobile for every customer? And not just a different color or options, but one designed from the ground up specifically to meet each buyer's driving needs? Seems a little extreme."[22]

It is certainly more cost-effective to produce a few *standard* parts or products than to make unique designs for every customer order. The costly engineering (or fashion) design, process and tooling design, and manufacture and machine programming for a standard item can be amortized over hundreds or even millions of pieces produced, while items produced to custom specifications would incur outrageous costs for these preproduction activities and tooling. For example, *Fortune* reported that the Toyota Motor company, widely acknowledged as the world's premier auto maker, until recently sold twenty-six separate lines of cars, more than any other manufacturer in the world, even GM.[23] The article noted, "Developing all those models, most of which sell in relatively small numbers, is hugely expensive. Toyota is gradually reducing the number of model variants it makes and reorganizing product development to operate more efficiently." A National Semiconductor case example adds to the evidence favoring narrower prod-

---

22. William A. Pasmore, *Creating Strategic Change: Designing the Flexible, High-Performing Organization* (New York: Wiley, 1994), pp. 73–74.

23. Alex Taylor and reporter associate Sally Solo, "How Toyota Copes with Hard Times," *Fortune,* January 25, 1993.

uct lines. As a result of analyzing the costs of its products, it found far too many contributed nothing to profits or revenue. As a result, it slashed 45 percent of the products from its line. These and other steps combined to help cut its delivery time (thus pipeline inventory) by 47 percent and distribution costs by 2.5 percent.[24]

Advocates of expanded custom-product offerings, however, are right in terms of retail customers wanting a wider variety of product features and options from which to craft a product according to their unique functional and aesthetic wishes. Industrial users are, one hopes, most interested in functionality and less in aesthetics. Meeting customers' needs, without vastly complicating the process of developing custom order specifications, demands a relatively simple structure of basic products and applicable options. As GE Fanuc in Charlottesville, Virginia, learned from its drive to meet customer needs by expanding its catalog to tens of thousands of part numbers and specifications filling four binders, "its expansion strategy exposed its customers to a great deal of complexity."[25] The benefits of reducing its product offerings to the three hundred products accounting for over 90 percent of customers' needs with packages and options that met the needs were that the company was able to shrink the time required to deliver products by 75 percent. Individual orders can now be fully specified in about ten minutes compared to the outmoded methods that typically took about one day per order.[26]

The predictable costs of product proliferation are not its only adverse aspects. The far-reaching effects spread throughout an organization, creating chaos for the company and its customers. Gwendolyn Galsworth put it as follows: "We think organizational gridlock and profit erosion are high prices to pay for product diversification. The culprit is unwarranted variation and the complication it can generate. Even when your hot-selling products reach the end of their productive life and are retired, even when parts are obsoleted and removed, the complexity that surrounded these remains."[27]

---

24. Ronald Henkoff, "Delivering the Goods," pp. 64–78.

25. Joe Pine, "Customers Don't Want Choice," *Wall Street Journal*, April 18, 1994.

26. See appendix 2 for reference to more about product line rationalization.

27. Gwendolyn D. Galsworth, *Smart, Simple Design: Using Variety Effectiveness to Reduce Total Cost and Maximize Customer Selection* (Essex Junction, VT: Oliver Wight, 1994), p. 276.

My approach to product standardization, which originated on a Briggs & Stratton project in the 1960s and was enhanced on my Yamaha Motors project in Japan in the 1970s—with resulting reductions in product offerings in the range of 75 percent—is basically simple, entailing the development of a matrix of products and their components.[28] Such a matrix makes it simple to see product similarities and differences and helps to understand customer preferences. However, to capitalize on the knowledge gained must involve working with customers to give them logical reasons to want to buy certain product designs—those that will underlie the company's ability to provide better service and higher quality at lower cost.

Completely automated systems for economically producing consumer products unique to each customer's specifications have never been, are not now, and are unlikely ever to be practical. It is always most economical to produce high-volume standard designs, or custom combinations of standard options.

MERGER MANIA: A NATURAL PHENOMENON

There was a time, in the past, when the United States automobile industry consisted of numerous small manufacturers. Eventually, through the merger and acquisition process, the number of manufacturers evolved into just three. Two or three producers of any product are enough to ensure that the economies of operations that concentrated investment provides will keep the product price/value relationship highly favorable. Too many producers inevitably force prices higher. One has simply to look at the rapid rise in average prices of automobiles in the last decade or two to see vivid proof that fragmentation of the market by vastly increasing the makes, models, and styles offered reduces the benefits of mass production. The cost of design development and tooling can no longer be amortized over high volumes, and since tooling costs are so high, it becomes impractical to produce an automobile in more than one factory. Compared to automobiles produced in very high volume, where the volume alone *dictates* that multiple factories be built in various areas of high market concentration, the distribution costs for the single lower-volume plant

---

28. For reference to additional reading about the matrix bill of material, see appendix 2.

are outrageous. For years I bought and picked up my automobiles in Detroit, and so I was made intensely aware of the distribution cost when the manufacturers adopted the practice of adding uniform delivery charges to the sticker price, regardless of the distance delivered, thus equalizing the competitiveness of dealers regardless of their location in relationship to the location of the factory. Because of that, I must now pay several hundred dollars more for each new vehicle.

The need and benefits of natural consolidation of the number of producers is not limited to automobiles. In the United States, the contraction of the number of companies producing appliances has been dramatic. In Europe, liberating national markets to free cross-border competition has already triggered a fantastic wave of merger and acquisition. Inefficient, low-volume, previously protected producers who can no longer compete now need to merge their local marketing and distribution resources with larger producers. In the best of cases, national producers continue to produce, since some of their national volumes are great enough to support local, focused factories while reducing product and process development costs by sharing the resources of the larger organization and producing identical products. In the worse cases, the factory is far too inefficient to remain in operation, thus the short-term impact has to be to cut the number of facilities. In the long run, however, as soon as the recent recession ends, the new larger firms will develop more new highly efficient regional factories.

Nor will the mania for merger be limited to producers. Many service industries, with visions of the probable future, already realize the benefits of acquiring and/or merging with both related and potentially related businesses. Not a single entertainment, telecommunications, or computer company is ignoring the inevitable boom in home shopping. Thus in recent years the daily business news has seen a plethora of announcements of business combinations and partnering of enterprises interested in being on the leading edge of interactive home shopping. (For example, on the day of this writing, Ameritech, one of the baby Bells created by the split-up of AT&T, announced "its plan to buy an equity stake in a company that publishes a home-shopping directory."[29]

---

29. Jon Van, "Ameritech Eyes Home Shopping," *Chicago Tribune*, June 2, 1994.

The realization is growing that Japanese producers face extinction, since the world has almost caught up with their product and process technology. As a result of this and other political and economic factors, Japanese costs are now too high to overcome their unavoidably high distribution costs. The inevitable next step in Japan will be massive restructuring of fragmented industries. Whereas seven significant automobile producers now compete fiercely with a fantastic variety of similar products, mergers will reduce the number to two or three. As a result, the producers will again (at least temporarily) be competitive as exporters.

A word of caution is in order. The majority of *diversification* mergers have failed, in that they have lowered rather than raised stockholders' equity and have usually led the acquiring business to divestitures. As Gary Hamel and C.K. Prahalad point out, these failures often stem from the fact that weak management has gone on an acquisition binge to obscure the poor performance of their core business.[30] The message is clear. Generally, it is better to limit acquisitions to those related to the business's core business, and then only if management is as strong as will be necessary to successfully maintain or increase the acquisition's profitability while blending its operations and culture into those of the new parent. Nor is it always safe to charge into mergers with companies that have related core businesses. The critical factor will always be the competency of the management of the acquiring enterprise, in terms of its ability to manage the expanded business. In fact, the recent merger boom should be disquieting for shareholders, simply on the basis of the track record of companies merging in the past. For example, when *Fortune* asked the former co-chairman of Goldman Sachs, Leon Cooperman, to name a single big merger that lived up to expectations, he answered, "I'm sure that there are many success stories out there, but at this moment I draw a blank."[31] The same article cited a thirty-year research project that studied mergers over

30. Gary Hamel and C.K. Prahalad, *Competing for the Future: Breakthrough for Seizing Control of Your Industry and Creating the Markets of Tomorrow* (Boston: Harvard Business School Press, 1994), p. 292.

31. Terence P. Paré and Patty de Llosa, "The New Merger Boom: New Combinations Are Reshaping America's Largest Industries, with Consequences for All," *Fortune,* November 28, 1994, pp. 95–106.

the last eight decades and came to the conclusion that "on average, mergers are bad." Nevertheless, unrelated business combinations may be in a company's vital interest.

A MANUFACTURING AND LOGISTICS VISION

Manufacturing employment as a percentage of the total work force (see exhibit 4–3) has decreased constantly over the past two decades in every major industrialized country.[32] The factor that will continue to contribute to the decline of work necessary in these industries is the reinvention of business processes which, except for computerization, have been basically unchanged until recently. However, new technology will eventually be the primary force behind the eventual virtual elimination of the need for labor. Jeremy Rifkin's observations in this respect were summarized in his publisher's news release of January, 1995:

> We are on the road to a near "workerless" society in the coming century. Sophisticated computers, robotics, telecommunications and other cutting-edge technologies are fast replacing human beings in virtually every sector and industry—from manufacturing, retail and financial services, to transportation, agriculture and government. Many jobs are never coming back. Blue collar workers, secretaries, receptionists, clerical workers, sales clerks, bank tellers, telephone operators, librarians, wholesalers, and middle managers are just a few of the many occupations destined for virtual extinction.[33]

Additionally, the most highly industrialized countries have lost jobs in manufacturing to developing countries. However, that production will return as the incomes of the developing nations rise, and as their manufacturing processes continue to be automated. The costs of supplying markets from thousands of miles away will just be too great to compete with factories in local clusters. In my long-range vision, the products of manufacturing and the transportation and distribution networks will change radically. For example, the use of private automobiles will eventually decline and most wheeled industrial and trans-

---

32. "The Manufacturing Myth," *The Economist,* March 19, 1994, pp. 91–92.

33. Jeremy Rifkin, *The End of Work: The Decline of the Global Labor Force and the Dawn of the Post-Market Era* (New York: Jeremy Tarcher, 1995).

EXHIBIT 4–3

Percent of Total Employment

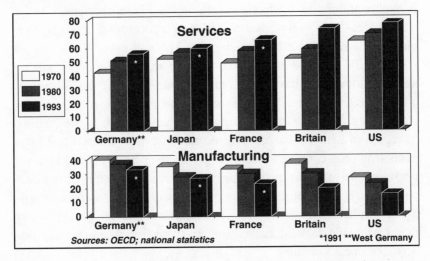

portation equipment will be operated by computer-controlled robots. Automotive manufacturers must heed the history of horse-drawn vehicle manufacturers, the majority of which went out of business because they saw the trend too late to join the ranks of the new automotive producers. Further, the typical factory of the future will no longer consist of slow, massive, expensive, and relatively inaccurate machines and armies of assemblers. Revolutionary changes will lower the percentage of the population working in factories as radically as the industrial age lowered the number of agricultural workers between the turn of the century and today. Matsushita Electric's Utsunomiya television factory output per employee, for example, has already soared 568 percent between 1971 and 1994.[34] Continuation of its drive to increase productivity will surely virtually eliminate labor in the next quarter century, if not sooner.

Our production and distribution industries must continuously increase productivity, but *not* to improve their global competitiveness (a statement that many will erroneously perceive as the epitome of naivete). Paul Krugman shares my viewpoint, cleverly leading with a

---

34. Steven Butler, "Matsushita Tries To Change Channels," *U.S. News & World Report,* August 15, 1994.

statement on the need for competing in the global economy, and then debunking it as follows: "The problem is: It's baloney. In reality, there is almost nothing to our fixation with national competitiveness, or its central idea—that every country is like a giant corporation slugging it out against rivals in global markets."[35] The real need is to compete successfully with *domestic* rivals, because remote producers will be unable to overcome the disadvantages of noncompetitive distribution costs, in the long run. The most successful multinational companies already compete globally by producing what they sell in the country or region in which it is sold. Nor do the best firms transport components from one country to another, giving their products and components expensive world travel. The competitive edge that multinational companies enjoy is primarily that of the lower overhead costs and superior results of product design and research and development spread over worldwide demand, decreasing the shared overhead for the products sold in each country.

My previous books detail the modern keys to unlocking the door to unparalleled productivity in production and distribution. They state, in summary, that industry leaders must perpetually and doggedly pursue the reduction of operating costs and capital investment requirements (buildings, equipment, and inventory). Simultaneously, they must continuously improve the value (quality/price) of their products and services. Further, no individual company, by itself, can achieve these ends. Therefore, every company must work harmoniously with its suppliers who must also achieve the same investment, operating cost, quality, and service objectives.

PRODUCTION AND DISTRIBUTION CLUSTERS

Two major changes will drastically alter the economics of frequent home delivery. The first will be clusters of smaller, more productive factories and those of their suppliers and distributors in every market location, and the second will be the new, highly productive home delivery services depicted in exhibit 4–4. Historically, several factors have combined to make home delivery infeasible for all except the

---

35. Paul Krugman, "Competitiveness: Does It Matter?" *Fortune,* March 7, 1994, pp. 109–115.

most affluent neighborhoods. For one, individual retailers who have tried operating their own delivery trucks have not had enough volume on each route to keep the cost per delivery at the lowest level achievable. Even United Parcel Service residential service must be relatively costly due to the infrequency of deliveries in any neighborhood.

The type of home delivery service depicted in exhibit 4–4 will be provided by an exclusive common carrier for each neighborhood, serving every private home and public and private enterprises. Thus the exclusive carrier will automatically have a much higher volume within each neighborhood than any of today's retail businesses, factory and distributor trucks, or trucking companies. Exhibit 4–4 depicts a representative truck route that begins with stops at each factory and distributor in the neighborhood to load deliveries for consumers on the route. Next the truck travels the residential streets, stopping for deliveries to most homes at least once daily, although the neighborhood delivery volume will likely be great enough to justify two or more deliveries per day. At boundaries between adjacent neighborhoods, the truck in neighborhood one will stop at a cross-dock facility to off-load deliveries to neighborhood-two trucks for delivery to its homes and enterprises. The neighborhood-one truck will also on-load items from the neighborhood-two truck. Finally, the truck completes

EXHIBIT 4–4

Production and Distribution Clusters

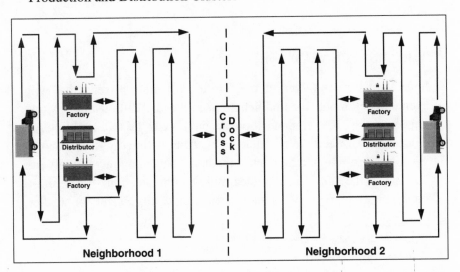

home deliveries then stops at factories and distributors to off-load transshipments from other neighborhoods and on-load goods for the next delivery cycle.

Another factor inhibiting low-cost, frequent home delivery has been that the total volume of home deliveries has been low, although the recent surge in catalog orders has started a dramatic increase in home delivery loads. The advent of the home system module and earlier primitive interactive shopping systems will drastically increase the frequency and volume of home deliveries, thus shorten each delivery route and distances between stops (see chapter 2, subsection "Virtually Real Home Shopping").

Companies of all sizes and products should take heart that clustering of supplier factories in local areas is a short-term, achievable, and high pay-back option. Ronald Henkoff's Compaq case example helps to prove this point.[36] Compaq did two things, one not-so-good—and the second, ideal. The ideal step was to convince seven of its sheet metal suppliers (why seven?) to move to the immediate vicinity of its Texas factory. However, it also "dragooned" thirty-five major suppliers to lease a warehouse in the area, and to feed the factory from it, a less than ideal step. This latter move undoubtedly helped Compaq to cut its factory inventory and to receive components on schedule. It is unlikely, however, that the suppliers were able to add the warehouse into the supply chain without adding to *their* cost. It would be quite surprising if they would "eat the cost" versus eventually recouping it in their price.

THE DISAPPEARING MIDDLEMAN

Several important waves of the future are behind a trend that will eventually eliminate the middleman from the distribution chain. Modern computer and communications technology is the tool enabling retailers to link directly to manufacturers. Thus, as Jeremy Rifkin wrote, "Wholesalers, like middle management, are becoming increasingly redundant in the age of instant electronic communication."[37] The most important trend, perhaps, is the movement towards clusters of smaller

---

36. Henkoff, "Delivering the Goods," pp. 64–78.
37. Rifkin, *The End of Work,* p. 151.

manufacturing and supplier facilities in the center of regional markets.[38] When producers and their suppliers have factories in every market region, a multitier distribution system will no longer be necessary. Second, the new interactive home shopping systems of the future can work just as effectively linked directly to the supplier, thus the added costs of middlemen can be eliminated.[39] Third, consumers are already increasingly switching from shopping in retail establishments to purchasing from catalogs. Contact lenses, for example, are a recent addition to the long list of products now available through catalog sales.[40] Catalog buyers of contact lens pay as much as 50 percent less than those purchased from optometrists (the savings is somewhat less when compared to purchase from a discount store). What makes the difference is the significantly lower overhead required by a mail order operation. People who work full-time find it difficult to make time for shopping trips, and when they do so on weekends, the rush of traffic and crush of customers in retail stores are unpleasant experiences best avoided. Homemakers with time to make shopping excursions a social event are largely a phenomenon of the past. The fourth wave of the future that will lead to the demise of the middleman will be incredible cost-effective home delivery systems that will cut the cost of small package home delivery, providing further impetus to the use of interactive home shopping.

I am not alone in predicting a radical decline in the middleman's market share. As exhibit 4–5 indicates, Steve M. Samek's Arthur Andersen & Co. study for the National Association of Wholesaler-Distributors projects a decrease from an estimated 46 percent market share in 1992 to 36 percent in 2000. Samek is quoted as saying, "The middle is going away, and what we have left is the small niche distributors and the giants. The middle-size company is in trouble."[41] I see no reason not to anticipate a continuing downward trend. The question is less one of *will* market share drop to zero than *when* will it do so.

---

38. See appendix 2 for reference to more about regional production clusters.

39. See appendix 2 for reference to more about the future home shopping system.

40. Yumiko Ono, "Contacts by Mail Change Industry's Look," *Wall Street Journal,* October 11, 1994.

41. David Young, "Middlemen Caught in Evolving Market", *Chicago Tribune,* November 29, 1993.

EXHIBIT 4–5

The Disappearing Middleman

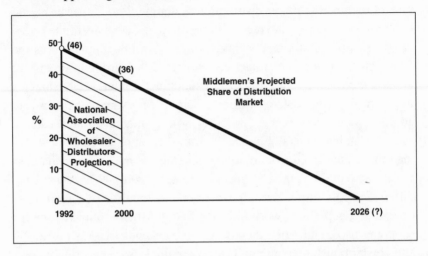

However, the inevitable decline is being delayed by those distributors attuned to customers' burning interests such as just-in-time delivery. Andersen Consulting's 1993 study and report for the National-American Wholesale Grocers' Association defined a new name for wholesalers with the vision to provide such exceptional systems and logistics operations—"market maximizers."[42] On average, wholesalers have already cut the distribution cycle by 50 percent over the last decade, from three days to one and one-half, according to Young. Improved computer systems and modern techniques such as bar-coding are a major factor behind the push for massive cuts in inventories within the distribution industry and for the customers it serves.

When wholesalers disappear from the chain, the reduction of steps in the distribution network will not have been completed. The next dominos to fall will be the retail outlets that also add unnecessary cost to the ultimate consumer. However, distributors and retailers need not rush to exit from their fields. If they are in the forefront of developing the interactive home shopping and delivery systems, those systems will eventually be their greatest asset. The end result for these compa-

---

42. Andersen Consulting, *Wholesale Food Distribution: Today & Tomorrow* (Falls Church, VA: National-American Wholesale Grocers' Association, 1993), pp. 29–31.

nies will be either to merge with large producers or to become a service center providing these services to many clients. Ultimately, however, each community will need, and have, a single home shopping system service that will permit the home shopper to compare competitors' goods, services, and prices, a capability that could not be economically provided by different systems for different suppliers.

THE COMING AGE OF COMPLETE ASSEMBLY AUTOMATION

Slowly, but inexorably, people on complex assembly lines are being replaced by robots, a fact not readily obvious when one walks along the world's people-intensive lines today. One reason that so many people are still required is the amount of work that must be done in spaces in which it is close to impossible to use robots. The key that will unlock the door to drastic improvements in assembly automation lies not with improved robots, but rather with improved product designs suitable for complete automation. H.J. Warnecke and M. Hueser put their fingers on the problem, writing: "One of the problems with converting a product to automated assembly is its design. Some products are not designed to be assembled by machines. Designers must take a close look at each product and consider the ability of machines that do the assembly work. By studying both the design requirements of a product and the ability of the robot or other machines, it is possible to design a device of better quality and have it assembled by a machine."[43] They point out that Volkswagen's Golf plant is one of the most highly automated and yet its level of automation is still only 25 percent. There are still giant improvements awaiting better design for automation! However, automation is ineffective if it merely duplicates existing processes on existing products. Manufacturers must first simplify engineering product designs and factory processes if automation is to produce quantum productivity and quality improvements.

The interior of an automobile is an example of a small space in which considerable human assembly is still required. However, the

43. H.J. Warnecke and M. Hueser, "Technologies of Advanced Manufacturing," in *Organization and Management of Advanced Manufacturing,* Waldemar Karwowski and Gavriel Salvendy, editors (New York: Wiley, 1994), p. 24.

EXHIBIT 4–6

Robotic Module Assembly

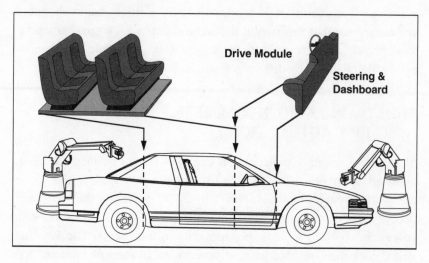

perfect design would be of an interior assembly module (exhibit 4–6) that could be lowered into the body using fully automated equipment for joining the body and interior. The interior module, with no side, floor, or roof barriers to robot access, could first be assembled on a completely automated subassembly line. The drive module, consisting of the steering, shifting, and dashboard functions, might be another subassembly. Ford Motor Co., for one, is already working in the direction of simplifying its car design to cut components and reduce its assembly costs by working on a new modular, integrated instrument dash panel.[44] In years to some, these pioneering efforts will be seen as the first primitive steps on the way to complete robotic module designs. Not all automation investment is designed properly: the goal is not merely to duplicate the actions of a human worker, but to perform far more productive work by virtue of not being human. Poor automation design for example, was behind Leroy (Pete) Peterson's comment when he was asked by *Fortune,* "how effective were the billions that Roger Smith poured into robots?" Pete's answer was, "Companies like GM spent on automation and didn't get a return, so management

---

44. Alan L. Alder, "Ford's Dash(ing) Idea," *Chicago Tribune,* October 16, 1994.

is skeptical."[45] Pete has told me that GM could have bought Toyota several times over for the amount expended on automation.

Michael Williams reports that at a Sony plant in Kohda, Japan, camcorders, which were once assembled on lines of fifty workers, are put together on tables by groups of four workers, each of whom assembles an entire product.[46] Williams also reports instances in which "craft work" is inappropriate, including circuit board assembly and other high-volume assemblies. It is thought that this process design is 10 percent more efficient because each worker is free to work at his fastest speed, versus the assembly line where every worker is paced by the speed of the slowest worker, and because time is saved by eliminating the need for each assembler to pass the camcorder to the next person. That this opportunity for improvement exists and is significant is shameful. I recently spent time in a Gold Star VCR factory in Korea that illustrates the alternatives. An automated line carried the product from one worker to the next when the first worker touched a foot-pedal switch. Since the worker was reaching for the next assembly component at the same time, absolutely no labor was lost in the product movement. Moreover, the time per worker was so well defined that every worker completed their operation in *precisely* thirteen seconds. This thirteen-second tact time was as fast as *reasonable* in any shop other than a sweatshop. If the Sony camcorder cycle times were considerably longer, assembly line assignments should have been based on worker ability rather than *standard* time.[47]

Assembly procedures in which each individual worker produces an entire complex product are doomed to eventual extinction. Who, for example, could begin to imagine the complex automation required to deliver all of the components of a locomotive to a single assembly robot responsible for an entire locomotive? Or the waste time and motion of that one robot walking down an assembly line on which it would assemble one locomotive. Not to mention the waste of the du-

---

45. Ibid.

46. Michael Williams, "Back to the Past: Some Plants Tear Out Long Assembly Lines, Switch to Craft Work," *Wall Street Journal,* October 24, 1994.

47. I define the line designed to make worker jobs equal to individual workers' speed as one having "cooperative recovery."

plicate equipment for each robot "worker." Since all assembly operators will eventually be robots, it is ludicrous to imagine that "one
worker, one product" is a reasonable design for the future. Its proponents praise the complete product assembly by the individual as being
more rewarding to the worker and as yielding higher quality because
of the individual's resulting pride in the product. And although some
cite direct labor savings in assembly, few openly admit that indirect
labor costs in material "kitting" in the storeroom and increased time
and cost in training assemblers have usually exceeded direct savings.
Who cares about how rewarding work is to a robot? Don't those with
quality problems understand that fail-safing product and process designs are the *only* way by which perfect quality can be achieved?

HIGH-SPEED MACHINING: PHENOMENAL PRECISION AND EFFICIENCY

Twenty-first century machine shops will undergo revolutionary
changes that will catapult their precision while lowering production
and tooling costs. Machine tools will have dramatically higher cutting
speeds, lighter weight, more durable ceramic bearings (cutting the
amount of machine rebuild and maintenance costs) and low-cost lin-
ear motors for high speed and accuracy. For example, leading-edge
chief engineer Jochen Zenker, of the Precise Corporation, predicts
"We will see spindle speeds of 250,000 rpm and cutting at over 1,000
ipm."[48] Machine tools have traditionally been massive, a necessity in
order to dampen the natural vibrations that cause cutting tools to wan-
der from the center of specification tolerance ranges. New hardware
and computer software that dynamically track the workpiece location
and keep the cutting tool in the ideal position vis-à-vis the workpiece
will alter this need and therefore radically reduce the amount of material required for, and the resulting cost of, machines.

Maintaining competitive position requires manufacturers to ride
the crest of this new machining technology. As it develops and becomes commercially available, shops predominantly populated with
older, slower, less reliable, and imprecise equipment will be forced to

---

48. Robert B. Aronson, "Machine Tool 101: Machine Tools of the Future," *Manufacturing Engineering,* July 1994, pp. 39–45.

change massively in order to survive, if competitors are early to re-tool. Strategic plans must include budgets for working closely with machine manufacturers on their research and development projects to be prepared to adapt the factory and tooling to the use of the new technology and to preplan new machine specification modifications suitable for the factory's products.

Producers with superior machine and tool designers and makers will (and already typically do) dominate competitors, because the best tools are necessary to produce the highest quality products at the low-est possible cost. In this regard, American companies are seriously threatened by the continuing decline of the U.S. machine tool indus-try. For example, "The U.S. has slipped to fourth place in machine tool production, behind Japan, Germany and Italy. Japan has been spending twice as much on machine tools as America, where the aver-age age of metalworking equipment is now the highest in half a cen-tury."[49] I deem the revitalization of the machine and tool design and manufacturing education, training, and employment to be the single most important facet of manufacturing competitive advantage. So much so that I have listed doing so as a *tactical* issue rather than a strategic initiative.[50]

SUMMARY

Far too few manufacturers and distributors have implemented the types of practices that lead to quantum improvement in their factories and warehouses as detailed in my previous "Reinventing" books. Even fewer have extended the scope of such initiatives into the pipelines of supply, starting with their suppliers and ending in deliv-ery to their ultimate customers. Most companies still need to set and to achieve target improvements in the range of 50 percent and better, just to maintain the continuous improvement pace of their most ag-gressive competitors. However, while pursuing these short-term tar-gets they must also keep their eyes on the future.

Manufacturing and distribution, like agriculture in the twentieth

---

49. Edmund Faltermayer and Wilton Woods, "Invest or Die," *Fortune,* February 22, 1993.

50. For specific reference to my comments on improving tool design and manufacturing skill de-velopment, see appendix 2.

EXHIBIT 4–7
Growth Industries and Occupations

Factory Automation

Outsourced Business Services

Computer Utilities

Business Computer Software

Product Design

---

century, will undergo radical change in the twenty-first. Exhibit 4–7 lists some of the future's growth industries and occupations. Producers of factory automation, especially the virtually untapped market for assembly equipment, will be high-growth companies. The product design field cries for new armies of designers to accelerate the pace of product improvement, especially as regards products compatible with automated assembly, product and product line simplification, and product cost reduction. In the short term, enterprises with bloated bureaucracies will find it expedient to outsource as many functions as possible. New outsourcing service providers, vitally interested in their own profitability, will operate lean processes with quantum improvements in productivity over in-house operations. These outsource businesses will form the nucleus for developing the "best practices" suitable industry-wide, and will begin to spawn the computer utilities and universally applicable business software that will serve to eventually eliminate in-house programming and computer operations.

Business executives will continue to be in high demand. However, their roles will be greatly simplified by the decreased role of personnel in their operations. Larger staffs of more highly educated and trained product and process designers will support lesser involvement of higher management in these aspects of operations. Marketing will play

EXHIBIT 4–8
Waning Industries and Occupations

Assemblers

Machinists

Distributors

In-house Programming

---

an ever more important role in an enterprise's success, but the channel of marketing efforts will be almost entirely the information highway. Information skills will be a prerequisite for all surviving occupations.

Like agriculture before them, the percentage of employment in manufacturing and distribution will plummet as a result of ever-increasing factory and delivery automation and improvements in product design that support still further automation. Some of the industries and occupations that will be waning in the twenty-first century are listed on exhibit 4–8. For those inclined to feel anxious or offended by the definition of some industries and occupations as waning or dying, there are several important points to keep in mind. These following points are repeated briefly in every chapter, because many readers are expected to read only selected chapters. First, the change may not occur in the foreseeable future. Second, the future continuous reduction of work will be universal. As a result, society must and will reduce average workweek hours in order to maintain full employment. Third, the era of reduced work and increased leisure time will be one of unprecedented quality of life and affluence. Fail-safe equipment design and self-diagnosis systems will reduce the amount of maintenance required, thus the number of millwrights, electricians, and other specialists.

5

REINVENTING COMPUTING

Will Big Brother Be Watching You?

Computer and related communication technologies lie at the very heart of every important public and private enterprise's strategic and tactical initiatives. Recognition of a few foreseeable, short-term advances in these technologies is the initial subject of this chapter. However, the longer-term, unimaginable power of future innovations, also subjects of this chapter, will not see a slowing of the trends already evident. Rather, these trends are most likely to accelerate. Therefore, the second part of this chapter consists of longer-term but likely visions that will challenge the reader to burst the confines of today's world and leap into the future. My purpose in doing so is to guide readers in a fascinating exercise. Executives in private and public enterprises will be able to grade their own performance in projecting backward from their visions (which will not necessarily be mine) into current tactics and strategies for accelerating the race into the future in their own operations, products, and services.

The broad sweep of technological improvements during the twenty-first century will affect every aspect of product design, production, distribution, consumption, and services. Numerous monumental innovations will be preceded by timid steps forward, due to private and public resistance to change. Another reason that changes

125

will be slow in coming is that technicians are incredibly slow to produce simple, user-friendly devices and software systems. They simply
do not understand that the general public is not now, and never needs
to be, computer literate enough to enjoy the advantages of modern
technology. Three of the timid steps forward, the next subjects of this
chapter, are the electronic book, newspaper, and check register.

The challenging visions offered later in this chapter are founded on
the premise that every individual will have an address on the same information streets and highways as public and private enterprises.
Their entire data bases will be maintained on computer utilities for the
economic benefit (and speed and quality of service) of each individual, business, and government. And the computer and automation will
take over increasingly complex functions of human professionals and
technicians as well as both simple and complex blue-collar labor, creating a need to replace "work" with new activities that will make future life considerably more enjoyable and rewarding.

EXECUTIVE CHECKLIST: SELECTED
COMPUTER/TECHNOLOGY ZINGERS

The primary purpose of executive "visioning" is not to end the
process with an idealistic view of some remote, impossibly long-term
program for the enterprise. Rather, the process must continue until the
present and future are bridged by strategies that, pursued vigorously
in the short term, will keep the enterprise in the forefront of innovative steps that will ensure its moving ahead of or at least no slower
than its competitors. The strategy must embody a realistic approach
for maintaining and enhancing short-term profitability, quality, and
superior customer service. The role of information systems is already
vitally important to every enterprise's success and will continue to become even more critical. For example, Stephen Schur explains the
need every enterprise has for timely, accurate, and low-cost information processing: "Whenever a company lacks knowledge about important business issues such as its resources, customers, bank accounts,
sales or inventory, such ignorance impairs corporate performance."[1]

This executive checklist summarizes what I consider essential

---

1. Stephen G. Schur, *The Database Factory: Active Database for Enterprise Computing* (New
York: Wiley, 1994), p. 6.

short-term operating tactics and strategies as well as visions for the future.

1. Massive amounts of business data are still being communicated between customers, suppliers, and service enterprises. In today's age of electronic data interchange and interactive touch-tone telephone data entry, every business must be working at breakneck speed to discontinue the costly process of manual data capture.
2. Possessors of extensive customer and supplier data bases should immediately begin to work with other companies with duplicate or similar needs, to capture, maintain, and use the information more cost-effectively. Cooperative ventures could be likely forerunners of the future's computer utilities.
3. Scanning technology, the process of converting conventional documents to computer data, is a powerful tool for converting massive conventional document files to far lower-cost, fast-retrieval electronic form. It may also be an effective way of lowering data entry costs in many applications until even better paperless processes are developed.
4. Electronic "printing" is on the threshold of replacing printing on paper. Every enterprise that produces paper products for widespread distribution must be actively preparing to replace them with electronic alternatives. As a result, the cost of production and distribution will be reduced to a small fraction of the paper predecessor.
5. Electronic catalogs are already being used in commercial applications such as dealer service centers and distribution. The era is rapidly approaching when electronic catalogs will be retailers' most important marketing tool.
6. Computer kiosks are a new tool that can bring interactive computer/video systems to the masses much faster and at lower cost than home systems. Enterprises that could benefit from interactive communications (i.e., home shopping businesses) should be working on development and widespread use of these systems.

FUTURE VISIONS

1. Community data base utility networks will vastly reduce the costs

of capturing and processing information concerning business, government and individuals. New security legislation and methodology will be the keys to resolving privacy and security concerns. Suppliers of the best software and system management professionals will be of overwhelming importance.

2. The explosive proliferation of catalog retailers in recent years is but a prelude to an even more convenient form of interactive home shopping, in which the consumer will be able to browse though catalogs of choice and enter and pay for orders on a new "home system" combining telecommunication, television, and computer technology in a completely user-friendly, nontechnical, simple system.

3. English is the almost universal business and government language. An even better, simplified English is likely to be the foundation of the future international business and government network and is vital to achieving the ultimate global usefulness of computer technology because it will make talking to computers simpler.

ELECTRONIC DATA INTERCHANGE: TODAY'S "INFORMATION STREET"

Some form of electronic data interchange dominates almost every private and public modernization initiative. The fairly recent invention of scanning devices by which printed data are converted to computer-processible electronic media, for example, is a short-term way in which the costs of data capture can be minimized and resulting electronic "documents" can be retrieved in seconds, reducing conventional paper document file search, retrieval, and refiling time from as much as hours to minutes or seconds. As a result, projects at companies such as the United Services Automobile Association (USAA) have enabled customer service to respond to inquiries while the customer is on the telephone, not several hours or even days later.[2]

The practical focus of the recently popularized "information highway," to date, has been on the interactive computer/cable television and its ability to bring vastly more entertainment into the home. However, the primary emphasis on entertainment is shortsighted, consider-

---

2. Nancy Baumgarten, "Insuring Victory: USAA Uses Technology to Improve Customer Service," in *Outlook* (Chicago: Andersen Consulting, 1993), pp. 32–33.

ing the vast array of services such as interactive home shopping, billing, payment, and education that the highway will carry between enterprises and their customers. Political leaders in the United States lag far behind the most advanced-thinking governments of other countries. For example, the Republic of Korea already has initiated a master plan for "installing microwave networks and optical fiber cables covering all households by 2015."[3] Vast product and service cost reductions will result from the elimination of the expense of millions of people involved in the manual and computer processing of data when the true potential of existing technology is used to pave the information streets and highways.

In manufacturing, for example, tens of thousands of companies still have armies of people processing the customer orders received in each day's mail through their computer systems to determine the required raw material and component purchase requirements. These purchase requirements are still, all too often, sent to their suppliers in the form of printed orders which in turn are processed by the suppliers' armies of data entry people. The armies disappear as soon as customer computers communicate with supplier computers, which in turn communicate with *their* suppliers' computers. My project with Yamaha Motors in Iwata, Japan, was one of the first in which a Westerner participated in a Japanese computer system project for processing customer requirements into instant electronic schedules for multiple tiers of suppliers. Such systems reduce from days and weeks to hours the time required to pass end assembly schedules, in paper form, to every tier. Since then these "Japanese" techniques have been brought to Western companies. General Motors, for example, has been able to reduce inventory in the pipeline by 80 percent in an initial project, while cutting transportation costs by 67 percent in concurrent reengineering initiatives.[4]

And in retailing, interactive home shopping is clearly the most important focus of technological development. For example, hundreds of my colleagues are currently working on an electronic catalog/order

---

3. Kim Yong-bom, "Korea Launches 1st Stage of Info Super Highway Project," *The Korea Times* (Seoul), April 23, 1994.

4. For reference to more information about the General Motors "electronic kanban" system, see appendix 2.

entry system for one of the world's largest retail companies. The company executives have, by their dedication of major resources to the project, expressed their confidence in the extreme importance of electronic catalogs to future retailing.

The electronic kiosk will rapidly put the convenience and speed of computer systems and modern telecommunications into the hands of the masses, far sooner than many might imagine. For example, the state of California recently installed one hundred electronic kiosks in shopping malls and supermarkets. The public can use these systems to make credit card payments, register cars, and renew drivers licenses, among other conveniences.[5] Innovations of this ilk will soon move massive amounts of inconvenient, clerk-oriented customer-to-business interaction into the mode of customer-to-computer interaction.

ELECTRONIC PAPER: A STEP TOWARD THE PAPERLESS FUTURE

In the 1950s and 1960s, the first decades of my career, the volume of paper printed by enterprises and stored in file cabinets was a small fraction of that now found in most businesses. After the Xerox machine was invented, an avalanche of copies was loosed to flood industry and government with an unparalleled volume of "information" to be processed and filed. Now the paper revolution is about to end. The inevitable decline of paper is about to begin. Technology, in the form of ever-improving laser discs and computers, is the weapon that will kill paper.

As computer (better still, home system) prices continue their precipitous plunge, and as computer programs continue to expand the uses to which the computer can be put, both hardware and software will be simplified and, thus, user friendly. Eventually every household will own a computer or home system. Further, competition in communications services will eventually pay off, in terms of lowering the costs of communications. In the end, every form of communication now laboriously written and keyed into systems or printed on paper will be telecommunicated from the system on which it originates to

---

5. George de Lama, "Citizens Plugging into Computer Government," *Chicago Tribune,* November 14, 1993.

any other system, electronically. At that time, there will be no further need for printing on paper.

Compact disc technology, applied to computer systems and fed by scanners that help to capture volumes of data at minimal costs, is already moving some printed paper products to far less expensive electronic forms that make accessing data faster and more convenient. For example, Amdahl Corporation now scans new office equipment manuals, using Xerox's Docu Tech to scan, store, and print manuals on demand, thereby cutting inventories of manuals by 73 percent.[6] Had Amdahl started the project to convert to electronic imaging just a little later, its primary emphasis would undoubtedly have been on "printing" and distributing manuals on laser disc, thereby providing a source of information much more convenient for repairmen to carry with them, and virtually eliminating space required to store manuals. Thus, Xerox is moving in the right direction in capturing and storing electronic images, but its primary design path for the twenty-first century will need to be interfacing less with paper printing and more with electronic "printing" using laser and computer disc devices.

Every business with routine needs to distribute masses of large printed documents should be reengineering the process to begin to replace paper with electronic alternatives. And electronic manufacturers should be gearing up to produce the "user friendly" electronic readers that will accelerate the decline of paper.

THE ELECTRONIC NEWSPAPER: MERGED WITH OTHER MEDIA

Newspaper readership in the United States has been on a long decline, with only about 50 percent of the population subscribing, and 50 percent of the future generation—those ages eighteen to twenty-four—don't read newspapers at all.[7] In my opinion, what is wrong with big city newspapers is clear: they are not "user friendly." For one thing, the ratio of advertisement space to news is very high. Reading the

---

6. Linda Grant, "Green Light for Growth: Xerox Bets on a New Generation of Digital Office Equipment," *U.S. News & World Report,* August 15, 1994.

7. Vic Sussman, "News of the Wired: The Perils and Promise of Electronic Newspapering," *U.S. News & World Report,* May 16, 1994, pp. 60–62.

newspaper involves skipping over many pages of advertisements to get to the news. Further, news and advertisements are intermingled on the same pages, causing the news reader to leaf through far more pages than otherwise necessary. Of course, the spaces closest to the most newsworthy news items are those most coveted by advertisers, because the reader is automatically exposed to *their* ads and may skip over the pages filled with ads only. Thus, newspapers can price this space higher. Worse, almost every front-page story is broken into two or more parts, requiring the reader to flip back and forth between the front page and following pages. (Most magazines seem to be able to concentrate all advertisement in the front and back sections and to keep stories on contiguous pages—why not newspapers?)

The classified ad section in metropolitan newspapers is difficult to use because of the vast number of ads in each category. Most often, when readers call sellers to get more information, they learn that the advertised item is not what they want or that it has already been sold. Furthermore, most newspapers try to be everything to every reader, thus newspaper sizes are humongous and production and distribution are so expensive that the cost to both reader and advertiser is too high. Another drawback is that because television and radio news coverage can be instantaneous, most potential readers have heard the latest news long before it can be printed in the newspaper. Those who prefer not to read can listen to the news programs and even see live and taped news scenes. On the plus side, newspapers can devote much more space to in-depth coverage than can television and radio whose coverage is limited to "sound bites" of a few seconds.

The electronic newspaper will address these shortcomings and will be "user friendly" as follows.

1. Media companies will be merged and the news and classified ads will be delivered through common information channels. Thus, the differences between "newspaper," magazine, television, and radio will become almost imperceptible.
2. Readers will be able to specify their reading priorities on their home system module, which will then access the news and present it in the sequence of the individual reader's interests. Entire sections equivalent to newspaper and magazine sections and radio and television segments can be ignored.

3. The reader will have the option of either reading or hearing news and classified ads. Live action and still scenes will also be available.
4. The news media company will offer continuous and instantaneous updates, making the electronic newspaper and all other media news equally current.
5. The tremendous duplicated cost of news gathering and reporting will be eliminated as the media merge. Huge investments in printing equipment and facilities will no longer be required, while materials and labor costs of printing and distribution will also disappear.
6. Retail advertisers will no longer put advertisements in the newspaper or other media. They will use electronic mail to put their ads in targeted individuals' electronic mailboxes, resulting in far better response.
7. The reader of electronic classified ads will no longer need to review massive numbers of offerings to narrow the candidates to a manageable few. Instead, the reader will give the home system module specifications and the system will select the ads fitting those specifications. Then the "reader" will be able to see the items advertised, without the need to go to the seller's home or business. Should the "reader" elect to buy an item, the deal could be closed instantaneously, payment transferred from the buyer's account to that of the seller, and the ad would be deleted immediately.

As the world awaits the advent of truly "user friendly" electronic newspapers, less usable ones have already recently started to become available in a format that could only be considered desirable by a dedicated computer "jock." For example, in commenting about Dow Jones News/Retrieval and Knight-Ridder's Dialog, Nancy Hass notes that "both offer on-line access to huge collections of statistics, news reports and scientific articles. Both services, however, are notoriously user-unfriendly."[8] Exhibit 5–1 is an example of one "electronic newspaper." Reading and using such a newspaper is not only unnecessarily complex but also grossly impractical, as compared to a printed page, in terms of the amount of "written" news displayed and need for manual

8. Nancy Hass, "Bound to the Printed Word: The Info Highway: Should the Nation's Newspapers Stick to the Business They Know Best?" *Newsweek,* June 20,1994, pp. 52–53.

EXHIBIT 5–1

Computer Jock Newspaper

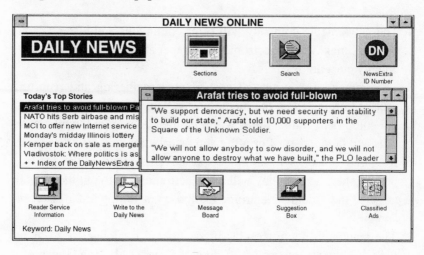

advancing to scan through an entire article. The mistake made, in terms of complexity, was to use windows-genre software features to operate the newspaper, which appeals only to "computer literates" and is even shunned by countless computer "jocks" who are disgusted with its low productivity. Nevertheless, pioneering steps in this direction will lead to better products eventually, and I salute leading-edge newspapers for starting their journey into the twenty-first century.

Exhibit 5–2 illustrates and summarizes the most important characteristics of the twenty-first century multimedia company. The most important point is that all news-gathering media (cable television, newspapers, magazines, and radio stations on the exhibit) will merge, and merged media suppliers will deliver all news to the home system module via the information superhighways and streets and computer utilities. Doing so will lower the capital investment and production and distribution costs, and reduce news gathering staff, thus lowering consumer prices. The new, interactive home system module will let the user select only the news and classified ads desired. Reporting will be delivered free of commercials and business advertisements. All news forms will be instantaneously updated and available to the worldwide public.

EXHIBIT 5–2

News Media Merger

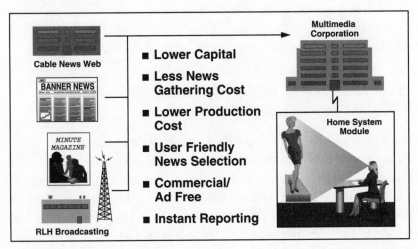

In a 1994 nationwide survey, only 15 percent of those surveyed said they relied on newspapers as sources of news, a shocking revelation which should spur newspapers to reinvent their products and processes.[9] Leading publishers such as *Time* and the *Chicago Tribune* are already beginning to enter the electronic publication arena. However, their electronic offerings require computer literacy and equipment and thus strictly limit the number of persons likely to use them in the short term. The burgeoning but still limited compact-disk–read only memory (CD-ROM) "book" business illustrates the problem. As Jessica Seigel reported of the annual American Booksellers Association convention, "Though booksellers said they were interested in new electronic products, many were concerned about high prices, getting computer-equipped kiosks into their stores and training personnel to demonstrate."[10] Despite the extremely high interest in electronic publishing (2,700 newspapers dabbling in electronic ventures), few

---

9. Tim Jones, "Time Pinch Controls How Americans Use Media," *Chicago Tribune,* November 7, 1994.

10. Jessica Seigel, "Many Booksellers Say They See the Interactive Handwriting on the Wall," *Chicago Tribune,* June 1, 1994.

appear to have a clear vision of the twenty-first century newspaper.[11] Obviously, those publication and broadcast media with the strongest conviction concerning the future of the electronic newspaper must pursue their vision in the format of the printed media. The single most important key will be the merger with other media forms.

THE ELECTRONIC BOOK AND READER: KEEP TREES IN THE FOREST

Publishers and electronic manufacturers are potentially on the verge of an exciting avalanche of transformation. Some, like Alfred C. Sikes, vice president and head of Hearst Corporation's news media and technology group, believe strongly in the future of interactive publishing media. Sikes predicts that a "fairly large segment of our population will be embracing" it.[12] Nor will the CD-ROM fit the need. With its capacity of approximately one thousand books per disk, far too much capacity would be wasted if each book were recorded on a separate disk. The conventional three-and-a-half-inch and five-and-a-quarter-inch floppy disks' capacities are far better matched to the size of an average book. As Spectrum Presses' Dan Agin points out, "Right now the most economical means of getting new fiction to the public is the floppy disk." He estimates the cost of publishing a disk as one-tenth that of printing a book. However, as Robert Jordan, publisher of *On-Line Access* magazine said to John Blades, "You just can't open an electronic book. It has to be loaded into a four-pound laptop or a desk-top PC (personal computer)."[13] What consumers need is a book reader that looks like a book and can be read like a book, without being tied to a computer.

Electronic manufacturers should be inventing a new electronic book reader now! A low-cost compact portable reader has a potential market of hundreds of millions of units in the home and in business. A new "button," a small magnetic storage disc for books, newspapers,

11. Vic Sussman, "News of the Wired: The Perils and Promise of Electronic Newspapering," *U.S. News & World Report,* May 16, 1994, p. 60.

12. Nancy Millman, "Magazines Turn Page on Ad Crisis, Seek New Ways to Make Money," *Chicago Tribune,* November 28, 1993.

13. John Blades, "Books on Disk: An Idea Whose Time Has Come," *Chicago Tribune,* July 12, 1994.

magazines, and catalogs will temporarily have a market potential for sales of hundreds of billions of units. I believe telecommunication transmission of published data will be a longer-term delivery medium, in that home computer systems and software capable of routinely ordering, receiving, and storing electronic "printed" books are too complex and too expensive for the average homeowner. Further, the complexities of systems for collecting the publication price and copyright protection may take some time to resolve. The book reader can be so cheap that publishers may well supply it gratis to subscribers in order to capture their business. Publishers should be working on seamless publishing of electronic books, merging their authors' word-processing output and the publisher's editing networks and feeding the results into the electronic "button" production (reproduction) process. The venerable Encyclopedia Britannica Publishing group is just one recent example of a publisher bowing to the pressure of lower sales and profits to move into electronic publishing. Its recent steps, as reported by James Coates, include making a CD-ROM available, selling a computer hard-drive version for local area networks and businesses, and making the encyclopedia available to students and faculty through the Internet's Worldwide Web.[14]

The computer, forest products, printing, and mail delivery industries are examples of businesses that I expect to undergo radical change in the twenty-first century, as a result of electronic publishing. In fact, most will become obsolete and will disappear as a result of technologies already emerging. Consider, for example, the evolution of books and magazines from paper to electronic media. I predict that the book of the future, in personal and business book libraries, may take the form of a new micro-magnetic medium. In its new form, an entire book (magnetic "button") will be the size equivalent of a postage stamp. Entire library buildings will no longer be needed since their entire contents would be maintained on a computer file and accessed from the home system module. Further, the physical size of computer files will continue to decrease, perhaps shrinking to a thousandth of the size of present storage forms by the end of the new century.

There is no reason, even today, for leading-edge electronic compa-

---

14. James Coates, "Promiscuous Path: Britannica Sheds Loyalty to Ink on Paper," *Chicago Tribune*, December 12, 1994.

EXHIBIT 5–3
Electronic Book

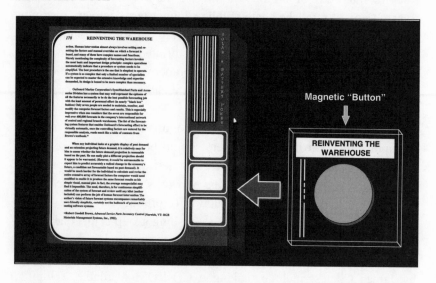

nies to delay beginning to design and produce the first crude electronic book readers. In their simplest, lowest-cost forms, the electronic book, magazine, newspaper, and catalog reader (exhibit 5–3) will consist of: (1) a book-size flat screen; (2) a single purpose magnetic media reader (very low cost due to the slow speed necessary); (3) an extremely simple computer chip, designed to read the magnetic input sequentially or by direct access to a page; and (4) simple controls to page through in sequence, or to access specified pages. Initial production costs of the electronic book reader would probably require pricing in the range of $200 to $300, but soon mass production would drive the costs and, therefore, price to under $100. The extremely simple electronic book and its low cost will extend its market potential to the entire reading public. For most households, the device would pay for itself in a few months. The cost of "printing" and distributing/mailing electronic books, newspapers, magazines, and catalogs should be no more than a fourth of the paper alternative. These costs will be even lower when and if the distribution is via computer-to-book reader or computer-to-computer telecommunication.

Electronic manufacturers are no less aware of the coming revolution in book readers. While in Germany gathering material for this

EXHIBIT 5–4
Reader Prototype

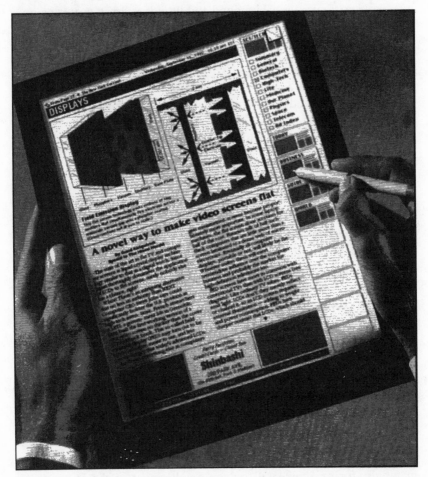

book, I found an article covering the new Xerox reader, the characteristics of which are seen in exhibit 5–4.[15] As computer buffs can see, the design is somewhat similar to the computer software windows-genre format, a feature which will be welcomed by millions of computer jocks but hated by tens of millions of others. Time Inc.'s Curtis G. Vibranz explained that *Time*'s first on-line magazine version read-

---

15. Steven Dickman, "Eleckronische Zeitung: Die Digitale Allgemeine," *Focus* (Frankfurt), October, 1993.

ership is the "globetrotting, Apple [computer] Power-Book user."
However, this market is a small but growing fraction of the masses
who have no computer background and little interest in acquiring one.
Most electronic engineers and computer analysts continue to make the
mistake of designing products that are not "user friendly" for the
computer illiterate. For example, Apple Computer's Newton flopped
when it hit the market, largely due to unrealistic reliance on the computer's ability to read handwritten input and failure to include a keyboard for those whose writing is unintelligible.[16] To make users comfortable, a book reader should look like a book and have booklike
controls. For example, the operation keys on the electronic book in
exhibit 5–3 are marked "turn page" and "turn back." Armies of book
readers who read during their daily commute would find an electronic
book significantly less than convenient if it were larger than book
size—fortunately, it need not be. Finally, the color screen price of exhibit 5–4 would exclude millions from buying the device until its cost
drops to more affordable levels. And although bright colors will ultimately be universal, book and newspaper readers will be perfectly
content to read in black and white until the price is right.

The impact of electronic "printed" material is not restricted to the
printing industry. Producers of electronic book readers and magnetic
book reproduction machines will be big gainers. The environment
will be massively benefited as a result of virtual elimination of most
paper products, because the need to harvest trees will be sharply reduced. In the future, most "paper" will be "stored" in the forest and
on our computer systems (exhibit 5–5). Certain industries and their
employees will be hit hard by the new technology. Electronic reading
materials, for example, will reduce employment in the logging and
paper-making industries. Post office volume will decline to a small
fraction of present levels when books, magazines, newspapers, and
catalogs are shifted to electronic media. Eventually, all subscribers
will receive and send mail electronically, eliminating the remainder of
printed material from post office distribution, leaving nothing but
packages. As a result, the salaries of most of the 700,000 U.S. postal
employees and their related costs will no longer be borne by the pub-

---

16. James Coates, "Key Part in Pocket PC? The Keyboard, Stupid," *Chicago Tribune,* June 5,
1994.

EXHIBIT 5–5
Future Paper Storage

lic and private enterprises.[17] Heavy industrial equipment manufacturers of printing presses, paper machines, and logging and pulping equipment will be hit heavily by the rapid demise of printed paper products. They would be well advised to start planning for conversion to alternative products. Sudden, unplanned business failures and unemployment can be avoided only if these industries start to plan for the future.

Publishers forming the earliest strategic alliances with electronic manufacturers and telecommunication companies for the purpose of developing electronic book systems will emerge as the survivors in a paper-printing industry which is doomed to eventual extinction. The transformation from printed to electronic book and magazine media will come faster than imaginable and, once started, will radically change the industry with amazing speed.[18] The speed of conversion is likely to be the same as that of the transformation from long-playing audio records and magnetic tape to compact disc. In retrospect, the

---

17. Hanke Gratteau and Sarah Talalay, "Delivering Changes: Sweeping Reform Sought in Mail 'Culture,'" *Chicago Tribune,* May 31, 1994.

18. Jessica Seigel, "Many Booksellers Say They See the Interactive Handwriting on the Wall," *Chicago Tribune,* June 1, 1994.

disappearance of grooved vinyl records seems to have been virtually overnight.

BENEVOLENT BIG BROTHER:
COMMUNITY DATA BASE

Almost every aspect of the world of the future will depend on processing by computer utilities via vastly improved telecommunication technology that will be applied to the construction of immensely efficient "information streets and superhighways." The current broad array of costly duplicate computer systems and data bases will be substantially reduced as continuous improvement by software and hardware suppliers results in the field being narrowed to the purveyors of the best-value products. Further, private and public sources of goods and services will be similarly consolidated. The future's new computer utilities, information hubs on the information streets and highways, will most likely be publicly owned but operated by private enterprises periodically bidding for each community's business. Others prefer a vision of privately owned computer utilities, which is another feasible scenario for the future. Ownership and management of these utilities is a point of probable disagreement, since many looking at government today see it as especially badly managed. In the longer term, my own vision includes reinvented government (chapter 9) and new, smaller community units (chapter 11). These predictions, which are not the only possible future scenario, are merely one person's very long-range vision. However, I believe that the integration of all information, transaction processing, and telecommunications would not be economically feasible if the services were to be provided by a patchwork of privately owned companies; thus I consider the most reasonable outcome to be a combination of public ownership of the processing and data storing computer utility with management of the utility by privately owned management firms.

Enterprises that create, maintain, and operate unimaginably more powerful software systems for various individual, public, and business processes will be among the most important businesses of the future. Cross-functional computer-literate specialists will be those in highest demand. Doctors capable of programming computer-oriented patient diagnosis and treatment regimens, for example, will dominate this field of medical practice, since the number of physicians required for this function will decline sharply as new software systems prove to be capable of far better, more consistent diagnosis.

Robert Heldman, whose book outlines most of the major information networking applications of the world of the future, also provides a futuristic vision of the global information society.[19] He wrote (as if reviewing the future as the past):

> As time passed, the new, planned cities were built near each major city. They were designed so there would be minimum commute time between residences and the workplace. Fiber optic cable was deployed to every home and to every desktop in satellite work centers. New switching systems and transport controllers ensured that both security and survivability were achieved, as well as network integrity and personal privacy. Information exchange enabled the multimedia flow of voice, data, text, image, graphic, and video conversations. There was now an exciting array of new customer-premise equipment as well as numerous specialized databases to provide financial, legal, medical, and architectural information, and information on protection, education, entertainment, and sports.

Horrified cries of outrage are one expected reaction to the notion of big computer networks with extensive data bases not only for public and private enterprises but also for every citizen. Visions of Big Brother watching us would be a valid reason for concern if it were not a fact that safeguards against invasion of privacy can and will be integral components of the future's computer utilities and information streets and highways. The reduction of the hundreds of manual and electronic files in which personal data is kept to a single data base will enable far better security measures to be put into effect.

A conservative estimate of the number of data bases in which the average middle-class citizen's name and personal data appears must be in the hundreds! Social security, federal, state, and local tax authorities, various licensing agencies, schools, employers, doctors, hospitals, insurers, utilities, credit card companies, credit agencies, banks and savings and loan institutions, mailing lists, magazines and newspapers are only a few. The ultimate cost to consumers (indirectly, in

---

19. Robert K. Heldman, *Future Telecommunications: Information Applications, Services and Infrastructure* (New York: McGraw-Hill, 1993), p. 112.

that they ultimately pay the cost of every data base in higher prices and taxes) must be a staggering sum. For example, no one who has had occasion to receive health care can fail to recognize the extraordinary waste involved when asked to provide the same medical history for the hundredth time. After all, even if no one bothers to read each copy of the history, we know that every page will be carefully filed and refiled for several years. Further, individuals have a logical reason to worry about the privacy and accuracy of information stored in so many different locations. And data that is kept in hundreds of files is not only of low security, it is also highly likely to be inaccurate in some of those files. It is impossibly difficult for the keepers of each file to maintain the completeness, accuracy, and current status of information in a mobile society where people move frequently from one neighborhood to another, from city to city, and from one employer to another. Thus, many data bases, such as medical records, are filed away where they are no longer accessible, and of no further use.

The ultimate, more effective society, including business, will inevitably come to the realization that a single common data base, resident in a community computer utility, would be far better than hundreds of files containing duplicate data. I am not alone in my vision of the information utility, although others such as Gary Hamel and C.K. Prahalad have not gone as far as conceiving the utility to be a public enterprise.[20] Their work has led me to concur with the probable linkage of the utility to portable access devices. "But what if there was an 'information Utility,' " they ask. And further, "Instead of carrying an electronic organizer or cellular phone, one would carry an 'InfoPort,' a small device replete with screen, telephone link, and data input device (stylus, keyboard, or microphone). The InfoPort would connect our happy user to his or her own small corner of the AT&T world, or British Telecom world, or Bell Atlantic world. In that little corner would reside all the user's files, safe from the neighborhood cat burglar, electrical surges, and other dangers."

However, to get started, groups of data base owners must work to-

---

20. Gary Hamel and C.K. Prahalad, *Competing for the Future: Breakthrough for Seizing Control of Your Industry and Creating the Markets of Tomorrow* (Boston: Harvard Business School Press, 1994), p. 87.

gether on merging, creating, and maintaining common *local* data bases. For example, one starting point could be the development of community mailing lists (soon to be superseded by the *electronic* mail list). Such lists, consisting of a composite of information from their predecessor data bases, will contain a wealth of facts on the life circumstances and buying habits of the individuals listed. The mailing list company will serve as a utility, providing information to local and to national companies in response to their specified target markets within the local data base area. Medical personal data base utilities are likely to be some of the earliest to be developed. However, public utilities are among the best sources for obtaining name and address information for home occupants, as they add and delete information as residents move about. The ultimate individual data base evolution will be the merging of *all* specialized data bases into the single community data base, maintained by the community data utility.

One of the most important users of name and address information is the census bureau. Every ten years, this agency, which normally employs about seven thousand full-time people, hires four hundred thousand people to work on the gathering of population information. After all of the census information is gathered, the consensus is that a substantial number of people, typically the poorest, are missed. Further, the small number of census questions that are practical to ask each person surveyed in the process is far less than those for which government and business would like to have answers. The establishment and use of community data bases for individuals will, within the next century, virtually eliminate the ten-year census cycle. Interconnecting the community data base utilities via the new information streets and highways will enable the census bureau computer, mainly a "black box" system, to maintain a *current* census of not only people, but also data of importance to government and business, gleaned from computer utility records.[21] This system will virtually eliminate the need for both full-time and temporary census employees.

In every company that maintains name and address information, realization eventually dawns on management that their data base has

---

21. For readers not familiar with the term "black box," it means a computer system that automatically initiates action free of routine human intervention.

value beyond routine use for their own purposes. For example, a Swiss emergency automobile road service insurance company, whose clients include over 99 percent of all Swiss drivers, recently pulled back its mailing list from an outside computer service bureau because of the value of their client list and the possibility of it being stolen dawned on the company's executives. Such a valuable asset must be protected from unauthorized duplication and theft, especially by potential competitors.

Again, I am completely aware that a horrified cry will surge from those concerned with data privacy issues, upon hearing the premise of personal data banks. The ultimate fears are epitomized by Howard Rheingold:

> If totalitarian manipulators of populations and technologies actually do achieve dominance in the future, I predict that it will begin not by secret police kicking in your doors but by allowing you to sell yourself to your television and letting your supermarket sell information about your transactions, while outlawing measures you could use to protect yourself. Instead of just telephone taps, the weapons will include computer programs that link bar codes, credit cards, social security numbers, and all of the other electronic tell-tales we leave in our paths through the information society. And the most potent weapon will be the laws or absence of laws that enable improper uses of information technology to erode what is left of citizens' rights to privacy."[22]

Unreasonable fears concerning misuse of personal information will best be resolved by strict new laws, as Rheingold intimates and as I describe in following paragraphs. First, however, it would be logical to examine less dramatic circumstances in which personal information could conceivably be misused. I believe that there are three primary reasons for concern. The first reason is that those individuals involved in outright illegal, criminal activities or borderline shady tax avoidance practices would be detected by automated government audits of the data base information. Society should decide whether to endorse the use of such data base information or to prohibit it. In the case of

---

22. Howard Reingold, *The Virtual Community: Homesteading on the Electronic Frontier* (New York: Addison-Wesley, 1993), p. 293.

tax evasion, my opinion is that by the end of the twenty-first century reporting procedures in the moneyless world will eliminate any potential for tax evasion, thus this worry will no longer be of concern. As to criminal detection, I personally would favor legislative authorization to government law enforcement agencies permitting the routine use of data base utilities for crime detection (therefore prevention). Since every citizen would be aware that every computer transaction would be subjected to crime detection analysis, this would be likely to virtually eradicate illegal transactions.

The second reason for worry about the secrecy of private records is the concern that unauthorized persons would learn of illnesses such as venereal disease and mental disorders—news of which would be embarrassing or damaging to an individual's social life or career. To this concern, a new remedy is proposed: namely, that severe, draconian penalties be assessed on *anyone* making unauthorized use of information and on anyone aiding and abetting in its illegal use. More important, however, is the question as to how vulnerable the single community data base will be versus the hundreds of data bases now in existence. I contend that the extensive security measures feasible and cost-justified in the new, single, unduplicated data base are impossible to imagine in hundreds of independent computer and manual files now existent. These new and better security remedies are of equal value concerning the third privacy worry, use of seemingly innocent information to torpedo careers and social life. For example, in the United Kingdom, the opposition recently revealed that a politician's credit card records included a purchase of champagne. In a district of working-class people, this indication of immodest lifestyle was enough to cost the imbibing politician the election. Such invasions of privacy would become much rarer in the future due to the combination of the draconian penalties and the superb new security provisions.

Business and government must go to work educating the populace on the huge monetary rewards that will accrue to every citizen as a result of integrated networks of community data bases for each individual's personal information. More important, work on consolidating the hundreds of thousands of existing data bases must be started in earnest, soon, and the benefits should start to flow to consumers in the form of lower prices and taxes.

COMMUNITY DATA BASE NETWORKS: FUTURE SYSTEMS FOUNDATION

The information age is barely dawning. The acquisition, storage, processing, and delivery of information-based products is outrageously inefficient and costly. Some of the reasons that information storage and processing are so costly bear repeating. The government, for example, maintains innumerable data bases containing data on every citizen and every private and public enterprise. Information is sometimes duplicated and is often inaccurate or conflicting. Duplicate medical information is maintained on dozens, perhaps hundreds of data bases—by health care providers, insurance companies, employers, and government agencies. Every utility and telecommunication company and credit card company maintains records. All of this wasteful duplication carries with it a tremendous cost, which is ultimately borne by the consumer.

One of the inevitable developments of the next century will be the establishment of data bases on each community's computer utility, accessible through international telecommunication networks (see exhibit 5–6). The privacy of these future repositories of *all* historical and current information pertinent to individuals and public and pri-

EXHIBIT 5–6

Community Computer Networks

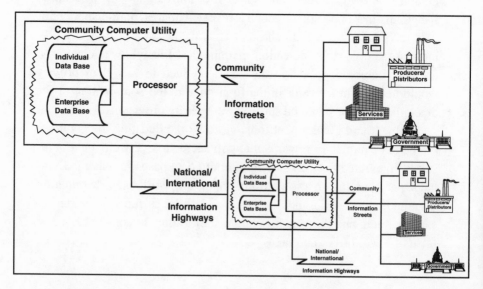

vate enterprises will be guarded with extremely strict security methods and protected by severe penalties, criminal and civil, for unauthorized use or disclosure. They will evolve from a natural progression towards consolidation of existing data bases. For example, electric, gas, and water utilities will discover the economies of common customer data bases and billing programs. Hundreds of businesses maintaining mailing lists will discover similar benefits by using a single common mailing list in which the buying habits and interests of individuals are recorded, permitting mailings to be better targeted to potentially receptive customers. As a result, businesses will cooperatively begin the process of merging all data bases into far fewer, better, shared electronic information treasuries.

Every community's computer utility should eventually be connected via telecommunication "information streets" to every residence and to every public and private entity in the community, as illustrated on the exhibit. Even later, telecommunication hookups via the national and international data highways will permit international access and transaction processing. This linkage will ultimately include such services as direct video-telecommunications and interactive computer travel accommodation booking. Thus, the single computer utility will also be the major telecommunication network node.

THE ENTERPRISE COMPUTER UTILITY: SAVING WITH COMMON SYSTEMS

The community computer utility's data base for enterprises (see exhibit 5–7), will be available to be processed and updated by producers, distributors, and service providers, including public entities. However, the incredibly strict security provisions of the computer utility will limit access to only the data required by the application being processed. For example, a single payroll computer program, used to "pay" every employed individual, would access the employee name and address information, and would automatically post (but not have access to) the government portion of an individual's information (i.e., the tax and social benefits segment shown on exhibit 5–9, below). Insurance withheld will be posted to the individual's account and automatically credited to the account of the insurer. The employee's equivalent of net pay would be added to his accumulated

EXHIBIT 5–7

Enterprise Data Base

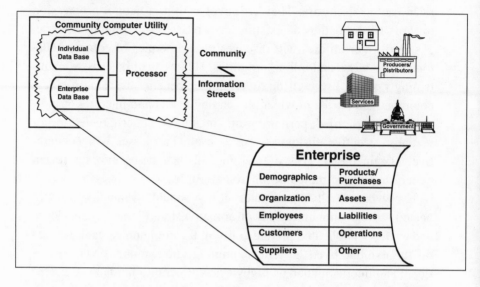

earnings account, from which his payments to creditors would be deducted. Virtually all such "payments" including those of the utilities would be transferred electronically to the recipients' accounts. The utilities would "bill" an individual's account, using a common utility computer process to calculate the charges and transfer the funds.

The long list of common computer applications that all enterprises will be able to use will, globally, cut application design and development costs to the bone, since it will no longer be necessary for each enterprise to develop or customize its own application programs. Further, since all development expense will be limited to just a few software supplier companies' products for each specific application (such as bill paying), these companies will be able to afford more improvements and, thus, all users will have access to the best software currently available. And while standardization of business practices required to enable an enterprise to use common application software is a massive undertaking, it will ultimately be achieved, surely sometime within the next century.

The enterprise data base, the hub of all business processing, will include the segments illustrated on exhibit 5–7, described below.

1. *Demographics.* The unique number assigned to the enterprise to identify it in the worldwide information network. The enterprise name, address, business codes, and other demographic information.

2. *Organization.* The organizational relationships of personnel in the employee data base and of other facilities in the same or other communities that are part of the enterprise's business.

3. *Employees.* Employee data will be much more concise than in today's enterprises, since each individual's personal data base will be where year-to-date payroll and deduction records will be maintained. The employee's educational and work experience records on his personal data base would also be available at the time of the initial job interview and updated as the employee gained additional valuable skills and experience.

4. *Customers and suppliers.* As in the case of employees, a wealth of data such as demographic information would be accessed in the suppliers' and customers' data bases. Therefore, the cost of capturing and maintaining this data at both the supplier and customer ends of the pipeline would be eliminated.

5. *Products and purchases.* The data base for each manufactured, purchased, and distributed product, component, and material, stored in this segment, would permit their suppliers to maintain specifications, prices, and other item information. Customers, through access to the supplier's item data base, would be able to generate electronically transmitted schedules of their requirements and forecast needs.

6. *Assets, liabilities, and operations.* Inventories of products, work-in-process, and purchases would be stored in the enterprise's data base, as would detailed inventories of equipment, real estate, and other assets. The computer utilities' financial accounting application programs would, thus, be used to routinely update the enterprises' balance sheet. And, because all financial transactions would be processed, operations information would be used to maintain an up-to-date operating report and sales statistics.

Jim Snider and Terra Ziporyn have a more limited vision of the data bases and their processors of the future. They foresee centralized, national, government-sanctioned, quasi-private organizations, one of which they have labeled National Institutes of Product Information.[23] My own vision of a network of smaller, local, public utility and data base processors has the advantage of greater simplicity, lower bureaucracy, and smaller, more manageable volumes of data to be stored and processed by each utility. However, the issue is not which specific vision will prove to be correct at some far-distant time, but what are the implications of either of these visions on every enterprise's short-term strategies, if any.

BUSINESS INFORMATION HIGHWAY: LINKING CUSTOMERS AND SUPPLIERS

Even in the most modern companies, the time lapse between an end-customer purchase (or order) and processing the resulting change in demand through the distribution, production, and supplier computer networks is a long process taking a minimum of days, and more often, weeks and even months. Each step in the network typically processes information through its own computer system, passing the resulting requirements and forecast back to the previous supply chain link, all too often in the form of paper orders or schedules. Because the time required to cascade requirements back through the supplier pipeline is so long, the majority of industries are *always* working on forecasted demand of some sort, rather than real-time demand forecasts based on end-customer actual consumption or orders as they occur. As an inevitable result, just-in-case inventories at all levels of the pipeline are outrageously high, and still unanticipated shortages occur.[24]

In the short term, enterprises need to continue to work on adopting limited use of electronic data interchange to transfer demand, forecast, and inventory data received from customers and forwarded on to suppliers. Companies that have mastered the single-level use of these telecommunication links to suppliers and/or distributors need to expand their networks farther into the pipeline of *their* suppliers and suppliers' suppliers and/or out to their ultimate customers. At any point in time, a high percentage of enterprises are feverishly working

---

23. Jim Snider and Terra Ziporyn, *Future Shop: How Future Technologies Will Change the Way We Shop and What We Buy* (New York: St. Martin's Press, 1992), pp. 262–267.

24. For reference to more about cascading pipeline requirement, see appendix 2.

to upgrade their current systems to better utilize the latest available computer and telecommunication power. (Systems, especially *integrated* ones, are so complex that these upgrades are often multiyear projects, guaranteeing that the software used will no longer be able to take advantage of the very latest computer hardware and telecommunications technology by the time a major upgrade is completed. Worse still, the cost and time required to upgrade systems is so great that most companies undertake major systems overhauls as infrequently as every ten or fifteen years).

Future community computer utility business demand network systems will be the channel for all customer, distribution, production, and supplier demand management networks. Since all enterprises and their customers will use one or both of the two demand-type *common* systems (custom and standard products, see exhibit 5–8), the power of the common software, shared by computer utilities nationally and even internationally, will be much greater than any one enterprise could now afford. Further, since a single software system will be used, it will be far easier to maintain it to best utilize current technology. Exhibit 5–8, a schematic of the common business processors, will serve to illustrate how the computer utility's business processors will direct the exchange of demand data in the local, national, and international networks of supply and demand. The process starts, for standard products, with an order or consumption of a producer's product by a local consumer or retail outlet on the community's information streets. In the case of retail outlets the consumption will be processed by the electronic transmission from point-of-sale devices (i.e., computer cash registers). Consumers will also order home delivery, using the same customer demand subprocessor. The retail sale might be merely replacing a previously forecast demand, and as such requires no forecast update. If, however, the order is not "covered" by a forecast, the customer's demand forecast processor would recast his forecast and transmit the order and updated forecast to the supplier's computer utility. The supplier's system would schedule shipment and transportation of the item ordered, using the customer demand and transport management processors. When the shipment is made, the supplier's inventory (quantity and asset value) will be updated, as will the customer's, using the inventory management processor. If customer and supplier are not in the same community, national and international telecommunication channels (information highways) facilitate the information travel.

If shipments are made from the producer's stock and the demand does not simply replace one previously forecasted, the producer's revised forecast will be developed by the demand forecast processor. When the forecast *is* revised, the scheduling and capacity management processor will schedule the item. (The interactive maintenance processor on the exhibit will maintain an enterprise's factory equipment data base). Next, the materials planning processor, using the product bill of material for the item, will generate updated component and raw material requirements. (The product maintenance processor will be used to maintain an enterprise's bill of material data base.) The demands for items purchased from suppliers thus generated will then be transmitted to suppliers' computer utilities. The suppliers' utilities will process the new or revised final product producers' requirements and, again, using the bills of material for the items they supply, generate demand for the components and materials produced by *their* suppliers.

The custom product processors, used by enterprises which assemble or manufacture to customer specifications, consist of several sub-

EXHIBIT 5–8

Common Business Processors

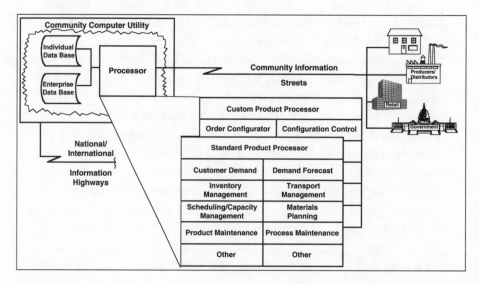

processors that are quite similar to those of the standard product processor. However, custom producers also have some unique needs such as the order configurator processor which will help to generate custom bills of material based on a customer's specifications and will interface with a product engineering system to obtain bill of material specifications for items requiring custom engineering. In addition, the custom product processor will provide a configuration control processor for capturing every custom product's "as built" configuration for purposes of subsequent service.

The schematic of the common business processors is not intended to be a complete depiction of all of the subprocessors that will be available to all enterprises through the community computer processor of the future. In fact, these same systems or personnel functions have always been part of every supply and production business. However, the processors of the future will operate with new business operations practices which will greatly simplify processing needs. Examples of two extremely important simplifying business practices are the shift to single sources of supply and discontinuance of the use of purchase order numbers.[25] When all "orders" are electronically broadcast from an enterprise's computer to the supplier's computer, it is easy to understand that the conventional concept of an authorizing purchase order must be sent to suppliers each time a purchase decision is made. As soon as systems are ready to operate in the new mode, there is no longer a need for a purchase order number. The need date of the requirement, in the new process, is the only mutually understood "authorization."

INDIVIDUAL COMPUTER UTILITY: ACCOUNTANT, BANKER, LAWYER, AND DOCTOR

The community computer utility's individual data base (exhibit 5–9) will ultimately be the sole repository of all information and the heart of all computer systems dealing with an individual. Artificial intelligence and continuing technological advances will bring personal electronic "accountants," "bankers," "lawyers," and "doctors" to individuals in their system modules at home. And the cost of these services,

---

25. See appendix 2 for reference to more material about single sources of supply and invalidating the need for "orders."

EXHIBIT 5–9
Individual Data Base

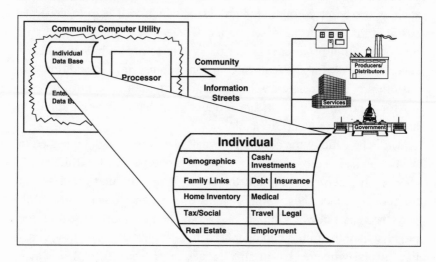

compared to human counterparts, will be negligible—consisting primarily of telecommunication and computer utility charges. It bears repeating that, since completely personal data can be accessed only from this location and by tightly controlled authorized private and public enterprises, security measures can be designed far more effec-

EXHIBIT 5–10
Individual Data Segments

Personal Statistics	**Accumulated Earnings**
Tax & Social Benefits	**Investments**
Utility Records	**Real Estate**
Medical	**Legal History**
Travel/Vacation	**Family Relationships**
Insurance	**Product Interests**
Employment	**Other**

tively than in today's world where bits and pieces of the same information are in hundreds of smaller document and computer files in numerous enterprises. Some of the data segments listed on exhibit 5–10 are as follows.

1. *Demographics.* The individual's unique identification number will be the only number universally used by private companies and public agencies. Thus separate numbers for bank accounts, driver's licenses, and credit cards, to name just a few of the wasteful separate identifiers now used, will become a thing of the past. The individual's home address will be key to electronic delivery of all forms of mail.

2. *Family links.* The hierarchical family structure linkage to parents, in one direction, and to children in another will have practical use in providing rapid access to family medical history. A human side of this linkage will be the practical ability to better maintain family bonds across the generations.

3. *Home inventory.* Purchases made through the business and individual transaction processes could be automatically added to the individual's home inventory. Such an inventory would be invaluable in terms of providing adequate insurance coverage, obtaining insurance reimbursement for theft and casualty loss, and for estate disposition.

4. *Tax/social.* Information basic to public programs such as social security should be integral to the individual's data base. Tax calculations should be automatically performed by public processors on the community computer utility, based on information from employment, investments, and real estate segments of the data base.

5. *Real estate.* Real estate sales should be transferred from one individual's or business's data base to that of another as the transaction occurs, while public records would be updated simultaneously. An individual's (or business's) "wealth," for purposes of establishing credit limits, would consist of real estate, personal property (home inventory), and cash/investments.

6. *Cash/investments.* An individual's "money" account and investment records should be incremented by an employer's payments and those of earnings from other enterprises, via the information highway. Purchases and payments for service and entertainment,

made via the home ordering system or at an enterprise via an electronic "money card" should be simultaneously deducted from the individual's data base and added to that of the provider.

7. *Debt.* Since all of the individual's debt is available to the community computer utility, the computer processor can establish credit limits based on the complete financial, employment, assets, and personal qualifications of the person. This will virtually eradicate instances of personal bankruptcy due to overextension, now often caused by too easy access to numerous different credit cards and personal loans.

8. *Insurance.* Life, health, home, and all other insurance information should be resident in the individual's data base and automatically updated to ensure adequate coverage consistent with the individual's own self-insurance objectives.

9. *Medical.* Complete, accurate, and up-to-date medical records, accessible only by the individual and used and maintained by authorized medical personnel will serve to enhance the quality of medical services while lowering their cost by eliminating duplicated documentation. Medical processors resident in the medical industry community computer utility can record medications prescribed as well as other therapy and perform analyses to preclude errors in prescriptions and suggested treatment. Links to the health insurer computer processor should facilitate timely transfer of insurance payments to the medical provider.

10. *Travel.* Future world citizens will have the time and wherewithal to spend much more time traveling as tourists or to visit distant relatives and friends. Therefore every individual's record of travel preferences should be of significant importance. One of the community computer processors should permit the individual to interactively plan a trip, order "electronic tickets," make accommodation reservations, and electronically transfer payment.

11. *Legal.* In the simplified future world legal system, where justice (not rule or rote) is demanded as the end result, the individual will have access to simplified electronic forms of contracts for various transactions requiring legal (albeit electronic) documentation. Examples might be wills and trusts, leases, and purchase and sales agreements. It would take the simultaneous action of both individ-

uals or private and public enterprises involved to record the document on the data base of each.

12. *Employment.* One of the most important aspects of an employment record is the individual's life experience as it relates to job qualifications. Therefore, a key part of the employment data base will consist of educational and training experience, job experience, and other related work qualifications. Performance on the job is also vitally important, thus the employee's work history should also be recorded. Links to current and past employers data base records should also be a fundamental provision.

SUMMARY

Current computer technology is incredibly underused, in terms of its potential contribution to reinvention of enterprise processes and transformation of entire industries. The problem of rapid advances in technology is exacerbated by the ever-increasing complexity of new software and its computer-technician orientation. The complexity of enterprises' existing computer systems often precludes patchwork improvements, while completely replacing these technological dinosaurs requires years and millions of dollars. Moreover, the time taken to develop and implement systems is so long that, by the time they are completed, the computer technology employed is already hopelessly out of date. Thus, executives and managers must improve operations by first simplifying them to begin to reap the rewards of lower-cost operations even before the computer software is finally revamped or replaced. And simpler manual operations help to simplify the related computer system. Thus simpler systems will be developed faster and can be upgraded more rapidly and at lower cost as soon as future advances in computer technology and continuous operation reinvention require it to be.

Thinking executives and managers are by now starting either to agree with some of my predictions or to formulate their own visions. In both cases, readers must begin to see that radical changes are now occurring and are bound to continue in the next century. It follows that they will be paying great attention to the growth industries of the future, some of which have been identified in this chapter and are

EXHIBIT 5–11
Growth Industries and Occupations

Short Term:	**Media/Telecommunication Conglomerates**
	Electronic Data Interchange Software
	Electronic Books & Newspapers
	Interactive Television
	Electronic Catalogs
	Computer Scanners
	Video Telephones
Long Term:	**Home System Module**
	Community Computer Utilities

listed on exhibit 5–11. Growth of many future industries is already underway. For example, entertainment and telecommunication industries are beginning the merger process that will inevitably lead to the few giant conglomerates of the next century. And work is well underway to bring electronic "printed" materials to home and business

EXHIBIT 5–12
Waning Industries and Occupations

Books	**Newspapers**
Copiers	**Facsimile**
Catalogs	**Service Manuals**
Scanners	**Order Processors**
Paper:	**Computer Printers**
Logging	**Printing**
Pulp Mills	
Making	**Post Office**

computer systems. In the short term, computer scanners will help businesses and individuals to rapidly, and at low cost, capture data that will persistently continue to arrive in printed form. However, in the longer term, scanners will disappear as more and more data is exchanged electronically. The biggest future industries in the long term will be the home computer system module producers and the community computer utilities.

At the same time some future industries develop and grow, the inexorable decline of human labor requirements and growth of automation cannot be ignored. Some of my predictions of additional waning industries and occupations, highlighted in this chapter, are listed on exhibit 5–12. For those inclined to feel anxious or offended by the definition of some industries and occupations as waning or dying, there are several important points to keep in mind. These following points are repeated briefly in every chapter, because many readers are expected to read only one or more selected chapters. First, the change may not occur in the foreseeable future. Second, the future continuous reduction of work will be universal. As a result, society must and will reduce average workweek hours in order to maintain full employment. Third, the era of reduced work and increased leisure time will be one of unprecedented quality of life and affluence. Electronic books, catalogs, and mail will radically reduce the number of lumberjacks needed, by obsoleting paper. For the same reason, pulp and paper mills and printers will disappear from use, as will the manufacturers of the heavy equipment used by them. Electronically transmitted mail and neighborhood delivery systems will eliminate the need for the post office. The home system module, a combination computer center, entertainment center, and telecommunication center will replace the need for stand-alone devices such as facsimile, telephone, and stereo components. It is my hope that industry executives and managers in areas directly and indirectly effected by the tide of these changes may find these lists helpful in casting visions, strategies, and tactics for their enterprises.

6

REINVENTING
HEALTH CARE

Cure the Cause, Not the Symptom

In recent history no single problem has undergone such intensive scrutiny nor received such generally inadequate proposed remedies as in the field of health care. Radical short-term improvements in the costs of staffing, equipping, and performing health care are feasible. Of greatest short-term importance, many of the problems of high-cost medical care can be alleviated through "reinvention" of hospitals, clinics, and health care supplier factories and distribution systems. As seen in exhibit 6–1, *hospital costs are 40 percent of total expenditures for health care in the United States,* the single greatest expenditure, with salaries and fees for doctors, dentists, and other professionals a distant second at 29 percent. If the high cost of hospital care is the bad news, the good news is that the most important path to reduced cost is clear. The benefits of reinventing the hospital hold the *tangible and realistic* promise of radically reducing costs while dramatically increasing the quality of care provided. For, like many inefficient factories, the modern hospital houses state-of-the-art equipment and supplies but manages them in an environment of anachronistic practices and facilities. The experience of Lee Memorial Hospital in Ft. Myers, Florica, reveals a myriad of typical improvement opportunities. For example it has moved several support functions which are centralized in virtually every other hospital into a small focused hospital-within-a-hospital specializing in treating orthopedic patients. Doing so has enabled the hospital to reduce the full-time support staff by 37 percent. Inordinately large portions of health care and support personnel's working days were previously spent in scheduling patient movements to and from the centralized support departments (X-ray, for example) and actually preparing, moving, and attending them while waiting for service. The focused facility eliminates most of the movement time and simplifies the scheduling of services, enabling the patient to be served as quickly as he is moved from his bed to the service area nearby. Such simplification was instrumental in helping to slash the previous bureaucracy of hardworking nursing directors by 32 percent. Further, wasteful paperwork and travel time required to order and deliver supplies and drugs from the central pharmacy and storage facilities were slashed drastically by moving these items into focused storage in the hospital-in-a-hospital. These short-term improvements are the first and most important subjects of this chapter.

However, it is not logical to perpetuate today's health care delivery systems, which are geared primarily to treating illness and injury without also recognizing and addressing other real problems in the longer term. Some of the most significant reasons that health care is necessary include: (1) unsafe workplaces, streets and highways, vehi-

EXHIBIT 6–1

Health Care Costs (Health Services and Supplies)

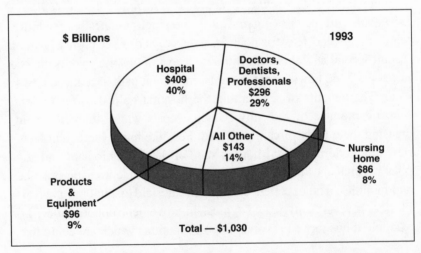

cles, homes, and appliances; (2) self-inflicted poisoning through smoking, drugs, overeating, and lack of exercise; (3) violent crime; and (4) genetic flaws. In the long term, developments in these areas will radically change the world of health care. Businesses providing the products and services in these fields will be some of the most dynamic short-term growth companies. The impact that these future solutions will have on health care are a second subject of this chapter.

In the meantime, however, some basic, elementary solutions to our health problems can be developed through methodical examination of their root causes and by application of *simple* new legislation to provide practical low-cost, permanent resolutions. The chapter concludes with a brief synopsis of the legislative changes that sooner or later will help to transform the industry.

EXECUTIVE CHECKLIST: HEALTH CARE ZINGERS

This executive checklist summarizes some of the tactics, strategies, and visions that every health care enterprise's top management should be contemplating.

SHORT-TERM TACTICS AND STRATEGIES

1. Today's hospitals and medical offices are bastions of inefficiency and poor service. Reengineering hospitals into smaller, more focused hospitals-within-hospitals can yield such radically improved results that every administration should be hard at work making the necessary changes to achieve this end.
2. Low occupancy rates and poor space utilization contribute to outrageous hospital overhead and labor costs. Rearranging hospital layouts, disposing of excess buildings, and constructing new highly compact hospitals can contribute significantly to lowering unnecessary costs.
3. Medical supply manufacturers and pharmaceutical producers are as subject to radical reinvention as any other companies. Such reengineering will contribute monumentally to reducing the production and distribution costs of health care products and equipment.

FUTURE VISIONS

1. Health care, as now practiced, will be revolutionized by the advent

of practical systems for genetic engineering and treatment, as well as fail-safe products and environmental systems that virtually eliminate disease and accidental injury.

2. Major strides in engineering fail-safe solutions to common accident causes will radically reduce injuries in the home, workplace, and in traffic.

3. Effective methods of controlling substance abuse will drastically reduce the wasteful costs of health care devoted to treating addiction and subsequent illnesses.

4. Diagnostic health care analysis and therapy programs can be, and should be, developed through the use of electronic "doctors."

5. Robot surgeons will perform operations using the world's best techniques achieving the highest quality of heath care possible.

Citizens of the twenty-first century will be fantastically more healthy and live much longer. However, in the meantime we can look forward to short-term improvements in the quality and cost of health care due to innovations such as the focused hospital-within-a-hospital, the most important subject of this chapter.

THE FOCUSED HOSPITAL: MODEL OF EFFICIENCY AND QUALITY

Blaming greedy doctors, drug companies, and malpractice insurance for rising health care costs only obscures one of the most important facts—that hospital costs are far and away the single largest health care cost component. The single greatest opportunity for improving the cost effectiveness of health care, modernization of hospital practices and facilities, does not depend primarily on extensive, new legislation or regulation. However, deregulation or regulation *simplification* will help speed the process, as will be seen in a later discussion of hospital aisle design.

My "focused factory" was the genesis of the "focused hospital," from which Lee Memorial Hospital in Ft. Myers, Florida, evolved its pioneering "subhospital." Andersen Consulting's health care specialists, exposed to the principles of the small factory-within-a-factory, were able to leap to the correct conclusion that exactly the same concepts, applied to the hospital, would dramatically lower its costs while improving the quality of health care provided.[1] In Lee Memorial's pilot hospital-in-a-hospital, orthopedic health care was reorganized by moving admittance, X-ray, supplies, laboratory, and pharmacy services from distant, centralized locations into the new module. Thus, the wasteful cost and delay of scheduling these services and traveling back and forth was eliminated. More importantly, the new entrepreneurial closeness of the compact hospital-in-a-hospital enabled health care suppliers, doctors, nurses, and technicians to provide higher-quality, more personalized services.

For example, one of the most exasperating hospital stay experiences is the typical delay between pressing the nurse call button (usually because of a need which to the patient seems calamitous) and the arrival of a nurse prepared to alleviate the distress. Modern technology which links the call button to the nurse via radio wave is only a partial answer. Lee Memorial's hospital-in-a-hospital goes a mile farther, by locating the nurse closer to patients and slashing the nurse's workload by eliminating absurd activities such as charting every observation even when those such as temperature are within a range deemed to be normal. As a result of these and other changes, the quality of health care provided by the pilot hospital-within-a-hospital improved by 62 percent, according to patient surveys conducted before and after the changes.

SPACE UTILIZATION: KEY TO CONTROLLING CAPITAL AND LABOR COSTS

Traditionally managed hospitals are models of inefficiency, with widespread opportunities for radical cost and service improvements. Few hospitals control wasteful expenditures on buildings and equipment although extremely low occupancy rates are the rule rather than the exception. Eli Ginzberg, writing about the failed Clinton health care proposal, pointed out that "this lack of attention to the future of the nation's hospitals whose current occupancy rates are, on the average, just above 60 percent suggests that the government does not con-

---

1. See appendix 2 for reference to more detail about factories-within-factories.

EXHIBIT 6–2

External Aisles

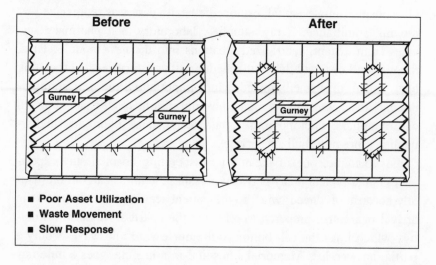

- Before
- After
- Gurney
- Gurney
- Gurney

- **Poor Asset Utilization**
- **Waste Movement**
- **Slow Response**

template any direct interference in their operations."[2] These low occupancy rates contribute mightily to the size of hospital bills, because the 40 percent of fixed overhead costs associated with the unused facilities must be absorbed by the patients using 60 percent. Ironically, the drive by government and insurance companies to hustle patients out of the hospital as quickly as possible has indeed reduced the average hospital stay, but it has failed to reduce the daily cost—in fact it has contributed to a cost increase spiral! However, low occupancy is not the only huge waste of valuable hospital space. Hospital aisles are broad avenues, the width of which is usually dictated by state and federal regulations concerned with providing space enough for two gurneys to pass in opposite directions while still accommodating two patients walking in opposite directions pulling their intravenous trees and bottles with them. Little thought, if any, has been given to the percentage of overhead and maintenance costs stemming from the overly wide aisles that in fact are occupied less than one percent of the time. The "before" side of exhibit 6–2 depicts the typical wide-aisle hospi-

2. Eli Ginzberg with Miriam Ostow, *The Road to Reform: The Future of Health Care in America* (New York: Free Press, 1994), p. 192.

tal design in which the aisle width is often the same dimension as the room size. Disadvantages of this type of design include the wasteful investment in the portion of the building occupied by aisles, the unnecessarily long distances traveled by health care and service personnel who move back and forth in the aisles, and the time it takes nurses, aides, and orderlies to respond to patient calls. The point is that, in the patient housing areas of the hospital, heavy traffic is *not* often, if ever, really experienced. Wide aisles are mandated throughout the hospital even though the only areas that come close to needing them are the central service areas to which all patients are brought for tests, surgery, and therapy (and those centralized services themselves cause unnecessary complexity and cost).

Simple hospital traffic control features such as one-way traffic patterns and alcoves to allow gurneys and even people to pass in opposite directions are just two of several hospital layout features that can reduce the size of the hospital. Exhibit 6–2's "after" side is a sketch of an improved layout with aisles half the width of those in the old hospital. Gurneys in this hospital can be moved into one of the side aisles in the rare instances where two meet traveling in opposite directions. Note that in this layout health care and service personnel have far shorter average distances to travel to the patient rooms, so the time required to respond to patient calls is shorter. The advantage of reducing the ratio of aisles to patient rooms is not limited to lowering investment (overhead) cost. It also eliminates the nonproductive labor cost that excessively long aisles engender. Anyone who has spent time in the hospital has seen armies of doctors, nurses, and technicians scurrying back and forth. Every minute spent walking is a minute of wasted time that could better be devoted to providing improved care. Unfortunately, at this moment the government bureaucracy refuses to accredit any hospital designed in violation of its liberal aisle standards—a serious barrier which heath care organizations must work to remove.

Waste space, excessive travel, and poor patient service caused by larger-than-necessary aisles is not limited to the hospital's formal corridors. Unnecessarily large *informal* aisles are often found within patient rooms, as illustrated on exhibit 6–3. The "before" side shows a long aisle leading past the room's private bath and its closet, that re-

EXHIBIT 6–3
Internal Aisles

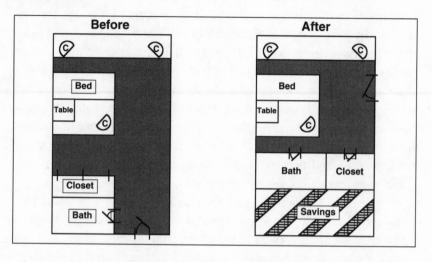

sults in considerable wasted space between the closet and the patient's bedside table and visitor chair. These nonproductive areas are eliminated on the "after" side of the exhibit, thanks to the new external aisle system which has the entry door opposite the patient's bed.

ILL HEALTH AND INJURY: THE REAL CULPRITS

The root causes of high heath care costs are *not* primarily doctors, drug companies, hospitals, insurance companies, or government. Health care costs are generated by genetic factors, abuse of our bodies, disease, and injury. The technical skills exist with which to virtually eradicate injury in its most prevalent environments: the home, the workplace (especially factories and warehouses), and in transportation. This should be exactly the same type of injury eradication engineering as that used for factory processes designed to produce fail-safe quality.[3] Clear evidence proves the effectiveness of safety engineering. The largest companies in the United States, with resources to devote to safety engineering and with the Occupational

---

3. See appendix 2 for reference to more about fail-safe process design.

EXHIBIT 6–4
Accidental Deaths

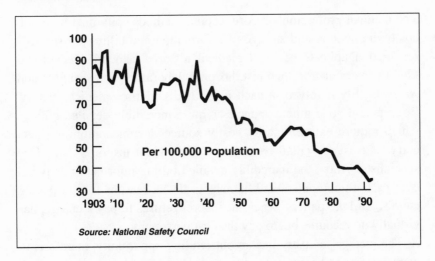

Source: National Safety Council

Safety and Health Administration policing them, have reduced their accidental death rate per thousand employees to one-fifth of a percent of the rate at the smallest companies.[4] Exhibit 6–4 shows that the nation as a whole has made dramatic progress in reducing the incidence of accidental death in the twentieth century. Industry and government cooperation on engineering fail-safe injury environments will eventually permanently eliminate most of the costs of trauma treatment.

People knowingly and unwittingly cause their bodies harm. They put all types of substances into and on their bodies that are the real root causes of poor health. Sweets, tobacco smoke, alcohol, meat, salt, mind-altering drugs, direct sunlight, and saturated fats are a few of the poisons that are killing us. Man is not a natural carnivore, but a plant eater. My own bout with cancer gave me an incentive to learn more about the proven beneficial effects of a high-fiber fruit and vegetable diet as preventative medicine. And though exercise *in moderation* is well known to be extremely beneficial in lowering health care problems, vast numbers of people live lives free of even minimal exercise.

---

4. Barbara Marsh, "Chance of Getting Hurt Is Generally Far Higher at Smaller Companies," *Wall Street Journal,* February 3, 1994.

HEALTH CARE SUPERHIGHWAYS: ROADS TO BETTER, LOWER-COST SERVICE

The medical profession's recordkeeping methods epitomize wasteful, costly duplication and storage of information and billing for services rendered. Duplicate personal medical histories abound, created and filed by every doctor, therapist, hospital, laboratory, and scanning and X-ray facility involved in each individual's lifetime medical history. Insurers and government agencies require incredibly detailed billings which require extraordinarily costly source documentation and data entry, and usually entail reentry by the recipient insurer's data entry specialists. Worst, the incredibly detailed billing information is pored over by both computers and humans to detect reasons for not paying claims. And the patient, when the insurer refuses to pay a charge, has virtually no recourse but to pay the cost personally.

The medical industry has an outstanding opportunity, therefore, to begin to reduce health care costs and deliver better services through modern information streets and superhighways. And work *is* underway. For example, the Illinois State Medical Society, in partnership with the Metropolitan Chicago Healthcare Council, have taken steps to initiate the development of the country's "largest and most comprehensive community health information network." This system will "link hospitals, physicians, insurers, employers, laboratories, pharmacies and other parties for the rapid exchange of clinical and payment information."[5] Systems such as these will be the early predecessors of the ideal community computer utility of the twenty-first century.

The individual data base (exhibit 5–9 in chapter 5), contains three summary-level segments related to health care (among other uses): the individual's medical records, family links (which provide access to the family's medical history), and insurance information. Exhibit 6–5 is an expansion of the individual data base medical segment into its most important components. Some of the subsegments of the medical data segment are described here.

History. A chronological history, in reverse date sequence, will highlight ill-health and injury episodes most likely to lead to

---

future complications. For example, childhood rheumatic fever often leads to heart disease in later years. Symptoms will be entered, by voice, by both patient and doctor. Test results will be fed directly from testing equipment computers into the patients' data bases and simultaneously reported, verbally and in display form, to the various medical specialists involved. *The test results will also be reported immediately to the patient, in plain English!* And physicians, therapists, and other health care providers will also be able verbally to input treatment rendered and prescribed, eliminating the need for transcription of recorded comments. In fact, using portable communication devices, their comments can be transmitted to the community computer utility as they perform examinations and medical and test procedures, thus reducing the risk of forgetting vital details between the performance of an action and reporting it.

Vital Signs. Current and recent blood pressure, pulse, heart rate, and other vital signs, in reverse chronological sequence, can be used by medical diagnostic processors, in combination with family and individual medical history, test and scanning results, and current and past symptoms, to produce computer diagnostics and suggest additional tests and examinations or medical treatment.

EXHIBIT 6–5

Medical Data Segment

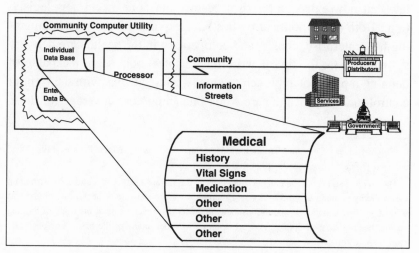

Medication. The medication subsegment will consist of an up-to-date record of medications in use. The computer utility will remind the individual, by voice message, when to discontinue a drug and to discard any remainder to prevent children and others from inadvertently taking a drug or using one whose shelf life has been exceeded. When the leftover drug has been discarded, the individual can tell the home system module, verbally, to update the system file. The system will be able to cross-check *all* medication prescribed, catching any possible dangerous interaction of drug combinations. Medications that have been tried and proven ineffective and those that have caused adverse reactions will be identified.

Physicians may be outraged at the suggestion that computers will diagnose and recommend testing and treatment, believing there to be no substitute for their skills. However, as medical programs such as APACHE are proving, the computer's vast and infallible memory often makes it "better than Dr. Welby" at doing just that.[6]

HEALTH CARE SOLUTIONS: THE LEGISLATIVE APPROACH

The root causes behind rising health care costs and lack of availability to all citizens lie not primarily with greedy doctors, lawyers, and drug and insurance companies but, in large part, with both the poor body of law that now exists and with necessary but nonexistent new legislation.[7] Both major political parties have espoused interest in maintaining free enterprise, choice, and competition in the health care delivery system, but (at the time I write this chapter) both seem incapable of defining a practical approach to empowering citizens with the right to control their own health care while financing *basic* coverage for those

6. Knight-Ridder, "Computer Technology May Someday Predict Which Patients Live, Die," *Chicago Tribune,* November 25, 1994.

7. The political strategy of hatemongering vis-à-vis the various health care entities has stirred up the public by pointing to "unconscionable" earnings and and denying of health care on the part of doctors, drug companies, and the insurance industry. However, some of the irony of bashing doctors has not escaped notice. Lawyers, a group to which many of the bashers belong, earn more than doctors, on average.

unable to afford it. Radical socialization is *not* required to achieve these goals, especially if reduction of costs makes it possible to extend the *same* health care access to all citizens.

Sweeping changes of the health care delivery system are stymied due to the citizenry's logical perception that it is not possible to get something for nothing. Misguided (and dishonest) proposals to have "business" pay the costs of health care for low-income and welfare people are transparent to the public. When business costs increase, prices for goods and services rise proportionately; thus the poorest in society, who spend the highest percentage of their disposable income on necessities, pay the cruelest tax of all. If the will of the people is to agree that the poorest in society are automatically entitled to free or lower-cost health care, the honest, most efficient way to account for the costs is to fund the subsidization through taxation.

Putting government between health care recipients and providers is commonly recognized to be an approach that leads to increased costs and poorer-quality health care. Nevertheless, present systems are not getting the job done, and it appears that legislative action, not interjecting government, is the only way to solve the several dilemmas.

Since many of the present problems with private health care stem from practices common to insurers, legislation designed to give the insurers the incentive and the necessity to solve these problems must be a primary goal. Several types of legislation should be involved in the ideal system. First, since private insurers at present are the best administrators of funds disbursement, insurance legislation requiring and enabling them to do so should be the cornerstone of the new system, and should simplify rather than complicate their operations. Second, entitlement legislation will be required to establish a body of law for better subsidizing health care for low-income families and welfare recipients. However, the system cannot be effective if universal health care is the goal but individuals are able to slip through cracks in the system and thus be uninsured. In recent years more and more employers have begun to offer multiple choices of insurance coverage to their co-insured employees. Simple choices, such as the amount of deductible (how much of her medical bills the employee herself pays) and the types of coverage (dental and optical coverage, for example) can reduce the cost of coverage. Thus, although *every* individual should be required to have at least the same minimum coverage, each individual with adequate income should be permitted to self-insure a portion of the coverage by putting money in a medical savings account. Doing so would be useful to young, healthy people, less advantageous to elderly persons more likely to have large medical bills. Requiring *everyone* to have insurance would be vital to avoiding the dilemma caused when insurance rates for everyone are equalized. The dilemma, experienced by New York insurers, is that equalized rates drive the costs to the young to very high levels (an immediate 140 percent increase, in New York) while lowering the cost to senior citizens.[8]

Third, the tax law requires substantial revision, given that the highest-paid employees are not taxed on their insurance benefits whereas the self-employed and those not covered by their employers are, since they are not fully deductible. Further, entitlement in the form of government subsidized payment of some individuals' insurance coverage provides no personal incentive to use health care judiciously as one does when personally responsible for payment. (Those covered by health insurance may go for treatment of every minor illness or injury, since it is free, whereas others—like me avail themselves of health care only when an actual problem is clearly too severe to expect the body to heal itself not only because the annual deductible is so high, but because of a long history of minor illnesses that go away by themselves. Finally, drug companies achieve profits higher than those of other enterprises, presumably to compensate them for the costs and risks of developing new drugs. However, in the long run, drug prices should be set at levels adequate to recoup their costs and provide profits consistent with average returns on investment no greater than all industries in general.

Following is a recap of some of the legislation features that I believe would address the needs of improved, universal coverage.

INSURANCE LAW

- Insurance companies should be required to provide the same coverage (multiple plans) to everyone, at the same price, regardless of age, sex, or prior medical history. A universal rate would greatly simplify the administration of health care pricing, and help to lower

---

8. Leslie Scism, "New York Finds Fewer People Have Health Insurance a Year After Reform," *Wall Street Journal,* May 27, 1994.

some insurer costs while spreading premiums equally over every individual's lifetime.

- Insurance companies should be required to make it easy for private individuals to obtain price and coverage information for their plans and to simplify enrollment.
- If an insured individual were to receive social support such as welfare, the premiums should be "deducted" from the social benefit payment and paid directly to the insurer in exactly the same manner that workers' premiums are deducted from their pay.
- Insurance should be universally required of individuals. Every employed individual should have a mandatory health care premium payroll deduction and the deduction should be taxable as earned income.
- Every individual, whether employed or not, should have the right to choose from *all* insurers operating in the region, and should have the right to switch from one insurer or plan whenever his insurance company fails to provide fast, courteous, high-quality service.
- The government should cease trying to operate as a health insurance company for various entitlement recipients. Instead, private insurance premiums should be deducted from the recipient's "paycheck" (i.e., the welfare recipient's medical allowance) and paid to the insurance company elected by the recipient. Thus, since every individual will be insured by private companies, all will have access to equal treatment.
- Insurance companies, *not government,* should be required to develop standard plans, used by all. Individuals shopping for insurance would then find it easy to compare prices for identical coverage. This will force the insurance companies to control their costs in order to be competitive.

ENTITLEMENT LAW

- People entitled to social benefits (unemployment, medicaid, and medicare, for example) should be "paid" for the cost of insurance coverage, but the premium payments should be treated as "payroll deductions" and treated as taxable income.
- Recipients of entitlement programs should be subject to the same insurance deductibles and co-payments as all other individuals, and each should "pay" for these costs from an entitlement account maintained for the individual.

TAX LAW

- Employer-provided health insurance should be treated by the employer and by the self-employed as taxable compensation.
- The intent of taxing employer-provided health care costs should not be to increase an employee's taxes but rather to provide a fair system for both employed and unemployed people. Therefore, tax rates initially should be dropped in an amount roughly equal to the increase in taxes due to making employer benefits taxable.
- The cost of government-provided health care such as medicare, medicaid, veterans hospitals, and welfare programs should also be treated as taxable income, although the recipient might still need pay no taxes, based on having low income or none at all.
- Henceforth, increased costs of health care insurance would be "paid" by the individual insured, not by the employer (albeit automatically deducted from the individual's pay).

FUTURE HOSPITAL: WHERE ARE THE PATIENTS?

Genetic engineering holds the promise of virtual eradication of most of the diseases (physical and mental) afflicting mankind today. Medical advances have the potential for radically slowing the aging process. For example, Dr. Steven Norvil, a member of the American Academy of Anti-Aging Medicine, has said "I've always believed, based on a lot of research I've read, that the body and its parts can live from 150 to 250 years in good health. And the exciting thing is that research is proving that."[9] Further, future engineering improvements to improve the safety of the home, transportation, and the workplace can be expected to reduce accidental injury to a small fraction of today's incidence. Wounds caused by criminals and family abuse will also decline sharply as an additional benefit of genetic engineering which is expected to eliminate genetic disposition to violence and criminality. Thus, sometime within the next century, the health care "crisis" will be reduced from a mountain to a molehill.

In the meantime, mounting health care costs are bound to cause a major shift in health care roles. Costs of nonintrusive tests and scans

---

9. Greg Beaubien, "Why Get Old," *Chicago Tribune,* October 20, 1994.

can be expected to drop, as a result of continuing technologic improvements, especially in the computer hardware and software fields. Further cost reductions will come from economies of scale, as higher volumes of medical equipment are mass-produced to meet the needs of convenient local access to test and examination equipment. For example, manufacturers of magnetic resonance imaging (MRI) equipment, which currently produces the best nonintrusive internal body images but requires a capital expenditure of over a million dollars, would be well advised to design the equipment for mass production, thus lowering the cost by as much as 80 percent. To not do so will continue to divert sales to much lower-cost ultrasound equipment which requires different (but lower-cost) machines for different body parts.[10] The ridiculous reliance on high-cost medical technicians and doctors to read and translate the results can be slashed by improved computer programs designed to tell the patient or his care provider specifically what has been found, and prescribe the necessary course of medical action, should further tests or treatment be required.

Surgical procedures, some time within the next century, will be performed by surgical robots, with uniformly high-quality results. No longer will the selection of a surgeon be a potentially fatal game of chance, should the individual selected possess inferior skills. The surgical robot can use the best-known operating procedure and work twenty-four hours a day, seven days a week, without suffering fatigue and the potential for mishap that occurs when human doctors work long hours in surgery.

Each individual's data base, within the next decade or two, will contain an in-depth family medical history. Interactive voice-computer systems will feature electronic "doctors" who will consult with individuals experiencing health problems and—using a description of the symptoms, the patient's medical history, and recent tests and scans—diagnose the most probable cause and order further tests or scans or treatment plans. The treatment plan, in many cases, will be executed in the individual's own home, perhaps by the family medical aid robot, perhaps by a local home-visit robot if complex procedures such as dialysis are involved. The medical computer system will

---

10. Amal Kumar Naj, "Big Medical-Equipment Makers Try Ultrasound Market," *Wall Street Journal,* November 30, 1993.

transmit medication orders to the pharmaceutical supplier for instant delivery via vastly improved home delivery service.

Prior to this medical vision coming to fruition, interim steps will be necessary. In part, this will mean systematic decoding of the unnecessary mystification of medicine. (I interviewed one surgeon in Germany who violently refuted the possibility that doctors would accept a standard operating method. This doctor believed that each individual would *always* use his own unique procedure. I was too polite to point out that this has always been the position taken by every skilled tradesman. In reality, however, this viewpoint has always been proven to be nonsense.) And leading-edge, computer-wise medical practitioners who develop the software and business structure to effect this transfer of simplified knowledge to nonphysician and nonsurgeon medical assistants will be founding the health care business of the future. As more and more knowledge is accessible, and as hardware and software are perfected, more medical diagnosis, testing, scanning, and treatment will be automated, and the cost thereof lowered.

Leading-edge developers should soon be bringing interactive self-diagnosis software to the market. Where symptoms indicate, with little doubt, that nonprescription palliatives would provide relief, a costly and time-wasting trip to the doctor's office could be avoided. And when symptoms alone would not be enough to diagnose problems adequately, new, improved, and readily available self-test kits would add depth to the diagnosis process, while neighborhood automated computer- and robotic-operated facilities for scanning, X-ray, and other tests could also be "ordered and authorized" by the diagnostic computer software. The results, automatically entered in the individual's medical records, might then be adequate to enable the electronic "doctor" to prescribe medicine. Computer-generated prescription will probably be far superior to that performed by today's doctors, since the individual's up-to-date medical history and record of current medications would be used to avoid prescribing drugs to which the individual has had adverse past reactions. The computer diagnostic program could also protect against new adverse reactions based on using drugs which, in combination with others, could have detrimental or even life-threatening results. Finally, when a diagnosis indicates the need for a doctor's involvement (surgery, for example), or when no diagnosis can be made, the computer could make the patient's entire record available to an appropriate specialist.

SUMMARY

The health care industry has unprecedented short-term opportunities for improving its costs and services. Reengineering projects, especially those based on organizing hospitals-within-the-hospital, are proving the quantum gains available in improved staff utilization. Medical record keeping has evolved into the recording and storing of huge volumes of vital signs and other medical data—whether significant or not—and recording it with little use of modern technology. Insurance companies and health maintenance organizations place additional layers of bureaucracy between patients and heath care delivery. Thus, health care managements' first priority must be to accelerate the pace of reengineering.

However, in the long term, permanent solutions to medical problems will transform the industry. In the field of medicine, continuing developments in genetic research will make those specialists and producers of genetic equipment some of the hottest occupations and industries in the twenty-first century. Other medical hot products, as seen on exhibit 6–6, include software for maintaining each individual's medical history, analyzing test and imaging results, and diagnosing medical problems. And producers of medical imaging, nonintrusive testing, and home test kits will benefit from explosive demand growth in response to radically lower prices—made possible by designing the products and production facilities for mass production. Robot surgeons, assisted by robot nurses and controlled by advanced surgical computer programs, will perform error-free operations, using techniques developed by the world's most outstanding surgery specialists, and enhanced daily as improved techniques emerge.

However, as those industries and occupations flourish, others (see exhibit 6–7), will wane and some will die during the next century. For those inclined to feel anxious or offended by the definition of some industries and occupations as waning or dying, there are several important points to keep in mind. These following points are repeated briefly in every chapter, because many readers are expected to read

EXHIBIT 6–6
Growth Industries and Occupations

Genetic Medicine

Genetic Test Equipment

Home Medical Tests

**Medical Diagnostic
Software**

**Non-intrusive Medical
Test Equipment**

**Do-it-yourself Test &
Imaging Centers**

**Surgical Robots
& Software**

**Medical Test & Imaging
Analysis Software**

**Medical Imaging
Equipment**

---

only one or more selected chapters. First, the change may not occur in the foreseeable future. Second, the future continuous reduction of work will be universal. As a result, society must and will reduce average workweek hours in order to maintain full employment. Third, the era of reduced work and increased leisure time will be one of un-

EXHIBIT 6–7
Waning Industries and Occupations

Hospital Construction

Doctors

Surgeons

Nurses

---

precedented quality of life and affluence. The vastly improved, universal good health and new do-it-yourself diagnosis will eventually eliminate most of the need for hospitals. And, when there are fewer hospitals, the need for janitors and maintenance specialists will also decline. With the automation of medicine, the need for all but a handful of the world's best medical, surgical, and nursing specialists will also decline markedly.

To achieve the goals of radical improvement, health care change agents must be capable of bringing fresh imagination, creativity, and substance to specific reengineering projects. Change managers and designers must be expert in every aspect of success—in today's age this means process (operations), people, and information systems—all working towards the enterprise's substantive visions and strategies. The enterprise should demand that every person contribute to a change process that will stretch them to meet its new, remarkably high but attainable goals.

7

REINVENTING
FINANCIAL SERVICES

Bankerless Banking

The financial services industry, perhaps better than any other, exemplifies the importance of information capture, processing, and retrieval to the achievement of profitable business operations. Banking, insurance, and financial investment companies reap giant rewards when their costs of information management are lowered by systematic application of the latest computer and telecommunication technology to constantly improved products, services, and rapid response to customers' inquiries and requests. An ideal goal, which is frequently being achieved by industry leaders, is a reduction of more than 99 percent (from days to hours) of the time required to process a request or inquiry.

Financial service organizations have traditionally employed armies of "back room" personnel manning telephones and processing transactions. Modern technology, applied to reengineered "back room" processes can easily improve productivity by 40 percent and more. Banc One Mortgage Corporation of Indianapolis, for example, recently completed a reengineering project that resulted in a 40 percent productivity improvement. And in the newly democratized nations, faced with moving from technologically primitive businesses to state-of-the-art processes, the productivity gains can be tremendous! For,

185

example, the Komercni Banka of Prague increased the number of various types of high-volume transactions processed per person by over 250 percent. In other industrialized European countries and enterprises the stakes are also high. For, example, a reengineering project for the Societé de Bourse (Paris Stock Exchange) produced significant stock broker "back office" gains and increased the exchange's own "back room" productivity in the range of 40 to 95 percent. Further, the number of unsolved trade transaction ("fails") corrections were cut by more than 99 percent.[1] Improvements of this magnitude are not the limit of opportunity. Because technology is evolving with breathtaking speed, every new reengineering phase should target another incremental productivity gain in the 50 percent range. In banking alone, over 40 percent of teller jobs have been replaced by automated teller machines, and projections of further reductions by the year 2000 are in the 90 percent range.[2] The First National Bank of Chicago has taken a drastic step to increase the number of customers processing their transactions at automated teller machines from the present 70 percent. It is charging three dollars for each teller transaction.[3]

Financial institutions' balance sheets typically include high-value buildings, furnishings, and equipment. As institutions continue to reduce the number of their employees through efficiencies gained by reengineering and as more employees work in offices in their homes (see chapter 3), they will benefit from savings due to reductions in the amount of space and equipment they will need. For example, a United Services Automobile Association (USAA) insurance company image-processing project improved the time required to respond to customer requests by converting from filed paper documents to electronic images. In the process, one tangible savings was that of over $7 million in floor space cost reduction.[4]

---

1. For more about the Banc One Mortgage Corporation, the Komercni Banka, and the Societé de Bourse successes, see the achievers list, Appendix 1.

2. Jeremy Rifkin, *The End of Work: The Decline of the Global Work Force and the Dawn of the Post-Market Era* (New York: Putnam, 1995), p. 144.

3. John Schmeltzer, "Tack On $3 for That Trip to the Bank," *Chicago Tribune,* April 26, 1995.

4. Nancy Baumgarten, "Insuring Victory: USAA Uses Technology to Improve Customer Service," *Outlook* (Chicago: Andersen Consulting, 1993), pp. 32–33.

One-stop financial services are a powerful business growth driver. Thus, financial service organizations need information systems data bases that contain every customer's account, portfolio, and financial profile to support their strategic plans to broaden their financial services. Creative and imaginative financial institutions are constantly inventing new products and customer acquisition promotions that require their people and systems to be speedy and flexible in adding the new products to customer portfolios, processing the promotions, and analyzing the results. Successful integration of the people element of new product and promotion operations is one of the highly important factors that delineate industry leaders from the also-rans. New products and promotions require an organization's people to *change* their daily operations to incorporate them. Thus, systematic change management, especially as it relates to training, is a vital necessity. The best of today's information systems integrate the new *processes* and *training*.

The next century's predicted advancements are lessons of importance to today's businesses. For example, any business involving high volumes of telephone contacts of routine (and also custom) content can and should be automated to provide instant customer service at radically lower cost. And though the use of invoices, bills, and checks was already an outmoded practice when I first started to decry it in the early 1980s, they nevertheless are still in use in the majority of private and public enterprises. Leading-edge banks, brokers, and other financial institutions have the wherewithal to begin to convert their operations to bankless, moneyless electronic services provided at minimal cost. Those that first do so will have unlocked the way to huge increases in market share and probable dominance of their industries in the next century.

As in every industry, many financial service companies' visions and strategies are remarkably devoid of the elements of longer-range imagination, creativity, substance, and goals that stretch the abilities of their entire organizations to the limit. The intense importance of information and technology in this industry will continue to drive it to operate close to the leading edge of technology and will continue to transform its products and business processes at an ever-increasing pace. Financial services organizations, collectively, have one of the largest and most comprehensive individual and business data bases. By pooling this critical resource, the industry is likely to be a pioneer of the first commercially developed computer utilities and information superhighways which represent a cornerstone of my vision of the twenty-first century. Preparation for this age requires financial services companies to begin to link their heretofore short-term strategies to longer-range visions.

Certain fundamental changes will impact the new way in which businesses will operate in coming decades. All enterprise and individual financial activity of the twenty-first century will take place in a cashless society in which community, national, and international computer utilities will transfer funds between accounts with breathtaking speeds. Enterprises that find the best ways to carve their operations into smaller, customer-oriented businesses-within-a-business will be those best equipped to meet customers' needs for high value and rapid, friendly service. Customer service must be the driver of all future operations. Accordingly, enterprises will need to respond instantly to customers' needs and deliver services within hours, even minutes. And the exchange of funds between customers and sellers will be unalterably changed in the dawning of the age of a universally wealthy populace and computer utilities that will replace banks as we know them today. This wealthy populace will increasingly become securities traders, and their avocation will be supported by low-cost, virtually brokerless trading. This chapter will lay the groundwork for understanding these critical, fundamental elements of the next century's business environment.

Not all visions are earthshaking revolutions. Many tiny steps into the future are, and should be, practical and simple improvements. One example will free hundreds of thousands of people from a common, onerous task. Time-consuming, complex reporting of business expenses by enterprise employees is now being improved by credit card companies, but is still far less than ideal. Improved systems, so far, do not completely free the person incurring expenses from the drudgery of writing explanatory information and still require enterprise input processors to key-enter the data into computer systems. Mundane advances like improved expense reporting, also a subject of this chapter, are today's forerunners of vastly improved future financial services.

EXECUTIVE CHECKLIST: SELECTED FINANCIAL SERVICES ZINGERS

Executives may find it useful to use the following "zinger" list to validate their enterprises' tactics, strategies, and visions. The two checklists are intended for two levels of management attention. The first summarizes the points of interest of the hard-nosed business realist, interested in improving business results in the immediate future. The second summarizes the main future-world topics of this chapter for the farsighted visionary.

SHORT-TERM TACTICS AND STRATEGIES

1. Electronic "money" is already starting to replace its coin and paper counterparts. Any business now paying and receiving payment by check and cash should begin to expand electronic receivables and payables systems and integrate them with automatic funds transfer systems, through their banks.
2. A hand-held, electronic check register will put electronic funds transfer into the hands of the masses, an important early step towards the elimination of paper-money transactions.
3. The costs of check and credit card fraud are staggering. Financial institutions' systems for detecting and controlling such fraud are woefully inadequate, thus those that reengineer their systems can expect to add very significantly to profitability by targeting a 50 percent or more reduction of loss.
4. Enterprises will soon be able to market and trade their stocks and bonds directly to investors, eliminating brokerage and securities firm charges. Trades will be processed in real time, eliminating some of the costs, time, and problems of settlement and payment.
5. The loathsome chore of bill paying will be eased or even eliminated by the universal adoption of automatic funds transfer systems. Bills will either be paid electronically upon receipt or automatically paid by transfer from the customers' asset or credit accounts to the account of the supplier. In the near term, every business can profit by reducing the costs of billing and collections by inaugurating funds transfer systems for their customers' increased convenience.
6. Various forms of automation such as automated teller machines and

artificially intelligent computer systems will continue to reduce the number of employees required by financial service enterprises. Every company needs a strategic plan for reducing staff, through automation, by at least 90 percent, over the next decade or two.

FUTURE VISIONS

1. Community computer utilities (owned by financial institutions in the foreseeable future), with comprehensive data bases for both individuals and enterprises, will operate systems handling every financial transaction, and do so much faster and at lower cost than present institutions.
2. National and international networks of community computer utilities will validate and process intranational and international financial transactions in real time.
3. New systems management firms will periodically bid to operate each community's computer utility financial systems for a stated term. Thus, these utilities, perhaps owned by local governments, will be operated by competitive, productive private enterprises.
4. Mutual fund managers will become financial investment computer utility system operators and financial investment analysis software purveyors.
5. Businesses and individuals will be able to process, almost instantaneously, loan and credit applications. Their complete, up-to-date financial information, available on the financial services system data base, can be computer-analyzed using artificial intelligence thus virtually eliminating the incidence of bad debt.

PAPERLESS BUSINESS PAYMENT: ELECTRONIC FUNDS TRANSFER

Major Japanese producers, decades ago, eliminated the flow of paperwork and support data for paying for goods they received. They adopted automatic funds processing to move funds automatically from their accounts to those of their suppliers based on their receipt of goods. And although computer links between suppliers and customers started to proliferate three decades ago in the West, electronic payment has lagged far behind. One reason is that western producers and customers have not learned how to eliminate complicating conditions

or how to keep them from interfering with extremely simple processing. For example, Christopher L. Wagner of the First National Bank
of Chicago explains that there are "hundreds of different items which
must be accounted and paid for. Adjustments for late delivery, dam-
aged goods and discounts for volume purchases are some of the complications of business bill-paying. Currently, a check from one big
company to another often is literally accompanied by boxes of computer printouts of remittance information."[5] The first major just-in-
time payment system in the United States, planned by the Chicago
Clearing House Association, will rapidly transact payments, but will
be expensive and unnecessarily complex, because it will recognize
that its clients will still be mired in the traditions where complicating
factors are accepted as necessary evils. By contrast, the major Japanese companies went to work long ago on permanent solutions to eliminate all but the rarest exceptions to detail-free funds transfer.[6]

Large companies in the United States have belatedly, but in
earnest, begun to work on their electronic funds transfer systems. In
1993, for example, more than 35 million invoices were paid electronically, an increase of 59 percent from the previous year. Dupont,
Chevron, Mobil, RJR Nabisco, Burlington Northern Railroad, and
General Electric are among the leading-edge companies making
and/or encouraging suppliers to make electronic payment. Converting
customers and suppliers to electronic payment cannot be done
overnight. However, the pace can be much faster than many would
suspect. Chevron, for example, converted 14 percent of its payments
in just the first nine months of its initiative.[7]

BILL-LESS BILLING: AUTOMATIC FUNDS
TRANSFER-PLUS

Every month, approximately one-half billion utility bills are com-
puter-prepared and mailed to residential and business addresses in the

---

5. Sharon Stangenes, "Banks Plan Computer Payment System for Business Clients," *Chicago Tribune,* March 14, 1994.

6. See appendix 2 for more about paperless supplier communications.

7. The substance of this entire paragraph is excerpted from Fred R. Bleakley, "Fast Money: Electronic Payments Now Supplant Checks at More Large Firms," *Wall Street Journal,* April 13, 1994.

United States alone. Americans receive and pay 104 *trillion* bills per year. Until now they have had few practical alternatives to receiving traditional bills. Upon receipt of these bills, most consumers and businesses prepare and mail checks to the creditors, who in turn process these pieces of paper through their accounts payable systems and forward them into the banking system for several stages of processing. A conservative, estimated annual cost of these mailings to the consumer is $20 *billion!* Within the next decade or two, it seems inevitable that automatic funds transferring systems will almost entirely replace this centuries-old method of payment, and consumers will gain billions in cost reductions.

In fact, automatic funds transfer systems are already in widespread use for a very small percentage of billing and payment transactions. For example, most banks and savings and loans have automatic funds transfer systems for mortgage payments. It is easy to do so, because mortgage payments are usually the same for a six- or twelve-month period. Thus, the mortgagee is able to plan to have funds in his account to cover the payment and can instruct his bank to post his account record with the payment on or in advance of the actual due date.

Electronic banking, fast gaining momentum in large American banks, including Bank of America, Citibank, Chase Manhattan, and Chemical Bank, is starting to blaze the trail for speeding automated funds transfer through the financial information superhighway of the twenty-first century. However, the already wide variety of software (Microsoft's Money, H&R Block's Managing Your Money, and CheckFree Corporation's system, for example) and communications alternatives will not serve to support the ultimate national and international common financial network.[8] Unfortunately, most of these systems still require the payee's bank to mail a notice of the transaction. Therefore, the bank's customers still pay some avoidable cost of the process.

The bill-less system of one or two decades hence will take some time for people to comprehend and accept. And there are practical roadblocks. For example, bill-less, automatic funds transferring requires that each customer have a "bank" account from which the bills

---

8. Andrew Leckey, "Electronic Banking Hits Home," *Chicago Tribune,* November 3, 1994.

can be paid.[9] In less developed countries and in the poorest segments of wealthy countries such as the United States, large numbers of citizens do not now have bank accounts. Also, although many of us have never bothered to look at the details of our utility bills, others pore over them for possible discrepancies. However, instances of most utilities being found to be in error are so few that it is usually practical to consider errors to be nonexistent.

Soon the use of "bank" accounts for automatic deposit of payroll and other income transactions will be universal. In the short term, it will be advantageous for poor people in the inner cities to receive welfare, unemployment, retirement, and any other income by direct deposit to their accounts. To do so will eliminate the possibility of checks being stolen from mail boxes or recipients being mugged for their checks or proceeds. Spending cards (debit cards, for example) for disadvantaged people will also provide a safer way to shop. (Spending cards may be a short-term need until the low-cost electronic check register—discussed later in this chapter—can be provided to even the poorest people). The disadvantaged often pay a penalty for not having bank accounts. "Currency exchanges" cash their checks and provide other financial services, but charge substantial fees. Limited, safe withdrawals of small amounts of cash could be disbursed from highly secure, armored automated teller machines in every neighborhood, making it less of a problem if there were no bank nearby.

Nor will it be logical, in the long term, to continue to make payment by check versus transferring funds electronically. The costs of bad checks to banks, goods and service providers, and individuals in the United States is well over $6 billion per year.[10] Almost every bank has a tremendous opportunity to reduce losses by reengineering check acceptance and clearance processes. Wells Fargo's recent check loss prevention system, for example, has cut losses by 25 percent. Thus, substantial

---

9. "Bank" is used in quotation marks because I consider the bank, as we now know it, to be unnecessary. The new community personal data base utility, discussed in chapter 5, will serve in place of the conventional bank.

10. Fred R. Bleakley, "How They Bounce! Bad-Check Toll Rises As It Becomes Easier to Pull Off Such Fraud," *Wall Street Journal,* December 2, 1993.

additional improvement could be undertaken, and continuous improvement initiatives should have an even greater improvement target.

Incidentally, some localities (Milwaukee for one) once made payments for welfare families' utilities and rents directly to suppliers and landlords. Modern, misguided thinking caused this practice to be discontinued, on the basis that recipients were degraded and would not learn to be responsible citizens. Now, many recipients play a game of moving when they get too far behind in their rent. Landlords wind up the big losers, abandoning properties right and left. Utilities try to cut off nonpaying customers but are sometimes forced to continue service out of concerns for sanitation. Thus, all conscientious bill-paying consumers are paying for these welfare recipient's utilities twice—once in portion of the welfare check designated for utilities, and again in higher utility prices necessitated by unpaid bills. Meanwhile, the welfare funds intended to pay for basic living expenses may go for drugs, alcohol, and gambling. An electronic check register system would earmark a portion of a welfare recipient's account for rent and utilities. Recipients will be able to pay their own bills but, should they not do so, the funds will be held in the account until properly disbursed. This will preserve the dignity of the recipients and do so in a manner that will require responsibility.

Even the Internal Revenue Service is getting into the act. For the past few years, it has been possible to file tax returns electronically, saving millions in data entry costs. However, electronic filing requires a paid tax preparer with computer and telecommunication skills. Until electronic filing is made user-friendly, its use will be limited to a mere handful of returns, and will continue to cost the taxpayers hundreds of millions for data entry and potentially billions in lost revenue compared to improved systems for enforcing the honesty and completeness of reporting.[11]

Incidentally, James Cortada identifies a leading credit card company as having the most effective billing practice, saying this came to light as a result of pursuing the latest hot fad, benchmarking.[12] As one

11. Marianne Taylor, "IRS Boss Looks to Compute a Higher Collection Rate," *Chicago Tribune,* November 7, 1994.

12. James W. Cortada, *TQM for Sales and Marketing Management* (New York: McGraw-Hill, 1993), p. 221.

recipient of its bills, the author finds this amusing, and the cost of benchmarking to determine this to have been wasteful. The company's practice of sending copies of each credit card transaction with the monthly bill is an anachronism that cries out to be reengineered out of existence. The prestigious company's cardholders are upscale and modern to a far greater degree than those of other card companies. Thus, a higher than average number of its customers probably possess personal computers and are prime candidates for payment by electronic funds transfer. Regardless of having cited this poor example of the classic benchmarking as an argument in favor of the notion of benchmarking, Cortada is one of the few brave souls with enough courage to even suggest that a minimal benchmarking exercise may be sufficient. He writes, "Benchmarking can be as simple as reading an article about a process and comparing it to your own."

THE MONEYLESS SOCIETY

Few citizens of the United States are aware that only a small percentage of the nation's "money" consists of currency and coins. In 1988, for example, about $185 billion in currency was in circulation representing about 25 percent of all Unites States' "money."[13] Technology is now available and should be rapidly put to work to replace paper money and coins. Carl Pascarella, president and chief executive officer of Visa U.S.A., for example, has said that the smart card (with its embedded computer chip) will give "a kind of *coup de grace* for cash" and "five years from now there will be a total relationship through a card."[14] The transition from money to electronic transactions is already well underway and gaining momentum. Credit cards and debit cards (debit cards transfer funds directly from the buyer's bank account to that of the seller, rather than creating debt which the buyer must pay later) are more and more often used in place of money. In the year ending 1989, the populace of the United States used 879 credit cards to purchase $414 billion in goods and services,

---

13. Edmond J. Seifried, *Economics for Bankers, second edition* (Washington, DC: American Bankers Association, 1990), p. 483.

14. Vincent J. Schodolski, "No Cash, Plastic: Soon We'll Ship Out Smart Cards to Upload, Download Money," *Wall Street Journal,* June 19, 1994.

creating an outstanding debt of $180 billion, according to Eric Compton.[15] Even the U.S. Internal Revenue Service has recognized the advantages of payment by credit card, a provision that would permit those short of cash to meet their required payment on time, increasing the timeliness of collections and lowering the cost of collection follow-up. It has, therefore, asked Congress to authorize credit card payment (the House of Representatives passed this legislation in May 1994, the time of this writing). Further, both Visa and MasterCard are working furiously on their smart card systems. These cards, with embedded computer chips, will be far superior to today's magnetic strip cards, in terms of their capacity to store information such as account balances.

Unfortunately, however, the charges per "plastic money" transaction to the consumer and/or seller are higher than necessary. Small wonder that those cards are offered not only by traditional banking institutions and credit card companies but also by every other conceivable enterprise of any size (telephone and automobile manufacturers, for example). Earnings on credit cards are impressive, despite the relatively high instance of uncollectible debt caused by liberal, greedy acceptance of low-to-marginal applicants and by undisciplined card bearers who accumulate massive debts with a fistful of cards from many different institutions.

The recent trend in the United States has been in two directions. The first, establishment of debit cards that transfer money from the owner's account to that of *any* establishment providing goods or services, is much more logical than the second trend—various goods and service providers "selling" stored value cards. The use of one such card, used by the Chicago Transit Authority, is illustrated on exhibit 7–1.[16] In this case, the passenger, as step one, inserts ten dollars in a vending machine, and receives a fare card containing that amount. When he travels, he inserts the card in a processor at the turnstile and the two-dollar fare is deducted. When the passenger makes a transfer later on the same trip, the card processor reads the date and time of

15. Eric N. Compton, *Principles of Banking, fourth edition* (Washington, DC: American Bankers Association, 1991), p.269.

16. Gary Washburn, "CTA Card May Open a New Era: High-tech Fare Method on Way," *Chicago Tribune,* April 6, 1994.

EXHIBIT 7–1

Stored-Value Fare Card

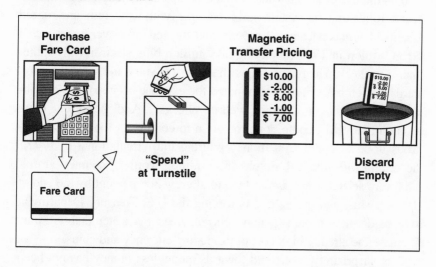

the previous fare charge and determines if the new charge counts as a transfer. If the last charge was recent enough to qualify, the processor charges the lower one-dollar transfer fee. When the entire ten dollars has been "spent," the card is discarded. Obviously, for every business to use its own stored-value card is nonsensical. A universal card would be far preferable, assuming that charges by the stored-value issuer to the selling establishment were suitably nominal.

Financial institutions are also keenly aware of the attractiveness of new plastic alternatives to paper in the forms of money and travelers checks. One such alternative is the First Bank System and Visa International TravelMoney card.[17] The card, which can be used to obtain cash at any of 200,000 automated-teller machines in eighty-three countries, can be purchased for any amount. When the amount has been withdrawn, the card is discarded. It can be used by anyone who knows the card's personal identification number, which is assigned at the time of its purchase. A proliferation of such innovative developments will be interim steps towards the completely electronic money of the future.

---

17. Sharon Stangenes, "Plastic Advances to Compete with Travelers Checks in Test," *Chicago Tribune,* December 13, 1994.

Government, for one, has the potential for massive savings as it adopts the use of stored-value cards (perhaps in conjunction with electronic funds transfer systems), for example, with its welfare and retired clients. Thomas McCarroll reports that the federal government saved $133 million in 1993 by paying 383 million bills electronically rather than by check. He further cites the state of Maryland's use of debit cards, which has virtually eliminated the expense of preparing, distributing, and accounting for its welfare checks.[18] And the age of electronic money will come none too soon to counteract the recent disastrous flood of counterfeit money pouring into circulation. "In 1992," according to Barbara Rudolph, "$30 million worth of counterfeit dollars were seized overseas" and the total grew 300 percent by the end of 1993.[19] This growing deluge is forcing the U.S. Treasury Department to consider new, more expensive currency designs, a step that will only increase the already high cost of producing currency and coins.

Not surprisingly, the trend towards moneyless money has not been limited to the highly industrialized West. Central Europe has been making great strides towards the adoption of "plastic money" even though "planting credit cards in Central Europe requires a cultural revolution."[20] As Brian Coleman reported, between 1991 and 1994, the number of cards in use rose from zero to 300,000 in Hungary alone, proving that the traditional reluctance to use banks, let alone plastic money, can be overcome in societies with deep, ingrained cultural prejudices. And the British, already leading the world in the speed of the decline of currency in circulation, are about to see the launching of a new smart card system that will further accelerate the demise of the pound note. The National Westminster Bank's Mondex system is a smart card that will hold cash and both pay and accept payment, and do so in five currencies.[21]

Once banks are able to receive funds from and disburse funds to

---

18. Thomas McCarroll, "No Checks. No Cash. No Fuss?" *Time,* May 9, 1994.

19. Barbara Rudolph, "Some Like Them Hot: A Global Lust for Dollars and Advanced Imaging Techniques Have Produced a Wave of Counterfeiting," *Time,* November 19, 1994, p. 76.

20. Brian Coleman, "Central Europe Finds Future Is Plastic as Banks Rush to Promote Credit Cards," *The Wall Street Journal,* April 22, 1994.

21. "The Smart Card Cashes In," *The Economist,* January 29, 1994, pp. 73–74.

smart cards, electronically and by telecommunication, the trouble-some drive to establish new, profitable bank branches, with the risk of making costly mistakes, can be eliminated. In fact, the costly real estate investment to house bank lobbies can be cut sharply, since the telephone will be a fast, low-cost substitute for trips to the bank.

TODAY'S BANKING PRACTICES:
A CENTURIES-OLD LEGACY

Banking enterprises of today, while extremely efficient in processing checks and credit card charges at nominal cost, are nowhere near as price-effective as they could be. For example, preparation and mailing of detailed account statements and sorting and returning of checks are costly anachronisms more suitable to the eighteenth or nineteenth centuries than to the twenty-first. Further, credit card services add cost to each transaction, in terms of the charge to the enterprise offering the goods or services, and interest charges to the individual who incurs the debt. Losses stemming from bad loans to both companies and individuals increase the amounts that the financial institutions must add to the interest rates charged to responsible debtors, reduce the interest given to depositors, and lower stockholder earnings. Further, some bank managements have been among the last to recognize their failure to control unreasonable bureaucracy by downsizing and reengineering their operations. One indication of management inattention to methodical control and improvement of efficiency is the occurrence of sudden and radical personnel reduction. For example, one bank recently announced that the imminent slashing of 4,300 employees (8.6 percent of the total) was prompted less from recognition of the inefficiency of operations than from losses on securities sold in erroneous anticipation of continued low interest rates.[22] However, the logical question that this raises is "if it is possible to slash employment now, why was the reduction not done long ago?" Mammoth organizations such as these all have a common problem. It is almost impossible to recognize the growing inefficiencies that stem from the

---

22. Matt Murray, "Banc One to Cut Work Force by 4,300 and Shut Down 100 Bank Branches," *Wall Street Journal*, November 22, 1994.

sheer size of their bureaucracies and widespread sprawl of their national and international operations. Fortunately, able managing executives like those at Banc One ultimately uncover the fat when declining profits in their organizations necessitate rapid improvement.

Another bank transaction that involves a morass of paperwork and complex decision making is the loan and credit approval process. Banc One Corporation's Financial Card Services Corporation Division is a pioneer in developing intelligent computer systems capable of reducing by more than 99 percent the time required to process a credit card customer's telephoned request for a credit increase, from days to seconds. Its TRIUMPH system has automated "the complex decision-making process typically performed by credit analysts."[23] While this feature is impressive, it is far more important that TRIUMPH has the flexibility to speedily support new products and promotions. No wonder bank companies in several countries have opted for versions of this system in their currencies and languages. These non-U.S versions will soon be servicing tens of millions of customers!

Advanced, computer-assisted *home mortgage* loan processing, much more complex than credit card credit analysis, is not just a future dream. The Federal National Home Loan Mortgage Corporation plans to inaugurate the Loan Prospector system in 1995. Supplied with a prospective borrower's financial information, the system will almost instantly analyze the data "by a combination of rule-based and statistical modeling systems. In the process, the computer will check the applicant's income, credit history and appraisal and title information through linked databases."[24] However, as Jane Dwight, director of automated underwriting, has indicated, although the decision to make a loan will take only minutes, the closing process may still take five to ten days. Obviously, loan closing preparation and completion processing also needs serious reinvention. A future system enhancement, the Desktop Originator, will enable borrowers to electronically analyze and submit their own applications using their personal computers.

The computer-based loan application processor of the future holds the key to solving the likelihood of racial discrimination in mortgage

---

23. William Jackson, "TRIUMPH Charges Forward: Giving Credit Where Credit is Due," *Outlook* (Chicago: Andersen Consulting, 1993), pp. 23–24.

24. John Handley, "Computer Loans a Laptop Away," *Chicago Tribune,* October 30, 1994.

financing so often and so sensationally reported by the media recently. The lack of data for realistically reporting the financial worthiness of loan applicants versus loan rejection rates by race is no excuse for media emphasis on the rates of rejection. Even when some decision rationale statistics have been gathered, the results have been misleading. For example, simply to compare the earnings of applicants, without considering their credit histories, job histories, and existing debts ignores the financial institution's responsibility to its owners and depositors to make secure loans. The Federal Financial Institutions Examination Council recently reported that the rejection rate for black Americans was 27.8 percent versus 15.3 percent for whites and 14.6 percent for Asian Americans. A less sensational and important message was that 72.2 percent of black American loan applications were approved! In fact, the acceptance rates for black Americans with income over 120 percent of the national median was 81.8 percent. And in the last four years, the rejection rate for black Americans has fallen 18 percent while the rejection rate for whites *rose* 6 percent. Donald G. Ogilvie, executive vice president of the American Bankers Association, was quoted as saying the report's data were "at best a flawed measure" because although the report grouped applications by incomes, it did not take into account such factors as applicants' previous indebtedness and credit records.[25] A nonsensational headline would have read, "Black American Loan Rejection Rate Plummets While White Rate Increases." By subjecting every loan application to a color-blind, dispassionate, and logical artificial intelligence-based computer review, using a single set of decision criteria, it will become impossible for decisions to be racially biased. Therefore, the sooner this technological advancement can be universally adopted, the better it will be for mankind.

REENGINEERED EXPENSE REPORTING

The process of recording, reporting, and data capture of business expenses took a turn for the worse when new U.S. government taxation laws vastly complicated the process. Now, instead of simply reporting

---

25. Associated Press, "Gap Still Broad: Twice as Many Blacks as Whites Rejected," *Chicago Tribune,* October 27, 1994.

an expense, it is necessary to break the expense into its nontaxable and taxable components. Untold numbers of enterprises and credit card companies have been working to relieve the burden by electronically transferring credit card charges from the card company to the companies that require their personnel to pay expenses with a corporate credit card. Alcoa, which previously processed conventional time and expense reports, eliminated much of the work required of individuals and the company's data entry and accounting personnel by adopting the system illustrated in exhibit 7–2.[26] A simplified explanation of Alcoa's new expense reporting procedures as described in *CFO Magazine,* includes the following key elements.

1. The person incurring the expense enters the accounting information required directly onto the charge card customer copy. (Previously, it was necessary to rewrite most of the credit card information onto the expense report.) The charge card bank copy is then sent to the bank (in this case, the First Bank Systems of Minneapolis). Most charges are telecommunicated from the seller establishment to the bank, providing lightning-fast availability of the data.
2. The person incurring the expenses mails the marked-up charge card copies to Alcoa's corporate Shared Services department.
3. First Bank Systems transmits charges to Alcoa Shared Services.
4. An Alcoa clerk, at a computer terminal, accesses the bank's record that matches the charge card copy mailed by the person incurring the cost, reviews the charge for compliance to policies, and enters the accounting data that was handwritten by the employee on the customer copy. The Alcoa computer uses the completed transaction to update the general ledger, prepares various report files, and prints checks for the bank.

After reviewing this procedure, I would suggest two avenues for future improvement. One would require the credit card company to provide a "user input" space on the customer copy. To do so would eventually eliminate most of Alcoa's remaining clerical tasks. However, it would add the burden of data entry to the establishment processing the charge. The second avenue would automate the tasks of the person who incurred the cost. For example, through the use of a

---

26. Ian Springsteel, "The Best Road Traveled," *CFO Magazine,* September 1994, pp. 103–106.

EXHIBIT 7–2

Expense Reporting

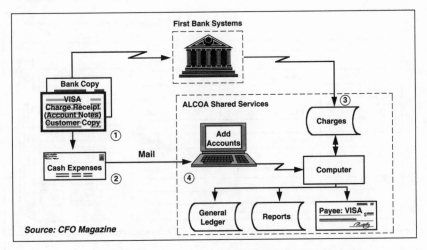

Source: CFO Magazine

notebook computer and small scanner, the charge card data could be captured and manually entered data could be added. Then, the data could be telecommunicated to the Shared Services department, and matched by computer to the bank's file (assuming that this data, now duplicated, would still be required, which it should not be).

Alcoa, so far, has reduced expense report processing costs by 77 percent! This is indeed an example of reengineering a business process that has yielded tremendous tangible improvement.

THE ELECTRONIC CHECK REGISTER

The electronic check register (exhibit 7–3), a precursor to vastly better twenty-first century systems, will soon be widely available. It has the potential for beginning to reduce some of the unnecessary costs of financial transactions, while giving consumers instant access to their account status. When the account holder plugs the electronic check register into any telephone outlet, the register will automatically dial the bank's automated system. When connected, the register gives the bank's computer the account number and transfers the manually initiated checks (numbered 101 and 102 on the exhibit), from the check register to the bank's computer. The bank's system, after merging the customer's manual checks with automated funds transfer (AFT) trans-

EXHIBIT 7–3

Electronic Check Register

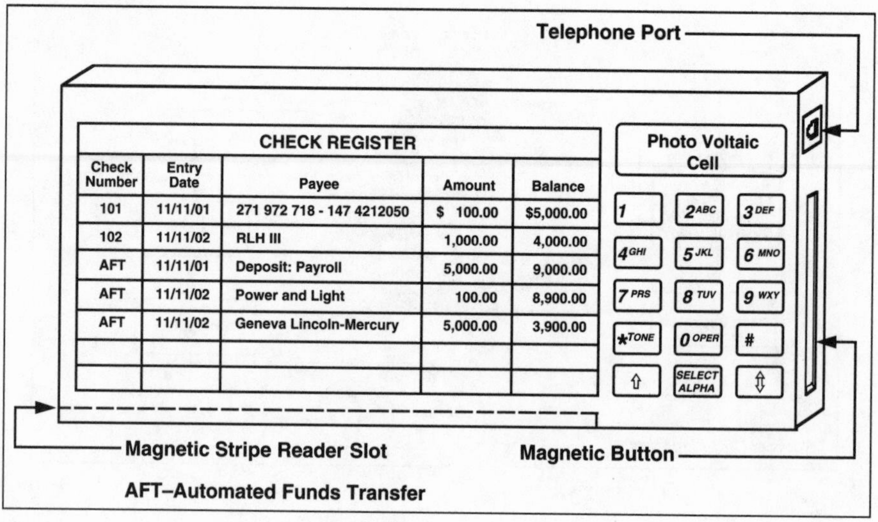

actions, puts the AFT transactions, which have not previously been transferred to the electronic check register, at the end of the list and updates the customer's register.

Check number 101, issued by the customer as an automatic funds transfer, specifies the nine-digit bank number and ten-digit account number of the payee rather than the individual's name. No paper check is required for this transaction. (The system could easily accommodate both the payee's name and numbers by entering the name or initials of the payee on the second line). Check number 102, issued to the account owner's son, has been recorded by entering the son's initials. The telephone transfer of information between the customer's register and the bank's data base enables the customer to reconcile his "checkbook" daily. Should the bank process a paper check in an amount erroneously different than the customer's previous electronic entry, the computer could make an immediate correction and flag the check for the customer's review. Since the electronic register and the bank's computer would perform all the calculations, arithmetic errors would also be eliminated. Because the bank would receive notification of the paper checks as they are written, the customer's register and bank's data base should always be in perfect synchronization, essentially eliminating the need to reconcile the two. The customer could also postdate automatic funds transfers due in the future, to keep them from being deducted from the account balance until that date. The magnetic button slot shown on the exhibit would permit the register owner periodically (annually, for example) to replace the year's magnetic button check history with a new one, and to put the button into an archive. The button might also serve as input to other home finance, tax, and budgeting systems through the simple addition of an account code for each check.

The advantages of the system should be obvious. The service to the customer would be superb, eliminating the necessity to mail monthly checks to various creditors. The options include authorization for the seller to initiate an automatic funds transfer transaction or for the customer to pay with one he initiates. Checkbook and bank statement would always be reconciled, and the customer could obtain current account balance information whenever necessary. Both payor and payee would benefit from lowering the cost of preparing and mailing statements and checks.

Although the electronic check register (or some other device serving the same purpose) is likely to be only a short-term, interim stage until the home system module becomes available (see chapter 2, subsection "Virtually Real Home Shopping"), it is only one of many devices that may address the same opportunities for simplifying payment by "electronic check." At the time of this writing, for example, Citibank is advertising a "revolutionary new way to bank" using one's personal computer (not public-friendly, considering how many people do not have their own computers) or new screen telephones. Citibank customers who do not own personal computers can now have access to home banking via a video screen attached to their Ameritech telephone.[27] Eventually, this low-cost alternative to interactive television will be used for interactive shopping.

The state of card technology in Europe is more advanced than that of the United States. It is truly a shame that the investment by companies in the United States in outmoded magnetic stripe technology (stripe readers for magnetically capturing the card owner identification and automatically dialing up the card company's computer if the

27. Jon Van, "Interactive Service Will Turn Home Telephones into ATMs," *Chicago Tribune*, November 10, 1993.

card has been reported stolen, or to authorize charges based on the remaining credit limit), has delayed adoption of the smart card. In France, the Carte Bancaire bank card organization already has 22 million smart cards in use, having formed the electronic charge coordinating function in 1984. The smart card's silicon microchip, embedded in a wallet-size plastic card, transforms the world of credit cards and banking to one of personal computer. The card is used for purchases and to pay all types of bills, and can store and retrieve data and be programmed for various tasks. A secret card-owner code stored in the card microchip must be key-entered when the card is used. This eliminates most of the possibility of a stolen card being fraudulently used. The card owner's available credit balance can also be maintained on the microchip. This feature eliminates the cost and inconvenience of calling a credit approval operator or computer for charge authorization. Since its introduction in 1991, the smart card's use has helped to reduce the costs of card fraud in France by 83 percent, to one-half that of the United States.

The march of progress will not end with the adoption of electronic check registers, smart cards, or screen telephones. The ultimate system will make coins and paper money obsolete.

THE WEALTH UTILITY: THE COMPUTER AS A FULL SERVICE BANK

Banks and other financial institutions are in the enviable position of being strategically positioned for a leap into the next generation of financial services. Their comprehensive computer systems and international telecommunications networks are the fundamental elements of the revolutionary systems of tomorrow and the next century (see chapter 5, subsection "Benevolent Big Brother: Community Data Base"). These ingredients are the framework necessary for the moneyless society and the ultimate wealth utility. The current vast array of financial service institutions in every community is far less than an ideal, cost-effective way to handle financial transactions. They create the unnecessarily costly requirement to channel financial transactions around a monstrous network of institutions in every corner of each country and between all countries. Each financial institution requires armies of back-rooms people to staff this complex operation. In the largely self-sufficient decentralized communities of the future, most financial transactions will be for goods and services provided by community businesses to other community businesses and citizens. A single "wealth utility" for each community, basically a "black box" computer system, will much more cost-effectively provide a more rational service. The recent furor over the proposed Microsoft-Intuit merger provides a window to the future. The combination is opposed by the U.S. Department of Justice on the basis that the merged company would dominate future home banking because it "would, in effect, turn every home computer into the equivalent of an automated teller machine."[28]

A financial institution's community computer data base of the future will be *the* repository of information for all citizens and private and public enterprises. The financial portion of these data bases will serve to facilitate an array of computer financial services. The asset and liability segments of individuals' and enterprises' data bases of the future will be repositories not only for monetary assets, in the conventional sense, but also for various properties and investments. (Charles Sanford, chairman of Banker's Trust, shares my vision of the wealth account as part of his vision of banking in 2020.)[29] Retirement funds, insurance cash value, stocks, bonds, and mutual fund investments are examples of cash-equivalent assets, while real estate, automobiles, and personal property are assets of less direct cash equivalents. Thus, the computer utility will maintain real-time balance sheets for both individuals and enterprises. The current financial status can then be used by the electronic "banking" program to process requests for credit.

The financial institution's community computer utility (exhibit 7–4) will have access to financial services processor programs integral to the financial processing systems. A few examples of these processors (of which there are two separate sets, for individuals and for businesses) are as follows.

1. *Assets*. The assets processor will maintain individuals' and businesses' detailed asset records and produce balance sheet informa-

28. James Coates and Jan Crawford Greenburg, "Microsoft Case Enters New Realm," *Chicago Tribune,* April 30, 1995.

29. "Bankers Trust's 2020 Vision," *The Economist,* March 26, 1994.

EXHIBIT 7–4

Financial Services Processors

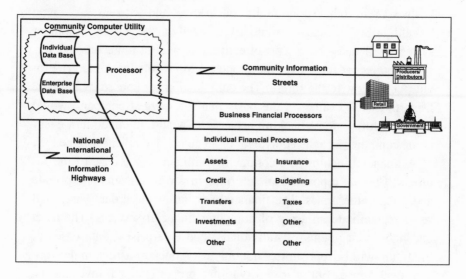

tion. For individuals, this will include home inventory, money equivalent account, investments, insurance cash value, and real estate. (The term "money equivalent" is used because coins and paper money will no longer be used. The electronic equivalent of money will be the wealth an individual or business has in a money equivalent account.) For business, the asset manager will also maintain all asset account details including inventory, facilities, and equipment.

2. *Credit.* The credit processor will maintain the indebtedness account, periodically deducting "money" from the asset account to reduce the debt account. Since *all* individual and business "loans" will only theoretically be backed by the tangible assets and intangible prospects of the borrower, "loan payments" will *not* need to increase the tangible assets of a lending institution and the loan will be interest free. (Instead, suppliers of goods and services will be "paid" for credit purchases by adding indebtedness to the borrower's debt account and to their own money equivalent account.) A borrower's credit limit will be determined by the credit processor.

3. *Transfers.* Every "purchase" of financial services, such as insurance, taxes, and investments will be transferred between buyer and seller accounts by the funds transfer processor.

4. *Investments.* The account holder's investment instructions will be maintained by the investment processor. This will include periodic automatic purchases of specified "stocks" and "mutual funds" and "government securities." (The quotation marks indicate that these investment forms may be radically different in the future.)

5. *Insurance.* The insurer and policy identification, rate, and benefit schedules will be accessed and maintained by the insurance processor. Periodic premium payments will automatically be transferred between the insured and insurance provider accounts. "Claims" will automatically be paid from the provider's accounts as medical, death, and loss transactions are processed against the insured's data base.

6. *Budgeting.* The budgeting processor, using financial history and current balance sheet, will provide budget projections for businesses and for individuals.

7. *Taxes.* Although tax calculation is a field in which there is fantastic opportunity for simplification, whatever complexity remains in the future world should be eliminated through the automatic use of the tax processor. It will calculate payments due and the funds transfer processor will automatically transfer the required payments from the asset or debt accounts of the person or business involved.

I have had extensive discourse with my colleague, Leroy Peterson, over the ownership of the community computer utility, and I have come to agree with Pete that banks are undoubtedly the enterprises that will own and operate these utilities over the foreseeable, practical future horizon. However, it seems unlikely that a vast number of banks, each with its own systems, will fit into the national and international network so important to achieving the economies of computer processing and data transmission that business and individuals should expect. Therefore, I anticipate a radically accelerating pace of banking mergers and reduction of the number of independent institutions. In the very long-range, almost inconceivable future, my vision of a more perfect democracy, in which citizens directly participate in passing and rejecting proposed legislation via the information superhighways, it seems likely that the computer utility might well become the property of small, local communities and neighborhoods. In this scenario, in order for competition to continue to flourish, the private enterprises responsible for developing, enhancing, and maintaining community data base services would periodically bid competitively to manage the operation for another contract period. Regional telecommunication network operations should also be competitively managed by private operators. However, each community's computer utility office facilities, data processing, and communications equipment and the data itself may be owned by the community in the very longest term. Leroy Peterson's comment as regards the practical, foreseeable future is that "banks and other financial institutions must become far more efficient if they are to live and prosper in this new environment."

The money changers of the world exact fees for services that, uniquely, add no value to the transaction and actually erode the value of the customer's assets. For example, an overseas traveler pays more for the currency he buys than the seller of the currency receives. And, if the traveler does not spend the entire amount purchased and must sell back the remainder, he will again receive less than the official exchange rate. Similarly, banking institutions pay a depositor interest on the funds he deposits, but far less than the interest the bank charges on the money it loans. A middleman can serve a useful, even vital, function in these two examples. However, present costs of these transactions are far too great in comparison to the alternatives offered by the latest technology. For example, Thomas McCarroll reports the financial institutions' cost of processing each check to be approximately $1.30.[30] Computer networks linking community data bases, not only in one country but around the world, will permit sellers and buyers of "currency" to make the exchange. The processing and telecommunications costs of all financial transactions are likely to be so small that they would be covered by the computer utility fee charged to citizens and businesses.

BANKLESS BANKING: THE CREDIT APPROVAL PROCESS

The financial institution community computer utility of the future will, through its "banking" system programs, process loan requests from the community's individuals and enterprises, making approved

---

30. Thomas McCarroll, "No Checks. No Cash. No Fuss?" *Time,* May 9, 1994, pp. 60–62.

credit available instantly. When checking an individual's credit worthiness, the system will be able to consider *all* of the person's assets and liabilities, earnings, credit history, and even more importantly, the individual's life record, in terms of education and job performance. In the normal case, credit will be approved and the available credit line amount will be entered on the individual's record. As the expenditures financed are transferred from the individual's account to that of an enterprise or another individual, the indebtedness amount will be deducted from the credit line, and added to her liability account.

The procedure for an enterprise obtaining credit will be quite similar, but the data base will contain far more information. For example, the enterprise inventory management system will maintain quantity and value information on inventories. The system of the future will be unlikely, however, to maintain accounts receivable and payable information, since all deliveries from supplier to customer would instantaneously trigger electronic funds transfer from one's account to that of the other. For small businesses, the use of their financial data base information in the loan request process will support almost instantaneous approval or denial, and will do so at far less cost. They will no longer need to complete the twenty-six-page business credit information form or pay as much as $25,000 for an audited financial statement![31]

"Black box" computer banking system features such as the credit approval process described in this section are among the factors that will relentlessly continue to reduce human labor in the banking process until the point of virtual elimination has been reached. Recent large personnel cutbacks have also contributed to the trend. And bank mergers will continue to offer opportunities for further economies. However, banking strategists need to recognize that "mergers among banks with redundant branch networks offer potential cost savings of at least 35 percent" and "a merger of two banks from disparate markets offers a potential cost savings of only 10% to 15%."[32] But few re-

---

31. Lee Berton, "New Form Seeks More Data from Business Borrowers: Banks May Require Additional Information to Help Cut Number of Bad Loans," *Wall Street Journal,* December 16, 1993.

32. Terence P. Paré with associate reporter Patty de Llosa, "The New Merger Boom: New Combinations Are Reshaping America's Largest Industries, with Consequences for All. Shareholders Could Be the Big Losers," *Fortune,* November 28, 1994, pp. 95–106.

alize that the long-term future of banks as currently operated is one of no banks at all! Nevertheless, Terence Paré and Patty de Llosa's indicate that such mergers alone will continue to reduce bank jobs, from a peak of approximately 2.2 million in 1990 to less than 1.625 million projected by the turn of the century (exhibit 7–5). If, however, banks and other financial institutions continue work on radically new computer-based processes, this projection will prove to be far too optimistic in terms of employment in the banking process.

In the very distant future, banking may become even more radically different. For example, future citizens will probably have higher moral standards (because genetic engineering will eliminate inherited tendencies to violence, crime, and sloth) and better education and career training. Therefore, credit rejection based on these factors will ultimately become rare. In fact, if my very long-range vision comes to pass, and the community and its citizens become the owners of the computer utility, individual and business interest—at rates that would be minimal—will be deducted from the borrower's "cash" and disbursed to the community's "depositors" in the ratio of their "cash" accounts to the community total, less a small amount to cover the cost of the computer utility's financial "banking" system operations. And if a community's "reserve" allowance (the amount of credit granted)

EXHIBIT 7–5
Bank Employees

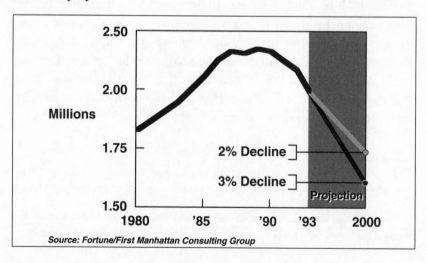

Source: Fortune/First Manhattan Consulting Group

exceeds community "deposits" by more than the reserve requirements, the community would instantaneously obtain credit from the
network of community computer systems, and would transfer interest
to the lending community's system. Such a contingency is mainly
likely when private enterprises plan expansion or modernization or
the community government needs to finance a large investment in infrastructure building or improvement. However, private enterprises
would also be able to issue financial instruments such as stocks and
bonds. Stock issues would be a superior way to obtain financing,
since they would not add to the enterprise or community's debt.

BROKERLESS STOCK TRADING

The world's financial investment networks are almost all patterned
after that of the United States, an abbreviated illustration of which is
presented as exhibit 7–6. The road from a producer's stock issue into
the hands of the stock purchaser is not only complex, but also costly,
because of the highly paid salaries and profits of the middleman brokers and exchanges and the exorbitant cost of government oversight
to business and consumers, paid through their taxes. Commissions on
sales and new stock issues substantially reduce the investor's capital

EXHIBIT 7–6
Financial Investment Network

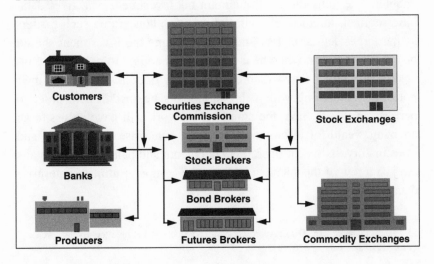

Customers

Securities Exchange
Commission

Stock Exchanges

Banks

Stock Brokers

Bond Brokers

Producers

Futures Brokers

Commodity Exchanges

and the capital delivered to the stock issuer's company, in the case of underwriting new stock offerings. And the network is even more complex than illustrated, since it must also have links to the networks in other countries.

A substantial case can be made for investment brokers, of which there are thousands in local offices in addition to each broker's central office (a factor that contributes substantially to the complexity of the network). The most powerful argument for these services is that they each employ research departments for the purpose of developing investment advice. However, the redundancy of researchers in all of the broker companies is extremely wasteful when compared to an ideal model in which a single super research enterprise is backed by computer utilities with access to every traded enterprise's data base and powerful new artificial intelligence analysis computing systems.

Individuals and enterprises in the future will be able to buy and sell stocks and bonds without costly payments to stockbrokers and institutions that underwrite stock offerings. In fact, a recent Securities and Exchange Commission regulation has already opened the door for companies to sell their stocks directly to consumers, bypassing brokers.[33] In the future, such direct stock trading will be the rule rather than the exception. The interactive home telecommunications network, through the local computer utility and national and international networks will provide a plethora of information for both the most sophisticated investor, the customer in exhibit 7–7, as well as the private dabbler. The individual will maintain his investment objectives database segment interactively with information concerning such matters as the target degree of risk and expected time the investment should be held. Thereafter, when he is interested in adding to or changing investments, the system will present various options, ranked by their potential for earning within the parameters he specifies. In order to perform in this fashion, the computer network will have access to an amazing wealth of information on every enterprise. Its financial and sales history, its recent operating statements and balance sheet details are just a few of the data available on the computer utility's enterprise data base.

---

33. Francis Flaherty, "The Direct Approach: No-Load Stocks to Let Investors Bypass Brokers," *Chicago Tribune*, February 20, 1995.

EXHIBIT 7–7

Future Financial Investing

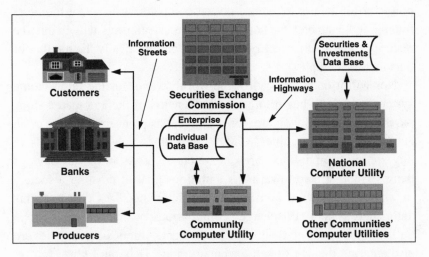

Just as the future will see virtual elimination of middlemen and retailers in the consumer distribution chain, in favor of direct producer-
to-consumer delivery, stockholders will benefit vastly from direct
sales of initial stock offerings from the company involved to the purchaser (see exhibit 7–7). Further savings will come from the virtual
"black box" central clearing house (resident in the national financial
institutions computer utility on the exhibit) that will match stockholders' offers to sell with buyers' bids. This is a step beyond First
Chicago Trust's pioneering internet shareholder/company communication system. This system, which gives investors access to company
financial performance, is expected to have proxy voting and dividend
distribution added in 1995. Eventually, according to Michael Foley,
First Chicago Trust vice president, the system will be expanded "to
access account information, initiate transactions and access company
information such as quarterly reports."[34] Because the stocks of the future will be electronic, recorded on the central securities and investment data base and on that of the stockholder's (either individual or
enterprise) computer utility, dividends and financial reports will be

---

34. William B. Crawford, Jr., "First Chicago Trust Opens Gates: Internet to Provide Stockholders Electronic Access to Companies," *Chicago Tribune,* December 13, 1994.

delivered from the stock's company through the central clearing house and on to the stockholder's data base. Additionally, another powerful artificial-intelligence-driven computer system that monitors trading and evaluates the soundness of stock offerings will enable the Securities and Exchange Commission to cut drastically the number of bureaucrats it employs.

Nor will it be necessary for the world to wait for the future home system module to begin to enjoy the benefits of the automated stock purchase system. Singapore, for example, has pioneered the use of an automated teller machine (ATM) system that enables individuals to buy shares from its six large commercial banks or postal savings bank: "Another step towards its ambitious goal of creating a society in which all financial transactions are automated."[35] Of course, this automated system still charges commissions, which the banks hope will help them recoup their large investment. American companies are also entering the age of self-executed trades. Deborah Lohse, for example, reported that there are only a few brokerage firms (such as Charles Schwab & Co. and Fidelity Investments) that are now accommodating trades by investors with personal computers. But Mark H. Goldstein, president of Reality Online, predicts that "by the end of the decade, 30 percent of all trading will be done on-line through discount brokerage firms."[36] The first such firm directly linking the customer's computer to a "stock exchange floor trading computer" will find that virtually all transaction costs will have been eliminated, and thus will lower its prices dramatically, winning a tremendous share of the brokerage business market.

COMMUNITY MUTUAL FUNDS: THE ELECTRONIC FUND MANAGER

There is no more place for mutual fund management enterprises as such, in the twenty-first century, than there is for any securities brokers. Old-fashioned securities analysts would argue that it would be impossible to "teach" a computer to recognize human emotional and

35. "Share Dispensers," *The Economist,* September 3, 1994, p. 73.

36. Deborah Lohse, "Log On: You May as Well Get Used to It: High-tech Portfolio Management Is Coming," *Wall Street Journal,* December 9, 1994.

political factors that underlie the success of the best securities analysts, although they generally admit that the speed and data base of the computer make its ability to analyze voluminous economic and financial fundamentals unsurpassable by any human. Informed analysts and computer specialists find it far easier to visualize the inevitable application of the new technology's "neural network" to *every* investment analysis problem.[37]

As soon as comprehensive analysis programs consistently outperform human analysts in making investment decisions and when computer utilities become available, the business of mutual fund management can be turned over to the much lower-cost system. Then, the fantastic earnings of mutual fund managers, usually at least one percent of the fund's assets, will be replaced by the small monthly computer utility charge covering not only fund trading but also every other computer and communications cost. Securities analysts will no longer be the kings of the investment world. Computer securities specialist firms will contract with the computer utility to manage its securities investment operations. These specialists, in turn, will manage the decisions regarding which software supplier's products to use, and manage the continuous upgrading of the system's capabilities. Today's mutual fund management enterprises will be best equipped for survival if they become the superior purveyors and managers of advanced investment management software.

AGENTLESS INSURANCE: COMMUNITY SELF-PROTECTION

The days of the insurance agent are numbered. User-friendly interactive computer systems with which any person will be able to obtain price and coverage information, define coverage needs, and prepare applications will soon be available to home computer owners, electronic kiosk customers, and on the interactive television channels. The advantage to customers of reduced costs of insurance will be significant and the reason for lower insurance prices or faster cash value accumulation will be highly visible. The agent, who often receives the

---

37. Ted Jackson, "The Human Touch: Computer Programs That Think Like People Put Some Money Managers on Cutting Edge," *Chicago Tribune*, November 29, 1994.

first one or two years of premiums as a sales commission, will simply disappear from the process. And the cost cutting will not end there. Many invisible costs, such as the processing of insurance applications, claims, and loan requests will also plummet, and will drop fastest for the companies that set the most aggressive strategic plans for transforming their operations. Target personnel reductions over the next decade should, for most insurers, be in the 90 percent range. Process reengineering is already making inroads on wasteful, bureaucratic operations. As Jeremy Rifkin reports, companies such as Mutual Benefit Life have found that claims which required only seventeen minutes of actual work took twenty-two days to be processed, during which forms were routed to nineteen people in various departments.[38] The reengineered process, which increased the productivity of the processors by 100 percent and reduced the days in process by 82 percent to four days has ample room for further improvement. After all, the remaining eight minutes of work per claim is still spread over four days!

In the long term, citizens and enterprises will benefit most from community self-insurance systems, operated by the community computer utility. Since these virtually "black box" systems will incur only computer operations and telecommunications costs, the price for insurance coverage will be nominal, and the earnings on invested assets will be returned to the insured accounts. Thus, cash value of the account holders will be faster. The insurance managers most capable of defining the systems and operations of these systems will be the professional system operators, developers and maintainers of the insurance business systems of the next century.

THE DAWNING OF THE NEW CAPITALIST AGE

Evidence of the industrial world's vast wealth is all around us. The huge government buildings, real estate, homes, parks, airports, office buildings, factories, automobiles, and retail and service businesses meet the eye in every direction, while the blight of slums and rural poverty are a small fraction of the landscape. And those of us who

---

38. Rifkin, *The End of Work,* p. 145.

have lived six or more decades can look back on continuous growth of all aspects of wealth.

Pessimistic projections of growing numbers of less affluent families ignore three extremely important trends likely to reverse the decline of average disposable family wealth. The first two factors are the decline of average family size and the increasingly longer periods between truly serious recessions or depressions (unemployment statistics mask the *less* serious impact of downturn in recent years, because the number of two wage-earner families is substantial—and many couples manage their finances wisely, protecting against the loss of income by one of the two). The result emerging is an obviously higher standard of life and a corresponding wealth accumulation enjoyed by all but the neediest families. The inevitable eventual gift and estate transfer that wealth accumulation and low population growth endow are creating people with greater affluence at a younger age.

The third factor that will influence the affluence of *all* citizens is recent, intensified, international legislative interest in solving problems of the chronically unemployed and long-term welfare recipients. Moving the poor and unemployed off the dole and into gainful employment will eventually extend the benefits of at least moderate affluence to every citizen. However, the spread of affluence is already underway. For example, Daniel Greenberg points out that a widely overlooked aspect of American consumers' failing to buy more than they have, recently, is because: "saturation of available closet and shelf space [is] to the point where it's difficult, if not impossible, to provide room for additional household goods and clothes." He adds that space in the home for new appliances is also in short supply.[39] As interesting as Greenberg's comments are, I believe that not only is lack of space limiting purchases, but many consumers have reached the point where they own almost everything they need and want. After all, in a household where there is already at least one television set for every family member, how many more sets can the family use? Further, some economic analysts anticipate a continuing growth of affluence as the population ages. Lowell Bryan and Diana Farrell forecast a boom in individual asset growth attributable to the aging baby

---

39. Daniel S. Greenberg, "Economic Villains: Overloaded Closets Help to Hurt the Economy," *Chicago Tribune,* November 4, 1994.

boomers who "are entering the period in their life cycle when they will save at higher rates. On average, their incomes will increase, and their liabilities will decrease. This means that they will enter their peak years for financial asset accumulation over the next two decades." They continue, "this group is saving at higher rates at every age than their parents or grandparents did, further contributing to the capital supply."[40] The factor that enables baby boomers to outperform their forebears is most likely that their parents (now most often two wage-earner families) have been able to accumulate wealth and thus provide a far better start for their offspring.

Viewing this tangible evidence of national wealth, individual citizens should realize that they are far wealthier than commonly acknowledged not only indirectly, in the sense of public assets belonging to the citizens, but also in direct terms. After all, businesses and all other tangible assets are owned by either other businesses or by individuals (stockholders or entrepreneurs) and those businesses owning others are in turn owned by stockholders.

Why, then, when the total wealth of all industrialized nations is so obviously huge, does the collective wealth of individuals seem far less? It is *not* because a nation's wealth is primarily owned by a small group of super-rich individuals. The fact is that many individuals' wealth is hidden because of its inaccessibility. Insurance companies and pension funds, for example, own massive amounts of securities and real estate. In 1992, for example, institutional equity holdings passed the 50 percent mark and continued steady growth, as seen in exhibit 7–8. Pension funds alone hold almost one-third of the financial assets of the U.S. economy, according to Rifkin.[41] The beneficiaries of these wealth holders are really the ultimate owners.

Further, a huge amount of public debt, owed to social security and medicare recipients, is not covered by issuing bonds to the beneficiaries that pay reasonable interest on the funds. And, unlike private insurance, the beneficiaries are denied the decision as to how the funds are invested to achieve the highest earnings feasible. For example, every citizen "owns" medical and retirement benefits which the gov-

---

40. Lowell Bryan and Diana Farrell, "The Savings Surge," *Wall Street Journal,* November 7, 1994.

41. Rifkin, *The End of Work,* p.228.

EXHIBIT 7–8
Institutional Holdings

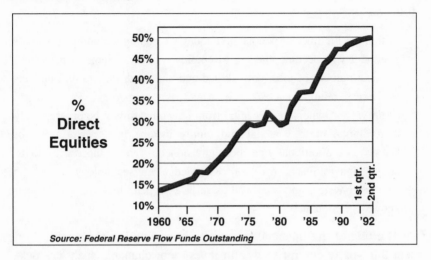

Source: Federal Reserve Flow Funds Outstanding

ernment routinely raids to finance deficit spending. However, were the individual issued treasury bonds for the amount of his and his employer's contributions he could either hold or sell them in order to make alternative investments. (The return on the investment would be much higher and he would now have documented, tangible ownership of their value under the two alternatives.) The rules governing the use of these retirement funds could be the same as for individual retirement accounts (IRAs), disallowing any use other than for retirement. In recent years, individuals with wealth partially hidden in life insurance and private retirement funds have gained a sense of ownership of this wealth by modern programs that permit, even encourage, them to make their own investment decisions and provide frequent statements of account balances. Thus, many individuals are increasingly more aware of their actual wealth and prospects for comfortably affluent retirement and estate transfer to their heirs.

Concurrent with the growth of assets, industrialized countries have experienced sharp declines of the average number of hours worked per year, although they have not seen any remarkable reductions in unemployment. I and many others expect the need for human mental and physical work to continue to decline to the verge of disappearance during the next century. And, therefore, the portion of individuals' incomes that is derived from the earnings of their wealth will eventually far surpass the income from their jobs. Lewis Perelman put it as follows.

Within the lifetimes of people alive today—certainly including America's youth—it will become cheaper to employ robotic systems to perform a growing number of jobs, both skilled and unskilled, than to hire humans at lowest minimal subsistence wage of the poorest Third World country. . . . Ownership of capital from now onward will be progressively more important to personal and family income than performance of "labor" as it traditionally has been envisioned, even for those with nominally "high" skills. The reason: Knowledge age technology makes the value of physical goods as well as services depend increasingly on their knowledge content.[42]

The tide of the financial future lies in accounting for wealth. Present third-party enterprise wealth investment channels such as stockbrokers and banks extract their operating costs and profits from investors and savers. Tomorrow's wealth utility will meet the need for wealth services at radically lower cost.

SUMMARY

The financial services industry is one in which success is most directly attributable to the quality and technological currentness of information processing and telecommunications. The unrelenting speed of change, not only in these areas, but also in the number of products financial service enterprises offer, is also tremendous. Thus, any enterprise without major, relatively short-term reengineering initiatives underway, or with timid goals and unimaginative visions and strategies, is bound to have substantial problems vis-à-vis more aggressive competitors. Financial services organizations, with their massive "back rooms" and huge customer service staffs and supporting facilities offer huge potential rewards to those companies that aggressively reengineer their operations and reduce the need for masses of employees. Citibank's recent decision to eliminate all electronic banking

---

42. Lewis J. Perelman, *School's Out: A Radical New Formula for the Revitalization of America's Educational System* (New York: Avon Books, 1992), p. 74.

fees, for example, is an indication that this leading-edge bank sees the huge advantage of reducing personnel costs by encouraging more customers to use automated teller machines and personal computers for bank transactions.[43] Further, banks have opportunities for quantum improvements in customer service by automating speedy and courteous responses to customer inquiries and requests for service.

In the very long term, ownership of all enterprises will rest primarily in the hands of the investing public, which will include most citizens. Businesses' managements must make informed decisions regarding the short-term survival and long-term success of their enterprises. When investors see the emerging future start to make inroads into the profitability of companies that lack systematic foresight, they will start to shift massive amounts of their capital from waning companies into those that ride the crest of change into tremendous growth in new arenas. Short-term profitability, while continuing to be vitally important, will not be any more important than long-term growth and continued viability to individual investors who depend on their investments for decades of income in their retirement years.

That growth opportunities will abound is readily seen on exhibit 7–9, a list of some of the growth industries and occupations identified in this chapter. The most important, in terms of long-term survival, are the financial system management companies that will eventually contract for the management of the community computer utilities' financial services processors and data bases. In the immediate future, firms offering low-cost electronic funds transfer services that eliminate printing and mailing bills, invoices, checks, and remittance advice documentation will flourish. Specialty services, such as those designed to lower the cost of employee expense reporting, will also blossom, as enterprises continue their quest for lower operating costs. In the not-too-distant future, specialty devices such as the electronic check register will bring high technology services to the vast majority of the population—those who are not yet computer literate—and will do so by their user-friendly similarity to their manual predecessors. Businesses will benefit from new financial services such as stockholder dividend payment systems that will use electronic funds trans-

---

43. John Schmeltzer, "Banking by Wire to Touch Nerves?" *Chicago Tribune,* May 24, 1995.

EXHIBIT 7–9
Growth Industries and Occupations

Financial System Management

Electronic Funds Transfer

Business Expense Reporting

Electronic Check Register

Electronic Dividend Payment

Smart Cards

Financial Services Software

---

fer technology for delivering payments directly to stockholders' accounts. And, credit card companies will soon find it necessary to upgrade their systems to modern smart card technology and capabilities. However, in the long term, among the most important financial services industries will be software development companies that de-

EXHIBIT 7–10
Financial Services Software

Individual and Business

Automatic Funds Transfer	**Balance Sheet**
Credit Check/Approval	**Loan Approval**
Investment Analysis	**Insurance Management**
Security Trading	**Tax Management**
Budgeting	

---

velop, maintain, and enhance the financial services software used by the future's community computer utilities. The various types of software, used by both individuals and public and private enterprises, are recapped on exhibit 7–10.

Enterprises at risk are also legion. Some of these are listed on exhibit 7–11. For those inclined to feel anxious or offended by the definition of some industries and occupations as waning or dying, there are several important points to keep in mind. These following points are repeated briefly in every chapter, because many readers are expected to read only one or more selected chapters. First, the change may not occur in the foreseeable future. Second, the future continuous reduction of work will be universal. As a result, society must and will reduce average workweek hours in order to maintain full employment. Third, the era of reduced work and increased leisure time will be one of unprecedented quality of life and affluence. The functions of banks, investment brokers, and mutual funds will eventually grow to be "black box" systems operated on computer utilities. In the meantime, these institutions will continue to evolve rapidly towards that end, by applying the latest technology to make even greater strides in reducing "back room" staffs and replacing "front counter" and telephone personnel with automated devices and voice and touch-tone customer

EXHIBIT 7–11
Waning Industries and Occupations

Banking	**Currency Exchanges**
Mutual Funds	**Securities Exchange Commission**
Investment Analysts	**Credit and Debit Cards**
"Back Room" Staff	
Investment Brokers	

service systems as described in chapter 2. Artificial intelligence computer logic will undergo continuous improvement and, as a result, will eventually eliminate the role of investment analysts and loan officers. Other new software will monitor financial reports and trading, eliminating the need for the watchdog role of the Securities and Exchange Commission. And credit and debit cards will soon give way, entirely, to smart cards. A limited number of these waning industries, those with managements of greatest precognition, will be able to reinvent their businesses and become their industries' leaders and survivors.

8

REINVENTING
EDUCATION

The School at Home

The education industry is poised on the edge of a radically new age in which learning will be moved out of the school classroom and into the electronic, home counterpart. For, as Michael Zey writes, "The university of the future will undergo a transformation so profound as to make it probably unrecognizable by current standards."[1] Movers and shakers in the education industry must, like private industry, begin a process of reinvention. To do so requires a tough set of goals designed to stretch their organizations to the utmost of their abilities. Examples of goals they should consider are as follows.

Percent

50	Instructor productivity increase
50	Facility utilization increase
25	Student achievement increase
50	More career-value subject content

Education, in terms of its potential for improvement, is one of the

---

1. Michael G. Zey, *Seizing the Future: How the Coming Revolution in Science, Technology, and Industry Will Expand the Frontiers of Human Potential and Reshape the Planet* (New York: Simon & Schuster, 1994), p. 234.

last great frontiers. In recent decades the continuous decline of its results proves that radical reengineering is necessary. However, short-
term reinvention will produce far lesser results than transformation,
and education is so far behind the march of technological advances in
almost every other private and public sector that truly transformational opportunities abound. For this transformation to take place,
though, it will be necessary to develop electronic courses and "teachers." Today's public education organizations and educators are highly
unlikely to contribute significantly to this development process, because the present system and its management are responsible for its
dismal failure to teach our children basic reading and mathematical
skills. Many prominent educators seem incapable of defining a reinvented educational system. For example, Eric Hanushek identifies a
need to measure the performance of educators and proposes an incentive pay system, but otherwise has no noteworthy suggestions for
transforming the industry. He seems pessimistic about the role technology can play in cutting the cost of education and improving its
quality. Regarding the start-up costs of new technology, he writes,
"Such expenditures might save money in the long run, but rewards for
saving money are not built into school systems."[2] Moreover, he fails
to grasp the vast potential of technology for improving student performance: "Therefore, it is not particularly surprising that little energy is
devoted to selecting and installing new technologies that primarily involve substituting capital for labor—especially if these substitutions
merely maintain existing levels of student performance."

Early moves of the private education industry, such as the five-year
contract between Education Alternatives, Inc. and the Hartford (Connecticut) board of education to operate its schools, may or may not improve test results or lower per-student costs.[3] Nevertheless, such moves
will lead ultimately to spectacular growth of this fledgling industry and
an explosion of electronic classroom products which are almost guaranteed to lower the costs and improve the results of education.

Nor is the need and potential limited to improved formal educa-

---

2. Eric A. Hanushek, et al. *Making Schools Work: Improving Performance and Controlling
Costs* (Washington, DC: Brookings Institution, 1994), p. 77.

3. Laurence D. Cohen, "Privatizing Public Schools Works," *Chicago Tribune,* November 25,
1994.

tion. Although large corporations, on average, are far ahead of public education in terms of technology employed in employee education and training programs, they suffer because the students delivered to them from formal education systems have almost no preparation for real-world jobs. Thus, they must continue to improve their own programs and to work with public and private educators to add content of career value to formal education. This chapter contains a description of the electronic classroom which will propel education and training light-years beyond today's outmoded, inefficient, and ineffective system. This is a vital prerequisite for quantum improvements in the mastery of all new technology. Nor is the futuristic interactive computer training and education system entirely beyond the range of today's practical application. For example, Andersen Consulting's Professional Education Division has created an interactive Change Management course which will be delivered to five thousand of its professionals around the globe.

EXECUTIVE CHECKLIST: SELECTED EDUCATION ZINGERS

Private and public executives are well aware that employees need vastly better education if they are to become qualified to work in the continuously more complex world of high-technology automation and computer systems. Educators should be equally aware and should be on the leading edge of developing new electronic educational and training material. Industry and enlightened academia together will need to work toward enabling the new technology to move into the homes and workplaces of all citizens. The following checklists of short-term and long-term changes and initiatives are intended to help every concerned executive and educator consider innovative methods by which to advance the science of education, which has seen little change since the days of the horse and buggy and one-room school. They are also a brief synopsis of the most important topics of this chapter for executives who need only a general overview.

SHORT-TERM TACTICS AND STRATEGIES

1. Education is a field in which privatization holds the potential for reinventing learning.

2. Private enterprises will soon develop massive amounts of electronic educational materials that eventually will be the foundation of twenty-first century tele-education.
3. Adoption of electronic topics, in the short term, offers the best potential for bringing the best, highest quality material to every student in the nation and in the world, eliminating differences in achievement due to the varying skills of individual teachers. Used properly, they will begin to lower the number and cost of teachers required.
4. Education must provide experience that will better equip students for their careers. This will require involving local employers in preparing and conducting topics of career value.
5. Private education and training companies must become much more active in developing materials for specific job training in industries in which shortages of personnel exist, and where employee turnover creates a need for frequent training of new employees.

FUTURE VISIONS

1. The electronic classroom will draw upon the best educators of the world for its methods and materials, virtually eliminating classroom educators.
2. A two-pronged attack on education reform will start with an interim program of privatizing largely traditional education. A second, more important prong will be the radical improvement of educational materials through privatization.
3. Vast public expenditures for building, maintaining, and operating educational facilities will be virtually eliminated by the classroom in the home.
4. The interactive educational system will not only permit each student to perform at his own level, it will also provide motivational encouragement when advances are achieved and will monitor "attendance."
5. Artificial intelligence will allow the computer and student to interact in question-and-answer sessions that will also include other peer-group students via telecommunication and virtual reality technology.

EDUCATION, KEY TO THE FUTURE,
FAILURE OF THE PRESENT

Education in the United States has been failing to do the job, as evidenced not only by falling performance on standardized tests but also by the performance of John and Mary in the workplace. Nationwide, scores on the verbal section of college admissions tests have plummeted by over nine percent in the last twenty years, as seen on exhibit 8–1. Unfortunately, the College Board, the organization that administers the Scholastic Assessment Test (SAT), faced with a two-decade decline of test scores as a result of increasingly poorer education, decided to "recenter" the scoring rather than continue to track the deterioration of educational results.[4] All too often, high school and even college graduates leave school unable to spell, write, or speak grammatically or to solve simple mathematic problems. Although critics tend to point at teachers and parents as the culprits, the fact is that the traditional classroom is an anachronism and traditional instruction is woefully outdated. And, studies like the *Reader's Digest* survey of a nationwide cross-section of 2,130 high school seniors clearly define the *real* problem—programs designed for *average* students are doomed to failure because students need courses designed for their individual learning paces and interests.[5] Following is one of the survey's forty questions of varying degrees of complexity (eight each in math, science, literature, geography, and history and government).

3 1/5 equals:
(a) 3 divided by 5 . (b) 3 minus 1/5 (c) 3 times 1/5 (d) 3 plus 1/5
(e) don't know.

A shocking *45 percent* of the students surveyed were unable to answer the question correctly. And, although the study's objectives were to attribute degrees of failure and success to the quality of family life (in which the study succeeded), an even more significant finding was

---

4. Ron Grossman, "SATs Get Dumber: New Scores Will Be Higher, but Standards Lower," *Chicago Tribune,* April 9, 1995.

5. Rachel Wildavsky, "What's Behind Success in School?" *Reader's Digest,* October 1994, pp. 49–55.

EXHIBIT 8–1

Average Verbal Scores (50th Percentile)

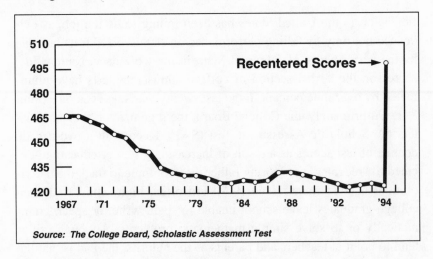

Source: *The College Board, Scholastic Assessment Test*

that the intelligence of students varied tremendously. That this is the case proves the critical need for education suited to each student's capabilities, and the inappropriateness of current education standards.

Today's crowded classrooms make it impractical for a teacher to give individual attention to groups of students with different learning skill levels and interests, let alone to give attention to single students. Nor is it practical to expect teachers to perform uniformly, to teach a uniform curriculum, and to use the same teaching techniques. With two-income households and long commuting hours, today's parents barely have time to do chores and prepare meals. They certainly do not have the time or tools to teach their children that which the school has failed to accomplish. Moreover, in the age of automation, traditional instruction is incredibly inefficient compared to electronic methods. Northern Telecom explains the problem and opportunity as follows.

In an age ripe with technology and access to information, our nation's educational infrastructure is in crisis. The traditional educational model of chalkboard and classrooms does not always provide equitable—or even efficient—distribution of scarce resources. Educational opportunities have traditionally been bound by distance, time and availability of classrooms and qualified teachers. The traditional model, however, is giving way to a new model based on interactive, two-way video—a model that spreads education resources through high-capacity, fibre-optic cable.[6]

The recently enacted Goals 2000 legislation, imposing nationwide testing on schools, has already proven that big government, with its armies of bureaucrats, is incapable of designing meaningful programs. What private citizen would not have expected a government agency such as that established by Goals 2000 to impose silly censorship such as deleting an author's passage describing a snowball fight on the grounds that it contains "violence"?[7] Government involvement in education cannot be the solution to the dilemma. Who but a government agency would create a test requiring students to write essays rather than answer multiple choice questions without taking into account the impracticality of uniformly grading the results or the massive resources required to even attempt to do so? Further, the notion of one standard test for everyone completely ignores the fact that the students' range of learning capabilities is extremely diverse, and that the real need is for education tailored to the individual's needs.

Fortunately a radical change in education is inevitable. Its basis will be the simple recognition that people are not uniform. In his checklist of potential future changes, for example, McKinley Conway writes, "A new doctrine for the development of the individual will assert that 'all men are created *unequal*' [italics added] and lay the basis for specialized development according to natural talents and abilities rather than attempting to make every individual conform to a norm."[8] Nor is it feasible to expect the nation to achieve better education simply by increasing spending for present educational methods. If so, the United States should have seen a vast improvement in test scores in the three decades between 1960 and 1990, a period during which per-pupil spending soared by 200 percent, as reported by David Warsh of

---

6. *Cornerstone Distance Learning* (Product Service Information) (Triangle Park, NC: Northern Telecom, 1995).

7. This and other examples are the subject of Sarah Lubman's article, "Tests to Gauge Student Ability Create a Furor," *Wall Street Journal,* May 31, 1994.

8. McKinley Conway, *A Glimpse of the Future: Technology Forecasts for Global Strategist.* (Norcross, GA: Conway Data, 1992.)

the *Boston Globe.*[9] The best improvement potential for education would lower, not increase education costs. For example, if video tapes of the world's best lecturer on each subject were produced and used in every classroom, tens of thousands fewer teachers would be required. However, it appears that the use of taped programming in the video age is woefully underutilized. The Cable in the Classroom organization, headquartered in Alexandria, Virginia, now reaches 33 million students, but only via cable television at odd hours of the day, and with very little programming specifically designed to supplant the teacher-conducted classroom with a cost-cutting alternative such as low-wage class monitors who would maintain discipline during the playing of tapes.

The old one-room schoolhouse seems to have been one of the most successful forms of education. The best teachers in those schools had to pay lots of attention to every student. Often, there were only one or two students in a grade, and the teacher had to keep several grades going at once. Since classes were so small, it was easier to adjust the pace of learning to accommodate both the slow-learning students and their brighter classmates. The brightest, most ambitious students were able to complete the assignments for their grade level, then involve themselves in the work of a more advanced grade. Students were rewarded individually for their progress and thus were highly motivated. The entire school heard about each student's triumph, and more importantly, every single student participated in schoolwide programs that were attended by family members and neighbors. Such education-oriented programs provided marvelous incentive to learn. However, a single-teacher school, like any classroom of today, is only as good as the teacher. And some teachers were less enthusiastic, less committed, less capable than others. Thus, some students benefited from the finest teaching available, while others were cheated of the opportunity to learn at the best of their ability.

Privatization of education and training holds the greatest promise for vastly improved quality at drastically lower cost, at least temporarily. Few public learning institutions have the experiences or cul-

---

9. David Warsh, "Study: More Choice—Not Spending More—Is Answer for Better Schools," *Chicago Tribune,* November 27, 1994.

tures to cast out their outmoded and failed teaching methods. Thus, one of the fastest growing private industries of the *future* will be professional businesses specializing in developing and marketing radically improved educational and career training programs, especially those that are electronic. The interactive, speech-recognition and voice-simulator computer will be the heart of the new delivery system. Vast public and private expenditures for mediocre results, produced in monumentally expensive facilities by armies of ineffective, nonproductive teachers will become history. In 1992, Lewis Perelman, senior fellow of the Discovery Institute, estimated public and private expenditures for education and training at over $600 *billion* even though the level of productivity—labor makes up 93 percent of its cost—makes it one of the worst industries.[10] It is clear that old educational methods must be replaced by delivery systems that will take education and training into the students' and employees' homes and workplaces. The worldwide savings potential of modern tele-schooling staggers the imagination.

Amazingly, the space-age solution to the crisis in education and training is to return to the excellence of the one-room system but through the modern wonder of computer and telecommunication systems capable of delivering the highest quality education with the best possible results, and at a far lower cost than present systems.

REINVENTING EDUCATION: A NEW WAY OF LIFE

Very soon the world will see the birth of an explosive new growth industry and a radical reduction in public expenditures. The field of education is the arena in which this new scenario will unfold. Mankind, as a result, will benefit enormously from huge improvements in the quality and quantity of *practical* education, designed to make *every* individual better equipped for a career and enriched with expanded life knowledge. Nor does the process of transforming the cost and efficacy of education require only reform of the traditional system. As Perelman writes, "the nations that stop trying to 'reform' their educa-

---

10. Lewis J. Perelman, *School's Out: A Radical New Formula for the Revitalization of America's Education System* (New York: Avon Books, 1992), pp. 97–99.

tion and training institutions and choose instead to totally replace them with a brand-new, high-tech learning system will be the world's economic powerhouses through the twenty-first century."[11] Radical reinvention using the best technologies of today and those of the future is what is needed!

Informed executives of private and public enterprises understand the need for two forms of education: one to enrich the personal life experience (the arts, for example), the second to prepare individuals for their working careers. Few in academia or in business and government would argue, with conviction, that our present education system delivers knowledge that will be more than nominally useful in subsequent employment. Even in imparting the most basic employment prerequisites, institutions of learning are failing to do what every business must do—continuously improve the quality and performance of its products. In the longest term, formal personal enrichment education will be a far smaller component of primary and secondary education, and career-oriented subjects will be a considerably greater proportion. Individuals who thirst for widespread knowledge will have a lifelong opportunity for formal and informal pursuit of those interests outside the mandatory education program.

In the relatively near future, the classroom will be transported to the home, borne by the hundreds of lanes of the information highway, and supported by marrying computer and video image technology to enable each student to interact with the system in a manner designed to individualize the learning process to the student's unique talents and previously acquired knowledge. The electronic classroom will provide curricula for basic skills (reading and arithmetic, for example) and for career-specific topics. But, in addition, the system will deliver topics to enrich personal knowledge. These largely optional subjects will be available at any time, to any individual interested. Not surprisingly, Asian countries, with their tremendous respect for the value of education, are likely to lead the world in the development of the electronic classroom. For example, the Republic of Korea is as advanced as any in the world when it comes to actions underway to enable the

---

11. Ibid., p. 20.

information highway to transport the classroom into the home. As reported by Yong-bom Kim, "Under the projection, all students will get access to the best schools, teachers and courses without regard to geography, distance and residence."[12] A vastly more efficient system for developing and delivering education will enable topic developers to produce material capable of competing with entertainment (movies and games) and made available on the same home system. Thus, the average individual, in his lifetime, will acquire a much broader knowledge base and the correspondingly higher quality of life.

Today, educators, computer and communications technicians, entertainment producers, and businessmen should be creating a new, explosive-growth industry by designing, developing, and bringing to market new educational products that will feature the best materials available in the world, presented by the most outstanding teachers. Separate private, competing corporations should be formed to select the best of these products for delivery to the world's public and private schools and, eventually, to the home, via the information highway. This approach, in which one group of competing businesses develops educational materials and separate competing distribution businesses select the products that will be used, will drastically reduce the cost of material preparation. (Today thousands of teachers and educators prepare hundreds of similar sets of subject materials for a single topic).

The quality of education delivered by individual teachers is now as variable as the different teaching skills of the thousands of educators conducting classes. By contrast, almost universal use of common topics, evaluated as the best currently available, will increase the quality of the products and improve the level of knowledge imparted. The average time required to master a topic will be much shorter than now possible, permitting students to learn far more in formative years. And most important of all, national and local budgets for education can be dropped to unimaginably lower levels by eliminating the need for most classroom educators and topic developers. In the long term, even the cost of the school building will disappear as the classroom moves into the home.

---

12. Yong-bom Kim, "Korea Launches 1st Stage of Info Super Highway Project," Seoul: *The Korea Times,* April 23, 1994.

REINVENTING TRAINING: VIRTUAL WORKPLACE REALITY

Development and distribution of on-the-job training media is another area in which a new private industry can be expected to have rapid growth. Far too little job training material is available, and since cyclic economic changes and normal turnover cause the frequent need to hire untrained workers, the cost of making new workers efficient and high quality producers is a significant, recurring business burden. Nor are government job training programs an acceptable substitute for those developed by private industry for use by private industry and government. Virtually every government job training and retraining program ever conducted, other than on-the-job, has failed to produce permanent benefits. Gary Burtless, an economist with the Brookings Institute, is quoted in reference to government training programs as saying, "With respect to training, I cannot think of a single study, based on convincing data, that shows it has helped workers."[13] The reasons are simple. First, if there are no job openings for a specific occupation, individuals trained for those jobs will not be able to find employment. Second, the number of jobs in which an individual might be trained is virtually limitless. Only a few of these jobs require specific, valuable skills. For example, a trained hair stylist's skills would be useful in any salon, however, training large numbers of stylists would be a tremendous waste if the number of stylists employed was already equal to or greater than the market demand. Many jobs, such as most in manufacturing, require product-specific or process-specific training which can be imparted only through on-the-job-training. An assembly worker needs to know how to put together the product of a specific factory. It is almost impossible to concoct a general training course that would prepare her for this job type.

In only one type of industry can government sponsor on-the-job training and then guarantee job availability by creating the demand. This industry category is public infrastructure maintenance and construction. As long as unemployment remains at an acceptably low level, public works programs, performed by private business, need not

---

13. Micheal Arndt, "Putting Careers on New Tracks," *Chicago Tribune,* October 23, 1994.

be launched to lower unemployment. However, when unemployment begins to grow beyond acceptable limits and businesses simply have no jobs to offer, government can create jobs by stimulating the economy or by launching new infrastructure projects to create the demand for labor. Superb pretraining and on-the-job training courses geared to infrastructure construction, repair, and maintenance, therefore, would help accelerate the speed with which the unemployed could be assimilated by construction companies, therefore dampening economic decline at the earliest stages of a recession. A successful program might even ultimately eliminate economic peaks and valleys.

Industry and government have incredibly ineffective on-the-job training programs which are simply incapable of transforming new employees into efficient workers producing high quality output. And, industry groups, academia, and professional societies are still far from efficient and effective in producing modern training programs for the job elements that are common to all businesses in any industry. (Academia produces the least amount.) As is the case with education, individual companies and professional societies and new private *training* development companies need to begin to create computer/ video-based, virtual reality, interactive training specific to unique, individual jobs and to work elements common to numerous companies and jobs. Absorption of new employees will then be easier and less costly and will keep government from intruding into an activity, job training, in which it has little chance of success.

THE ELECTRONIC CLASSROOM

Interactive computer-based education has the potential for improving the learning process—to achievement levels even better than the one-room schoolhouse—and it will be able to do so with vastly superior cost-effectiveness. Its "electronic teacher" can provide the same superb instruction to millions of students, and will always be bright and cheerful, as well as perfectly uniform in its frequent praise of its students' progress. Perelman writes, "For a technological revolution is sweeping through the U.S. and world economies that is totally transforming the social world of learning and teaching. This learning revolution already has made the 'classroom teacher' as obsolete as the blacksmith shop."[14] The electronic teacher of the future, to some extent, is at hand today. Interactive computer-based, multimedia educational and training materials are starting to be developed. The Massachusetts Institute of Technology, for one, is blazing a trail for the use of computers in higher education. Most of their students have twenty-four-hour computer access to "library catalogs, simulating laboratory experiments, questioning professors, reading electronic bulletin boards, sending love notes, carping to administrators, discussing the mysteries of the universe."[15] The best educational programs permit students to interactively mold the process of learning to suit their individual needs and skills. For example, inquisitive students who have read and viewed video media widely during their lifetimes will have acquired extensive knowledge outside of their formal education and chosen fields of study. If such a student finds she has already acquired the knowledge required by a given course—and she can successfully answer questions or solve problems embedded in the computer's interactive progress testing program—the computer-guided course can be dynamically and automatically modified to bypass nonproductive study and to focus on the subjects in which she is deficient, or which she finds of highest interest or value in career planning.

The future's community computer utility and its educational/training processors (exhibit 8–2) will be the focal point of tomorrow's teaching experience. Its data base, consisting of interactive written and audio/visual courses, and its processors will carry the classroom into the home. Its instruction processor will be the primary "teacher," incorporating lectures, texts, and audio/visual materials central to the educational process.

Objections to the home electronic classroom are easily anticipated and solutions provided. One of the obvious objections will be lack of personal interchange between student and "teacher." In this regard, I respectfully disagree with my colleagues, William Bramer and Charles Winslow, who write: "Only the worst Orwellian doom-sayers would point to computer training and see the end of person-to-person contact. Unless electronic training takes place within the larger con-

---

14. Perelman, *School's Out,* p. 20.

15. "Computer Catch-up," *FW Financial World,* March 15, 1994.

EXHIBIT 8–2

Educational/Training Processors

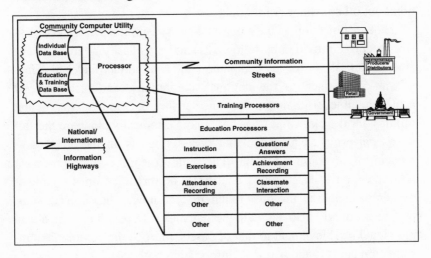

text of a learning organization, where conversation and sharing of knowledge is always taking place between people, it is likely to fail."[16] Perhaps their viewpoint was framed more in present than future likelihoods. My viewpoint is based on a far longer-term vision. For example, future technology will permit the computer's questions-and-answers processor, shown on the exhibit, to "listen" to students' questions, analyze their meaning, and formulate responses via voice, written text, and other audio/video means. Depending on the educational level, the three-dimensional video image of the "person" responding might be a warm primary grade "teacher" or a scholarly "professor." In conducting "conversations" with pupils, the computer "teacher" will never be cross, unfriendly, or too busy to attend to the student's special needs, thus the objections of those bemoaning lack of "warm and fuzzy" interchange will be answered. Further, the electronic "teacher" will never "put down" a student by saying an answer or comment is wrong. Rather, the "teacher" will use the ideal response,

---

16. Charles D. Winslow and William L. Bramer, *Future Work: Putting Knowledge to Work in the Knowledge Economy* (New York: Free Press, 1994), p. 203.

remarking on how interesting the student's viewpoint is and then sub-tly leading the student to improve his answer by asking questions that point out other avenues of thought.

Another objection to the electronic classroom, the lack of competi-tive incentive provided by fellow classmates, is easily overcome. The student can ask for (or the computer could routinely provide) his rank-ing in comparison to the national, community, and neighborhood achievement levels maintained by the network of community computer utilities. Or the electronic "teacher" may periodically compare the stu-dent's performance to that of her peers either as an incentive or as recognition for a job well done. The achievement recording processor will enter, on each student's data base, performance on the courses mastered, including the time required to complete the subject. Thus, the processor will also maintain the statistics with which to compare an individual's achievement to that of others, through the community "in-formation streets" and national "information highways."

Still, some will object to the loss of interaction with other students, a presumption that assumes that locating the classroom in the home would cause direct contact with neighborhood students of the same courses to be lost. The classmate interaction processor indicated in exhibit 8–2, however, can serve to keep the live interaction going dur-ing common question and answer periods, or during any rest period. It will be able, using the home system's virtual reality feature and the latest telecommunication links, to surround the student with his peer group classmates' voices and three-dimensional images. In a like manner, teamwork exercises, driven by the system's exercise proces-sor, will support nurturing cooperative solutions of problems and management of enterprise operations. The attendance recording processor will keep track of the time students devote to education, at least in early days of operation, prior to having proved that the new system will motivate students to spend more time on education than ever before. Just as the ultimate design of work should cause perfor-mance of labor to be rewarding, interesting, and motivating, the new courses should be designed to make education interesting, entertain-ing, and rewarding. After the system has proved that students enjoy "attending" classes, such attendance monitoring will be deemed un-necessary.

How long will it be until this dream of future education becomes reality? One educator, Mel Munchnik, a theorist in communications technology at Governor's State University, is quoted as follows.

> In 25 years, people will sit at home at their computers, looking at a big, flat TV screen in their entertainment and education center. They will log on. Get a listing of universities. Check courses. Develop a study plan. Register. They might see a counselor several times a year, or consult by telephone or e-mail. The display of information will be enormously sophisticated. There will be high-definition television. Better audio systems. Incredible sounds. Incredible pictures.[17]

Another educator, Dr. Arthur Levine, president of Columbia University Teachers College, opines that by 2050 there will still "be liberal arts colleges and research universities" and that "the rest of the students would go to school electronically."[18] I concur that this should be the norm by 2050, but the surge of change should begin far earlier.

I expect that one of the United States' sovereign states (perhaps one of the smallest) will lead the way in converting primary public education to the private, interactive telecommunication mode. Although the public has the right to expect the federal government to take the lead, this is unlikely to transpire, since most politicians today seem singularly lacking in vision. Several universities will be instrumental in the earliest innovations in higher education. However, the single greatest driver of the reinvention of education will be the proliferation of private firms helping industry and government by developing the material for the new information streets and highways.

PUT CAREERS INTO EDUCATION

The most serious flaw in today's education is lack of career-specific orientation. Basic change is therefore necessary and is bound to be forthcoming. In his prediction about future education, Michael Zey put it like this: "The curricula will be radically different. The subjects will be less theoretical and more practical, oriented toward preparing

---

17. Jon Anderson, "The Global Classroom: New Technology May Mean Never Needing to Go to School," *Chicago Tribune*, October 25, 1994.

18. Reuters, "In 2050, Computer May Be Collegian's 'Campus'," *Chicago Tribune*, November 7, 1994.

students for real careers."[19] On a recent public television program on secondary education, an educator was asked if his school had an adequate program for students who would not go on to college and pursue professional careers. In all seriousness, he answered that his school had an excellent program—they offered classes in auto mechanics and woodworking. This honest but seriously unrealistic assessment of the skills students will be able to use in their nonprofessional lifetime is symptomatic of the gulf so often found between academia and the real world. (Far fewer than one percent of all jobs in which nonprofessional workers are employed are in auto mechanics and woodworking.)

The practice of career training through apprenticeship, once common in the United States and still quite prevalent in Europe, may be a promising response to the abysmal failure of education to provide valuable career preparation. A combination of on-the-job training by prospective employers and synchronized formal education, like that of the typical German apprenticeship program, has the potential for preparing students not simply to perform the required menial tasks, but to bring additional value to the job by acquiring an understanding of the basics of efficiency improvement and the theory behind the mechanics of a job. For example, students aspiring to be medical orderlies, who have access to superb interactive computer studies in health care while they perform the dual roles of secondary education students and on-the-job trainees, will have much greater career potential.

However, even in Germany, which has one of the best apprenticeship systems, the number of applications for positions has fallen so far that in 1993 the number of students entering universities exceeded that of those enrolling in the combination educational and job training programs. Although some argue this is due to a need for increased numbers of university graduates, there is little proof that the number of "blue collar" jobs, as a percent of all jobs, has been decreasing.[20] Rather, the trend is more likely a result of the increasing disparity of lifetime earnings between university graduates and those pursuing the apprenticeship route. This lifetime lock into a lower income level is

---

19. Zey, *Seizing the Future,* p. 234.

20. "Education in Germany: The Next Generation," *The Economist,* August 20, 1994, p. 44.

unfortunate. Vast numbers of individuals with the technical skills to do work that must be done are not adequately recompensed, nor are they provided an opportunity for lifetime advancement through adequate educational programs.

Another proof of the need for massive improvement of industry-oriented education is highlighted by the failure of automation to transform thousands of manufacturing operations into "lights out" factories, operated without human workers. Much of the manufacturing world of the 1980s was caught up in an excessive enthusiasm for the fad of the decade, computer-integrated manufacturing (CIM). At the time, I was considered a hopelessly outmoded dinosaur for resisting the cry for high-tech, computer-dominated manufacturing, arguing that factory organization and management practices were so terrible that giant advances could be made with nominal investments in yet to be proven automation technology.[21] History has proven that the intense rhetoric about computer-integrated manufacturing was misguided, if only premature. For example, R.J. Badham commented on the emerging consensus: "Increasingly management and engineering consultants are emphasizing the faulty thinking that lies behind simplistic high-tech solutions to manufacturing productivity. Emphasis is increasingly placed on the detailed examination of companies' manufacturing processes before, and possibly instead of, computerization."[22] I believe this is because computer technicians are too often uneducated in manufacturing operations and personnel management, thus inclined to solve all problems by computer programming, while factory management personnel, immersed in both factory operations and personnel management, are not sufficiently computer-literate to realize that poor factory layouts and operating methods could be improved by computer programs that are incomprehensible to the average factory worker and manager. Badham also realized this and continued, "Moreover, the 'people factor,' the crucial significance of extensive retraining and difficult organizational restructuring, is now commonly regarded as a cru-

---

21. For reference to more of my thoughts about "computer *inane* manufacturing" see appendix 2.

22. R.J. Badham, "International Perspectives on Computer-Integrated Manufacturing," in *Organization and Management of Advanced Manufacturing*, Waldemar Karwowski and Gavriel Salvendy, editors (New York: Wiley, 1994), p. 311.

cial yet exceedingly difficult component of any transition toward CIM." Still, there are two avenues leading to the solution of the problem. One is to accept the assumption that automation must require routine and extremely complicated human intervention because it is so complex. (Computer technicians are famous for obfuscating basically simple concepts with an outrageous proliferation of acronyms and unnecessarily complex computer systems.) The alternative is to simplify the systems (factory equipment *and* computer-human interface design) to the point of achieving "black box" performance. The latter approach is still so far from coming to fruition that greater emphasis for education and training will be needed in the interim.

Motivation for employers to develop and operate apprentice programs could be provided by tax benefits tied to the number of students in their programs and the ratio of education and training hours to productive on-the-job work. Further, laws enabling employers to pay minimum wages and benefits to the apprentices for the productive work they perform are urgently needed. Incidentally, giving secondary-education students who might otherwise be dropouts the opportunity to earn while learning can be expected to do wonders for helping families keep their children off the streets at the same time it raises family income. And the early development of the rewarded work ethic may do wonders for lifting people out of welfare rolls and into productive work. Nor will future job preparation be limited to vocational training. As previously noted, Michael Zey predicts that "the university of the future will undergo a transformation so profound as to make it probably unrecognizable by current standards." He explains that "the subjects will be less theoretical and more practical, oriented toward preparing students for real careers." "Students will not necessarily be required to spend most or any of their educational career in the classroom," he adds, noting that "George Washington University, and others have already established a program in which students at a variety of locations receive instructions via fiber-optic transmissions."[23] The largest industrial companies can only maintain their preeminent positions if they also recognize and invest in both new apprenticeship programs and continuing electronic education.

---

23. Zey, pp. 234–235.

SUMMARY

In an era in which the continuous rise of public debt threatens the country's financial stability and the ever-declining quality of education threatens the nation's competitiveness, the situation cries out for radical transformation. The technology exists with which to dramatically reduce education's costs and improve its results. Thus, short-term reinvention of education must be a vitally important objective. However, today's backward instructional practices and the need for radical improvement might provide a unique opportunity to begin to transform education, rather than simply reengineer it.

Writers of general and career educational and training software will create innovative and high-quality programs, and enterprises will use the materials in apprentice programs geared to both lifetime career goals and individual talents. Thus, the businesses and occupations on exhibit 8–3 will be among the most dynamic growth opportunities in the twenty-first century. And the various educational and training processors, the drivers of the new electronic topics and administrators of the new home education system, will also be in high demand. New "Learn and Earn" programs which will better prepare young people for their initial jobs will replace old-fashioned apprentice programs and will be used in every private and public enterprise.

EXHIBIT 8–3
Growth Industries and Occupations

Electronic Topic Design
  –Educational
  –Industrial Training

Education & Training Software
  –Interactive "Teacher"
  –Interactive "Discussion" Driver
  –Achievement Monitor

Learn & Earn Training Programs

EXHIBIT 8–4
Waning Industries and Occupations

Industrial Trainers

Teachers & Professors

Government Training Programs

School Building:

– Construction

– Repair & Maintenance

– Administration

– Lunchroom & Library Operations

However, as the industries and occupations listed in exhibit 8–3 flourish, others, shown on exhibit 8–4, will wane and some will die during the next century. For those inclined to feel anxious or offended by the definition of some industries and occupations as waning or dying, there are several important points to keep in mind. These following points are repeated briefly in every chapter, because many readers are expected to read only one or more selected chapters. First, the change may not occur in the foreseeable future. Second, the future continuous reduction of work will be universal. As a result, society must and will reduce average work week hours in order to maintain full employment. Third, the era of reduced work and increased leisure time will be one of unprecedented quality of life and affluence. The electronic classroom will eliminate the need for schools and universities. With the automation of education and training, the need for all but a handful of the world's best specialists in these fields will disappear. The electronic home classroom will provide a lifetime tool for continuing education and for educational entertainment. It will cut the costs of education and training by eliminating most of the positions of teachers and professors. And most of the costs associated with school facilities will also no longer burden the taxpayer.

9

REINVENTING GOVERNMENT

Modern, Simpler, and Better

Government, more than any other enterprise, is ripe for massive reengineering improvement. Its ponderous slowness to react to technological improvements has kept the bulk of its operations firmly rooted in past practice. Thus modernizing and radically changing government processes holds the promise of dramatically more efficient and effective ways of serving the citizenry at far lower cost. Privatization of some government processes, for example, has cut their costs by as much as 90 percent, while reengineered computer processes have more than doubled the productivity of some government employees. The amazing performance of the new "focused factory-in-a-factory" has been heeded in numerous industries and in government as well.[1] The result has been an explosion of instances in which the amount of work required to provide better, higher-quality service has been reduced dramatically. In the public sector, one such example entails the use of interactive computer systems to register "clients" in local, state, and national welfare programs. Whereas welfare applicants in Merced County, California, used to have to make several visits to the human services agency, over several days, a new system

---

1. See appendix 2 for reference to additional material on the focused factory-in-a-factory.

guides the person registering the client through the maze of overlapping, conflicting, and duplicate data required by numerous agencies of the different government levels. Registration is now completed in two visits over two days, and each applicant requires 37 percent less time of the registration specialist. Further, the average caseload handled by each caseworker has been increased by 140 percent. This experience proves that great economies are feasible even in government, albeit more readily in local jurisdictions than at the national level. However, as in industry, merely changing government processes is not enough to realize the greatest benefits. Fundamental changes in the structure of government and its laws are also required.

For more than two centuries, the government organization defined by the Constitution of the United States has served to make this country one of the most successful in the world. In recent decades, however, the structure of government has become increasingly less effective, failing to control its costs, permitting unacceptable levels of unemployment, poverty, and crime, imposing staggering amounts of costly laws and regulations on business, local government, and the population at large, and, worst of all, thwarting the will of the people regarding the timely creation of bodies of law shaped to meet the desires of the majority. For the United States nothing less than a new Constitutional Convention to reshape the organization of government into an efficient, businesslike operation is needed in the *short term*. In the long term, titanic forces of change will increasingly dictate a vastly improved world organization. As Allen Goodman wrote, "the twenty-first century will encompass the longest period of peace, democracy, and economic development in history. The new century will be an intercultural one. The great and transcendent forces of the age—the idea of freedom and the application of technology to make people everywhere both freer and more able to control their environment—*will erode national boundaries and, eventually, the concept of sovereignty itself will become obsolete* [italics added]."[2] In the meantime, however, some basic, elementary solutions to our problems can be developed through methodical examination of the *real* root causes and application of *simple* new legislation to provide practical low-

2. Allen E. Goodman, *A Brief History of the Future* (Boulder, CO: Westview Press, 1993), p. 7.

cost, permanent resolutions. Further, many of the problems can be alleviated through less radical "reengineering."

EXECUTIVE CHECKLIST: SELECTED GOVERNMENT ZINGERS

Government, and the politicians who make up the only body capable of reforming it, may well be mankind's last wilderness frontier. Reinventing government, however, may prove to be the most difficult challenge of the coming century. Government is uniquely *un*equipped to lead the populace into the future, being virtually devoid of any meaningful vision for the next century's individual lifestyles or business operations, let alone for its own operations. That government has continuously increased its share of gross national product is clear. Nor has public spending been cost effective. While taxes have increased, the public infrastructure has deteriorated, the growing armies of public employees are assigned ever more nonsensical tasks, and bureaucrats daily write new regulations that burden businesses and individuals with unnecessary cost.

The following checklists summarize the long-range visions and short-range strategies that may be helpful to both local and national legislators for sponsoring and enacting bodies of law designed to relieve the public and business of the onerous legacy of poor government.

GOVERNMENT REORGANIZATION

Short-Term Tactics and Strategies

1. Privatization of all types of government processes should be used for fast reduction of operating costs and improved service to the public.
2. Every process in government should be analyzed and reengineered in the same systematic way that has been so successful in private industry.
3. A data base of *all* federal, state, and local laws should be created and used eventually to develop a uniform national law to replace similar but different laws in various jurisdictions with one that incorporates the best provisions of them all.

4. Regulations and legal precedents should initially be incorporated in national and international law data bases, but should be reviewed in the light of the overriding nature of a new constitutional law requiring justice over form, and discarded or radically simplified as rapidly as possible.
5. Electronic kiosks, an initial tool for putting the power and speed of the computer into the hands of the citizenry, should initially also serve as voting booths.

Future Visions

1. In an updated U.S. Constitution, justice should be specified as the overriding rule of law. Form and formality must not be permitted to frustrate justice.
2. Privatization of the dispensation of justice will be key to bringing economic sanity and professionalism to the legal process.
3. Government and its laws will be reinvented to be truly responsive to the wishes of its citizens and to guarantee justice as contrasted to strict conformance to the rules regardless of whether the end is just.
4. The power of the modern computer and telecommunications should be used to put direct governance into the hands of the populace. Lawmakers and regulators should propose legislation and regulations, but citizens should vote directly whether to pass or reject them. The information age will provide the tools for voting and for maintaining the necessary understanding of the issues.

CRIME

Short-Term Tactics and Strategies

1. The elimination of currency and coins and universal adoption of "electronic money" (see chapter 7) should be the basis for almost complete elimination of the opportunity for criminals to rob or steal money.[3]

---

3. How soon this comes to pass is debatable. However, pushing the continuous and accelerating growth of the use of plastic money as an important financial institution strategy is bound to cause this to occur far sooner than might be expected. Further insight into my reasoning can be gained by reading chapter 7.

Future Visions

1. The electronically generated fingerprint identification number of the not-too-distant future will eliminate the possibility of fraudulent misuse of others' identities and deny fraudulent access to others' accounts.
2. Modern prison colonies should enable cooperative offenders to live near-normal, productive lives while repaying society and their victims and paying for the costs of their prosecution and incarceration.
3. Genetic engineering will one day be able to minimize or eliminate inherited violent traits and other criminal tendencies. In the meantime, the futility of reforming genetically defective persons may require them to live apart from citizens of socially acceptable behavior.

WELFARE/UNEMPLOYMENT

Short-Term Tactics and Strategies

1. Private apprentice programs, for which employers would receive tax benefits, should be the main thrust of national job training programs.
2. An apprentice's work, other than that spent on nonproduction training and education, should be paid for at minimum wage levels, while on-the-job production should be paid for at going pay rates. This minimum wage will provide some incentive for employers to better train workers through apprentice programs.
3. The minimum wage should be substantially raised through systematic increases *over time.* To do so will increase employment, not decrease it. The result will be lower unemployment and welfare costs and higher business volumes and profits.[4]

Future Visions

1. National and eventually international work-week hours should be set by law to levels required to guarantee full employment.

---

4. I am well aware that this position is likely to be highly controversial, especially among my conservative colleagues. Since I am relatively conservative, it took a lot of study to come to this conclusion. I ask readers to read my reasoning, in a later section, before rejecting this notion out of hand.

GOVERNMENT REORGANIZATION

The world's systems of government and law are ponderously, but with growing momentum, staggering towards paralysis and chaos. I contend that woefully outmoded laws and legal systems—nationally and internationally—are the root of most of the world's social and economic woes. The notion that massive elected legislative bodies, consisting mainly of career politicians and their vast unelected staffs, are capable of managing entire countries on behalf of their constituencies is a centuries-old concept that needs to be replaced. For example, Tony Snow reports several examples of poor congressional management. Chief among these is an excellent example of bureaucracy run amok—*38,000* unelected congressional staffers oversee legislative processes such as those used to process law concerning children's programs which, to endure, "must survive a gauntlet of 52 committees and sub-committees."[5] A better, space-age system would put true control directly into the hands of the populace. To do so could shift the business of government management out of the hands of politicians and bureaucrats and could shift it into the businesslike purview of private industry. However, this will require a radically new body of enabling laws, a reformed government structure and legal system, and new, private, professional government management enterprises.

During televised debates, the week of this writing, Tom Foley, Speaker of the House, and other incumbents had the gall to argue for their reelection on the merits of the amount of federal money (pork) they delivered to their constituencies, something that a new representative without seniority is unable to deliver. As if the voters would be too stupid to understand that there is no free lunch.[6] For every dollar returned to a congressional district, another dollar's worth of pork is being delivered to every other district and it is all citizens who ultimately pay for the largess. The prospect of continuing to govern the country in a congressional organization in which seniority can be used to thwart the best interests of *all* citizens with respect to not only pork but also every other potential legislative act is intolerable and is the

---

5. Tony Snow, "Isn't It Time to Get This House In Order?" *Chicago Tribune,* July 25, 1994.

6. Fortunately, Foley's constituents were intelligent enough to understand how crass this argument was, and put him out of office.

reason that every state in which the populace has voted for term limits has overwhelmingly approved the proposition.

Reinventing Government: Much Smaller Is Better

In the United States, combined community, state, and federal government employment has grown, virtually unchecked, to its present ludicrous size. Most middle-class taxpayers now work almost one-half year before they have earned enough to pay their annual taxes. Lawmakers and government bureaucrats have managed to increase the government payroll despite periodic reorganizations which are touted as staff savings but in reality just move people out of one department and into another. However, a few shining examples have proved that even government *can* increase its productivity and still improve the quality of its services. The accomplishment of the U.S. postal service in cutting total employees almost 25 percent while handling 6 percent more mail, for example, is one such outstanding case (see exhibit 9–1).

If lawmakers were to act in their citizens' best interests, untold programs would be dropped and others never enacted. However, most of the populace doesn't even vote for the legislators who presumably represent their interests. Many, or even most, politicians are obviously incapable of exerting rational fiscal responsibility. Sooner or later this will

EXHIBIT 9–1
Government Can Cut

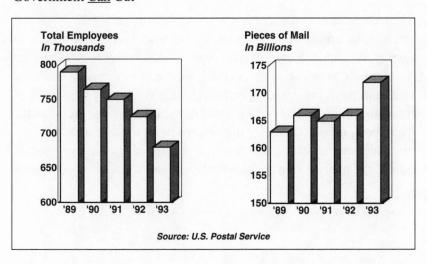

Total Employees
In Thousands

Pieces of Mail
In Billions

Source: U.S. Postal Service

change, supported by the outcome of a new Constitutional Convention in which the two-hundred-year-old government structure will be revised to limit lawmakers' responsibilities to writing proposed legislation for the citizenry to accept or to reject. Both majority and minority parties should draft legislation to be presented for voting by the populace. This will give all parties an incentive to be the one that drafts the best legislation which most accurately matches the majority consensus.

The information highway of the future will make it easy for all citizens to vote on proposed legislation, either from an interactive home system module or at a neighborhood kiosk. (See chapter 2 for more about the home system module.) Even earlier, electronic kiosks such as those recently installed in California will enable citizens to begin to directly participate in the acceptance or rejection of proposed laws and regulations.[7] Putting direct participation and approval into the hands of the populace will ultimately change governance into true democracy. The voice-recognition features of the future home system will make it easy to "enter" votes, and a voter who is uninformed about an issue can ask for and instantly receive an electronic presentation by the legislation's writer and another by the writer of the opposition's legislation. These interactive electronic queries will enable voters to ask for varying degrees of detail necessary to make informed decisions consistent with their desire for overview or detailed understanding.

Reinvented Government: Kick-started by Enabling Laws

The Constitution of the United States set forth an outstanding body of government organization law that has been the foundation of human liberty and rights. However, practical, modern provisions should be developed in response to the crushing burden of government and legal costs and the complexity engendered by the continuous expansion of the law and the findings of various courts. Like private industry, the institutions of government and law have become unnecessarily complex. Industry is solving the problem through *simplification*—reduction of the number of management layers and simplification, stream-

---

7. George de Lama, "Citizens Plugging into Computer Government," *Chicago Tribune*, November 14, 1993.

lining, and automation of processes—thereby increasing the speed with which higher quality goods and services are delivered.

Elective national government, so very appropriate when the representatives of the widespread citizenry had to travel days or even weeks to the seat of government to represent the interests of their constituencies, is now an anachronism. One has only to spend a few days or nights watching government in action, on C-SPAN cable television to understand how inefficient the process has become. Televised committee meetings are largely a farce—an opportunity for legislators to make speeches and then run to their offices, leaving those testifying to wonder what purpose their appearances have. Politicians seem to represent their constituencies at the pork barrel, but have little regard for the interests of the people of the nation in such basic matters as balancing the budget.

In the modern world, it is no longer necessary to elect representatives. The electronic highway will soon bring the voting booth into the homes of the electorate, enabling the populace to exercise the ultimate democracy—direct voting on budget *line items,* tax levies, and other unavoidable, permanent legislation. Further, the populace will be in a position to vote on the acceptance or rejection of private companies bidding to manage essential government functions for two- or four-year contract periods. The proponents of local government must triumph over those in favor of a big government which controls hundreds of billions of pork dollars for dispensation by the party in power and the politicians with the greatest seniority. Far too much government spending is in the hands of the federal government. Only strong local government will permit the populace to operate a real democracy, authorizing the expenditure of their taxes only on those items they approve by majority vote.

Space Age Laws: Creating Order from Chaos

The massive accumulation of laws, legal precedents, and quasi-legal, bureaucratic government regulations grows, unchecked, every day. As a result, the costs of government and justice continue to increase faster than the growth of the economy. Business is drowning in a sea of regulations, forms, and laws far too extensive to allow the most conscientious enterprise to employ enough specialists conversant with all legal requirements let alone to ensure compliance. The sad fact is, the direction lawmaking has taken is to formalize rules for virtually every aspect of public and private business and personal behavior. However, it is almost impossible to achieve this formalization objective. Age-long experience has proven the impracticality of putting a set of words on paper that clearly, precisely, and completely defines the intent of the law. In fact, the interjection of the language of lawyers, to insure specificity, obfuscates the meaning and intent of the law in terms of lay comprehension. Jeffrey Abramson, in defending the jury system, writes, "Law is massive and mysterious, inaccessible to the uninitiated; it takes professional study, not just natural reason, to understand its intricacies and details. Hence there must be a basic division of labor between jury and judge."[8] Thus, the United States economy must support hundreds of thousands of lawyers, paralegals, and other specialists to access and translate the laws and regulations. Even then, lawyers must admit that the law may be interpreted different ways by different courts. Thinking people, uninvolved in the practice of law, readily recognize that the problem is *not* the inability of lay people to access and understand the law. The problem is that the law is permitted to be too complex and should be transformed into easily accessible, simple, efficient, and common-sense language, a situation that would lead to the near-elimination of the need for legal specialists.

Clearly, intelligent computer systems of the future, with two-way voice communication, have the potential for eliminating the need for legal retrieval specialists. Computer data bases of laws and regulations (exhibit 9–2), translated into lay language, will be accessible by every business and home system. Inquiries will be made in everyday language and analyzed by the computer, and synopses of the applicable laws and regulation will be returned to the inquirer. However, the primary need is to mete *justice* logically, not to enable justice to be frustrated by the confusing, imprecise laws or regulations. An example of the rule of law taking precedence over justice is the tragic story of Joshua DeShaney. In this case, the state of Wisconsin child welfare system's officials "failed miserably at accomplishing their true task—protecting the welfare of a child

---

8. Jeffrey Abramson, *We, the Jury: The Jury System and the Ideal of Democracy* (New York: Basic Books, 1994), p. 9.

EXHIBIT 9–2

Law Data Base

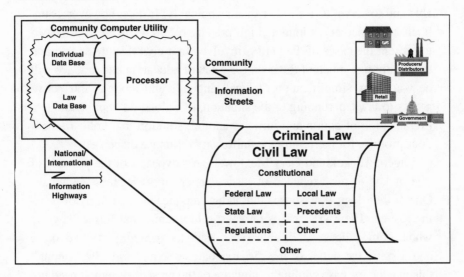

abused by a 'parent who became a predator.'"[9] "Justice was not served by the Supreme Court's stinging denial of Joshua's constitutional claim." Joshua, who suffered permanent severe brain damage at the hands of his father was denied justice by six justices determined to withhold their power to grant redress to Joshua and his mother, choosing instead to base their decision on the technicalities of the law, as they interpreted it.

Further, the formalities of courtroom procedure and the undue attention to form rather than substance have produced a maze of technicalities that all too often determine the outcome of legal proceedings at the cost of justice. A simple constitutional amendment specifying that justice (not the rule of law or technicalities) must be the overriding objective of every legal action will solve the problem. This amendment would minimize the need to rely on precedent and law specificity to decide legal issues and would ensure that logic be permitted to determine legal proceedings, not legal technicalities. Further, massive voidance of existing regulations and laws, on the basis of determining the need for them in light of the new legal requirement for judges and juries to make

9. Eugene W. Hickock and Gary L. McDowell, *Justice vs. Law: Courts and Politics in American Society* (New York: Free Press, 1993), p. 193.

just decisions should be undertaken. Laws and regulations determined to be necessary should then be systematically rewritten to be understandable and to serve justice rather than technicality. Justice, however, is unlikely to be served as long as high-priced professionals are still needed to present the cases of the parties involved in a civil dispute or criminal trial. Although much of the need for years of education and practice will be voided by simplification of legal language and modern, interactive access to laws, pertaining to the situation, this alone will not be enough. Privatization of courts and juries is another solution that holds tremendous promise for increasing the uniformity of justice dispensed.

Eugene Hickok and Gary McDowell are advocates of the primacy of rule of law to the exclusion of justice, as are most legal professionals. One of their logical reasons is that judges are incapable of fairly dispensing justice. They write, "It is unrealistic to assume that former lawyers who become judges will be able to cast aside the mentality of an advocate and assume the duties of the dispassionate seeker of truth."[10] Although this may be the case within the structure of the present system, it need not be true in a reformed legal structure. In a far better judicial system, professional judges, educated and trained specifically as jurists, should be employed by private businesses that run court operations under contracts that are periodically subject to rebidding. If citizens and public and private enterprises refuse to "buy" the jurists' services due to their reputations for dispensing poor justice, the judges would be as subject to demotion, discipline, or termination as any others in private business. Other independent legal businesses, responsible for processing appeals, would provide the checks and balances necessary to insure recourse for litigants convinced they failed to receive justice. However, career jury panels, specializing in certain aspects of justice, would also speed the legal process, help to bring uniformity and expertise to the dispensation of justice, and drastically lower its cost. And radical improvement of the jury system is an urgent need. Brandeis University professor of politics Jeffrey Abramson is quoted as follows: "The average jury rarely understands the expert testimony in an antitrust suit, a malpractice case or an insanity defense. . . . Trial by jury has thus become a trial by ignorance."[11] One addi-

---

10. Ibid, p. 218.

11. Joan Beck, "Practicing Stupid Jury Tricks: Picking 12 People Who Are a Cross-Section of the Population Is a Legal Nightmare," *Chicago Tribune,* December 15, 1993.

tional advantage of a privatized career jury system would be that privatized jurors could have career-long education and training in their fields. Thus the jurors would be relatively expert in antitrust, malpractice, or crime laws and their private companies might lose contracts with some communities if too many of their decisions were perceived as unjust.

Another constitutional amendment that would substantially improve the quality of justice would punish those who obtain evidence illegally, if they have *knowingly* done so, with a penalty consistent with the seriousness of their actions. The current alternative, prohibiting the use of that evidence at the expense of freeing a felon who would be proven guilty if it were permissible to use it, should be voided. At the time of this writing, the defense lawyers in the O.J. Simpson case were arguing for suppression of evidence obtained without warrant, alleging that the police lied about their motives for entering the property. In their summation, it was eloquently and fervently argued that the best way to punish the police was to rule the evidence subsequently obtained inadmissable. Any thinking person must understand that if this evidence were not injurious to the defendant—indeed if it should prove him innocent—he would clamor for its admissability rather than seek it to be barred. One interested in justice should be offended at the notion that barring the use of the evidence is just punishment for the *police,* as their long careers of otherwise meritorious service are unlikely to be seriously affected. However, the *families of the victims* would in effect be punished, forever living with the knowledge that the probable murderer of their loved ones was permitted to escape justice. Justice would be far better served, when police knowingly and illegally obtain evidence, if the law provided specific penalties on the guilty lawmen. Such a provision would be a far greater deterrent to illegal search than to free the offender by invalidating the evidence thus obtained.

REINING IN GOVERNMENT-BY-REGULATORY-AGENCIES

Government's legislative branch has abdicated its responsibility for creating and maintaining the law of the land by vesting regulatory agencies with the power to create regulations that have the power of law. It is bad enough that the regulatory bureaucrats burden citizens and businesses with insane, costly regulations. It is worse that they are empowered to usurp the rights of the courts to ensure that no individual or enterprise is denied the right to be presumed innocent until proven guilty in a court of law. In one recent example of unbridled power and mind-boggling illogic, the Transportation Secretary declared General Motors' pickup trucks with side-mounted gasoline tanks to be defective although they passed the agency's own safety standards and even though some of his own technicians disagreed.[12]

The regulatory power to propose fines for violators of any regulation, whether reasonable or not, is one that should certainly be changed by legislation that would return this prerogative to judges and juries. To do so would preclude instances in which penalties for proven violations would far surpass any logical level of punishment. As the aforementioned *Wall Street Journal* article indicates, the head of the Occupational Safety and Health Administration recently admitted that extraordinary fines were being used "to set an example" because the agency's inspection forces are understaffed and injury and illness rates are rising. This selective and harsh punishment can hardly be deemed fair and equal justice.

PRIVATIZATION: CURE FOR LUDICROUS COSTS OF GOVERNMENT

Can there be any serious doubt that management by government is the most efficient way to waste the taxpayers' contributions? Government operations of almost all varieties are fiscal disasters, yet most politicians seem intent on perpetuating systems in which employees cannot be fired due to sloth, incompetence, or even inefficiency. (Worse, in big cities like Chicago, numerous employees have drawn checks while rarely appearing on the job, and have even held other jobs during the same working hours.) Fortunately, more and more communities and states are discovering the savings possible through privatization of both services and government office operations. The benefits

---

12. Laurie McGinley, "Flexing Muscles: Clinton's Regulators Zero In on Companies with Renewed Fervor," *Wall Street Journal,* October 19, 1994.

can be enormous: When Indianapolis privatized street pothole repair, it was rewarded with a cost reduction of almost 50 percent![13]

Few elected or career government employees are equipped to manage a privatization drive. Their experience and training are bounded by the restrictions of laws and regulations accumulated over many decades, even centuries. However, overcoming the restrictions will be an area requiring the utmost political acumen since enabling legislation will be a vital prerequisite to the best results. Such legislation must free the privatized operations from any laws and regulations other than those to which every private enterprise is subject. In the meantime, every government entity—federal, state, and local—should privatize its privatization drive. Contracts should be awarded to professional private organizations capable of analyzing the government process, reengineering it, and developing the contract offering with which to solicit bids from private companies. Reputable firms willing to spearhead these programs will be more than willing to conduct the program at cost, with eventual profit dependent on the magnitude of savings achieved. Firms that offer these services will have one of the greatest potential growth markets, because the size of government is so vast and the potential for improvement so great. Reengineering of government by its own architects would be folly, since it would be unreasonable to expect the originators and operators of such systems to throw them out and to eliminate their own jobs. Outside, business-oriented productivity specialists will be the logical candidates for the awesome task ahead.

PRIVATIZED RETIREMENT: REENGINEERING SOCIAL SECURITY

Privatization of the social security retirement system is an outstanding example of one way by which an unreasonable government problem might be solved. As most citizens are aware, the pay-as-you-go system worked reasonably well in 1950 when there were sixteen workers to support every retiree, but it will be unable to function in 2030 when the number of workers is projected to be two per retiree. Examination of the system has shown there are tremendous opportunities for improvement.

---

13. Robert Becker, "Big Savings Found for Cities That Privatize," *Chicago Tribune,* March 15, 1994.

For example, a single, once-a-month process of preparing and mailing checks to retirees and other recipients is a costly anachronism. The peak monthly requirement imposes a higher than necessary capacity on both computer hardware and personnel. As soon as recipients receive their checks in the first week of every month, the two million among them who have questions swamp the agency's toll-free telephone number.[14] A far better process would spread the check preparation evenly over an entire month, reducing both personnel and hardware costs. Better still, all recipients should be required to maintain bank accounts into which their payments could be deposited electronically, eliminating entirely the cost of mailing checks and processing checks returned after cashing. And even better would be to put the computer system operations into the hands of private business, which is sure to operate the improved processes at the highest efficiency far earlier and at lower cost than if government employees continue to run the systems.

In the long term, the best solution of all would be to completely privatize retirement benefits, with laws requiring automatic employer withholding and payment of retirement insurance to private companies. The amount employers would be required to deduct from each employee's wages for their retirement accounts would be sufficient to insure financially comfortable twilight years. Such payments could be far less than the sums now contributed by employer and employee and still provide far better retirement benefits. In order to privatize the system, treasury bonds could be issued, one time, to each participating working and retired person in the amount of their contributions (in the case of future retirees) and in the amount of projected future benefits (in the case of those already retired). These bonds could then be held until retirement, earning interest, or could be sold and invested in commercial stocks or bonds in restricted individual retirement accounts. Jon Hull and colleagues describe a similar plan, backed up by a continuing government program to cover indigent retirees. However, they assume that current retirees would continue to receive benefits from tax revenues rather than one-time issuance of treasury bonds.[15]

---

14. Associated Press, "U.S. Planning to Streamline Social Security: Private Business May Do Some Work," *Chicago Tribune,* April 10, 1995.

15. Jon D. Hull, Ratu Kamlani, and Suneel Ratan, "Social Security: The Numbers Don't Add Up—and the Politicians Won't Own Up," *Time,* March 20, 1995, pp. 24–32.

These private pension funds would permit the majority of workers to continue to plan to retire at a reasonable age and enjoy their remaining years should they elect to do so. This would be far better than proposals that include cutting benefits and increasing the retirement age. Nor is such a plan untested. Chile inaugurated a plan in which 14 percent of an individual's income must be invested in a personal retirement mutual fund which cannot be accessed until retirement. There are several such closely monitored approved funds—which now account for 50 percent of the country's gross domestic product, according to Joe Klein.[16] The result has been phenomenal. The average fund has earned 14 percent on the individual's investment, and millions of participants have turned into active capitalists who avidly monitor the funds and switch their investments back and forth to maximize their gains.

PROCUREMENT RATIONALIZATION: STOP PAYING FOR PAPER

As a taxpayer, for years I have been outraged at the prices government pays. Having worked with companies that supply products to the government, I was not at all surprised to read what the government has paid for items such as hammers and toilets. To the uninformed these prices seem astronomical, but those accustomed to the costs of supplying the government readily understand that government specifications, even for these mundane items, are the most elaborate and complex in the world. Proving compliance to the quality levels required and segregating each government contract's inventories and financial accounts have burdened suppliers with unbelievably high costs as compared to those incurred by private enterprise for similar items. Recently the Pentagon announced its intention to switch its purchasing procedures from requiring a waiver to use commercial standards in place of military specifications to requiring a waiver to use military specifications.[17] (This practice is clearly not working—last week I saw a government order for two of my books. The order was three pages, one of which was a list of all of the government

---

16. Joe Klein, "If Chile Can Do It . . . Couldn't (North) America Privatize Its Social-Security System?" *Time,* December 12, 1994, p. 50.

17. Thomas E. Ricks, "Pentagon, in Streamlining Effort, Plans to Revamp Its Purchasing Procedures," *Wall Street Journal,* June 30, 1994.

specifications applicable!) Although the planned simplification of the entire procurement process is laudable, it is pathetic and characteristic that the Pentagon expects procurement costs to increase in the first year and not begin to decrease until the second! Only government would expect simplification for both supplier and customer to increase their costs.

All levels of government, from local to national, need to rationalize their procurement operations to mirror the new practices being adopted by most leading-edge private enterprises. One of the most radical, but most logical, is that of adopting "partners in profits," long-term relationships with single suppliers of a commodity.[18]

CRIME

Crime in the United States is out of hand and becoming more so each year. The prison population of over one million in 1994 is more than double the number just ten years earlier.[19] And, the country's percentage of people in jail (.0455) is the highest in the world.[20] Debates rage over the effectiveness of imprisonment as a way to reduce crime. Increasingly convincing evidence of the link between genetic disposition to violence and criminal tendencies is one factor supporting the need to segregate those inherently incapable of conformance with society's laws. Further, the drug generations of the second half of the twentieth century have given rise to an explosion of drug-related crime, just as the prohibition of alcoholic beverages did in the first half. Armies of criminals now wholesale, distribute, and retail the substances that have led hundreds of thousands to turn to crime to support their sad habit. Stemming the flow of illegal substances has been proven to be impossible, as a virtual tidal wave of drugs continues to engulf the ineffective barriers to their importation. Therefore, a lesser debate is beginning to gain momentum. Some recognize the certainty that legalization and decriminalization of the sale and use of drugs will rob the criminals of their lucrative occupation and enable addicts with a will to change to more readily seek help.

18. For reference to more about these new supplier/customer relationships, see appendix 2.

19. Associated Press, "Nation's Prison Population Now Exceeds Million," *Chicago Tribune*, October 28, 1994.

20. Associated Press, "U.S. Prison Population Near 1 Million," *Chicago Tribune*, June 2, 1994.

The plethora of guns in the United States is one of the factors most responsible for the country's unenviable position as having the world's highest murder rate. Recent tentative steps towards alleviating the problem—bills requiring a delay in buying weapons, to permit a police check, and banning certain automatic weapons—have had little impact in reducing the death toll. The Founding Fathers included the right to bear weapons in the basic law of the land when that right was essential for protection against marauding Indians. And the reason the colonists were successful in casting off the yoke of tyrannical government from overseas was that they were in possession of the arms required to win the War of Independence. Weapons are *no longer* necessary for personal protection, as many weapon-free countries have proven. And the responsibility for defending freedom and deterring crime is now and should continue to be the role of the military and the police, not individual citizens. The United States has a crying need to solve the weapons dilemma and will be able to do so only if the needs and rights of sportsmen, collectors, and hunters to use guns are protected but limited to the specific occasions on which they pursue these hobbies.

Plain, old-fashioned dishonest crime, including such offenses as theft, embezzlement, forgery, and income tax cheating, seems more prevalent today than in a more innocent age in which either a higher emphasis was placed on morality, or it was more difficult for perpetrators to go undetected. The currently popular political cry for a return to "family values" will *not* be the initiative that leads to a crime-free or even crime-reduced society. Concrete, practical steps must be taken to remove most of the possibility for all but the most petty profits for criminal acts by using new and improved technology. For example, elimination of the use of money, described in chapter 5, will be one way in which criminal activity will be harnessed. The tax processors (exhibit 9–3) in the networks of community computer utilities will have access to *all* "monetary" movements, because every future financial transaction will be electronic and will travel through the system's information streets and highways. The tax processors, used to automatically calculate federal, state, and local taxes and to transfer them from business and individual "accounts" to those of the government, will use the system's legality checker processor to routinely detect all but the most sophisticated illegal transactions. When criminal and civil illegalities are

EXHIBIT 9–3

Law and Tax Processors

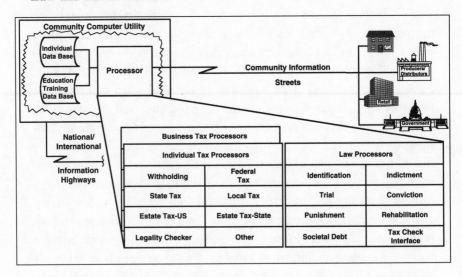

detected, the use of the law processors (exhibit 9–4) could be triggered to initiate investigation and to track prosecution, punishment, and rehabilitation. Awareness that illegal acts will be instantly detected and punished (with loss of wealth due to fines, penalties, and victim compensa-

EXHIBIT 9–4

Law Processors

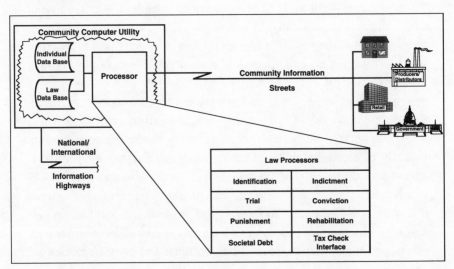

tion) will do more to reduce crime than any amount of preaching about morality. And the new, universal, individual identification system will help to eradicate forgery and crimes such as credit card theft.

The mounting costs of prosecuting and incarcerating criminals contribute to the dilemma of increased prison populations and lack of facilities in which to house them. This results in early release of felons who are ready to return to their lives of crime. The paradox is that large numbers of the prison populations would welcome the chance to work at productive jobs, enabling them to help support their families, relieve the dreadful monotony of idle time, purchase amenities, and improve their quality of incarceration. Unfortunately, competition by public or private enterprises that use prisoner labor is strictly limited by laws in some jurisdictions, banned entirely in others. This situation cries for legislation to liberalize inmate employment laws and encourage private industry to establish places of employment in prisons. Employers could return the difference between inmate earnings and average outside wages and benefits to the government to help finance victim compensation and recoup some costs of prosecution and incarceration.

Print Identification Number: The Basic Key

The world of the future will need a universal individual identification number system. The United States government has used the social security number for over six decades. Today, this number is assigned to infants almost as soon as they are born. However, illegal aliens and criminals have found it relatively easy to obtain false numbers or to illegally use valid numbers belonging to others. Widespread credit card fraud, just one rampant form of criminal activity, will be sharply curtailed as soon as a nearly fail-safe method for identifying individuals is adopted. While researching the reinvention of penal institutions, one of which was the Tennessee Department of Corrections, I stumbled on the fingerprint identification number used widely by law enforcement and penal institutions. As everyone knows, every individual's fingerprints are unique. One company has developed a machine that can read a fingerprint and, based on its unique configuration, assign the individual a unique identification number.

I predict that a lower-cost, mass-produced machine will be in widespread use within the next two decades. Such a machine, at every cash register, could be used to verify the identity of credit card purchasers. Startek, a Taiwanese company, is already selling a similar device which is the size of a kettle. *The Economist* describes the operation of the device:

> A tiny solid-state camera inside scans your fingerprint 30 times a second, and chooses the sharpest image. This thorough sampling lets the system deal with grubby hands. Special circuitry then reduces the image to a succinct digital description of the fingerprint's minutia, the interconnections between its distinctive whorls and loops. This code is then transmitted to a personal computer which checks it against records.[21]

This device is every bit as fast as swiping a magnetic stripe card through a reader and it offers far greater protection against fraud. The development of the additional computer software required to "calculate" the unique identification code matching the fingerprint would be a minor addition to this system.

Such a use of fingerprints may be common much earlier than one might surmise. For example, as Jon Van has written, "In Europe, tests are under way with equipment that puts a person's fingerprint information onto his or her credit card so a device at the point of purchase can compare the card's data to a fingerprint."[22] The machine could be used to detect illegal aliens, fugitives from justice, and parents who abandon their financial obligation for child support.

One not-so-major flaw of my vision is that not all people have fingers, nor do all people keep the fingers they now have. And, while the worldwide number of individuals in this category undoubtedly number in the millions, they still represent a small percentage for whom an "artificial fingerprint" card (or, perhaps, an electronically created fingerprint tattoo) must be provided. A criminal's professional zeal would really be exceptional if he were to steal an artificial fingerprint carrier's card and cut off his own finger or fingers to appear to be a believable card carrier. A colleague identified another hurdle to overcome: Infant fingerprints do not stabilize until age three. One solution might be a temporary infant identification number.

---

21. "Truly Digital," *The Economist,* May 21, 1994, p. 94.

22. Jon Van, "Fingerprint Scans Pose Uses, Abuses," *Chicago Tribune,* June 6, 1994.

EXHIBIT 9–5
Identification Numbers

Social Security	Customer Number
Driver's Licence	Patient Number
Insured's Number	Real Estate Tax I.D.

Finger Print

Credit Card Number	Prisoner Number
Library Card	Retail Licence
Vendor Number	Tax Identification

THE NEW, UNIVERSAL IDENTIFIER

Individuals and enterprises are, today, identified with dozens, even hundreds and thousands of different and unique identification numbers, a few of which are shown in exhibit 9–5. The need for, and cost of, various numbers should, in the world of the future, be eliminated in favor of an internationally recognized number, electronically assigned an individual as soon as feasible and closed by electronic recording at the time of that individual's death. Subsequently, the identity of an individual wishing to obtain a birth certificate, driver license, passport, and the like can be instantaneously verified by scanning his fingerprints and matching them to the individual's record on the tax/law data base. Thus, future criminals will be unable to obtain or use forged, stolen, or fraudulently obtained identification for nefarious purposes. Nor will criminals be able to access others' bank or credit accounts, since small, low-cost fingerprint scanner/encoder terminals will be able to verify the identity of account holders.[23]

Criminals, uncovered through the use of the fingerprint scanner/encoder or other means, who are tried and later convicted will be tracked through the justice system using the same universal identification num-

---

23. Ibid.

ber and the community computer utility's indictment, trial, conviction, punishment, and rehabilitation processors. On-line national and international access to the justice records of suspected criminals will greatly enhance the ability of law enforcement agencies to identify, locate, and arrest offenders. However, when a criminal has paid for his crime and is deemed to be rehabilitated, his record should be removed from access by any other than authorized law enforcement agencies.

DOMED PRISON COLONIES: PRISONERS AS PEOPLE

My dream of eliminating violent crime and criminal tendency through genetic engineering may or may not be possible in the next century. It seems unlikely that people born in the next few decades can be reengineered into more genetically perfect beings. It also seems unlikely that mankind will ever eradicate the human greed and passion that only rarely erupts into violent or criminal behavior. Thus, it will continue to be necessary to punish lawbreakers. The punishments of the future will inevitably be wiser, recognizing the need to lower society's cost of incarceration—especially the cost of imprisoning those first-offenders who would otherwise be productive, valuable members of society.

Future law should keep more offenders who are capable of rehabilitation at their jobs, where practical. It should, however, find new employment for them if their crime had been one against their employer. Financial punishment, community service, and confinement in the home except for working hours would be apt retribution for first-time offenders. Repeat offenders and those inherently violent and incapable of living normal lives need to be segregated from the law-abiding population but in a humane environment designed to minimize the cost to society, and one as close to that of the rest of society as practical. If some offenders, deemed incapable of rehabilitation, against all odds prove themselves redeemable, it should then be practical for them to "graduate" back into mainstream society.

Future prisons should closely resemble the domed communities of mainstream society (chapter 11, subsection "The Domed City: Eden on Earth"). Various classes of offenders should populate colonies of their peers. Sex offenders should live in colonies in which there would be no potential victims, whereas nonviolent criminals might live in colonies in which their families are also permitted to dwell. As in mainstream society, offenders should work to pay for their housing, meals, clothing, and recreation. Pay for such employment, however, would be fractionally less than in the mainstream, since the difference should be used to reimburse victims and repay the costs of administering justice and the oversight of the penal colonies.

The domed prison colony (exhibit 9–6) includes housing of varying degrees of comfort, as would be found in the mainstream. However, housing of minimum comfort would be used for those refusing to work productively and those who violate the rights of their fellow prison citizens, committing crimes of greed, violence, or sex. I, for one, believe that imprisonment should be a punishment of varying degrees of severity, not an enjoyable country club. For the worst offenders, this may still require old-fashioned, high-security imprisonment in cells. Otherwise, an ambitious, well-behaved, lifetime inhabitant should be able to accumulate wealth and live in a style that would reward productivity, honesty, observance of the law, and thrift. By contrast, inhabitants unwilling to conform to the law and those unwilling to work would live in a style consistent with their sloth or misbehavior. Access to the recreational zones of the colony should be used to motivate its inhabitants to conform to the normal laws of society. Withholding recreational privileges might well be one of the colony's

EXHIBIT 9–6
Domed Prison Colony

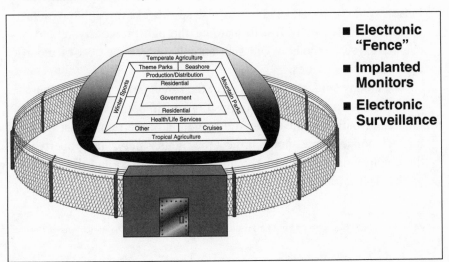

- ■ Electronic "Fence"
- ■ Implanted Monitors
- ■ Electronic Surveillance

most effective disciplines. For the best-behaved inmates, comforts and privileges could be close to "resort" class. However, the worst offenders or least well-behaved should certainly not be pampered as they are in some of today's institutions. Robert Bidinotto has identified several creature comforts that some felons enjoy today.[24] They include body-building programs that strengthen violence-prone felons so that, upon release, they can beat and intimidate honest citizens. (In days past, convicts served hard labor, now they exercise in comfort.) Other activities include watching color television (often in their cells), sports, music, little theater, music lessons, and college courses.

The major differences between mainstream domed communities and penal colonies would be that the dome and/or surrounding "electronic fence" would be impenetrable and travel outside the dome would not be permitted. The twenty-first century "electronic fence" is likely to be an energy barrier rather than a physical structure. Continuous electronic tracking of the whereabouts of every inmate by the use of an implanted transmitting device identifying the individual will be a likely supplement to the "electronic fence." Armored night-vision-capable video transmitters throughout the colony would continuously monitor and record activity in every nook and cranny, guarding against undetected criminal acts by inmates against other inmates or society. Thus, the danger to, and cost of, guards would be drastically lowered. Guards would need to enter the domed colony only if an inmate committed an offense that required outside intervention. Offenses would be as detected by surprise spotchecks through the monitoring systems and by fast-forwarding through previously recorded events. These methods would substantially reduce the cost of monitoring inmate activities.

The colony "citizens" should elect their own government and business "executives" would rise to positions of importance by virtue of their contribution to the successful operation of their enterprises. The inmate "police" force should protect the rights, safety, and property of the colony population, and should be responsible to and disciplined by the elected inmate government officials.

---

24. Robert James Bidinotto, "Must Our Prisons Be Resorts?" *Reader's Digest,* November 1994, pp. 65–70.

EXHIBIT 9–7

Time on Welfare

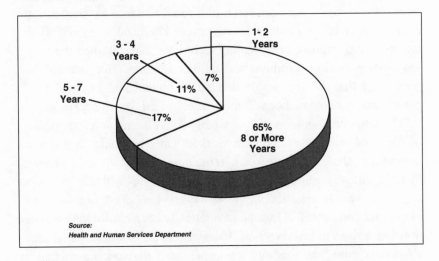

Source:
Health and Human Services Department

WELFARE/UNEMPLOYMENT

No country in the industrialized world has performed as spectacularly as the United States when it comes to creating a permanent, pervasive percentage of the populace unemployed and on welfare, as seen on exhibit 9–7. The ever-increasing percentage of women in the work force has unobtrusively raised living standards for the vast majority of the populace—the middle class—not only in the United States, but also in the other industrialized nations. One need simply compare the modest size of houses and apartments constructed in the fifties with the grandiose dimensions of those currently being built to see monumental differences in lifestyle expectations. In the last two and one-half decades, "the average single-family home (in the United States) has jumped to 2,100 square feet from 1,400, while the size of the average family has declined to 2.7 people from 3.6 people."[25] The number of automobiles, appliances, cameras, telephones, and all other accoutrements of those of moderate wealth has also risen correspondingly,

25. Neal Templin, "Wanted: Six Bedrooms, Seven Baths for Empty Nesters," *Wall Street Journal*, October 17, 1994.

as have the quality and amount of public services in the average middle-class community. However, as the number of working women has increased, to bring the work force into rough balance by gender, production capacity has finally started to exceed demand, as increased automation and improved reinventing techniques have slashed the hours required to produce products and deliver services. Nor is there any possibility that the inexorable decline of mental and physical work performed by human labor will moderate. Indeed, it will accelerate.

The long-term solution will inevitably be an international shortening of the number of hours and days worked. Only by doing so will it be possible to share the little work remaining among all able persons, thereby virtually eliminating unemployment. Nor will the trends to shortened work hours and fewer work days be long in coming—governments and companies in Europe have already been considering legislation and actions in this direction. Volkswagen, for example, had discussions concerning the four-day workweek with its worker's council in the midst of the 1993 recession.[26] As Volkswagen discovered, the seniority-conscious rank-and-file of the labor movement cannot be expected to generously share work with their lower-seniority brethren if it means lower pay for all. Nor would it be just for government to in any way legislate the number of employees a company must have or the hours they work in order to achieve a target level of national employment. To do so might reward companies operating inefficiently and punish those operating with lean bureaucracies. Thus, national and international laws regulating work hours per week for all employees (most importantly those in the highest management positions) would be the most logical way to eliminate unacceptably high unemployment. Better still, dynamic management of the hours per week in reaction to falling demand (potential economic recession) holds the promise for eliminating this source of heartwrenching job loss and economic hardship.

SUMMARY

The cost of government has increased to the point where it consumes a larger percentage of every citizen's income than any other expense.

---

26. Daniel Benjamin, "Giant Under Stress: With Unemployment Climbing in Germany, So Are Social Tensions," *Wall Street Journal,* November 4, 1993.

A portion of government expenditures, such as the costs of bridges, streets, and highways, contribute to higher quality of life. Few taxpayers would object to even greater spending of their tax dollars for still better quality of life projects. However, government has done a poor job of keeping pace with modern technology and methods of reinventing its processes. As a result, the potential savings of taxpayer's funds by reducing wasteful and inefficient spending is enormous. The beginning steps for most local, national, and international governments will be the reengineering and privatization of every feasible government process.

As in every private industry, radical changes in employment in government will be the tide of the future. Replacing computer systems, which generally lag far behind the capabilities of modern hardware and software, and embody the worst of antiquated processes and organizations will be the key to revolutionary change in government. For example, as exhibit 9–8 indicates, today's legal system will be replaced by software systems that will maintain and retrieve new, universal, simplified-language laws and regulations. Virtual intelligence software will permit interactive voice retrieval by *anyone* needing to access the laws, whether the person has legal training or not. In fact, the virtual-reality lawyer software will make a software "lawyer" in-

EXHIBIT 9–8
Growth Industries and Occupations

Legal System:
 – Law Data Base Software
 – Virtual Lawyer Software
 – Computer Management

Privatized:
 – Professional Judges
 – Professional Jurists
 – Welfare Management

Voting System:
 – Voting Software
 – Legislative Software
 – Candidate Software

Fingerprint Scanners

"Electronic" Fences

stantly available to every citizen. The court system also cries out for reform, and the most likely direction reform will take will be to privatize judges and juries, replacing them with career professionals. The same will be true of the administration of new privatized welfare administration management.

Voter systems, interacting with every voter through public computer kiosks or the voter's own home system module will maintain slates and candidate biographies and positions on key issues, enabling voters to become well-informed before voting. Another software system will maintain a data base of proposed legislation and synopses to provide voters with the knowledge necessary to vote directly for the acceptance or rejection of new laws and regulations.

One new product that will represent a growth industry—if a minor one—in the twenty-first century is the fingerprint scanner that will uniquely identify individuals, thereby virtually eliminating instances of identity fraud and mistaken identity.

The net effect of future changes in industries and occupations related to government will be even greater than in private industry, because government is generally much less efficient. Therefore, the losses of jobs in categories shown on exhibit 9–9 will exceed those gained in the growth categories. For those inclined to feel anxious or offended by the definition of some industries and occupations as wan-

EXHIBIT 9–9
Waning Industries and Occupations

Government Bureaucrats

Lawyers

Appointed/Elected Judges

Prison Guards and Administrators

Conventional Prison Construction

ing or dying, there are several important points to keep in mind. These following points are repeated briefly in every chapter, because many readers are expected to read only one or more selected chapters. First, the change may not occur in the foreseeable future. Second, the future continuous reduction of work will be universal. As a result, society must and will reduce average work week hours in order to maintain full employment. Third, the era of reduced work and increased leisure time will be one of unprecedented quality of life and affluence. Government at all levels, the single largest employer in the United States, will see a dramatic employment decline.

10

STRATEGIC
FUNDAMENTALS

The current rage of the business world, business process reengineering, will eventually be another buzzword that has been replaced by another fad. However, every important fad of the past twenty years has had at its roots a common objective—radical revision of processes to make quantum improvements in cost, quality, and speed of performance. This chapter, for example, will identify improvements such as those achieved in a reinvented Lee Memorial Hospital which simplified and lowered the number of organization levels by 44 percent, and Andersen Consulting's "hoteling" office concept which reduced the number of partner and manager offices it requires by 81 percent. Even government has been able to make giant improvements by reinventing its operations. One example (cited in chapter 9) is the Merced (California) county human services agency, which has increased caseworker caseload capability by 140 percent. Such quantum improvements truly deserve the label of reinvention or reengineering!

The problem facing most companies striving to identify truly revolutionary "reengineering" solutions is that few examples cited in books and articles are truly leading-edge ideas, and many are trivial. For example, Hank Johansson and colleagues cite one such process in an unspecified bank.[1] This bank had an incoming mail-sorting process that took several hours, thus delaying the addressees from acting on correspondence. The answer to speeding the process was to use several different post office boxes for different types of mail. By doing so, one simple initial sort of each box's contents would permit the mail to be delivered to its centers of processing. Seasoned executives and managers will readily understand that such improvements are *not* revolutionary or visionary breakthroughs (or breakpoints, as Johansson calls them). Rather, this is a simple technique used by tens of thousands of companies for decades. Seasoned executives also understand that the doing is harder than the decision. In this case, it would have been necessary to notify every customer of the new post office box in such a way that each customer's different, multiple types of mail would be addressed to the right box.

I have found it is not very difficult to identify process improvements—most are fundamentally radical simplifications of existing processes. The hard part is designing the new process in detail, getting people to buy in to it, and devising effective ways to convert from present procedures to the new. Of these difficult tasks, winning buy-in is perhaps the most difficult, especially when weak managements fail to infuse their organizations with enthusiastic acceptance of improvements. Uninspired personnel will too often object to new practices, needing evidence of their proven success. I intend this chapter to be helpful for convincing reluctant skeptics to begin the process of mindset alteration, by describing a number of the fundamental factors that have already molded the strategy of business leaders and proposing some fundamental changes that will continue to alter the world in which private and public processes will need to operate.

EXECUTIVE CHECKLIST: OTHER STRATEGIC FUNDAMENTAL ZINGERS

This executive checklist, like the others in this book, is intended to serve a dual purpose. First, it may be helpful to executives and their

---

1. Henry J. Johansson, Patrick McHugh, A. John Pendlebury, and William A. Wheeler III, *Business Process Re-engineering: Breakpoint Strategies for Market Dominance* (New York: Wiley, 1993), p. 125.

organizations to compare it to the operations (tactics), strategies, and visions of their own operations. Second, for the busiest reader, it summarizes many of the messages of this chapter. Thus, it may serve as a digest, in place of reading the remainder of the chapter, or it may help to identify topics of interest within the chapter that will trigger more in-depth reading.

SHORT-TERM TACTICS AND STRATEGIES

1. Organizations will continue to expand the reorganization of functional departments into far better, smaller "focused" businesses-in-the-business. The best of these will be organized around customers and/or product lines.
2. Simplification and automation will continuously reduce the labor hours required to deliver services and produce products.
3. "Stretch" goals—performance improvement targets set by management and adopted by an entire organization—will continue to be the most important factor differentiating leading enterprises from their competitors.
4. "Benchmarking" and imitating the "best practices" of other enterprises is *not* the route to competitive advantage. The goal is to invent a *new* process, and those who do so will win the race.
5. Enterprises must realize "leanness" in every aspect of their operations—not only lean staffs but also lean balance sheets. Acquired assets should be minimized and as economical as possible, since the organization with the lowest investment should have a competitive advantage.
6. Telecommuting (offices in the home, for example) and "hoteling" (shared offices for personnel rarely in the office) are two approaches that will be important in lowering the investment in and operating costs of offices.
7. Many enterprises vastly underutilize their expensive facilities and equipment—operating only eight hours per day, five days per week. Those that reinvent their operations to lower their investment and operating cost by increasing utilization will have a competitive advantage over less aggressive rivals.
8. The "meat-ax" approach to across-the-board personnel reductions will continue to be a painful but necessary tool for sharply modifying enterprises needing radical action to survive.

9. Business and labor should take steps to lower the costs of business downturn caused by layoffs. A far better alternative would be an agreement or contract to vary the work hours per week for all employees, consistent with the business volume.

10. Enterprise managements need to learn that people are not uniform, therefore performance reward and measurement systems are anachronisms that must be replaced with far better methods for matching people's abilities to jobs and to motivate them based on the almost universal need to have good performance recognized.

FUTURE VISIONS

1. The computer's new "ears" will transform work, leisure, education, and virtually every other aspect of life. They will do so by enabling every person to communicate with it in normal prose.

2. As a result of continuous simplification and automation, the average work week must ultimately be reduced in order to provide employment for all.

3. Imaginative new work schedules will ignore the outdated calendar and fully utilize expensive investments in equipment and facilities.

4. Government will learn how to react to business downturns by timely increases in infrastructure projects, thus trading nonproductive expenditures on unemployment and welfare benefits for productive infrastructure improvements that will benefit the public and keep people gainfully employed.

5. Peak-and-valley seasonal demand can and will be controlled at more moderate levels, greatly reducing problems of maintaining consistent levels of customer service, employment, and business profitability.

6. The growing gulf between low- and high-income people must be drastically moderated. This can occur naturally as a result of better availability of lifetime education and cross-training and by reinventing jobs to increase their inherent value.

7. English is already the language of business in most advanced and developing countries. An improved, simplified language (probably English) will eventually come into universal use. This will facilitate the transfer of computer, automation, and communications technology from country to country and lower the costs of resulting common systems.

FOCUS: SMALL BUSINESS IS BEST

The cornerstone of the new business structure is the development of customer, product, and/or process-oriented focus. The new focused businesses-in-a-business are units created by carving the functional departments of a big company into many smaller units—each with its own functional processes. For, as H.J. Warnecke and M. Hueser wrote, "The problems arising from a lack of communication can be solved by creating small autonomously acting units. This type of organization, which is either product-oriented or process-oriented, promotes the identification of the involved employees with their tasks, and it allows autonomous and responsible actions."[2] As enterprises have grown over time from small entrepreneurial operations into large, cumbersome organizations, two cost-related phenomena have occurred. First, the *direct* costs of products and services have always decreased, as a result of improved efficiencies achieved through higher-volume economies of scale. Unfortunately, the second phenomenon has been an increase in the ratio of all other costs to direct costs. Big business breeds bureaucratic growth and careless use of a company's assets. For example, few small organizations have the large and lavishly appointed executive and managerial offices often found in large enterprises. In a small business, every individual can readily understand that avoidable expenses will, if allowed to occur, lower profitability and competitiveness, thereby jeopardizing the pay and benefits—and possibly even the jobs—of all employees and owners. Small wonder then, that capital costs of office and equipment can be reduced radically (typically by as much as 50 percent) by a combination of reducing the bureaucratic organization *and* downsizing to a permanently leaner, more productive staff. Jessica Lipnack and Jeffrey Stamps described why bureaucracies fail: "*Functional* firms fail when they grow beyond their ability to fully use their special skills and machines. Divisions have a different problem. Typically, corporate executives *force* cooperation across divisions, undercutting the self-reliance and market sensitivity of the business unit."[3]

---

2. H.J. Warnecke and M. Hueser, "Technologies of Advanced Manufacturing," in *Organization and Management of Advanced Manufacturing,* Waldemar Karwowski and Gavriel Salvendy, editors (New York: Wiley, 1994), p. 6.

3. Jessica Lipnack and Jeffrey Stamps, *The Team Net Factor: Bringing the Power of Boundary Crossing into the Heart of Your Business* (Essex Junction, VT: Oliver Wight, 1993), p. 363.

Incidentally, in my first book I described the usefulness of the meat-cleaver approach to business downsizing as it applies to office operations.[4] William Barnard and Thomas Wallace explain why it is possible to make such arbitrary staff cuts and note that "allowing organizations to become over-staffed and under-utilized in the first place points to a deficiency in the decision-making process."[5] And I only partially agree with their observation that "subsequent downsizing with a meat cleaver rather than a scalpel only compounds the problem." I have seen numerous companies solve their problems, although not without some pain, by reducing the drain of excess employees on profitability and gaining time to reorganize into a permanently leaner, more focused organization.

Small wonder, also, that the smallest new business start-ups are those most likely to succeed. In explaining why, of the 250,000 business start-ups in 1985, most of the 175,000 surviving in 1994 were opened with fewer than twenty employees, Dun and Bradstreet economists say, "Larger start-ups are more sophisticated—that means they are likelier to adhere to a precise business plan that calls for terminating [the business] if it fails to meet a specified return on investment."[6]

In large organizations, the linkage between one small department's expenditures and the enterprise's overall success is too abstract to influence daily decision making. In fact, the widespread planning process of casting each new budget significantly higher than the last in order to ensure continuous growth and preserve and increase spending levels is not a sickness unique to government but is a fundamental pitfall of large private organizations. Further, the small organization is usually more agile in its ability to respond rapidly to new and changing customer needs. Everyone in the organization knows that it exists only because customers buy their services. Individuals in large enterprises tend to resent and resist changes—viewing them as disruptions to their routines. When customers request earlier delivery

---

4. For reference to more about the "meat-cleaver" approach to downsizing office staff, see appendix 2.

5. William Barnard and Thomas F. Wallace, *The Innovation Edge: Creating Strategic Breakthroughs Using the Voice of the Customer* (Essex Junction, VT: Oliver Wight, 1994), p. 7.

6. Michael Selz, "For Business Survival, Bigger Isn't Necessarily Better," *Wall Street Journal*, October 21, 1994.

or service, the typical reaction is not to find ways to meet the request but rather to find grounds for refusing it.

The focus solution works in two important ways. First, it restructures the big business with multiple operations in various corners of mammoth facilities and even in far-flung plants into smaller, more compact units. The people and processes common to a product, a service, and/or a customer are relocated into the new, small enterprise-within-an-enterprise. Second, the new enterprise is structured along customer lines, to provide each customer with a communication channel to every aspect of its product and service needs. In recent years, for example, the health care industry has seen the tremendous benefits of focus, in terms of both higher-quality service and greater efficiency in delivering that service. Modern hospitals are disbursing several central services to new, specialized care delivery units. Thus, the orthopedic unit typically will have its own X-ray, laboratory, pharmacy, and supply facilities, greatly reducing the work required to schedule procedures and tests and move patients to and from them. Lee Memorial Hospital in Ft. Myers, Florida was one of the earliest to adopt the Focused Care Center approach. Among other benefits, the number of management levels, from chief executive officer to supervisory/lead personnel was cut from a bureaucratic nine to a lean five.[7] Incidently, most hospitals with central services have long queues of patients waiting for their turn, hardly a way to spare the hospital's customers unnecessary additional trauma.

The new focused organization will have far fewer satisfactory results if people continue to function within the narrow stricture of their previous jobs. Radical changes in the business organization must also entail radical changes in the skills and value of the employees in the new organization. The focused, agile organization, staffed by a lean force of cross-trained and empowered employees, will be more efficient and responsible than today's enterprise. However, the organization can respond to new and changed demand only after it receives notification of it and processes the information. Today's "information street" can make the interchange of demand data lightning-fast.

---

7. William Johnson and Kurt Miller, "Lee Memorial Hospital Records Positive Early Results for First of Several Focused Care Centers, Foundation of Hospital-wide Conversion," *Strategies for Healthcare Excellence.* Santa Barbara, October 1992, pp. 1–8.

THE OVERWHELMING VALUE OF HIGH GOALS

Setting "stretch goals," targets so extremely high that they force an entire organization to expand to the limit of its abilities, is key to breaking the chains of convention and experience. Such goals enable individuals and their enterprises to adopt or invent revolutionary changes to operations. However, too many convention-bound executives and their managers have insisted on past micro-management practices. Doing so involves the notion that by virtue of "measuring" numerous "key performance measures" management can control their companies' improvement progress. As Robert Hall wrote, "No one can pay attention to a blizzard of performance measures. An improvement process that aims for company excellence must have clarity and focus."[8] He credits former Hewlett-Packard chief executive officer John Young as one whose company used a "single and commanding performance driver."

The alluring siren song of "worker involvement," after all, is that management need not play an active (demanding) role, since everyone else in the enterprise will be responsible. It would seem far easier for executives to just sit in their offices reading performance reports and writing scathing memoranda when improvement fails to meet expectations than to have more meaningful direction of the effort and be immersed in the plodding but, nevertheless, exciting process of reinvention. Executive management's first and most important contribution to the reinvention process is to define the improvement goals. Next, management alone bears the responsibility of convincing their organizations that they are serious, and expect the goals to be met. In order to do so, the best executives bring their wealth of experience and qualifications to the reinvention process, contributing meaningfully to the generation of ideas that simplify, speed, and improve the quality of the process.

OCCUPANCY COST: AN UNNECESSARILY HIGH BURDEN

The importance of space reduction, for any enterprise, cannot be overstated.[9] When companies use space lavishly, the space becomes occu-

---

8. Robert W. Hall, "Hallmarks of Excellence," in *Instant Access Guide: World Class Manufacturing*, Thomas F. Wallace and Steven J. Bennett, editors (Essex Junction, VT: Oliver Wight, 1994), p. 9.

9. For reference to more information about space utilization, see appendix 2.

pied with expensive excesses: (1) people and equipment spend too much time moving about causing there to be more people than necessary; (2) the space becomes full of inventory, equipment, and furnishings, assets which have little productive value; and (3) since the numerous costs of occupancy are directly proportionate to the area used, costs are higher by the same percentage of potential space reduction. Wasted space puts nonproductive assets on the balance sheet and increases the costs of operations. Conversely, reducing poorly utilized space can release capital for better purposes and permanently lower operating costs. Telecommuting and hoteling (maintaining shared offices for employees who usually work in the field or at home and only occasionally visit the office) are two means by which enterprises are drastically cutting overhead costs of space occupancy. As reported in *CFO* magazine, Andersen Consulting's pilot "hoteling" design in San Francisco reduced the number of offices from seventy to thirteen.[10] Worldwide, this concept is expected to cut occupancy cost "tens of millions of dollars."

BENCHMARKING: A FAD REVISITED

One fad that burst on the business scene in the late 1980s, benchmarking, continues to be popular. It seems to be the answer to many managements' unceasing search for alternatives to rolling up one's sleeves and going to work on reinventing every possible process to reduce time and cost and improve quality. My own views on the subject were first emphatically aired in my 1991 book.[11] In summary, I saw far too many companies that spent enormous resources to benchmark other companies' processes and, in doing so, delayed unnecessarily beginning to design and implement their own improvements. Worse, the practice led to copying what others were doing rather than inventing even better process improvements. In an age in which the reasons behind the Japanese success were widely published and the subject of countless seminars, it is ludicrous to see enterprises postponing the hard work they must do to improve the processes that have the potential for yielding the biggest return. These processes are easy to iden-

---

10. Nancy Bader, "It's About Time, It's About Space," *CFO,* September 1994, pp. 89–94.

11. For reference to additional reading on the subject of benchmarking, see appendix 2.

tify since they are almost always the ones with the highest operating costs and assets.

I am often queried about my perceptions of the Malcolm Baldrige National Quality Award, about which I am singularly negative. One reason for this is that winning the award requires companies to conduct benchmarking projects, many of which have spanned several months. In trying to explain why companies benchmark, Robert Boxwell has written, "Because it makes so much sense, that's why. Identify the best, study and learn from them; and implement improvements that will work in your organization based on that learning."[12] This would make more sense if a company had no access to consultants and lecturers who already have the desired knowledge and if the company's management were completely unable to identify the processes that need improvement. Fortunately, most companies have one or more executives with the knowledge, talent, and the ability to infuse their organizations with the will to improve in quantum leaps. Companies that have spent the most on benchmarking are those that are the largest, where bureaucratic inertia welcomes studies rather than immediate action.

Nevertheless, I recently came very close to succumbing to arguments that one company was in vital need of a benchmarking project. Executives from this heavy industrial equipment company came to Chicago from India to enlist my help in encouraging my consulting colleagues in Bombay to assist this manufacturer in performing benchmark studies. The pending opening of the Indian market to foreign competition was perceived as an imminent competitive threat by a handful of the company's executives, but not by most other executives and employees. The others, aware that the company had historically had a virtual monopoly in its own country, saw no reason for concern. The far-seeing handful of executives believed that a benchmarking process would help convince their compatriots that the need for change was urgent—that international competitors had superior processes and could offer faster delivery and better service.

Even though I explained my position concerning delaying improvement, the visitors' arguments almost swayed me. Fortunately, I

---

12. Robert J. Boxwell, Jr., *Benchmarking for Competitive Advantage* (New York: McGraw-Hill, 1994), p. 38.

consulted my colleague Leroy Peterson on this case, and Pete jerked me back to reality. The reality is that we are obligated, as consultants, to work with our clients to achieve *concrete business improvements.* It just does not satisfy our objectives to work on "studies," especially when these studies are unlikely to cause the company to make the changes necessary to ensure success. It is more important to deliver implemented solutions than studies that will gather dust on executives' shelves. And we know which processes industries need to work on, based on their potential for cost, quality, and service gains, and are able to implement change with years of experience in accomplishing the necessary stretch goals.

QUOTAS: PEOPLE AND CIRCUMSTANCES ARE NOT STANDARD

Perhaps the single most controversial of my disputatious viewpoints in *Reinventing the Warehouse* was the position that standards (numerical quotas) should be abolished. In recent decades, logistics executives have seen that using standards to measure the performance of warehousemen has substantively increased the volume of transactions handled per person per day.[13] However, the injustice and illogic of standards is so great that it is one of W. Edwards Deming's famous fourteen points. For example, Mary Walton cites Deming's example of the airline reservations clerk for whom a standard of twenty-five calls per hour (while requiring courteous and unrushed treatment of each caller) is used to measure performance.[14] If the computer response time often interferes with the clerk's ability to perform to standard, is it reasonable to use this measure? Should a clerk who masters rapid response stop taking calls when the daily quota is met?

My most eye-opening experience came while working in Japan when I asked my Japanese colleagues why so few companies there use standards. The answers were: (1) People are not standard, so work designed as though they are would be very inefficient, and (2) if detailed standards must be maintained they would inhibit change, be-

---

13. For reference to more material about my views on standards, see appendix 2.

14. Mary Walton, *The Deming Management Method* (New York: Putnam, 1986), pp. 78–80.

cause it would be necessary to revise the standards every time a process change was made. William Pasmore tells a poignant story that reinforces this lesson. The story was told to him by someone who had packed light bulbs for a living.[15] This man's natural human desire to excel, coupled with his better-than-average blue-collar education led him to find ways to improve his work to the point that he was eventually able to pack three times the "standard" quantity, and to do so without breaking light bulbs. Eventually, the industrial engineer responsible for the standard berated him unmercifully and threatened to have him fired because the engineer was no longer able to calculate the costs and determine the amount of daily output using the "standard." The bulb packer reverted to using the standard methods and periodically broke some bulbs to keep his breakage at the historic level! Eventually the plant was closed because it was not competitive with domestic and foreign facilities. My point in recounting this story is one that I have always made since my years working in Japan—standards often stifle innovation and individual incentive!

These examples are but a few of the reasons that standards are poor substitutes for motivation by empowerment and productivity gains through process improvement rather than driving people to work harder. Therefore, every business reinvention project and subsequent continuous improvements should address the twin issues of increased throughput by working smarter and motivation through empowerment. Those who advocate monetary incentives to spur productivity and quality miss the most important point. Although every person would like continuous pay increases, virtually everyone is more naturally motivated by the satisfaction of a job well done, and even more so if recognized by peers and management. And, whether or not the job performance is quantitatively measured, each individual *knows* when the output or quality of the process is better. If not, the process design is defective. The inevitable end result of automation and process improvement in the twenty-first century will be the elimination of standards, and companies leading the way will find that determining how to do so will make their processes better than those of their less enlightened competitors.

---

15. William A. Pasmore, *Creating Strategic Change: Designing the Flexible, High-Performing Organization* (New York: Wiley, 1994), pp. 81–82.

EARS FOR THE COMPUTER: A NEW AGE

Perhaps no single technology will contribute more to freeing mankind from working drudgery than the empowerment of our computers with the ability to converse with humans in normal prose. I expect that software advances in the next decade will begin to meet this difficult but not insurmountable challenge. As soon as this goal has been achieved, the general public will become "computer literate" without needing to become computer technicians. And this will happen without millions of people to having learn the incomprehensible jargon of computer technicians. Instead, the computer itself will convert the natural language of the user to the language it understands. Further, voice communication will reduce computer keyboards to museum relics. Data entry jobs will then disappear.

In fact, crude systems that are able to recognize a limited number of words and prompt the speaker to try again when the speech is not understood are already in use in numerous automated telephone response systems. An even more advanced speech recognition system, IBM's VoiceType Dictation, has been in operation for over a year, at the time this is being written.[16] As the *Chicago Tribune* reported, the user must spend about four hours to "train" the computer to recognize that person's speech patterns. Once trained, the computer is ready to "write" the user's spoken words on the computer screen, using its 32,000 word vocabulary. However, use of the computer to format a spreadsheet or perform more complex tasks such as order entry is still a far cry beyond this technology.

An even more exciting future prospect is that of direct linkage between brain and computer. And although I considered this possibility too "far out" when I first heard of it, subsequent serious thought has led me to an interesting conclusion—that while this is a perfect example of speculation on a matter for which there is absolutely no scintilla of evidence of feasibility, the possibility, though remote, does exist. As McKinley Conway suggests, the downloading of brain to computer and uploading of computer to brain would revolutionize the process of data capture and acquisition, thereby transforming mankind in a way totally inconceivable until we begin to envision the ef-

---

16. James Coates, "IBM Gives Windows Hearing," *Chicago Tribune,* November 9, 1994.

fects.[17] Conway projects the occurrence of this phenomenon in the next three decades!

SHARED EMPLOYMENT: PRECURSOR OF THE ONE-WEEK WORK YEAR

My vision of the future appears, on the surface, to doom untold millions to the roster of the unemployed, no matter what rosy predictions I make about new products and services. However, mankind's fate is not destined to be one of idle poverty, but one of affluent leisure. Far fewer human hours will be spent providing better products, services, and infrastructure, hence far more hours can be devoted to pleasure activities. How, then, can unemployment be avoided? The inevitable solution for eliminating the massive unemployment caused by fantastic improvements in productivity, infrastructure transformation, product design simplification, and automation is to shorten the hours worked. In fact, even today, the fact that society permits nonproductive and persistent unemployment to exist is completely irrational. Any unemployment cascades into additional idling of the work force. Cutting an individual's income to the level of unemployment or welfare compensation reduces spending for goods and services, ultimately putting others out of work. Worse, it channels the taxpayer's money into nonproductive use when it could be put to much better use.

Obviously, whenever the true rate of unemployment falls to 5 percent, changing *everyone's* workweek to 95 percent of normal would be the easiest way to achieve full employment. Employers whose demand volume had not fallen would need to add people to continue to satisfy it, since they would also reduce work hours by 5 percent, thereby immediately taking up some of the slack. Further, the public infrastructure is always in urgent need of repair and expansion. Roads and bridges are in sad disrepair, streets and highways woefully inadequate for the volumes of traffic. And practical, safe, and comfortable mass transit alternatives to single-person commuting and shopping by automobile are virtually nonexistent. Therefore, one early and rapid response to the first sign of increased unemployment should be the

---

17. McKinley Conway, *A Glimpse of the Future: Technology Forecasts for Global Strategists* (Norcross, GA: Conway Data, 1992), p. 16.

automatic upturn of public works. To do so would require every level of government to maintain plans for this contingency—plans designed to accelerate the public works projects that will have the greatest impact on creating jobs. Road and bridge construction projects, for example, create immediate jobs for workers and for the overhead staffs required to schedule, procure, and manage labor and materials. Of greater importance, perhaps, is that the projects would increase demand in several industry segments. Earthmoving equipment, concrete, and steel suppliers would be the first to see the new demand wave, followed shortly by their suppliers. However, for such a scenario to take place is outside of the capability of government as it functions today. For, as Michael Niemira and Philip Klein write of economic cycles, "Moreover [and thought provoking indeed, is this observation], they seem to occur regardless of whether the governments are interventionists or not."[18] However, I hold that the type and scope of intervention has been ineffective, mainly because intervention has begun far too late, usually after the economy has already turned the corner and is beginning to recover. When government is reinvented— putting into place businesslike management capable of rapid reaction and meaningful corrective action of grand scope—the peak-and-valley economic cycle syndrome may finally become history.

Just as obvious as the above simplistic solution to unemployment is the fact numerous difficulties must be overcome before such a plan can be put into effect. For example, reduced workweeks would be disastrous to businesses if they were to continue to pay employees as much as they receive for full employment. Therefore, some of savings from unemployment compensation should be used to offset part of high employee pay reductions. The government should reimburse workers for pay reductions only to the extent that such a reduction would truly impose a hardship. For example, a 5 percent pay cut should be a relatively minor inconvenience to most people, and infinitely better than the drastically lower unemployment compensation alternative, thus government reimbursement might be provided only to those workers at or near minimum wage.

---

18. The bracketed remark is mine. Michael P. Niemira and Philip A. Klein, *Forecasting Financial and Economic Cycles: How to Understand and Predict Changes in the Stock Market, Interest Rates, Inflation, Industries, Regions, Global Economies* (New York: Wiley, 1994), pp. 450–451.

Employers could ill afford to pay 100 percent for 95 percent output if 5 percent of payroll costs plus benefits were equal to two or three times profit. The employer's costs of continuing fringe benefits for the workers who would otherwise be unemployed could be reimbursed to the extent that company shareholders would otherwise suffer losses greater than those of their employees. Incidentally, a company's highest-paid executives and managers should have compensation cuts even higher than (perhaps double) the cuts of other employees. Compensation at the upper organization tiers of many companies has reached unconscionably high levels, thus top management should be able to afford larger cutbacks than the rest of the organization.

A serious impediment to relocation of the unemployed to areas where labor is in demand occurs when unemployment occurs in pockets, often due to large factory closings in small communities. People whose families have lived in the same communities for generations often find it impossible to contemplate relocating, and thus they join the ranks of long-term unemployed. This despite the fact that there are almost always labor shortages in other regions. Even when the cultural reluctance to relocate is overcome by the predominant human will to work, homes in communities of high unemployment cannot be sold or are sold only at distress prices. Thus, permanent relocation often causes loss of a family's single greatest asset—its home.

One quick way to put the unemployed back to work would be to use the equivalent of unemployment benefits to pay the individual's out-of-town living expenses in another community where a suitable job is available, temporarily. If the individual is happy in the new location and is able to sell his home at an acceptable price, such payment would end as soon as the person relocated. Meanwhile, industry and government must work cooperatively to organize permanent, routine practices to locate new facilities and cottage industries in the highest areas of underemployment. When this occurs, residents who have been temporarily working out of town could again return.

One would think that both management and unions would readily see the merits of such a full-employment scheme and rush to put some such plan into operation. The union's rank and file would benefit through elimination of full-time unemployment of its members with least longevity, while management would benefit from the dramatic reduction in costs of layoffs, eventual rehiring, and retraining. In Europe, the need for reducing workweeks has been more readily recognized and government and industry are exploring plans to adopt shorter hours. Volkswagen, for one, won union concessions to cut the workweek to four days by publicly announcing it would otherwise need to cut 30,000 people.[19] However, although this has saved the company approximately $1 billion, the employees lost approximately 13 percent of their earnings. Society cannot afford to force individual companies and their unions to unilaterally cut work hours in order to solve the community, regional, or national unemployment problem. Progressive governments must someday systematically legislate universal workweeks in order to avoid lowering the lifestyles of large numbers of their citizens, including the unemployed and the taxpayers who must support unemployment benefits.

Industry leaders need not wait for the government to put new programs into operation. They may be retired before national governments enact necessary legislation and learn how to manage fast response to developing economic trends. Individual enterprises, their unions, and all employees stand to gain from the practice of sharing available work. Therefore, management and labor, if truly interested in the economic welfare of their business and community, must go to work on new contracts with these types of work-sharing agreements. Local and state governments can also help to ensure the economic well-being of their constituencies if they develop infrastructure programs coordinated with the current local unemployment status.

THE ONE-WEEK WORK YEAR

The twentieth century has witnessed a sensational plunge in the average hours per week worked in industrialized nations—driven first by the mechanical technology that gave one man the "strength" of hundreds and most recently by electronic technology that has given one man the clerical and mental speeds of thousands. That the average workweek has not plummeted even more in the last few decades, as seen in exhibit 10–1, is misleading. Between 1850 and 1950, the aver-

19. Audrey Choi, "VW's Flexible-Hours Plan Could Boost German Competitiveness—If It Spreads," *Wall Street Journal,* October 27, 1994.

EXHIBIT 10–1
Average Workweek

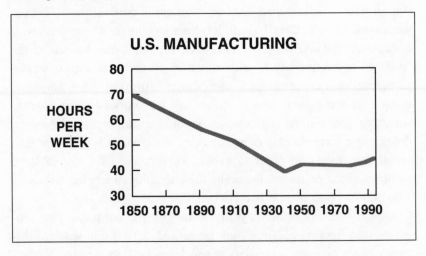

U.S. MANUFACTURING

HOURS PER WEEK — Hours per week

age workweek in manufacturing fell from seventy hours to forty.[20] During the following decades, millions of women have moved into careers outside the home, temporarily delaying the relentless decline by using their earnings to increase consumption. The twenty-first century will see a resumption of the inevitable trend, and will perhaps close with the amount of human physical and mental work required being no more than one week per year per person.

I am not alone in recognizing the inevitable trend toward permanent job elimination. George Church, for example, quotes Stephen Roach as saying, "The labor market is in the midst of a profound structural transition where we are really moving away from the traditional sources of hiring." Church adds, "Into what? A not-very-brave new world in which, even after the recession is a faded memory, no one can be quite sure where the big surge of new jobs will come from."[21] The amount of work requiring human physical and mental labor is perceptibly shrinking and will continue to do so! The current

20. "Workaholics Anonymous: Why Do Americans Work So Hard?" *The Economist,* October 22, 1994.

21. George J. Church, "America's Frightening New World of Work: Jobs in an Age of Insecurity," *Time,* November 22, 1993, pp. 34–39.

worldwide phenomenon of high unemployment is too commonly accepted as a temporary downturn of demand. However, one of the recent drivers of unemployment in the United States has been a drastic productivity improvement in response to the "Japanese" model of lean production. Although the challenge has required leaps of productivity in factories, the bloat of white-collar bureaucracy was the area in which the most serious lack of productivity was found. Now that major companies have discovered the new economies of downsizing business units and operating with lean white-collar staffs, it is doubtful that they will ever forget the message and return to operating with more paperwork processors than production workers.

Before the end of the twenty-first century the world must, therefore, see the dawning of a new lifestyle—one in which the work requiring human participation is so minimal that the only way for countries to keep their citizens gainfully employed will be to ration available work equally to all citizens. The work regimen might then be retitled from "days per workweek" to "workweeks per year." However, human nature seems to cry for activity. Thus, the future will see an explosive growth in enterprises and services providing entertainment, education, and recreation to replace the disappearing work.

AROUND-THE-CLOCK ACTIVITY: INCREASING RETURN ON CAPITAL

Massive amounts of capital investment are permitted to sit idle because of human wake/sleep cycles. Enterprises with low asset utilization need not delay increasing their return on capital employed. It requires little initiative to increase the hours and days per year during which the business operates, mainly by manipulating shifts on which their employees work and the hours during which the doors are open to customers. Many enterprises are already doing this—retail establishments that have recently extended business hours include such giants as "Wal-Mart, Venture, Caldor, Dayton Hudson, Barnes & Noble, and Blockbuster Music."[22] In some instances, staying open longer hours may also be a key factor in increasing market share. For exam-

22. Karen Blumenthal, "Stores Tinker with the Hours They Stay Open," *Wall Street Journal,* October 28, 1994.

ple, eighteen months ago Sears Roebuck & Co. made a decision to keep its retail stores in the Chicago area open until nine o'clock on Saturday nights. Now they find that up to 25 percent of Saturday's sales occur after six in the evening, and the additional sales have been enough to necessitate adding staff.[23] Since many high-volume stores have employees such as stock-replenishment staff and cleaning crews working during the wee hours, it is quite simple to man the cash registers even when the volume of business is not high, because the cashier can do stock replenishment and cleaning tasks during slow times. Many of us, myself included, find that late night and early morning access to retail establishments is one of the best customer services. The low traffic and short lines in the store have made these establishments more attractive than their competitors who do not yet provide the same service.

Employees' wishes regarding unusual hours must of course be considered. Employees are not universally adverse to working hours other than the "prime shift." For example, Bill Arenburg, president of the Columbia Pipe & Supply Co. of Chicago, told me of a recent experiment in which several of his employees elected to work a night shift and were deeply disappointed when the experiment was ended. Without a doubt, they discovered the delight of shopping, going to banks, getting haircuts, and finding myriad other opportunities to enjoy the lack of crowds during hours when most other people are at work. Incidentally, Columbia, a distributor, is frustrated in its ability to improve the cost of delivery by doing so when traffic is almost nonexistent—at night. The problem is that their customers, including plumbing businesses and construction sites, are closed then. However, there is still hope for the future when the managers of the customer companies are convinced of the advantages *to them* of receiving at night. Fast-food restaurants, for example, commonly hire part-time employees to come whenever deliveries are scheduled, and work only as long as it takes to unload the shipment. Every business with the potential for improving the costs of delivery can benefit by arranging such special work hours with one or more employees. Risk of theft, where it is a concern, can be minimized by walling off a limited area for access by the night worker(s) and changing the lock whenever the

---

23. John Schmeltzer, "Saturday Night Fever," *Chicago Tribune*, November 7, 1994.

person with access leaves the company's employment. Especially innovative distributors might even make arrangements with their customers for their *bonded* delivery personnel to be provided access to the limited receiving area for the dual purpose of delivery/receiving, thus eliminating the need for the customer to have an employee present. Even with around-the-clock operation, however, capital requirements for facilities and equipment will still be far greater than necessary if demand is permitted to peak in certain seasons and on certain days of the week.

In my very long vision, artificial sunlight and new energy sources will be used by the future's domed community, as described in chapter 11. This will enable people to vary the daylight hours in different neighborhoods, thus opening new vistas of full-time utilization of expensive real estate and equipment. For example, amusement parks, which have limited nighttime operations, will be able to operate in full daylight for two or three "shifts" of citizens. This will increase the enjoyment of the experience, since crowds on each shift will be smaller, and at the same time reduce the investment currently required to accommodate much larger peak crowds. Further, eliminating the artificiality of the seven-day week, with its two nonwork days, and scheduling different holidays and vacations for different neighborhoods will cut peak crowds and discomfort in every imaginable retail, recreational, or service enterprise.[24]

SEASONAL AND DAY-OF-WEEK DEMAND PEAKS: LEVEL THEM

Before seasonal and day-of-week demand peaks are leveled through future environmental and sociological changes, as described below, businesses need to better manage their present people, facilities, and equipment assets and thus stay in the forefront of the competitive race. One way to manage manpower peaks is to schedule work throughout the year and within each month and week equal to the actual demand. Doing so requires new flexible work schedules which in turn often involve long negotiations with unions. Some companies

---

24. I have addressed the opportunities that industry has to increase asset utilization in previous writings. See appendix 2 for reference to more about work hours and work calendars.

will be forced to adopt flexible work hours in order to stay or become profitable. Volkswagen, for one, wants to vary workweeks according to seasonal demand, according to Chairman Ferdinand Plech.[25]

The domed community of the far-distant future will virtually eliminate many of the natural seasonal phenomena (see chapter 11, subsection "The Domed City: Eden on Earth"), by providing constant, year-round temperatures in its various temperate, winter, and tropical zones. This will be crucial in terms of supporting improved lifestyles, because food processing plants and distribution facilities will be the size required for year-round harvesting and processing and thus require less investment in facility and equipment than facilities sized for once-a-year processing of an annual harvest. In fact, every production and distribution facility and their equipment requirements will be smaller, if bursts of seasonal demand such as that of the Christmas and New Year holiday period are controlled in the future.[26]

FUTURE JOB ELIMINATION

Today, relatively little education and training is available for job-specific skill development or enhancement. In fact, when politicians and academicians talk of retraining programs to give unemployed workers new job skills, they sound incredibly naive. The jobs for which education and training can be fruitful are generally lower-paying jobs for which there may be relatively few openings. Two such job types that come to mind are hair care (beautician and barber) and clerk-typist. In both these cases, the future world will have virtually no jobs to offer. Hair care (one of 143 common job titles listed in exhibits 10–2 through 10–5) is a skill that will easily be replaced by low-cost, powerful computers guiding vision-equipped robot barbers. In-home systems will permit both men and women to "try on" various hairstyles and colors, using virtual reality technology. Their own three-dimensional image will "model" the hairstyles for them. When they have made a selection they will simply tell their system, in normal language (not computerese) that the household robot should proceed to perform the hair care task.

25. Choi, "VW's Flexible-Hours Plan."

26. I have written some tips for leveling demand seasonality in a prior book. See appendix 2 for reference to more about this subject.

EXHIBIT 10–2

Common Job Titles—1

Accounting	Automatic Screw Machine	Chemical/Chemistry
Administrative Asst.	Bakery	Chemist
Advertising	Banking	Clerical
Air Conditioning	Bartender	Collections
Airline	Benefits	Construction
Architect	Biology	Computer
Artists	Bookkeeping	Cosmetologist
Assemblers	Brokerage	Credit
Attorney	Buyer	Customer Service
Auditor	Cabinet Maker	Data Entry
Automotive	Cable	Data Processing
Auto Sales	Carpentry	Dental

As for clerk-typist jobs, progress in computer voice recognition and synthesizing technology will be perfected and, as in all logic-based applications, the hardware and software costs will decrease to the point that every household and business person will have systems that convert spoken input to "written" electronic form for storage, re-

EXHIBIT 10–3

Common Job Titles—2

Dental Hygienist	Environmental	Heating
Designers	Estimator	Horticulture
Dietician	Factory	Hotel
Dispatcher	Financial	HVAC
Distribution	Firefighter	Human Resources
Drafting	Floral Designer	Inspectors
Driver	Food Service	Installer
Editorial	Fund-Raising	Insurance
Education	General Office	Interior Design
Electrician	Graphics	Inventory
Electronics	Hair Stylist	Janitor
Engineering	Health Care	Journalism

EXHIBIT 10–4
Common Job Titles—3

Laboratory	Media	Paralegal
Landscape	Medical	Payroll
Law Enforcement	*(see Health Care)*	Personnel
Legal	Microbiologist	Pharmacists
Library	Model Maker	Photography
Machinists	Moldmakers	Physical Therapist
Mail Room	Municipal	*(Health Care)*
Maintenance	Nuclear	Plastics
Manicurist	Nursing	Pressman
Manufacturing	Office Manager	Printing
Marketing	Operations	Production
Mechanics	Optician/Optometrist	Proofreading
	Painter	Psychologist
		(Health Care)

trieval, and written or voice playback. Thus, legions of filing, clerk-typist, and word processing jobs will disappear. Nor will executives need to be retrained as typists, a skill currently demanded by today's personal computer systems. Alvin Toffler's humorous "dream ad" for a group vice president listed typing as a required skill. However, I am

EXHIBIT 10–5
Common Job Titles—4

Public Relations	Sales	Tool & Die
Purchasing	Secretarial	Transcriber
Quality Control	Security	Transportation
Radio	Service Manager	Travel
Real Estate	Shipping & Receiving	Truck Drivers
Receptionists	Social Services	Typesetting
Recreation	Switchboard	Typists
Research	Teacher	Urban Planning
Restaurants	Technical	Warehouse
Retail	Telecommunications	Word Processing
Roofing	Telemarketing	Writer
Safety	Television	

convinced that progress in the new voice technology will be fast enough to preclude this happening.[27]

Each reader is challenged to review the common job titles listed on exhibits 10–2 through 10–5 and to conclude whether there is any potential for conducting classroom retraining programs that have promise for putting massive numbers of unemployed people back to work. It should be clear that many of the professional job categories—such as architect, engineer, law, and research—require not only college-level training but also the prerequisite aptitude for higher education. Clearly, there are legions of people with no interest in or aptitude for these professions or for higher education. Further, of the other hundred-plus job titles, one must ask whether, having completed classroom or even laboratory training, there are even a few job titles for which hundreds or thousands of jobs are available in any local job market. Unfortunately, the answer is most often a resounding no!

Can classroom (and/or laboratory) training really prepare people to step into the jobs available? How many jobs listed in newspaper classified sections specify "experience required"? In my experience, a vast number of jobs are unique to a specific company, industry, or product. Thus the most valuable training, from an employer's perspective, is on-the-job training. And employers simply have little, if any, interest in training people for whom they have no need.

The messages are clear. First, little will be gained in government programs to retrain unemployed people if the number of available job openings does not correspond to the number of people trained. Training more people than the job market requires can be very demoralizing for those who study conscientiously only to learn jobs are not available. This was the case of eighty laid-off California aerospace workers who spent eight weeks training for jobs in hazardous materials handling. Less than one-third were able to find jobs in this specialized field.[28] Second, the amount of available human work is decreasing. For example, Marshall Burns writes, "fabrication facilities are already realizing hundredfold and thousandfold productivity increases in terms of output per machine operator. While this influence has been

---

27. Alvin Toffler, *The Third Wave* (New York: William Morrow, 1980), p. 179.

28. John Greenwald, reported by James Willwerth, Joseph R. Szczesny, and Adam Zagorin. "Retrained for What," *Time,* November 22, 1993, p. 38.

resisted by large American manufacturers and their unions, there is underway a relentless decline in the amount of human effort needed to produce manufactured goods."[29] Thus, the logical way to achieve full employment is to revise the per-person hours worked. However, it will ultimately be necessary for nations or even global governments to adopt, as Burns suggests, "a global agreement on reduced working hours, causing expanded opportunities for working people and expanded markets for leisure products." And, during the shorter-term transition years, success in reducing unemployment first requires new jobs to be created. The only way for government to directly add *productive* jobs in the economy is to launch public infrastructure construction or maintenance projects. Private industry can be expected to train or retrain new employees as long as demands for their products and services require the workers. However, if the demand is less than required to keep everyone employed, and the objective is full employment, the only logical solution is to cut per person work hours.

VALUING WORK ACCORDING TO WORTH

The difference between a fast-food restaurant employee's wage and that of the chief executive officer of any major corporation is obscene. The indecent difference could be leveled in two ways. Taxing the incomes of the highest earners certainly appeals to politicians crass enough to invoke class envy as a vote-getting ploy. However, the dollars that would be added to the federal coffers as a result of doing so would be relatively insignificant. A far better solution would be to dramatically, over time, increase the earning of the lowest wage earners and expand pay-equity reform. Women and children, as a group, earn far less than males doing work of comparable worth. However, relief is in sight because local governments are taking action. For example, as June Lapidus and Deborah Figart reported, "Minnesota, Iowa, New York, Oregon and Washington have already implemented pay equity."[30] I consider low wages in an industrially developed country to be immoral and illogical.

---

29. Marshall Burns, *Automated Fabrication: Improving Productivity in Manufacturing* (Englewood Cliffs, NJ: Prentice-Hall, 1993), p. 296.

30. June Lapidus and Deborah M. Figart, "Cut Welfare by Pay-Equity Reform," *Chicago Tribune,* July 26, 1994.

If anything, jobs of low desirability should be among the highest paying, rather than the lowest. Who among us would be willing to forego the products and services provided by low-income workers if the alternative would be to increase their wages over time?

Sadly, Congress infrequently considers updating the minimum wage mandate, then enacts timid increases, worried that larger boosts would reduce the number of low-paying jobs. Lawmakers reason that employers would need to increase prices for products and services and this would reduce revenues as customers unable to afford or unwilling to pay higher prices cut their purchases. The fallacies in the logic of anticipating job loss when substantially raising the minimum wage are several. First, the vast majority of citizens (the middle- and upper classes) for the most part would *not* cut back their expenditures for fast food and various services and products provided by minimum wage workers. Further, as minimum-wage employees earned more, they would spend more on, among other things, fast food. Therefore, even if some earners in the fringes between low-income and middle-class wages cut back fast food expenditures because of price increases, other workers whose wages rose would increase their purchases. Still better, higher beginning wages would exert upward pressure on the next higher wage tier. Thus, even these workers would receive raises and would be unlikely to cut their purchases. Additionally, the infusion of higher wages in the economy and increased spending on all products and services would cascade through every product and service industry. The global demand increase would raise both the number of employed and the profits that would reenter the economy though increased purchases and business investment.

Finally, because substantially increasing the minimum wage, over time, could be expected to increase employment, the number of people on welfare rolls would drop and they would join the ranks of taxpayers. The net improvement in government operating expenditures and revenues resulting from increased economic activity could be used either to reduce the deficit or to increase spending on improving the nation's infrastructure. As citizens, workers, and businesspeople, we must begin to demand of our legislators that they undertake reform of minimum wages. To do so will raise average incomes, reduce welfare costs, increase the gross national product and tax revenues, and help reduce crime and drug use.

Nevertheless, the amount of human work required by society in developed nations has fallen and will continue to do so as technology continues its inexorable march. While waiting for this to happen, all human work should be valued equitably and jobs should be redesigned to have greater intrinsic value.

EMPLOYEE VALUE ENHANCEMENT INCREASES ENTERPRISE AGILITY

Massive numbers of enterprises have still not recognized the potential for improving their organizations' efficiency and customer service agility through employee value-enhancement programs. Millions of employees are closeted in narrowly restricted, highly specialized jobs, most of which require relatively little expertise. When customer requirement changes necessitate a different mix of work by these single-skill specialists, the need can be met only when some work long hours, while others are underutilized. When every employee is systematically cross-trained to perform a variety of jobs, people can be moved smoothly from one responsibility to another to efficiently match the shifting workloads. This value-enhancing cross-training should be rewarded by increased pay and benefits, consistent with the tangible rewards of improved customer satisfaction and lower costs of operation. Thus, the employee will be the focal point of two powerful motivating forces—job satisfaction and monetary reward.

Far too much press has been given to "employee empowerment" and far too little to cross-training as its vital prerequisite. It is relatively easy to fall into the trap of believing that simply declaring employees to be empowered will magically create an environment in which titanic improvements will be realized. At a blink of the eye, I could empower my wife to operate my personal computer. However, the net effect of doing so would be nil unless she received training and education in the software basics and their most efficient application to various computer jobs. (It would be an even more challenging job for my wife to "empower" me to cook.) Numerous enterprises have learned this the hard way, having enthusiastically heralded a new era of empowerment in their operations, only to fail to see much accomplished. Empowerment before cross-training and education is like divorce before marriage.

UNIVERSAL BUSINESS LANGUAGE: NEW ENGLISH

Companies headquartered in all industrialized nations will continue to expand their operations into other countries. The biggest players such as SKF, Philips, and IBM have recognized for decades that far-flung international operations demand that management personnel have a common business language. They conduct all business meetings in English, because it has been the most frequent second language of choice in most countries and because English is used as a universal language for the majority of international business transactions and product and process documentation. I deem it likely that an improved English language will eventually come to be the world's first language.

Japan is an example of a country that needs to replace its own language in order to survive in the coming century. What will Japan be able to offer other countries when all nations have very nearly the same manufacturing capability and equal labor costs? It is unable to feed its population without importing about 40 percent of its needs, due to its extremely limited amount of arable land. Nor can it export raw materials or energy—it has none. Therefore, Japan's survival will rest on whether it can massively produce "brain products" (for example, book and movie manuscripts, product instruction manuals, and computer programs). Although the Japanese spend huge amounts of time studying English, the poor quality of their educational material and the absence of ongoing use of the language combine to make them among the least able to communicate with businessmen of other nationalities. In addition to spending years learning the English language and alphabet, Japanese students must learn their own three alphabets, one of which, with its roughly three thousand characters commonly used in daily life, is one of the world's most complex. I believe students in Japan spend more time on reading and writing than any other industrialized nation's students. Therefore, the hours each student spends in school and doing homework are far less productive than their counterparts in the other nations. Since Japan will need a populace able to produce brain products for other nations, the Japanese will need to methodically replace their own language with one that becomes the language of the rest of the world. In fact, as soon as this need becomes clear, Japan, faster than any other country, will rapidly set the wheels in motion to convert to English.

However, the English language is unnecessarily complex, making its mastery difficult and lengthening the time required by non-English-speaking students to become reasonably fluent. For an example of the complexity of English, a comparison to Japanese will be helpful. The Japanese language has a single sound for each vowel, whereas English has several (e.g., the letter *a* has a different sound in each of the words f*a*t, f*a*te, f*a*ther, and f*a*ult). Further, some English words are spelled differently but are phonetically identical (e.g., reel, real, read, red) or have two different sounds for a single spelling. Worst of all, the language is full of irregular verbs. The rules of punctuation and capitalization are another cross English speakers bear. The Chinese and Japanese, somehow, are able to read and write quite well without either punctuation or capitalization. No rational person designing a language from scratch would ever unnecessarily complicate it in these ways.

A new, simplified language, based on English, would certainly increase the amount of study time students can spend on more useful subjects such as science, mathematics, physics, and chemistry. Learning writing skills, after New English is in use, will relieve the student of petty concern for unimportant technicalities found in the "Old" English, allowing the student to concentrate almost exclusively on pithy content rather than frothy form. Most important of all, a simplified language, used universally, will speed delivery of existing and new knowledge to every corner of the world. This will help to minimize the waste that results when people speaking one language are busily working to reinvent a technology that has already been developed by people in another country.

Simplified voice-recognition and voice-generation computer systems will become possible, and eliminating the plethora of strange pronunciation rules and other complexities will be a far better alternative than programming the convoluted logic required to adhere to the existing illogical structure. And the universal language of the future will facilitate using common computer programs worldwide and instantly. Thus, wasteful costs that arise when different countries develop similar systems at the same time can be eliminated. As a result, every country (including those less developed) will be able to adopt new technology more easily, faster, and at far lower cost.

SUMMARY

Most other chapters' summary sections have focused on growth and waning industries and occupations, because I believe that most of the improvements that enterprises must make in the short term, in order to achieve competitive value and customer service, will entail employee reductions which must occur at the same time that quality, service, and cost are improving. If executives and their organizations understand these changes and the reasons behind them, they will be better prepared to pursue the necessary improvements.

The fundamental nature of the subjects in this chapter makes them integral components of all industries and occupations; thus there is no need to repeat these changes here. Monumental and revolutionary changes will turn the worlds of industry and public enterprises as well as individual lives upside-down in the twenty-first century. These changes will proceed apace, under the leadership of the world's movers and shakers. My future visions may be of especial interest to these all-too-rare individuals. However, it is hoped that *every* reader will be stirred to apply the lessons of future projection to today's enterprise operations, and to begin to apply the fundamentals of today's and tomorrow's wisdom to the process of reinvention.

11

REINVENTING
THE WORLD
Distant Visions

The first and foremost priority of every chief executive officer and every management team must always be to focus on short-term profit continuation or improvement. However, if they do so at the expense of visionary planning, they may fail to recognize some of the best opportunities for additional short-term profit and may unwittingly set the stage for disaster should unforeseen changes put their company into the category of dying and fading industries at the very time it is investing in outmoded operations. My colleagues believe that most chief executive officers of the world's largest companies are almost totally uninterested in investing in the long-term success of their companies. Smaller company executives, especially those with major ownership of their companies, are much more likely to invest in their companies' futures. For example, Joseph Engelberger, founder of Transition Research Corp. of Danbury, Connecticut, plans to spend $15 million over ten years to develop a series of household robots.[1] However, most company boards and stockholders demand maximum current profits—which almost precludes investments in future profitability or even

---

1. Chuck Murray, "U.S. Focused on the Wrong Vision," *Chicago Tribune,* October 19, 1993.

business viability. In fact, when I began to implement the use of "Japanese" methods in Western enterprises, it was incredibly difficult to convince most companies to invest in the necessary improvements, although the failure to do so put them on the verge of demise.

The answer to the dilemma of lack of vision is no different today than it was then. All investments must be managed in a way that will closely control the short-term need for profitability while laying the groundwork for far more important future profitability. Thus, I have always pursued the objective of controlling my clients' projects to achieve payback of their required investment in one to two years of operation.

Most reasonably grounded visions of the distant future should not only serve as a strategic road map into the future, they should lay the foundation for immediate actions that can accelerate realization of the vision and shift some of the vision's beginning stages into short-term profit improvement initiatives! For example, the railroad industry seems to be well aware that it has the potential for outperforming the trucking industry to the point of causing long-distance trucking to disappear. The industry, vitalized by this realistic vision, is making gargantuan strides towards its realization. As a result, productivity improvements in the rail industry, over 8 percent per year, were three times more than those in the trucking industry between 1979 and 1992. It is no surprise that these gains are closely linked to transformational computer systems that "link tracks to computers" as Michael Arndt puts it.[2] If I have succeeded in my objectives for this book, I will have directed much attention to immediate cost and profitability improvement, but will have done so in full awareness of the long-term prospects for the subject industries.

The single most difficult barrier to achieving breakthrough future vision is the need to grasp the broad sweep of all of the radically new conditions of future life and business, none of which would be possible without every other new condition. For example, it was impossible for the populace in the early twentieth century to envision the newly invented automobile traveling on networks of paved streets and roads from one coast to the other—the cost of paving such a vast net-

---

2. Michael Arndt, "Rail Workers Feeling Efficiency's Sting," *Chicago Tribune*, February 27, 1994.

work would have appeared far too great to be conceivable. It was also impossible to contemplate because early automobiles were much less reliable than horses. They frequently broke down, and their tires were constantly going flat. Who could have envisioned engineering technology and design improvements that would virtually eliminate breakdowns and flat tires? When it rained, the muddy streets and roads were impassable for automobiles whereas horses were merely slowed. It was impossible to imagine that streets and highways would eventually be paved, eliminating this problem. And, of course, the locations at which gasoline could be purchased were far and few between. What a leap of imagination was required to envision hundreds of thousands of gas stations spread across the land!

Businesses geared to the use of the horse (i.e., harnesses, saddles, wagons, and carriages) failed massively in the early decades of the twentieth century, while those related to the automobile proliferated and grew like wildfire. The changes of the next few decades (and all decades to follow) will be every bit as revolutionary as those during which the horse was replaced by the automobile, truck, and locomotive. Which enterprises, today's equivalent of horse-and-buggy businesses, can afford to ignore the inexorable march of progress as it will affect their operations?

The primary purpose of this chapter is to provide at least one radically different view of the future world along with some of my far-out predictions. These visions may or may not come to pass. The accuracy of the predictions is not the point. My intent is to help break the shackles of experience and free the mind to explore the unknowable—the future. Towards this end, this chapter explores many facets of the infrastructure of the future, including the community, utility services, and transportation. Every enterprise's management should spend at least a few hours "visioning" each year, exploring possibilities not only for the world at large but, more importantly, developing a vision for their own industry and company. Having done so, if they are unable to see bridges back to short-term strategic initiatives, they might consider the visioning process to be complete. However, fortunate managements, by freeing their imaginations through this process, might identify an opportunity for transformational change and their resulting strategic plans may ultimately lead them to become leading-edge companies in new products, services, and processes.

Nevertheless, readers whose sole interest is short-term profit, quality, and service maximization, those who prefer their own visions and are unable to view those of others as thought-provoking, and those who feel offended or threatened to hear predictions about the future that include pessimistic forecasts about their own industries may choose to skip this chapter.

The community I envision for the future, discussed at length in this chapter, will be a largely self-sufficient entity, under a dome that will provide an ideal climate. Those realists who scoff at the notion of domed cities as science fiction should heed the words of numerous leading professional futurists. For example, McKinley Conway recently wrote, "Domed structures providing protection against weather will become key elements of many city plans. New domes will cover not only sports complexes but also entire mini-cities." Nor does Conway view the domed city as I do—as a very far distant vision. He points out that "there's definitely a fast-moving trend toward widespread and innovative use of huge tent-like structures. Made of fabric or plastic and supported by cables, light frames or compressed air, they are already being used to cover a variety of facilities, including sports arenas, air terminals and industrial projects."[3] Further, as Herman Maynard and Susan Mehrtens point out, "The science fiction stories of the past are now becoming reality, and this will increasingly be so as we move forward, our powers of creativity and ingenuity unleashed through the synergism of intuitive and rational mental processes. Only our imagination and our ethical commitment will limit the possibilities of what can be created."[4]

Transport, within and outside the dome, will be almost exclusively by vastly improved, low-cost mass transportation, another fundamental future vision explored in this chapter. And, because nearly all work still performed by humans will be done in home offices and will require only a few hours per year per person, a massive new industry centered around leisure activities will come into existence. Various leisure industries may well be the single largest future business.

---

3. McKinley Conway, *A Glimpse of the Future: Technology Forecasts for Global Strategists* (Norcross, GA: Conway Data, 1992), p. 36.

4. Herman Bryant Maynard, Jr., and Susan E. Mehrtens, *The Fourth Wave: Business in the 21st Century* (San Francisco: Berrett-Koehler, 1993), p. 138.

A common utility conduit, which will substantially lower the cost of bringing utility services and small packages to homes and businesses, is another of my visions described in this chapter, as is home and business power generation, first for individual buildings and ultimately for entire domed communities, another utility-related vision that will lower energy costs and conserve nonrenewable energy resources. The most progressive subdivision developers and community planners will almost immediately put new utility conduits and neighborhood mass transit systems into their plans. In fact, planning for entire communities should be based on integrating business and local utilities with residential areas. Thus, the new, smaller community unit of the future will focus employment, residence, retail and service suppliers, utilities, leisure activity establishments, and public services in convenient compact packages. As a result of the proximity of all of the goods and services and places of employment to residences, the community mass transport systems will be the lowest-cost and most convenient form of transportation. Therefore, the use of automobiles for travel within these new and remade communities will be unnecessary. Although the decline of the personal automobile is almost certainly inevitable, worldwide production is bound to continue growing in the early part of the next century and is unlikely to plunge much earlier than mid-century. Therefore, automotive manufacturers and their suppliers must continue to aggressively improve their product designs and production processes, to lower costs and increase product value.

Some readers, upon learning that I have defined their company's industry as dying or fading, might be inclined to panic and desert the ship, even if that death or decline is unlikely to occur in the immediate or even foreseeable future. I hope to make it unnecessary to head for the life rafts. Whenever possible I will outline strategies for short- and long-term transformation of the doomed industries into winners of the future. Some of my visions may take most of the coming century to come to full fruition. For example, automobiles will eventually become unnecessary, and they may even be replaced by personal airmobiles, if Leroy Peterson's vision comes to pass. But certainly this should have no impact on automotive manufacturing in the foreseeable future and no component suppliers need yet contemplate their demise. However, legions of entrepreneurial executives and inventors (especially those in automotive companies) should get to work on the conception of radically improved, practical designs for the new generation of *neighborhood* mass transit systems and the linkages to long-distance mass transit networks. The automotive component suppliers should view themselves as the logical candidates to manufacture the mass transit system components, and automotive assembly companies should plan to enter the neighborhood mass transit car assembly business.

EXECUTIVE CHECKLIST: SELECTED FUTURE WORLD ZINGERS

The following checklists are intended to meet the author's two objectives for this chapter. The first is meant to demonstrate how some long-term predictions may indicate the need for formulating shorter-term strategies and tactics. The future visions list contains some of the scenarios that I consider to be feasible predictions of the future world. My intent is to stimulate executives to formulate similar or alternative visions as they contemplate a future world in which their businesses will thrive or wane.

SHORT-TERM TACTICS AND STRATEGIES

1. Breakthroughs in lower-cost wind and solar technology, in the near term, will spark an era of home and business power generation. Investments in these technologies today will reap huge profits in the future.
2. An explosion of demand for mass transit in the Pacific Basin, with its populace of billions, is beginning to emerge. Companies with potential to become producers should gear up to share in the huge new Asian market and coincidentally should prepare for a similar future boom in the industrialized Western world.
3. Continuous growth of rail passenger and freight systems as cars and trucks become outmoded will make them one of the best long-term investments.
4. Transportation companies, automotive and rail, should be preparing to capitalize on the expected boom in mass transportation. Every automotive company should establish or acquire a mass transit rail production division and actively pursue the new Pacific demand.

5. Automotive and air travel related enterprises will eventually see a drastic decline of these modes of transportation. They should begin to acquire or establish rail transport businesses if they intend to remain profitable through the twenty-first century.

6. Labor, in industries such as mining, agriculture, and transportation, will be sharply reduced when computer and telecommunication technologies put robotic controls into the driver's seat. Satellite vehicle guidance and control systems will be one of the exciting new growth industries.

7. Agricultural, construction, transportation equipment, and electronic and telecommunications companies' research and development budgets should begin to make heavy investments in computer software and guidance systems that will make human operators unnecessary.

8. Entrepreneurial businesses, especially those involved in polymers and photovoltaic panels, should be positioned to design and market the first small-scale dome systems and building climate control systems.

9. Most utilities' office and field service personnel will be able to work at or out of their homes. And in the longer term, home and business energy generation will reduce required supply from utilities. Thus, utilities' investment in offices and shops will be minimal.

FUTURE VISIONS

1. The future's domed city will entail climate control of the complete environment, not just of individual buildings. The dome has the potential for built-in power generation and solar heat shielding.

2. The domed community of the future, virtually self-contained with respect to its own manufacturing and agricultural enterprises, will have a *neighborhood mass transit system,* eliminating the need for automobiles. Local sources of goods and foods will also reduce the need for truck traffic.

3. Home shopping and direct delivery via an underground tube will further help to decrease the need for trucks and automobiles.

4. Offices in the home will eliminate most of the need to commute to a place of employment, further supporting the removal of the automobile from the urban scene.

5. Hands-free agriculture, requiring far fewer person-hours per acre

and no herbicides and pesticides, will deliver fresh produce to domed communities' consumers year-round.

6. A common utility conduit, carrying all energy, water, waste, telecommunications, and even small package deliveries has the potential for radically reducing the original costs of installing utility services and subsequent maintenance and repair costs.

7. Massive power generation stations are likely to give way to community, individual business, and even neighborhood alternatives. This will cut the loss of power due to long-distance transmission and eliminate most of the costs of building and maintaining expensive transmission lines and equipment.

8. Fast-food restaurants and supermarkets are additional examples of businesses that will undergo radical change. Electronic home and office ordering systems, coupled with lightning-fast delivery systems, will facilitate easier, traffic-free, home dining and grocery shopping.

THE DECENTRALIZED COMMUNITY: EVERYTHING FOR EVERYBODY

Community planning and construction in the United States will experience an unprecedented, explosive growth sometime before the end of the twenty-first century. The impetus for growth will stem from the mass migration of jobs from giant office buildings in mammoth cities to offices in homes in more pleasant, safer small communities. The movement to telecommuting is already underway. Those who worked at home at least some hours per day totaled 7.6 million in 1993, an increase of 15 percent over the prior year.[5] Radical advancement of telecommunication technology will be the factor enabling businesses to further decentralize workplaces. For example, rural Nebraska towns are already seeing high technology bring jobs, reversing the trend of population decline. As Bill Richards writes, "Almost unnoticed are recent census figures showing an abrupt turnabout in the rural diaspora: more than 400 counties whose population shrank during the 1980s are

---

5. Jon Van, "Next Cost to Be Cut: The Office," *Chicago Tribune,* February 13, 1994.

now growing."[6] The combination of high technology and people yearning for a return to the simple life is a potent rural restorer. In Nebraska's case, a network of 6,700 miles of fiber-optic cables is helping to attract businesses to towns where costs of operations and payroll are lower—where many people prefer to work. The businesses that move into middle America's vastness are those like telemarketers, credit card companies, and other service companies able to locate operations anywhere good telecommunications are available.

Further, new clusters of producers and their suppliers will continue to find suburban and rural areas lower-cost, safer sites for their operations than large urban alternatives. Individuals and their families will continue to prefer the quality of life in smaller communities, too, and will continue to migrate outward in ever increasing numbers. For example, the population of the major city nearest to me, Chicago, plummeted 23 percent between 1950 and 1990.[7] The decline, in light of the overall growth of the nation's population during the same time frame, is dramatic. And the rate of decline has been accelerating in most of the recent decades, with decade-end decreases of 2 percent in 1960, 5 percent in 1970, 11 percent in 1980, and 7 percent in 1990.

The population decline of the central city has also been extending outward to mature "collar communities." "It's a continuation of a pattern that has existed for a long time—the decline of the population as people move out to the suburbs where jobs are and there's less crime."[8] Thus, as the population migration continues, an opportunity arises to plan and construct new, ideal communities.

THE DOMED CITY: EDEN ON EARTH

As government becomes more businesslike, community planning will be transformed from an unimaginative, helter-skelter process into a

6. Bill Richards, "Many Rural Regions Are Growing Again; A Reason: Technology," *Wall Street Journal,* November 21, 1994.

7. Patrick T. Reardon, "More Chicagoans Find It Isn't Their Kind of Town," *Chicago Tribune,* November 28, 1993.

8. Sue Ellen Christian, "Leaving City, Cook Behind: Inner Suburbs See Own Losses," *Chicago Tribune,* November 18, 1994.

EXHIBIT 11–1

The Domed Community

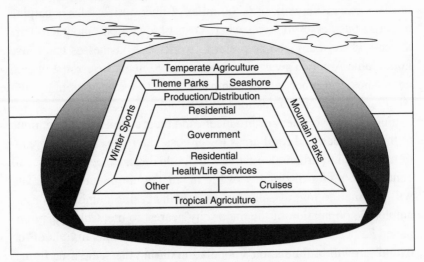

farsighted visionary one, encompassing such futuristic technology as neighborhood inter- and intra-community mass transit systems, common utility and home delivery conduit networks, and community data base utilities. However, sometime before the end of the next century, the most dramatic innovation in community life will be the construction of new domed communities. Exhibit 11–1 is a schematic of my vision of the relatively small but almost self-sufficient domed community of the future.

The residential area, and most of the rest of the surrounding zones will be climate-controlled. The enclosing dome will serve to provide year-round comfort, eliminating the need for individual heating and cooling systems for each home or business. (Heating and cooling manufacturing will thus be virtually nonexistent in the future world. The dome will serve several new purposes. In times of temperate weather, it might be "opened" via ducts designed to filter insects and other undesirable pollutants from the air entering the dome. At other times the dome will insulate the community from unpleasant hot and cold weather. Its new, perhaps transparent, super-efficient photovoltaic cells will gather solar energy to drive the community's heating, cooling, and electrical systems. K. Eric Drexler and colleagues, for example, foresee the development of a paint containing solar-gathering properties, made possible by new molecular engineering and manufacturing. Thus, every structure (or dome) could become a "solar panel."[9] Super-efficient underground storage batteries will accumulate energy during sunlight hours so that citizens will no longer be burdened with large utility costs. And even if it is not completely transparent, the dome will not reduce the community's "daylight." Vastly improved light bulbs, like the system being developed by Fusion Lighting Inc. and promoted by the Energy Department, will increase the amount of high-quality light by 12,000 percent per bulb while reducing energy consumption 60 percent.[10] This artificial daylight will enable various neighborhoods in the domed city to be on different day-night schedules. The advantage of doing so is that areas such as those zoned for recreational activity will be able to enjoy daylight twenty-four hours per day. This will cut the peak crowds in half, thus increasing the enjoyment of leisure activity, and can cut the recreational facility investment required accordingly, because the facilities will have smaller peak crowds to accommodate. Further, spreading energy consumption over both day and night will level the load, reducing the maximum capacity required to meet the most extreme demand. This will also reduce the investment in energy generation equipment.

Nor will large amounts of the earth's limited supply of rainfall be permitted to flow back to the oceans while communities suffer shortages. Giant reservoirs will efficiently collect every raindrop and snowflake that falls on the dome for use by the community's homes, businesses, and agriculture. Community waste treatment facilities will efficiently reclaim sewage and reuse extracted pure water, and will convert waste by-products to agricultural fertilizer. Better still, water and sewage treatment and reclamation may start with mini-systems for each residential building and enterprise facility. Recycling of water, already an important aspect of space flights, could significantly reduce the size of required community water distribution and sewage treatment facilities. Public understanding and perceptions of the qual-

9. K. Eric Drexler and Chris Peterson with Gayle Pergamit, *Unbounding the Future: The Nanotechnology Revolution* (New York: Morrow, 1991), pp. 157–158.

10. Associated Press, "New Light Bulb Seen as Future Energy Saver," *Chicago Tribune,* October 22, 1994.

ity of reclaimed water will undoubtedly need to undergo transformation. For example, Miller Brewing Co. found its $25 million water recycling program in the vicinity of its San Gabriel Valley, California plant to be a potential nightmare. The plant's public relations manager, Victor Franco, was quoted as saying "No amount of information or education can convince consumers at large that this water is safe."[11] However, while I agree that very few consumers will be convinced in the immediate future, long-term prospects of better educated people will overcome this roadblock to inevitable progress.

Workplaces, of which there will be very few in the world of the future, will be in a zone surrounding the residential district. The few remaining workplaces will be mainly highly automated manufacturing and distribution centers, including all of the community's food processing facilities. The community's entire food needs will be provided from the outer temperate and tropical agricultural zones, thus the community will have lower-cost fresh fruits and vegetables year-round, eliminating the need to process and store foods of lower nutritive value and the added processing cost. All health and life services will also be in the zone surrounding the residential area, although the need for these services will be greatly diminished because of giant leaps in medicine and in engineering safer, accident-proof environments in the home and outside surroundings. Thus, the community's mass transit system will carry citizens to workplaces and services in just a few minutes.

Because the components of the community's next zone, amusement, sport, and vacation facilities, will also be domed, they will provide a year-round choice of winter and summer vacation and sport activities. Artificial, lifelike beaches, oceans, and mountains will make daily excursions to habitats designed for swimming and skiing a practical reality. Vastly expanded amusement and entertainment facilities will be one of several vital ways to fill the void created when the amount of work necessary per person will be no more than a few days per year. Do-it-yourself hobbies are also likely to be one way people will satisfy their inborn need for meaningful, productive activity. Home gardening would be my first choice. Others might prefer wood-

---

11. Hugh Dellios, "Brewer Fights to 'Stand Clear' of Recycled Water," *Chicago Tribune,* November 23, 1994.

working or making their own clothing. Still others will spend significant time in home production of inventions, architectural designs, script and book writing. Activities that will permit people to supplement their earnings will help them satisfy another inborn need—the compulsion to achieve greater financial success than their neighbors.

The community's agricultural zone will operate year round, providing fresh produce of all types, regardless of the season outside the zone. Robots and other automated machines will perform all of the work, including planting, irrigating, harvesting, and delivery to the food processors. Complex distribution systems that transport agricultural products hundreds and thousands of miles will no longer be required. Maintenance of agricultural equipment will also be performed by robots, although improved designs and materials will greatly extend machines' trouble-free lives and dramatically reduce the amount of preventive and repair maintenance needed. And since water, energy, and fertilizer will be supplied as by-products of the dome, the costs of foodstuffs will be minimal.

Some of the messages to private and public executives that derive from the vision of the domed community, with applicability in the short term, include the following.

1. Producers of wastewater treatment facilities and equipment should be designing, manufacturing, and aggressively marketing smaller, low-cost equipment suitable for residential and business applications. These systems should not just dispose of treated water and sewage, but recycle them. New suburban community planners should require that developers use these systems, thus lowering the taxpayer burden from large community systems.

2. Manufacturers of photovoltaic panels, plastics, and paints should jointly begin the process of developing new materials and systems with domelike qualities. Initial products would be used as the outer shells of large buildings and, later, private residences. As soon as cost-effective systems are available, a boom in new home facilities to switch back and forth from the electric utility to self-generated power, and to sell and meter electricity to the utility will begin to occur.

3. Computer software and telecommunications for linking small power generation systems and the community power utility will also be a thriving business.

Nor should an enterprising executive's company ignore the opportunity to be one of the leaders in commercially developing the domed community and "bubble farms." If the predictions of visionaries like Conway come to pass, these new forms of communities and farms will be in operation within the next two decades![12]

AUTOMOTIVE TRANSPORTATION: GOING THE WAY OF THE HORSE

The automotive industry is the single most important producer that any advanced industrial nation must protect and developing nations must nurture in order to advance into the ranks of the economically advantaged. The reason for this is twofold. First, the populations of advanced countries use large numbers of cars, trucks, and buses, the production of which requires the largest number of workers of any manufactured product. The automotive industry, therefore, is a huge wealth generator that powers entire nations' economies. In the 1970s and '80s, the Japanese transformed themselves from a low-wage nation into one of international economic prowess. By making inroads into the world automotive market, which had always belonged to American companies, they threatened U.S. economic stability. However, in the 1990s, American companies, following years of arduous improvements in design, quality, and productivity have started to turn the tide, as seen in exhibit 11–2 which shows the worldwide production of American and Japanese companies between 1964 and 1994.

Automotive transportation, more than any other single product, transformed the world from a rural, agrarian society into the modern industrial age. And exploitation of the earth's energy resources made possible the fueling of the internal combustion engine that gave power to this overwhelmingly important product.[13] In just a few decades, the horse, buggy, and wagon gave way to the tractor, automobile, and truck. The world now stands at the threshold of a new transportation

---

12. Conway, *A Glimpse of the Future,* pp. 36–37.

13. Alex Lidow, chief executive officer of International Rectifier Corporation, gave the author food for thought when he ascribed industrialization and national wealth to the availability of energy resources. Upon serious reflection, I agree.

era in which the replacement of the automobile by superior neighborhood mass transit or perhaps by airmobiles (a scenario preferred my
colleague, Leroy Peterson) will begin. In addition, locating producers
and their suppliers where their markets are, rather than transporting
their products to the market, will shrink the needs for long-haul truck
transport.

The industrialized world of the twentieth century has revolved
around the automotive industry. The vast number of jobs dependent
on automotive sales has always been highly visible—when car sales
drop or recover, the entire economies of modern nations quickly follow suit. However, the boom in automotive technology has created serious quality-of-life problems at the same time it has been the driver
of economic betterment of entire countries. The ravenous, gas-guz-
zling machine has been spewing noxious fumes, damaging human,
animal, and plant life around the globe, and rapidly depleting the
world's nonreplenishable petroleum reserves. Automobiles clog the
world's streets and highways and are gradually turning urban areas
into vast oceans of concrete. And many in industry and government
recognize the growing need to harness the outrageous public infrastructure cost and environmental damage the automobile entails. For

EXHIBIT 11–2
Worldwide Production

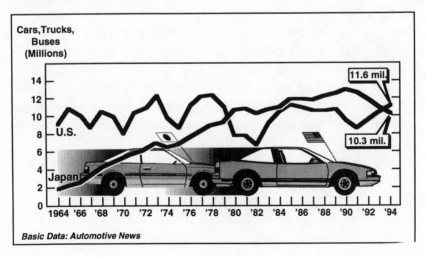

Basic Data: Automotive News

example, John Norquist, mayor of Milwaukee, is a futurist. He sees a need to replace city freeways because, "There is just not enough money to pay for these things."[14]

The eventual (not imminent) decline of the automobile will wreak havoc with manufacturing employment in the coming century, because over 14 percent of all jobs in the United States are automotive related. The new mass transit systems will require considerably less labor, thus few automotive jobs lost will be replaced (even fewer because of increased factory and office automation). Mass transit equipment's greater degree of standardization (every passenger car on the train is the same) will support development of factories with more automation than is currently possible in automotive production. Further, the cars and structures of the new transportation network will have useful lives several times longer than those of present automobiles, further reducing the labor required to build and to maintain them. Under these circumstances, it would behoove the automotive industry to acquire new core competencies in the design, marketing, and production of mass transit equipment and, perhaps, mass transit construction. Acquisition of mass transit capabilities would help to ensure the survival of automotive producers in the next century and increase the speed of construction of new mass transit systems. Therefore, automotive manufacturers would be well advised to build or acquire mass transit equipment production facilities, in preparation for the long-term automotive decline. In fact, at the time this is being written, Fiat's rail division, which already accounts for almost 10 percent of the company's revenues, is a leading contender to supply $600 million of tilting trains to Amtrak.[15] Every other likely bidder is also non-American! By working aggressively on designing and starting production of the future's mass transit systems, the industry in the United States can not only prepare to survive as a revitalized business, but can also help to accelerate the march into transportation's world of the future.

The automotive world should continue to heed the experience of

14. Gary Washburn, "Expressways Are Doomed, a Mayor Says," *Chicago Tribune,* June 13, 1994.

15. John Tagliabue, "Fiat Out to Tip Amtrak in Its Favor," *Chicago Tribune,* November 27, 1994.

EXHIBIT 11–3

Japanese U.S. Sales

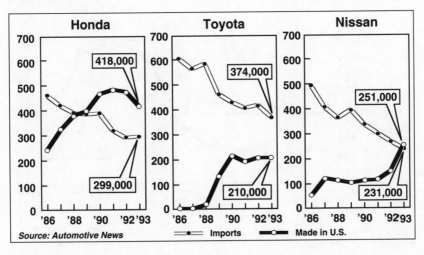

American auto companies in the 1950s and '60s, during which time they expanded their worldwide sales, not through exports, but by producing in the countries in or nearest their market. The Japanese, in the 1980s and '90s, also learned that this was the only viable way to achieve and then maintain market share. As exhibit 11–3 shows, United States sales of locally produced cars of two of the three biggest Japanese automotive companies making cars in the United States were 50 percent or more of their total United States revenues in 1993. Further, this trend will accelerate, rather than decline, because Honda and Toyota plan over 61 percent increases of their combined U.S. production by 1996. Ronald Yates astutely observes that Detroit cannot afford to rest following its recent regaining of U.S. market share, because the newer transplant factories of the Japanese have significantly lower cost due to the younger labor force and tax advantages and other incentives given them by the states in which the plants are being built or expanded.[16]

The nationalization of U.S. production in the 1980s and '90s has not been limited to automotive final assemblers but also involves their

---

16. Ronald E. Yates, "Detroit's Windshield of Opportunity Shrinks," *Chicago Tribune,* October 24, 1994.

EXHIBIT 11–4

Tire Imports

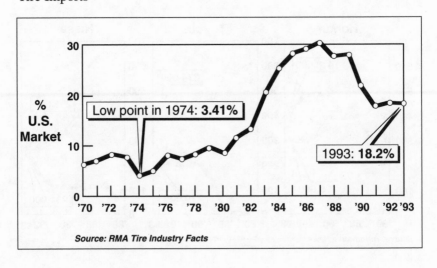

Source: RMA Tire Industry Facts

suppliers. Tire imports as a percent of the U.S. market have fallen 40 percent in the six years between 1987 and 1993 (see exhibit 11–4), largely as a result of acquisition of U.S. tire producers by Japanese and European companies (for example, Bridgestone/Firestone, Sumitomo Rubber Industries/Dunlop, Yokohama Rubber Co., Ltd./Mohawk, Michelin/Uniroyal Goodrich, Pirelli/Armstrong, and Continental AG/General Tire).[17] However, increased U.S. output of tires has not brought higher employment, because tire makers have simultaneously increased productivity, lowering employment by 39 percent in less than two decades (exhibit 11–5). The best strategy for American companies, therefore, should not be to expand present facilities, but to build new smaller, focused ones closer to their markets than those of the Japanese, and to expect their suppliers to establish plants in local clusters.[18] Automotive producers, especially tier-two suppliers, need to work much harder at reinventing their manufacturing and office process flows. As Don Wingard, Andersen Consulting partner, noted, an An-

17. Stephen Franklin, "Union vs. Tiremakers: Wearing Battle Gets Down to Rules of Road for Both," *Chicago Tribune,* October 23, 1994.

18. For reference to more about smaller focused factories and regional clusters, see appendix 2.

EXHIBIT 11–5

Tire Maker Employees (000's)

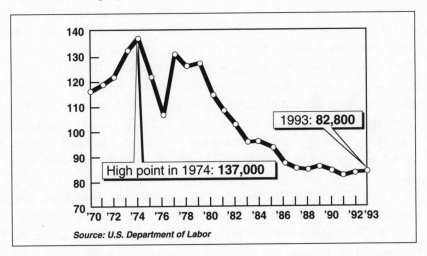

Source: U.S. Department of Labor

dersen Consulting worldwide study of auto parts makers found that the tier-two suppliers of U.S. companies had defect rates seven times higher than Japanese companies, although U.S. tier-one plants are very close to achieving quality parity.[19] And, worldwide, of seventy-one automotive plants surveyed in this study, only thirteen were rated as world-class.

NEIGHBORHOOD MASS TRANSIT: DISNEYLAND REVISITED

There will be no place for the automobile in the domed city of the future! Mankind, especially in the United States, will come to realize that vastly improved mass transit, designed for near optimal convenience, can be far superior to the automobile. As Philip Kotler and colleagues write, "From the provider's vantage point, mass transit can be less costly than expanding and maintaining road systems; it also provides environmental benefits through cleaner air, more trees and

19. Jim Mateja, "A Big Gap Among Makers of Auto Parts, Study Finds," *Chicago Tribune,* November 4, 1994.

open spaces, and less concrete."[20] The cost and benefits are even greater when mass transit networks include the small neighborhood systems described here. One problem with almost all existing local rail transit is that it does not provide stations conveniently near citizens' doorways and close to all of their travel destinations. (I reject the notion that bus mass transit will ever be popular. Buses jerk from start to stop, have uncomfortable, small seats, travel slowly—paced by other automotive traffic and traffic lights—and are crowded, expensive, and smelly.) The error common in the design of virtually all rail mass transit systems is the assumption that they must carry large numbers of people in order to be cost effective. Often, this conclusion has been driven, in part, by the assumption that trains must be operated by humans. The neighborhood mass transit system of the future, illustrated by exhibit 11–6, will address these design flaws. For example, the Disneyland-like transit cars will be small, and neighborhood trains will contain only as many cars as warranted by the amount of traffic. The system may be elevated, allowing foot and vehicle traffic below it, while minimizing the area occupied and its cost. The cars can be as comfortable as luxury automobiles and virtually dedicated to the person or group traveling from one point to another. For example, the rider might talk to the "traffic controller" (interactive voice-communication computer) on the train platform, telling it his destination station. The next empty car about to pass the station, or a car stopping to let passengers exit, would be assigned to the rider, and would bypass stops at stations between the start of his trip and its end, except for picking up passengers with the same destination, if the car had adequate space.

The regional mass transit system (exhibit 11–7), shows how the small-scale neighborhood lines will intersect and share transfer stations with larger express lines which will carry traffic between neighborhoods within the domed city and to other even larger-scale systems used to transport passengers between national and continental communities. The neighborhood stations on the exhibit would be close together, rarely requiring people to walk more than a block or two to the nearest station. The savings of these lines can be monumental. Citi-

---

20. Philip Kotler, Donald H. Haider, and Irving Rein, *Marketing Places: Attracting Investment, Industry and Tourism to Cities, States and Nations* (New York: Free Press, 1993), p. 113.

EXHIBIT 11–6
Neighborhood Mass Transit

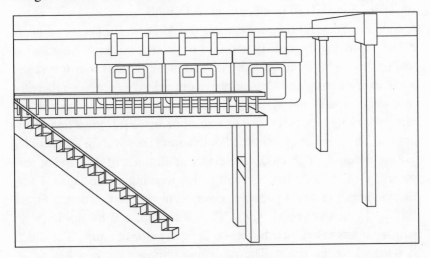

zens will no longer need to invest in their family private automobiles
and pay to fuel and maintain them. The neighborhood line will require
far smaller capital investment than the aggregate total of automobiles
for every neighborhood family, much less maintenance, far fewer re-
placements due to wear and tear, and less energy. Further, the commu-

EXHIBIT 11–7
Regional Mass Transit

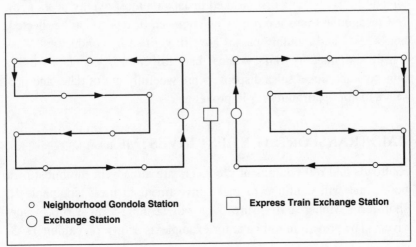

○ **Neighborhood Gondola Station**   ▢ **Express Train Exchange Station**
◯ **Exchange Station**

nity will enjoy pollution-free air and virtually no traffic accident injuries and deaths. Little wonder that I am heavily invested in rail transportation and rail product manufacturing!

While waiting for the future, there should be no slackening of interest in improving the quality and cost of present systems. Automation and process reengineering offer city and intercity mass transit systems ways to trim costs and thus attract more riders. Chicago's relatively new intra-airport train system, which operates between terminals and remote parking lots, is just one example of a driverless mass transit operation. The number of trains and number of cars per train are flexible, giving uniformly high customer service at all times of day, and at reasonable cost. And during my most recent working trip to Japan, I saw that thousands of ticket-puncher personnel have been taken out of their subway system in recent years. They were replaced by machines in which patrons insert their tickets on the entry side of a turnstile, which is released by the ticket. The passenger retrieves the punched ticket after passing through the turnstile. At the end of the trip, a similar machine checks the ticket to make sure the passenger has paid for the correct number of stations. The passenger is passed through the turnstile if the ticket is correct. Otherwise, a displayed message directs the passenger to a fare-paying window. These systems are not new, but are not yet in use in every mass transit system. For example, when I make one of my rare trips to downtown Chicago on the Regional Transit Authority train, I buy tickets at a manned window (or tokens from a machine). Ticket vending machines are not used (although such machines were already in use when I first worked in Japan almost twenty years ago). In Chicago the trains are run by an engineer, tickets are still collected, and weekly and monthly passes are still verified by conductors. Mass transit and intercity rail systems that still employ people as ticket punchers and ticket sales dispensers are woefully out of date, and present a major opportunity for improvement.

RAIL TRANSPORT: THE BEST INVESTMENT

Railroads and rail equipment producers are already in the midst of a boom that will continue to make investment in these companies a short-term winner and ensure they will be long-term earnings survivors. The growth in rail cars, for example, is shown on exhibit 11–8.

EXHIBIT 11–8
New Rail Cars

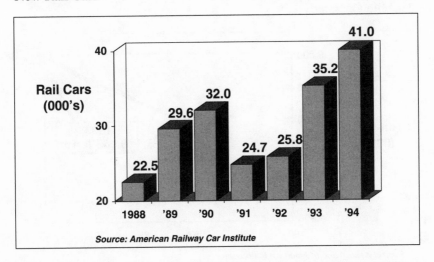

Source: American Railway Car Institute

Not only the new community people movers and intercommunity trains, but also high-speed intercity trains and freight traffic can be expected to boom in the twenty-first century. The impetus for growth stems from the railroads beating long distance trucking costs by 40 percent, and at the same time increasing both the efficiency and scheduling precision of existing operations and the amount of inter-modal freight. And the more than 20 percent growth in the ten years between 1983 and 1993 (see exhibit 11–9) is only a minor indication of things to come, as the predicted decentralization of communities increases the need for better intercity connections. As improved passenger networks and high-speed trains evolve and as leisure time soars, passenger mileage can also be expected to increase.

The increase in rail ton-miles has already caused a corresponding boom in new railcar production, which has increased by over 82 percent in the six years between 1988 and 1994 (exhibit 11–8). And every other supplier of railroad equipment has had the opportunity to hitch its caboose to the dependable-growth locomotive of its customers. Anticipated growth of high-speed rail transport in the United States can also be expected to dramatically increase the amount of crossing equipment, because present rail systems have so many crossings not yet protected with automatic gates and light warning

EXHIBIT 11–9
Rail Ton-Miles
Per Mile Operated

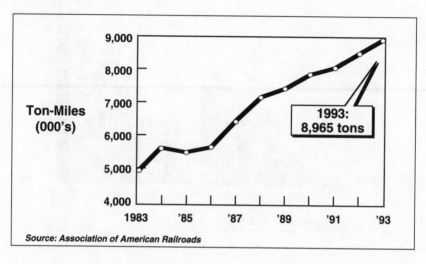

Source: Association of American Railroads

systems.[21] However, railroad and railway suppliers must duplicate and better the productivity achievements of their customers in the segmented competition now fighting for supremacy. The ABC Rail Products Corporation, maker of switches and crossover tracks, is one company that saw the writing on the wall (or red ink on the operating statement) and began to come to agreement with their union on forming teams to design quality and productivity improvements and with their vendors on tighter quality specifications and just-in-time delivery.[22] The need for the most basic improvements, just-in-time, for example, is far from being satisfied. Therefore, the basics must be part and parcel of reinventing or reengineering manufacturing operations.

Finally, continuing developments in the design of tomorrow's high-speed train, "known as *maglev* . . . from the words *magnetic* and *levitation*" promise eventual speeds in excess of four hundred miles

21. Stanley Ziemba, "Train from Spain Fit for Plains," *Chicago Tribune,* November 27, 1994.

22. John M. Maclean, "Rail Equipment Company Learns ABCs of Success: With Doom Barreling Down, Management, Workers Switch Tracks," *Chicago Tribune,* November 6, 1994.

per hour.[23] As Michael Zey says, "At that speed, this mode of transportation will challenge current aviation technology for cross-continental and regional travel and freight transportation." The even greater future boom in large-scale rail transportation should give even greater motivation for present producers and for others such as the automotive industry to make investments to stay or become one of the eminent players in an exciting new era.

AIR TRANSPORT: JOINING THE HORSE AND BUGGY?

The twentieth century was the age of the automobile and airplane. The twenty-first century is almost certain to see the decline of the automobile, as much more comfortable and lower-cost neighborhood mass rail transportation and high-speed long-distance trains proliferate. Now the question is, what does the future hold for air travel? Three major developments will impact air travel. The first is vastly improved video telecommunications, which will virtually eliminate the need for almost all business travel (see chapter 3, subsection "Video Teleconference: Attending in Virtual Reality"). Most business travel in the United States is by air, and far fewer businesspeople will be flying. Secondly, the far shorter work hours that stem from automation of most factory and office work will greatly expand the opportunities for leisure travel, the overseas portion of which is likely to continue to be by air (see chapter 1, subsection "Future Work: Hours Per Year"). Finally, and perhaps of greatest impact, high-speed trains, criss-crossing every continent, will speed intercity travelers to their destinations in far greater comfort and at lower cost than possible with air travel. Travelers with no pressing business demands and with no vacation time limits will want the roomy comfort and relaxation that high-speed rail travel will provide. The recently opened tunnel under the English Channel and its high-speed trains are but one example of the advantages of rail travel. Travel time by train between downtown London and downtown Paris will be three hours. And the comfort is superb! As Ray Moseley writes:

---

23. Michael G. Zey, *Seizing the Future: How the Coming Revolution in Science, Technology, and Industry Will Expand the Frontiers of Human Potential and Reshape the Planet* (New York: Simon & Schuster, 1994), p. 54.

No more long, expensive ($63) taxi rides to Heathrow Airport, complete with traffic jams. No more checking in an hour before departure, standing in line for passport checks, killing time in crowded waiting lounges. No more getting off planes and being told that takeoff is being delayed because of heavy traffic or flying in holding patterns over Paris or Brussels for the same reason. The seats and aisles are wider than on planes, and the whole experience is far more relaxing than flying.[24]

The net effect of the redawning of the age of rail transport, new video telecommunications, reduced work hours, and increased leisure time will be a sharp decrease in the amount of intracontinental air travel while overseas flight loads are likely to increase, but be less subject to tourist seasonality. Tourists will be traveling year-round in the twenty-first century. Thus the impact on airlines, airplane manufacturers, and other air travel related products and services will be profound. As automotive producers need to prepare for the future by acquiring or establishing new rail divisions, so too must air-travel related businesses.

However, in the meantime, the costs of providing air travel are substantially higher than necessary, and reinvention of its business and operations processes should be of high priority. One such revolutionary change, already underway in experiments by United Airlines, Delta Airlines, and Southwest Airlines, involves the elimination of tickets. Few outside the industry appreciate just how expensive the ticketing process is. Jonathan Dahl found it to be in the range of fifteen to thirty dollars per ticket, or approximately a billion dollars per year, enough so that eliminating tickets would triple airlines' profits over the course of a year.[25] Initial programs being tested require flight reservations to be booked by the airline, a procedure that threatens the revenues of travel agencies. The passenger is given a confirmation number which can be used at the airport to retrieve a boarding pass. (If the reservation is booked far enough in advance, United mails an itinerary.) At the airport, credit card and other identification is typically required to retrieve the boarding pass, a procedure that helps to ensure against fraudulent

---

24. Ray Moseley, "Channel Tunnel Train Flies into the Future," *Chicago Tribune,* November 20, 1994.

25. Jonathan Dahl, "Airlines Try Ticketless Systems, Giving Passengers New Gripes," *Wall Street Journal,* November 30, 1994.

or mistaken issuance. Passengers who previously received boarding passes in the mail or from their travel agents have found the airport procedure which now requires them to stand in line a source of annoyance that airlines will need to solve. Passengers can then use the boarding pass, itinerary or credit card billing to submit to their companies for expense reimbursement. Better still, their companies should be using the type of reengineered expense reporting described in chapter 7, subsection "Reengineered Expense Reporting." (Morris Air, a low-cost airline based in Salt Lake City, is another pioneer of ticketless travel. It has saved sending out 12,000 tickets per day.[26])

All is not sunshine and roses in new ticketless systems. For example, the corporate, bureaucratic world has initially resisted the ticketless system. Bureaucrats, accustomed to policing and enforcing adherence to travel policies find it next to impossible to accept change. Hewlett-Packard, for one, prohibits its 25,000 U.S. employees from using ticketless travel, according to Dahl, "because of the way the company's accounting system is designed." Corporate executives, at the highest levels, need to recognize the long-term reduction of airline travel costs that will occur in both the airline industry and *by providing an opportunity to simplify their own travel procedure, thus cutting the number of bureaucrats who can inhibit the march of progress.*

Eventually, airline reservation and travel agent personnel will be removed from the ticketing and boarding pass loops by the technological advances and improved systems illustrated on exhibit 11–10. Future passengers will converse with airline computer utilities from their home system modules when making airline reservations (see chapter 2, subsection "Virtually Real Home Shopping"). On the travel date, the passenger will take the neighborhood mass transit network to the airport, avoiding the frustrations of traffic and finding and paying for airport parking space. (James Hirsch identifies ten major airports with severe parking restraints, although parking at almost all airports is considerably less than convenient and low cost.[27]) Once at the airport, the traveler will go to the airline gate where, by putting his hand over

---

26. James S. Hirsch, "The Paperless Society Takes a Leap Forward With a Ticketless Airline," *Chicago Tribune,* October 22, 1993.

27. James S. Hirsch, "Add 'No Place to Park' to Flier's Airport Laments," *Wall Street Journal,* November 30, 1994.

EXHIBIT 11–10
Paperless Travel

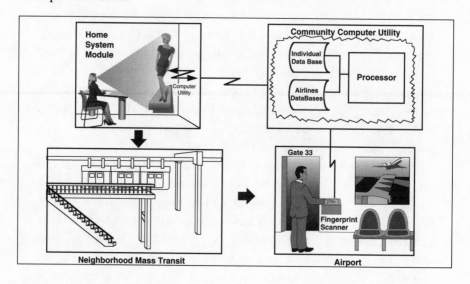

the fingerprint scanner (see chapter 9, subsection "Print Identification Number: The Basic Key"), a seat assignment will be verified and the gate turnstile released, permitting the traveler to board the aircraft. Fraudulent or erroneous boarding pass issuance will, thus, be virtually impossible. In the meantime, feedback to the computer utility will trigger an automatic transfer payment from the account of the traveler, or his company, to that of the airline. Reinventing today's new airport and reservation operation and system processes should not ignore these futuristic features. Rather, airlines should start to make the future begin today!

MOTORCYCLE OR AIRCYCLE?
A RECREATIONAL VISION

Few Western manufacturers have grasped how huge the developing world's demand for motorcycles will be in the dying years of the twentieth century and the dawning years of the twenty-first. Japanese motorcycle producers, however, are well aware, and are prepared to continue to dominate Asian and other developing markets, first for motorcycles and then for automobiles. James Abegglen says, "Honda executives note that motorcycle sales gain ground when a bike [meaning motorcycle] can be purchased with three to four months of salary, and that auto sales sprint ahead when an annual average salary will buy a car."[28] And Harley-Davidson's continuing success in marketing vast numbers of very large, expensive motorcycles has shown that one of the final stages of growing affluence is a return to the motorcycle, this time primarily for leisure-time enjoyment.

Developing nations (and regions) have been all too aware of the extreme value of developing a domestic automotive industry. A thriving demand, satisfied by local producers, will account for one out of every six or seven jobs in manufacturing, as it does in the United States. Thus, developing nations have always had severe restrictions on imports and liberal concessions for companies willing to establish local factories partially owned by foreign companies. Japanese manufacturers, as Abegglen notes, have already captured over 90 percent of the market in Thailand, Indonesia, and the Philippines, over 80 percent in Hong Kong, nearly 70 percent in Singapore, and almost 50 percent in Malaysia, leaving nothing but crumbs for American and European companies.

It is not too late for aggressive expansion of American and European automotive assemblers and component suppliers into the blossoming Asian markets, especially now that the recent General Agreement on Tariffs and Trade (GATT) has been adopted. However, the world's non-Japanese producers will have a much harder time gaining ground on Honda, since Honda is the sole producer savvy enough to have a product line that can win the loyalty of a consumer when he buys his first low-cost motorcycle, and keep it through the years when he upgrades to larger sizes and finally graduates to his first automobile.

In the long-term, though, the automotive industry is going to fade, as I have postulated in this chapter. And just as automobiles will give way to new forms of small, convenient networks of local mass transit and larger intracity and intercity mass transit, the use of small, inexpensive motorcycles for primary transportation will also fade. In the end, one of two forms of leisure transportation will boom for the companies with the foresight to plan ahead. With most individuals' time

28. James C. Abegglen, *Sea Change: Pacific Asia as the New World Industrial Center* (New York: Free Press, 1994), pp. 218–219.

for leisure activities expanding to nearly full time, one activity that is likely to flourish is motorcycle races and rallies. Thus, thousands will enjoy roaring over the hills and trails outside their domed cities. And my client of almost thirty years, Harley-Davidson, a premier manufacturer of leisure activity motorcycles, is in a position to be one of the survivors. Taking the longer view, personal "aircycles," the aerial equivalent of the land motorcycle, are likely to fill the skies with their enthusiasts!

ROBOT MINING, AGRICULTURE, AND TRANSPORTATION

Space vehicles are already traversing the vast reaches of the solar system with almost unbelievable accuracy and without the benefit of on-board human pilots. The computer and telecommunications technology for eliminating labor from far simpler operations such as mining, manufacturing, and transportation is now at hand and is starting to be put to other uses. In mining, for example, workers have long suffered physically and mentally from the danger, dirt, and discomfort of working hundreds of feet below the earth's surface in spaces too confined to stand upright in, often in cold and damp environments with the ever-present potential for cave-in, explosion, and gassing. Everett Henderson, part of an engineering team at Inco, Ltd. of Ontario, Canada, is putting robotic control to work in place of human drivers.[29] By continually increasing remote control of drills, scoops, and trucks, Inco has shown it feasible to reduce the number of workers required by almost 22 percent by 1997. Just imagine how few will be required by 2020! And the drivers of all types of agricultural equipment are also becoming unnecessary. Use of modern satellite location control and computer-guided robotic drivers is on the verge of eliminating the human driver's dusty tedium of dawn-to-dusk operation of tractors, combines, balers, planters, and the like. (As Laurie Goering explains, the global positioning satellite system, which pinpoints any location on earth [accurate within three feet], "is becoming cost effective for use on the

---

29. Mark Heinzl, "Inco Moves to Take Miners Out of Mining," *Wall Street Journal,* July 6, 1994.

farm and in other applications such as aviation."[30]) In fact, there is no reason that operating hours need be restricted to daylight. Around-the-clock, seven-day-per-week operation will increase equipment utilization and dramatically reduce the amount of equipment required. These changes are imminent. In the medium-term future, the safety of every mode of freight transportation—rail, boat, air, and truck—will rise to the new levels as robotic control systems use ever better fail-safe accident prevention mechanisms now being invented. An example of one such mechanism is the anticipated "positive train control" which the Federal Railroad Administration is expected to mandate by the year 2000. In fact, the Burlington Northern and Union Pacific railroads, in early 1994, announced the inauguration of a satellite/radio project to test these new technologies on 750 miles of track.[31]

These technological changes in the reduced maintenance, longer life, and higher utilization of robot-operated equipment will have a profound effect on the amount of human work required in the industries directly involved, with cascading reductions in employment in their equipment manufacturers and in the manufacturers' component suppliers. While work in these areas declines, robotic and electronic guidance and control system component industries' production will increase, and the volume of computer programming required to control the robots will expand. A few specific new products that will soon come to the market include the following:

1. Satellite communication systems and ground location tracking and control software
2. Robot equipment operators
3. Robot refuelers and load exchangers
4. On-board computer robot and machine operations controllers and software

For example, the government-owned Global Positioning System, used effectively by the military in the recent Gulf War, is now being

30. Laurie Goering, "High Tech Is Fertile Ground for Farmers: Satellite, Computer Control Join the Tractor," *Chicago Tribune,* November 7, 1993.

31. Daniel Pearl, "Railroads Are Being Pushed by the U.S. to Hasten Installation of Safety Systems," *Wall Street Journal,* July 13, 1994.

put to use by the Federal Aviation Administration in "the biggest revolution in aviation in 50 years."[32] Rockwell International's potential
market for satellite receivers is vast. Reuters offers some suggestions
for future private use (other than those I have cited): "Back-country
hikers can calculate their position with pinpoint accuracy, rental cars
with on-board navigation can steer drivers through strange cities,
yachts can be put and kept on course." The huge potential use of these
devices holds tremendous exciting prospects for companies like
Rockwell, in on the ground floor.

REINVENTED AGRICULTURE: THE COMMUNITY'S HANDS-FREE FARM

Agriculture's continuous improvement, through labor automation, hy-
bridization, and chemical fertilization and weed, pest, and insect control, have vastly increased crop yields per man-hour over the past century. Corn production by the best "master farmers" in the United
States, for example, has increased approximately 60 percent in
slightly more than three decades, as shown in exhibit 11–11. And, in
1994 American farm corn production reached a new all-time high of
over 10 billion bushels, indicating that the improvement trend will
continue. Thus, if all corn producers were to follow the practices of
the world's best corn farmers, they would be capable of feeding a
world population of 10 billion people and, as the exhibit 11–11 indicates, average Iowa farmers are already producing at the level necessary to provide subsistence meals to that many. Further, while agricultural yields have been increasing, the prices consumers pay for food
have been declining, a natural reaction to the law of supply and demand. In fact, the decline from peak prices within two recent decades
has been approximately 70 percent, as shown on exhibit 11–12. Nor is
the improvement near utopian levels. For, as Zey writes, "The impact
of biotechnology on agriculture can and will be dramatic: It will obliterate hunger and even force the human species to re-conceptualize issues like scarcity and abundance."[33] Genetic plant engineering in the

---

32. Reuters, "FAA Navigates New Uses for Satellite Technology," *Chicago Tribune,* November
20, 1994.

33. Zey, *Seizing the Future,* p. 165.

EXHIBIT 11–11

Corn per Acre

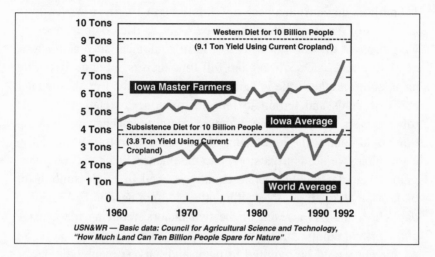

USN&WR — Basic data: Council for Agricultural Science and Technology, "How Much Land Can Ten Billion People Spare for Nature"

next century will produce plants of staggeringly higher size and yield. And these plants will be spoilage resistant, reducing the loss between harvesting and delivery to consumers. Thus, the acreage required to support the population's needs will be far less than currently required.

The labor remaining in today's agricultural operations is radically

EXHIBIT 11–12

World Food Price Index
(1900 = 100 Constant Dollars)

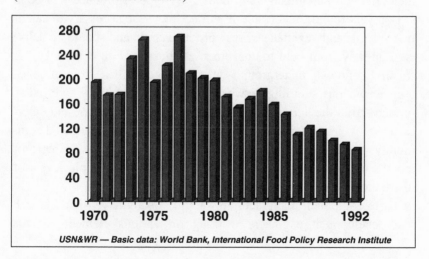

USN&WR — Basic data: World Bank, International Food Policy Research Institute

lower than it was fifty years ago (in November 1994, the U.S. Census Bureau reported that the number of American farms had dropped to 1.9 million, down from a peak of 6.8 million in 1935). However, farm labor is still far greater than should be required if modern technology were brought to bear. For example, farm equipment such as tractors, combines, and balers still require full-time drivers, a tediously boring occupation. It takes little imagination to envision the use of computer maps of fields and terrain to feed instructions to relatively simple robot drivers. Slightly more complex computer/mechanical automation could control the interfacing of harvested crop transfer to delivery vehicles, or seeds from storage to the planter. Since the computer-guided vehicles would operate equally as well in bright sunlight or darkest night, operation of equipment would not need to be limited to daylight hours. As a result of the two factors, reducing the acreage and working equipment twenty-four hours a day, far fewer pieces of equipment would be required to plant and harvest mankind's needs. And although the cost of automation will continue its steady decline until it is as low as it must be to justify (by itself) full automation, the greater yields from smaller fields will make hands-free farms feasible.

Further, each community's domed agricultural zone will enable its operators to virtually eradicate animal and insect pests and undesirable weeds from its climate- and access-controlled environment. Thus, herbicide and pesticide chemicals, which may be causes of ill health, will no longer be necessary. And since the agricultural zone in the dome will be climate controlled, every type of produce will be in season year round. As a result, it will no longer be necessary to can or freeze fruits and vegetables. Fresh produce could and should be delivered directly from field to consumer, as illustrated on exhibit 11–13. In all likelihood, underground delivery tubes, filled from produce transfer wagons shuttling between the harvester and tube, will carry produce from the agricultural zone to a distribution center, and delivery tubes will transfer it to the consumer's home. The automated community produce-distribution facility will drastically cut the cost of today's expensive long-distance transport with its multiple levels of distributors, wholesalers, and retailers.

Farm equipment manufacturers should already have their research and development engineers working on various elements of the

EXHIBIT 11–13
Produce Delivery Automation

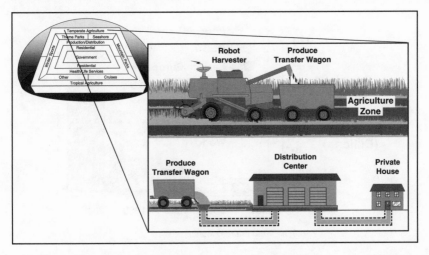

hands-free farm of the future. The logical starting point is the application of computer and mechanical vehicle guidance and driver technology, while a secondary effort would be the design of automated load-transfer and refueling devices.

THE UTILITY AND DELIVERY CONDUIT

The race to completely deplete the earth's limited unrenewable energy sources has barely begun to accelerate into high gear, as the world's most populous nations (China and India) are poised to begin a surge that will move them into the ranks of industrialized countries. For example, the ultra-conservative estimate of the World Energy Council is that the growth of energy consumption by the developing countries alone between 2000 and 2010 will be more than today's consumption in Western Europe (exhibit 11–14).[34] Thus, fuel and electric utility companies will need to anticipate massive conversions to alternative, renewable resources before the end of the twenty-first century (Shell International Petroleum, for one, predicts that renewable power will

---

34. "Energy: The New Prize," *The Economist,* June 18, 1994, pp. 3–18.

EXHIBIT 11–14

Energy Demand

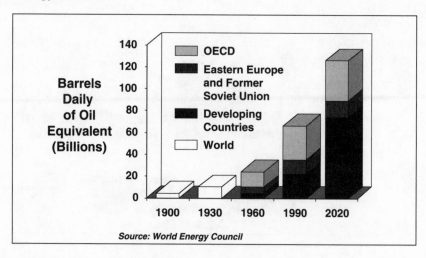

Source: World Energy Council

"dominate world energy production by 2050," which means a steep ramping up long before mid-century).[35]

The two largest replenishable energy sources now known to man are nature's sun and wind. But technological development of practical means to harness them has been stalled by the temporary decrease in the price of oil. However, imminent breakthroughs in economically harnessing both wind and sun power are commonly expected and even close to fruition. For example, Eugene Linden reports that Amory Lovins of the Rocky Mountain Institute believes the next generation of wind turbines will lower the cost to a level below that of oil. He also reports that scientists at the University of New South Wales in Australia have designed new photovoltaic cells with the potential for reducing their cost by 80 percent, which would bring the cost to levels competitive with conventional power generation.

Recent waves of privatization and decentralization in Europe and South America have not been limited to industry but have also encompassed utilities. This should provide additional strong testimony to the inability of national governments to provide public service at

---

35. Eugene Linden, "A Sunny Forecast: Always Cleaner Than Fossil Fuels, Renewable Power Sources May Soon Be Just as Cheap," *Time*, November 7, 1994, pp. 66–67.

costs commensurate with the benefits provided. The newly privatized British Northwest Water Engineering company swung rapidly into action to reorganize the business. Its twin objectives were to lower costs while increasing its customer service. Its reorganization resulted in a fantastic productivity increase, having raised the workload capacity of its personnel by approximately 200 percent! Under national government administration, numerous small shops served as home base to the administrative staff responsible for responding to customer calls for service and scheduling the repairmen's activities. The servicemen previously used the facilities as a home base, a place to check into and out of work, receive assignments, store repair supplies, and report on work performed.

Now the repairmen work out of their own homes. Their work vans are equipped with modern telecommunication and computer terminal equipment, enabling the new service center to broadcast assignments to them, and allowing them to report on their completed work. Periodic replenishment of the van's supplies from a central depot, which was already in the distribution network, has proven to be even more cost-effective than maintaining small local stocks. The expenses and overhead costs of these facilities were completely eliminated by closing them and moving operations into a new computerized service center. Incoming calls are almost always answered within one or two rings, a speed of response unimaginable in the old fashioned service centers, in which all representatives' lines might often be busy, and the manual recording of the need for service and its subsequent scheduling combined to lengthen the time required to put a repairman at the site of the required service. Now, as soon as a call is received, the customer's entire profile is available to the service representative, the call is recorded on the computer terminal and instantly entered into the queue of jobs of the repairman closest to the site. In most instances, the customer can be immediately advised as to the repairman's approximate time of arrival.

Although the most modern communities have invisible, underground utility lines, older cities and much of our countryside are blighted by ugly (and perhaps unhealthy) electrical and telecommunication lines. In the world of the next century, long electrical transmission lines will be rare, perhaps extinct, because power generation will originate from the community dome, the community generating system, or even home and business systems. Although I am unable to imagine a practical, safe, radical new power source of immense energy, my vision must rely on the assumption that vastly improved versions of present sources will be developed. Thus, a compact generating system dedicated to a single relatively small community or building will be aesthetically pleasing to the community and will be infinitely more economical. Local systems will reduce power loss and cost (and perhaps health hazards) of long distance transmission. The electricity produced by the community power station should be carried to homes and businesses in new underground utility and delivery conduit systems, reducing the volume of electricity carried and insulating the remaining power better than high-volume overhead transmission lines.

It is both amusing and sad to watch the development of a new subdivision rising out of farmland—funny because the methods used to install utilities are so ill-conceived, and sad because of the unnecessary cost. Over a period of time, one observes the arrival of equipment used to open a trench, trucks laden with sewer pipe, cranes to lay the pipe, workers to join the pipe and to seal it to construct access points, and earthmoving equipment to fill in the trench. A little later, a second set of equipment, pipes, and people arrive on the scene to install water. Still later, separate additional teams install electricity, natural gas, telephone lines, and coaxial cable and/or fiber optic lines for video and telecommunication services. What waste of resources!

Farsighted contractors, community planners, and manufacturers of various forms of present utility conduits should at this very moment be developing plans and strategic alliances for the application of a new generation of common utility and delivery conduit and service access products (see exhibit 11–15). This combination conduit, carrying all forms of utilities, should be prefabricated in much longer lengths than now commonly used, to lower the cost of installation. The utility carriers, such as electric, telephone, and coaxial cables might be pre-installed at the factory with fast, snap-together connections. There must be various sizes of conduit for the various applications: main lines from utility centers, trunk lines to neighborhoods, neighborhood lines for each subdivision, and, finally, conduits to bring utilities and deliveries into the consumer's home or the indus-

EXHIBIT 11–15
Utility and Delivery Conduit

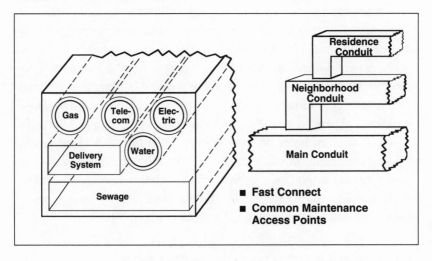

trial facility. Since communities can and should be carefully pre-planned, outlet points along the various conduit lengths can also be preplanned and designed with fast-connect, plug-in features to further minimize installation costs. Perhaps newly deregulated, farsighted utilities are already recognizing their potential commonality of operations. For example, A. David Silver mentions electric utilities which have put start-up capital into local telecommunications companies, waste management enterprises, and electronic manufacturers.[36]

A somewhat more futuristic feature of the common conduit, illustrated on exhibit 11–15, is the "delivery tube." My vision of a century hence presumes the virtual disappearance of retail establishments. Home shopping—in which the shopper can sit in the midst of his system or that of a recreational and social facility such as a restaurant, talk to the system about the item(s) in which he is interested, view the offerings of various suppliers, and instantaneously order them for im-

---

36. A. David Silver, *Strategic Partnering: How to Join Forces With Other Companies to Get: Capital, Research and Development, Marketing, Product Testing, Sales Support* (New York: McGraw-Hill, 1993), p. 2.

mediate delivery—will replace retail shops (see chapter 2, subsection "Virtually Real Home Shopping"). Appliances, furniture, and other items too large for the delivery conduit will continue to be delivered "overland." But smaller items, including clothing, groceries, and notions can and should be delivered via the delivery conduit.

The power source of the delivery system might be something as mundane as electricity or pneumatics, or it might be something entirely new. Whatever it turns out to be, it is clear that the cost, time, labor, and energy expended as a result of individuals going to retail stores far exceeds that of the home delivery system of the future. And the benefit to the environment, through reduced automobile emissions, is also of great potential importance to the future of the world. Aesthetically, landscapes devoid of automobiles will be considerably more pleasant than streets and highways clogged with smelly, noisy traffic.

HOME POWER GENERATION: PRECURSOR OF THE DOMED CITY

The eminent prospect of low-cost solar, wind, and other power generation will soon solve the problem of its competitiveness vis-à-vis conventional fuels. However, lower cost will not alone bring nature's energy into businesses and homes. The area that would be required by solar collectors and wind turbines would be massive if entire communities were to be powered by conventional utilities. Fortunately, homes, factories, shopping centers, and office buildings provide a probable alternative to wasting land by filling it with power generation gear, because the area around, on, and above these structures will accommodate arrays of both photovoltaic panels and wind turbines. Even today's turbines and solar collectors, although not cost competitive, are entirely adequate to meet the average needs of a typical home. However, windless and cloudy days dictate the need for either new, improved energy storage or backup supplies from conventional utilities. New home and business power generation equipment should be connected to the utilities' power grid so that excess power can be "deposited" in the grid during peak wind and sun generation hours, and "withdrawn" in periods of cloudiness and wind calm. Incidentally, hydrogen is one of the most abundant elements and has tremendous energy generation potential.

Conway, for one, predicts that it will become one of the most important power sources within the next two decades.[37]

As regulated industries, many utilities (those with which I am familiar) have historically worked harder than the average enterprise at increasing productivity. Deregulation, however, has forced an entirely new environment on utilities. For the first time, consumers have the option of moving to competitive sources of energy. Nor are all potential opportunities for increased productivity exhausted. Indeed, the restructuring brought about by deregulation has caused, major new avenues of improvement to surface—not only of new operations but also of traditional practices. With the advent of utility deregulation, power generation companies have had to learn to compete with low-cost producers, and to time massive new facility investments carefully to meet increased demand when it occurs, not far earlier. When the added capacity of any facility outstrips demand, the newly deregulated companies will lose market share and have problems remaining competitive if there is not enough power demand to absorb fixed overhead costs. When home and business power generation starts to escalate, utilities will face a continuous decrease of demand and will need to discontinue operations of their least productive facilities.

Eventually, domed cities' solar collectors and radically improved devices for lighting, heating, and other power applications will virtually eradicate the need for large generating plants. And the time may come sooner than many might imagine. For example, Georgia Power Co. has recently concluded a one-year test of a solar array that produced power enough to supply an average home at a cost of six cents per kilowatt hour, a rate comparable to conventional fuels.[38] Energy utilities need to be in the forefront of solar and wind technology in order to survive when home and business power generation begins to reduce dependence on massive power generation facilities. And potential producers of solar panels will become world leaders only if they have the vision to enter the high-stakes business of investing in a new technology. Japan's Canon is one such visionary company, hav-

---

37. Conway, *A Glimpse of the Future,* p. 15.

38. Cox News Service, "More Light Shining on New Solar Technology," *Chicago Tribune,* December 5, 1994.

ing formed joint ventures with Plasma Physics and Energy Conversion Devices (American companies), because Canon has as one of its goals, "to make solar energy cells a commercial product by the turn of the century."[39]

THE DOMED CITY: FREE POWER AND CLIMATE CONTROL

Cities in temperate zones expend enormous amounts of energy to heat homes and businesses in winter and cool them in summer, while those in tropic zones consume at least as much on air conditioning and humidity control. Continued future use of today's inefficient single-residence and business climate control equipment is inconceivable. Shielding communities from the sun will be a far more cost-effective method of cooling, while the harnessed power of the sun will certainly be the best source of power for climate control.

For decades, one popular feature of conceptual, fictional sketches of cities of the future has been the transparent dome encapsulating them in a uniform, controlled environment. Such a dome, in my hundred-year vision, serves to do far more than simply enclose the environment. The dome should provide shade, cooling, heat, and electricity, helping to maintain a clean and healthier atmosphere at the same time it drastically reduces the drain on nonreplenishable energy sources. Remarkably improved solar panels and sun-focusing panels should be used to generate both heat and electricity for the super-efficient new storage batteries and energy cisterns that will meet the nighttime and winter needs of the domed community. Importantly, the clean air and uniform seasonality of the dome should also contribute substantially to the reduction of respiratory and seasonal diseases.

This is not to imply that mankind will be unable to enjoy the benefits of the seasons. Neighborhoods within the dome could easily be zoned and climate controlled for year-round winter sports or beach activities. Availability of such recreational activities will become much more important as the average workweek length continues its rapid decline in the next century.

---

39. Louis Kraar and Seiichi Takikawa, *Japanese Maverick: Success Secrets of Canon's "God of Sales"* (New York: Wiley, 1994), p. 64.

VACANT BUILDING REHABILITATION: GROWTH INDUSTRY

The huge increase in numbers of workers moving from office buildings to home offices, radical reduction of the number and size of distribution facilities, conversion of consumer buying to home shopping (which will eliminate the need for retail shops and grocery stores), and emphasis on factory design of vastly better space utilization will flood the market with surplus buildings. This could be either a problem or an opportunity. A landscape dotted with vacant buildings, and the financial losses associated with facilities which were once productive and useful could become a significant social and economic disaster if nothing is done to put the buildings back into productive use.

Considering the masses of low-wage people now living in small and marginal houses and apartments, rehabilitating the new surplus of buildings into roomier, low-cost residences is one avenue that will put construction crews to work and make the quality of life better for new apartment owners. Further, the future massive reduction of work will drive up the demand for new recreational facilities. Imaginative new theme-park style facilities could well become one of the answers to expanding the array of leisure time activities while making use of some of the newly vacated buildings. For example, factories and warehouses might be converted into indoor sport facilities such as basketball and handball courts, ice skating rinks, and billiards and ping-pong facilities.

THE FAST-FOOD FACTORY

The new speedy home-delivery wave will not be limited to providers of goods, but will soon spread into the fast-food arena. In fact, successful fast-food home delivery service is already an established fact. Pizza restaurants have provided home delivery service for decades, and fast-food chains will inevitably follow suit. As the home delivery business continues to expand because customers become addicted to the comfort of ordering for delivery and eating in, fast-food outlets will come more and more to resemble food factories, not restaurants.

In recent years, the intense competition between the chains, combined with an explosive growth in the number of new restaurants has

EXHIBIT 11–16
Where's the Beef?

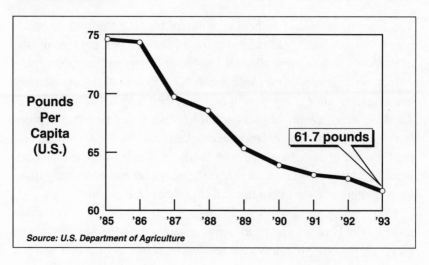

Source: U.S. Department of Agriculture

forced the chains to expand their product lines into those of other specialty fast-food providers. For example, Kentucky Fried Chicken was *the* chicken fast-food provider for years. Recently, numerous competing chicken specialty chains have sprung up. Even more recently the hamburger chains have also made moves to enter the fierce chicken market. The market for chicken has continuing growth potential and will boom even faster as more and more evidence emerges that poultry is far healthier than red meat. And, although the red-meat restaurant business is still booming, the long-term trend to reduced consumption (exhibit 11–16) continues and eventually can be expected to impact fast-food beef and pork sales.[40] Continuation of this trend, which has seen an annual per capita reduction of approximately thirteen pounds in just eight years, would completely eliminate beef by the year 2031. Further, the fast-food chains have not been alone in recognizing the new market for poultry. Major grocery chains and even some gas station convenience stores now offer roasted chicken. Dominick's, a grocery chain in my home area, for example, opened a new section in No-

---

40. David Young, "Beef on the Comeback Trail; Restaurant Steak Sales Sizzle," *Chicago Tribune,* July 6, 1994.

vember 1993, offering not only rotisserie chicken but also gourmet pizza and fresh pasta.[41] The grocery chains find the fast-food business attractive because the profit margins can be several times higher than those of their other, conventional grocery store products.

In the highly competitive fast-food race it will be differentiation of the customer service rendered that will ultimately determine who dominates. The ultimate in customer service will be the lowest-cost delivery of hot, fresh, high-quality food directly to the home and the workplace. McDonald's may have been one of the earliest to recognize this fact. In November 1993, McDonald's inaugurated a test home delivery service that may ultimately revolutionize the fast food industry.[42] If thorough preliminary investigation and methodical implementation have been done, the new service is likely to be a smashing success. One dimension of success will be the number of orders received well in advance of the requested delivery time. An objective of moving to home delivery should be an ability to preplan the delivery load and route so that both restaurant and delivery people will be able to preplan their workloads and delivery routes efficiently to make every trip a multiple-delivery occasion. If its test fails to provide the expected additional volume and if McDonald's abandons the effort, it will only be a matter of time until it or another chain will adjust to compensate for the shortcomings of the initial experiment, and the boom in fast-food home delivery service will begin.

There will be various hurdles to overcome in order to deliver hot, high-quality food speedily and at reasonable cost. Some food items, notably french fries and hamburgers, lose some of their taste appeal shortly after they are cooked, and keeping them warm only briefly extends the time during which the deterioration is acceptable. Mobile mini-kitchens may well emerge as the perfect solution to timely, high-quality delivery. Second, the cost of delivery driver's insurance may be far more than tolerable if a high percentage of drivers are young. This problem could be minimized by hiring retired people, but such a strategy may well run afoul of age discrimination laws. A third hurdle is the risk to the driver. There are urban and suburban neighborhoods

---

41. Nancy Ryan, "Dominick's Takes Stab at Takeout," *Chicago Tribune,* November 14, 1993.

42. Nancy Ryan, "McDonald's Paves the Way with New McDelivery Service," *Chicago Tribune,* November 24, 1993.

where a driver's life would be in jeopardy because the criminal element realizes that the driver carries money. Thus, the driver can be a source of free food and money, at the same time. Avoiding this danger might require "redlining" neighborhoods and/or requiring customers to pay by credit card. Portable, electronic, radio frequency credit card readers will, therefore, be a product in high demand.

Before the really big shift to home and office delivery, the fast food business is likely to continue the shift away from sit-down facilities to those almost exclusively devoted to drive-through customers. Checkers Drive-In Restaurants Inc., Pepsico Inc.'s Hot 'n Now, and Rally's Restaurants, leaders of this new fast food trend have had mixed results. Commitment to executing successfully means earmarking sufficient capital for the business-building phase of any enterprise. These start-up operations are commonly thought to be suffering from their lack of funds to compete with the advertising budgets of large existing chains of conventional restaurants such as McDonald's and Burger King.[43]

Even before or while the new wave of drive-through restaurants is developing, the apparently overbuilt fast-food industry needs to reexamine existing and new restaurant design concepts, and adopt many of the principles of the latest, highest-productivity factories, including designing work in the kitchen to eliminate excessive movement, especially that of individuals who run around gathering the components of a customer's order. Nor are the order-taking and cashiering functions of the fast-food restaurant world class, in terms of utilizing the very best of existing and soon-to-emerge technology. Ultimately, customers should enter their own orders, which will become increasingly more practical as voice communication systems are improved. Further, electronic money will eventually replace cash (see chapter 7, subsection "The Moneyless Society"), and fast food restaurants need to begin to install credit card systems to be prepared for the cashless society.

SUMMARY

As community domes become a flourishing reality, a boom in their construction will occur, creating a large demand for dome materials

---

43. Eleena De Lisser, "Fast-Food Drive-Throughs Lose Speed," *Wall Street Journal,* October 27, 1994.

production, especially for alternative energy equipment such as solar panels. Thus, exhibit 11–17 lists not only domed community construction as one of the growth industries and occupations of the twenty-first century, but also its components such as artificial lighting and climate control systems. The smaller, highly efficient power generation and waste reclamation systems of the future will radically change these fields from ones in which utility companies must deliver to the home and business, and convey waste from them. The transportation of people and goods will be undergoing fantastic alteration, as local mass transit and continental networks of intercity rail transport replace automobiles and large numbers of airplanes. All types of equipment operators and drivers will be replaced by robot controllers of high reliability.

In the interim, opportunities for huge savings in delivering utilities to homes and residences will generate a demand for new multiutility conduits. And as leisure time continues to increase, leisure businesses will boom, as will every enterprise providing hobby equipment for activities such as gardening, woodworking, and sewing.

However, as some industries and occupations flourish, others (see exhibit 11–18) will wane and some will die during the next century. Those who may be working in industries or occupations that are pre-

EXHIBIT 11–17
Growth Industries and Occupations

Domed Community Construction	**Robot:**
	– "Drivers"
Artificial, Low-Energy Sunlight	– Mining, Agriculture and Manufacturing
Community Climate Control	
Home/Business Energy Generation	**Common Utility/ Delivery Conduit**
Mini-Waste Reclamation Systems	**Leisure Recreation**
Neighborhood Mass Transit	**Hobby Supplies:**
High-Speed Rail	– Gardening, Woodworking, etc.

EXHIBIT 11–18

Waning Industries and Occupations

Automotive, Trucking and Busing

Highway, Street and Bridge Construction

Office Buildings

Air Travel

Business Equipment

Utilities

Home Climate Control

Herbicides and Pesticides

Canned and Frozen Foods

---

dicted to decline should keep several important points in mind. These following points are repeated briefly in every chapter, because many readers are expected to read only one or more selected chapters. First, the change may not occur in the foreseeable future, especially those far-out notions predicted in this chapter. Second, the future continuous reduction of work will be universal. As a result, society must and will reduce average work week hours in order to maintain full employment. Third, the era of reduced work and increased leisure time will be one of unprecedented quality of life and affluence.

12

CONCLUSION

It is with great happiness that I look back over more than six decades of progress—to see with great clarity the unbelievable changes that have occurred in my lifetime. As a lad, I helped in harvesting crops with horse-drawn equipment. Later, I watched the landing of man on the moon and the takeoff of space vehicles bound for other planets. I grew up in an era in which telephones, radios, cars, and large homes were luxuries, and today live in a world where multiple family cars, color television, and cordless and cellular telephones are found in almost every large home. During my lifetime average life expectancy has soared by three decades. And, the best is yet to come.

It is with some sadness, but boundless pride, that I realize that I will not be here to see the world of the distant future. I am proud, because I expect our progeny to continue the process of transformation. The world of the future holds the promise of incredible health, affluence, education, and quality of life. The movers and shakers in industry have been the driving force behind progress to date, and will be the first to usher in the new world. Let us begin!

Appendix 1

THE ACHIEVERS

This list includes benefits achieved by a few of Andersen Consulting's thousands of clients who have implemented many of the business process flow and systems improvements, strategic initiatives, and management techniques described in this book. The achievers appendixes in previous books listed over three hundred companies, many of whom have implemented the same types of changes.[1] Names and office locations of Andersen Consulting or persons are shown in parentheses for the convenience of readers who desire more information.

MANUFACTURING

ABB Process Automation, Inc. Columbus, OH, process controls. Reduction of time required to close financial statements, 85%; reduction of remote computing expenses, 75%.

Berol Corporation, Empire Berol USA, Shelbyville, TN, writing instruments. (Stephen J. Anderson, James Fry, and Jeffrey O'Keefe, Nashville, TN.)

---

1. Roy L. Harmon, and Leroy D. Peterson, *Reinventing the Factory: Productivity Breakthroughs in Manufacturing Today* (New York: Free Press, 1990); Roy L. Harmon, *Reinventing the Factory II: Managing the World Class Factory* (New York: Free Press, 1992); Roy L. Harmon, *Reinventing the Warehouse: World Class Distribution Logistics* (New York: Free Press, 1993).

Capacity increase, 53%, labor reduction, 27%; and productivity increase, 45%. Six month payback.

British Aerospace, Chester, UK, aircraft wings. (Peter Roberts, London.) Manufacturing cycle time reduction, 35%.

Fiat Group: New Holland, Modena, Italy, and London, agricultural and earth-moving equipment. (Renato Dedonatis and Alberto Proverbio, Turin.) Inventory reduction, 40%; personnel savings, 30%; customer service improvement, 50%.

Geon Company, The (was B.F. Goodrich division), Cleveland, OH, PVC (resin and compound). (Karl E. Newkirk, Cleveland, and Bill McKearn, Milwaukee.) Raw material investment, 45% reduction; improvement in meeting shipment dates, 70%; inventory accuracy improvement, 50%; manufacturing lead time reduction, 33%; process engineer productivity improvement, 50%.

Gonvauto, S.A., Barcelona, automotive blankings. (Juan Pedro Raurell and Salvador Cuadras, Barcelona.) Increased production per line, 60%; increased labor productivity in tons, 135%; finished goods stock reduction, 50%.

Harley-Davidson, Inc., Milwaukee, motorcycles. (Thomas Arenberg, Milwaukee.) Market share, 60% gain; productivity increase, 40%; reduced scrap and rework, 65%; setup cost reduction, 75%; warranty cost reduction, 35%; factory space savings, 25%.

I.E. duPont de Nemours & Company: Agricultural Products Business Unit, Wilmington, DE, crop protection chemicals. (Thomas P. Harig and R. John Aalbregtse, Chicago.) Finished goods reduction, 20% (target 25%–30%); sales increase attributable to product availability, 5%; capital spending improvement, 50%; product development time reduction, 15%.

ITT Fluid Technology Corporation, New York, pumps and valves. (A. William Kapler III, Roseland, NJ, and Robert C. Kane, Jr., New York.) Personnel savings, 50%; improvement in capital utilization, 15%.

Johnson Matthey, Materials Technology Division Europe, Manchester, U.K., precious metals mining, refining, and manufacturing. (Peter Roberts, Gary North, and Philip Monks, Manchester, U.K.) Reduction of production facilities, 50%, and of national distribution locations, 75%; lead time and inventory investment reduction, 50%.

Montgomery KONE, Moline, IL, elevators. (Roger G. Willis, Chicago, and Gene A. Gutman, Dallas.) Bid development time reduction, 66%; fewer bids requiring custom engineering, 17%; setup time reduction, 95%; backorder reduction, 100%; improved space utilization, 50%; faster overall inventory turns, 185%; lower total lead time, 63%; better work-in-process inventory turns, 255%; higher supplier on-time delivery, 216%; on-time shipping improvement, 890%.

Nissan, Tokyo, cars and trucks. (M. Mori, Tokyo.) Reduction of late deliveries, 59%; number of orders unable to schedule promise date, 44% reduction; orders made to order (versus sold from inventory) increased, 62%; reduction of customers dissatisfied with delivery performance, 52%; order scheduling delay, 89% reduction.

Nokia-Maillefer, Ecublens, Switzerland, cable machinery. (Patrice Massat, Paris.) Order lead time reduction, 50%; inventory investment reduction, 25%; net working capital reduction, 20%; reduced fixed costs, 15%; hierarchical (organization) levels reduced, 43%.

Octicon A/S, Glasgow, hearing aids. (Jens Darket, Copenhagen). Sales increase, 30%; headquarters staff reduction, 15%; increased return on sales, 100%.

Pilkington Optronics: Barr & Stroud Ltd, Glasgow, defense optical systems, including periscopes and sights. (Paul Burgess, London.) Management tier reduction, 55%; sales per employee increase, 184%; inventory reduction, 72%; on-time delivery increase, 900%; increased inventory record accuracy, 96%; inventory turn increase, 334%; productivity increase, 30%.

Ruiz Food Products, Inc., Dinuba, CA, frozen foods. (Douglas W. Cunningham, Orange County, CA, and A. Lee DeNova, Atlanta.) Bottom line improvement, 2–4%; material cost reduction, 6%.

Yokohama Tire Company, Salem, VA, tires. (Roy K. Phelan, Cleveland.) Tire engineer and compounder productivity increase, 40%; reduced specification development lead time, 60%.

RETAILING

Damark International, Inc., Brooklyn Park, MN, catalog sales. (Dale Renner, John Nash, and Paul Cameron, Minneapolis.) New employee training time reduction, 60%; Carpal tunnel injury claims reduction, 50%.

Sears Canada, Inc., Toronto, department store and catalog sales. (Gary C. Garrett and Mary Tolan, Chicago.) Inventory reduction, 27% to date (projected to improve to 50% by the end of 1995); stockout reduction, 59%.

FINANCIAL SERVICES

Allstate Insurance, Chicago, multiline insurance. (David E. Hoffman, Chicago.) Reduced time required to issue new business, 89%; reduced cost to issue new business, 50%; reduced cost to renew business, 33%.

Banc One Mortgage Corporation, Indianapolis, mortgage servicing. (Stephen A. Elliot, Toronto, and David A. Stadler, St. Louis.) Increased productivity improvement, 40%; capacity increase, without staff increase, 100%; data accuracy improvement, 100%; cross-selling improvement, 15–20%.

Deutsche Bank AG: Regional Head Office, Singapore, full service bank. (Willie Cheng, Singapore.) Productivity improvement, initially, over 20%.

Komercni Banka, Prague, full-line banking. (Pat O'Neill and Tom Cox, Frankfurt, and Mark Eyen, Columbus.) Increased transactions per teller per day, 250%; increased customers per customer service representative, 287%; increased loans per loan officer, 53%; reduced outward international payment processing time, 79%; reduced inward international payment processing time, 76%.

Societe de Bourse (Paris Stock Exchange), Paris, securities trading. (Patrick Lacombe, Paris.) Back-office client broker and back-room productivity increase, 40% to 95%; unsolved trade transactions ("fails"), over 99% improvement.

DISTRIBUTION

Canada Post Corporation, Ottawa, Canada, postal and distribution services. (Christopher Brennan, Ottawa.) Reduction of supervisor's work processing employee time reporting, 66%; reduction of production volume reporting errors, 30%.

ICA Handlarnas, Stockholm, food. (Richard W. Hill, Stockholm, and Joseph Van Winkle, San Francisco.) Inventory reduction, 35%; revenue increase, 15%; workforce reduction, 30%.

Mazda Motor of America, Inc., Parts and Service Division, Irvine, CA, service parts distribution. (Douglas R. Willinger, Irvine.) Service parts operating costs as a percentage of sales, 11% reduction; distribution center operating costs as a percentage of sales, 13% improvement; outbound transportation cost reduction, 21%; corporate administrative cost as a percentage of sales, 20% reduction; dealer order entry elapsed time, 99.98% reduction (to less than one minute).

SLS Sears Logistics Service, Itasca, IL, distribution services. (Gary C. Garrett, Chicago.) Strategic partnering transportation cost reduction, 40%.

Printing and Distribution Services, Andersen Consulting/Arthur Andersen and Co., SC, St. Charles, IL, on-demand printing and distribution. (Kenneth A. Winters, St. Charles, IL.) Production time reduction, 80%; work-in-process inventory reduction, 87%; production flow distance reduction, 80%; reduction of jobs printed for stock (versus for immediate delivery), 88%; printing cost reduction, 30%; printing and warehousing space reduction, 50%.

GOVERNMENT

Canada Post Corporation. See entry under DISTRIBUTION, for this privatized postal/distribution service.

Irish Department of Social Welfare, Social Welfare Services, Dublin, welfare administration. Improved claims processing time, 30%; reduction of inquiries stemming from previous long claim processing time, 60%; personnel reduction, 20%.

Merced County Human Services Agency, Merced, CA, welfare assistance services. (M. Kenneth Bien and Jens Egerland, Sacramento, CA.) Faster eligibility determination, 89%; lower agency employment turnover, 75% improvement; initial client input work reduction, 37%; average caseload handled per caseworker, 140% increase; preprinted forms eliminated, 46%; increased supervisor span of control, 42%; error rate reduction, 75%; reduction of mainframe computer charges, 70%.

United Kingdom Department of Social Security, London, welfare benefits administration. (Ian Charles Watmore, Manchester, UK.) Efficiency improvement, through personnel reduction, 20%.

HEALTH CARE

Kaiser Permanente: Permanente Medical group, Sacramento and South San Francisco medical centers, laboratory services. (James B. Hudak, Jennifer Hinshaw, and Bob Rebitzer, San Francisco.) Reduction (leveling) of peak workload period, 40%; peak period test turnaround time improvement, 20% and 40%.

Lee Memorial Hospital, Ft. Myers, FL, patient care. (Newell I. Troup and Kurt H. Miller, Pittsburgh.) Fewer nursing directors, 32%; central departments full-time equivalents reduction, 37%; length of stay reduction, 12%; quality of care improvement, 62%.

Maricopa Medical Center, Phoenix, AZ, patient care. (Robert B. Lemon, Seattle.) Higher than budgeted cash collections, 43%; higher cash collections, 30%; reduced days in receivables, 50%; productivity increase in billing and collecting, 60%.

CONSTRUCTION

Cubiertas y MZOV, Madrid, all types of construction. (Luis Vassal'lo and Francisco Aguado, Madrid.) Faster closing of the financial books, 75% improvement; speedier materials and subcontracting payables processing, 90% improvement; significant revenue increase due to administrative personnel cost reduction in regional offices and purchased material and subcontracting cost reduction.

TRANSPORTATION

SAS—Scandinavian Airlines System, Stockholm, in-flight services. (Lennart Ulvskog, Stockholm.) Cost reduction, 10%.

UTILITIES

Compania Sevillana de Electricidad, Madrid, electricity. (Basilio Rueda, Madrid.) Billing cycle, 95% reduction; productivity, 20% increase.

Thames Water Logistics, London, water. (Ian Lomas, London.) Reduced the number of water districts, 70%; reduced the number of depots, 56%, and warehouses, 95%.

OIL AND GAS

BP Exploration (Europe) Operating Company Limited, Aberdeen, Scotland, North Sea oil fields. (Norman Cook, London.) Accounting services cost, 18% improvement; reduction of required credit line, 70%; reduction of routine reports, 50%; meeting due dates, 100%; supplier invoices paid by due date, 40% improvement; reduction in joint venture audit claims, 35%; reduction of the value of late unapproved intercompany invoices, 94%. (Also see listing under planned benefits.)

As this book neared completion, a number of Andersen Consulting's clients had projects in process and had not yet implemented all of the changes planned. The following are some of those companies and the goals they plan to achieve.

MANUFACTURING

Geon Company, The (was B.F. Goodrich division), Cleveland, OH, PVC (resin and compound). (Karl E. Newkirk, Cleveland, and Bill McKearn, Milwaukee.) Raw material investment, 75% reduction.

Montgomery KONE, Moline, IL, elevators. (Roger G. Willis, Chicago, and Gene A. Gutman, Dallas.) Bid development time reduction, 99%; fewer bids requiring custom engineering, 66%; improved space utilization, 75%; faster overall inventory turns, 471%; lower total lead time, 83%;

better work-in-process inventory turns, 400%; higher supplier on-time delivery, 233%; on-time shipping performance, 900%.

Quantum: USI Division, Chicago, polyethylene. (Thomas P. Harig and Terence A. Andre, Chicago.) Cash flow improvement, this project, 501%; inventory reduction, 20%; distribution cost reduction, 15–20%; time required to deliver customer orders, 25–30%.

RETAILING

Sears Canada, Inc., Toronto, department store and catalog sales. (Gary C. Garrett and Mary Tolan, Chicago.) Inventory, 50%.

FINANCIAL SERVICES

Komercni Banka, Prague, full-line banking. (Pat O'Neill and Tom Cox, Frankfurt, and Mark Eyen, Columbus.) Increased transactions per teller per day, 430%; increased customers per customer service representative, 350%; increased loans per loan officer, 67%; reduced outward international payment processing time, 93%; reduced inward international payment processing time, 92%.

HEALTH CARE

Hillington Hospital NHS Trust, Uxbridge, Middlesex, UK, hospital care. (William M. Lattimer and Katherine Barnes, London.) Reduction of absenteeism, 25%; length of hospital stay, 22%; X-ray and laboratory testing reduction, 15%.

United Hospital, Grand Forks, ND, patient care. (Richard D. Monroe, Brian E. Younger, and Ronald L. Anderson, Minneapolis.) Reduction in management levels, 25%; reduction in job positions, 60%; key business process cycle time reduction, 30% to 80%; improved documentation cycle time, up to 90%; supply material handling time reduction, 50% to 75%; fewer days of accounts receivable, 20%; patient stay reduction, 5%.

GOVERNMENT

State Superannuation Investment Management Corporation (State Super), Sydney, government employee investment management. (Paul V. Greenhalgh and James Bromfield, Sydney.) Reduced operating cost, 37%; payback period, under 2 years.

TRANSPORTATION

SAS—Scandinavian Airlines System, Stockholm, in-flight services. (Lennart Ulvskog, Stockholm.) Cost reduction, 24% with the same or better customer service.

OIL AND GAS

BP Exploration (Europe) Operating Company Limited, Aberdeen, Scotland, North Sea oil fields. (Norman Cook, London.) Accounting services cost, 24% improvement. (See another entry under completed projects to see previous achievements).

FOOTNOTE REFERENCES TO THE AUTHOR'S PREVIOUS BOOKS

Reinventing the Factory:
Productivity Breakthroughs in Manufacturing Today

By Roy L. Harmon and Leroy D. Peterson

Reinventing the Factory II:
Managing the World Class Factory

By Roy L. Harmon, Foreword by Leroy D. Peterson

Reinventing the Warehouse:
World Class Distribution Logistics

By Roy L. Harmon, Foreword by William C. Capacino

The author's previous books are frequently footnoted sources of definitions and background information for the subject matter covered in *this* book. To help minimize the clutter that numerous footnote references to the one source would cause, this appendix was developed. Footnotes in the book, referencing *Reinventing the Factory, Reinventing the Factory II,* or *Reinventing the Warehouse,* will direct the reader to this appendix. (The cross reference below uses the identifications I, II and *Warehouse* for the three books). Readers interested in selected chapters of this book may wish to first read the portions of the prior books in which important background material can be found. This appendix is organized to facilitate such use. The duplication in this appendix is intentional, intended to be of help to those electing to read only certain chapters, based on their job responsibilities or interests.

Chapter/Footnote   Subject and Source

1/4	Empowerment: *Warehouse,* p. 74.
	Focused business-in-a-business: I, chapter 2.
1/7	Visions, tactics, and strategies: *Warehouse,* pp. 12–13.
2/2	Kanban and electronic kanban: I, pp. 208–15, and *Warehouse,* pp. 212–15.
2/5	Shrinking middlemen: *Warehouse,* pp. 19–22.
2/15	Interactive home shopping: *Warehouse,* pp. 272–73.
3/1	Productive space utilization: I, pp. 5–7, and *Warehouse,* pp. 239–42.
3/4	Factories-within-factories: I, chapter 2, and II, chapter 3.
3/7	U-Form cells: I, pp. 118–23.
3/8	Video teleconferencing: *Warehouse,* pp. 307–12.
3/11	Warehouse design: I, chapter 6, and *Warehouse,* entire book.
4/1	Improvement goals: I, chapter 1, and *Warehouse,* chapter 1.
4/4	Partners in profits: II, chapter 4.
4/9	Cost management: II, chapter 7.
4/11	Economies of scale: I, chapter 2 and p. 259; II, pp. 35–36.
4/12	Multiplant systems: I, pp. 224–25.
4/15	Supplier schedules: I, pp. 220–23.
4/17	Capacity planning forecasting: II, pp. 223–27.
4/21	Resistance to change: II, pp. xv–xviii and pp. 89–92.
4/26	Product line rationalization: II, pp. 182–87.
4/28	Matrix bill of materials: II, pp. 172–75.
4/38	Regional production clusters: II, chapter 2.
4/39	Middleman elimination: *Warehouse,* pp. 19–22.
4/47	Line balance: I, pp. 93–97, 138–41.
4/50	Tool design and manufacturing skills: II, pp. 30, 45.
5/4	Electronic kanban: I, pp. 261–65.
5/24	Pipeline requirements: *Warehouse,* pp. 205–11.
5/25	Single source suppliers: II, pp. 123–26, 220–23.
6/1	Factories-within-factories: I, chapter 2, and II, chapter 3.
6/3	Fail-safe quality design: II, chapter 6.
7/6	Paperless supplier communications: II, pp. 145–49.
8/21	Computer inane manufacturing: II, pp. 14–17.
9/1	Factories-within-factories: I, chapter 2, and II, chapter 3.
9/18	Supplier/customer relationships: I, pp. 257–65; II, chapter 4.
10/4	"Meat-cleaver" downsizing: I, pp. 265–66.

10/9	Space utilization: I, pp. 5–7; *Warehouse,* pp. 240–43.
10/11	Benchmarking: II, pp. 54–56.
10/13	Labor standards: I, pp. 149–51; *Warehouse,* pp.148–49.
10/24	Work hours and business calendars: *Warehouse,* pp. 59–62, 171–75.
10/26	Seasonal demand leveling: *Warehouse,* pp. 77–81.
11/18	Factories-within-factories: I, chapter 2; II, chapter 3.
	Regional production clusters: II, chapter 2.

Appendix 3

DETAILED CONTENTS

Including Chapter Subheadings

BIBLIOGRAPHY

"**B**ooks and papers" and "articles" are the two major sections of this bibliography. The two reference types have been separated to make it easier to identify and obtain personal or business copies. Most of the books are new or still in print and should be easy to obtain. Articles, especially those printed in other countries and for limited distribution are less readily available. Both book and article subsections are further subdivided into works of general interest and works of primary interest to those involved in a specific industry or function, as follows.

BOOKS AND PAPERS

I. General

Abell, Derek F. *Managing with Dual Strategies: Mastering the Present, Preempting the Future.* New York: Free Press, 1993.

Abrams, Malcolm, and Harriet Bernstein. *More Future Stuff: Over 250 Inventions That Will Change Your Life by 2001.* New York: Penguin, 1991.

Bailyn, Lotte. *Breaking the Mold: Women, Men, and Time in the New Corporate World.* New York: Free Press, 1993.

Balm, Gerald J. *Benchmarking: A Practitioner's Guide for Becoming and Staying Best of the Best.* Schaumburg, IL: QPMA Press, 1992.

381

Barnard, William, and Thomas F. Wallace. *The Innovation Edge: Creating Strategic Breakthroughs Using the Voice of the Customer.* Essex Junction, VT: Oliver Wight, 1994.

Batra, Ravi. *The Myth of Free Trade: A Plan for America's Economic Revival.* New York: Scribner, 1993.

Boxwell, Robert J. *Benchmarking for Competitive Advantage.* New York: McGraw-Hill, 1994.

Burleson, Clyde W. *Effective Meetings: The Complete Guide.* New York: Wiley, 1990.

Byham, William C., with George Dixon. *Shogun Management: How North Americans Can Thrive in Japanese Companies.* New York: Harper Business, 1993.

Cali, James F. *TQM for Purchasing Management.* New York: McGraw-Hill, 1993.

Champy, James, and Michael Hammer. *Reengineering the Corporation: A Manifesto for Business Revolution.* New York: Harper, 1993.

Collins, James C., and Jerry I. Porras. *Built to Last: Successful Habits of Visionary Companies.* New York: Harper Business, 1994.

Conway, McKinley. *A Glimpse of the Future: Technology Forecasts for Global Strategists.* Norcross, GA: Conway Data, 1992.

Cornish, Edward, ed. *The 1990s and Beyond.* Bethesda, MD: World Future Society, 1990.

Corrado, Frank M. *Getting the Word Out: How Managers Can Create Value with Communications.* Homewood, IL: Business One Irwin, 1993.

Cortada, James W. *TQM for Sales and Marketing Management.* New York: McGraw-Hill, 1993.

Covey, Stephen R. *The Seven Habits of Highly Effective People: Powerful Lessons in Personal Change.* New York: Simon & Schuster, 1989.

Crosby, Philip B. *Running Things: The Art of Making Things Happen.* New York: McGraw-Hill, 1986.

Dauphinais, William, and Paul O. Pederson, et al. *Better Change: Best Practices for Transforming Your Organization.* Burr Ridge, IL: Irwin, 1995.

Davis, Stan, and Bill Davidson. *2020 Vision: Transform Your Business Today to Succeed in Tomorrow's Economy.* New York: Simon & Schuster, 1991.

Freemantle, David. *Incredible Customer Service.* London: McGraw-Hill, 1993.

Fuld, Leonard M. *The New Competitor Intelligence: The Complete Resource for Finding, Analyzing, and Using Information About Your Competitors.* New York: Wiley, 1995.

Giscard d'Estaing, Valerie-Anne. *World Almanac Book of Inventions.* New York: World Almanac Publications, 1985.

Glass, Harold E., ed. *Handbook of Business Strategy.* Boston: Warren, Gorham & Lamont, 1991.

_____. *Handbook of Business Strategy: 1991/1992 Yearbook.* Boston: Warren, Gorham & Lamont, 1991.

_____. *Handbook of Business Strategy: 1992/1993 Yearbook.* Boston: Warren, Gorham & Lamont, 1992.

Glass, Harold E., Brent N. Cavan, and David Willey, eds. *1994 Handbook of Business Strategy: 1992/1993.* New York: Faulkner & Gray, 1993.

Goodman, Allan E. *A Brief History of the Future.* Boulder, CO: Westview Press, 1993.

Hamel, Gary, and C.K. Prahalad. *Competing for the Future.* New Canaan, CT: Harvard Press, 1994.

Heskett, James L., and John P. Kotter. *Corporate Culture and Performance.* New York: Free Press, 1992.

Johansson, Henry J., Patrick McHugh, A. John Pendlebury, and William A. Wheeler III. *Business Process Reengineering: Breakpoint Strategies for Market Dominance.* New York: Wiley, 1993.

Kaplan, Daniel I., with Carl Rieser. *Service Success! Lessons from a Leader on How to Turn Around a Service Business.* New York: Wiley, 1994.

Levering, Robert, and Milton Moskowitz. *The 100 Best Companies to Work for in America.* New York: Doubleday, 1993.

Lipnack, Jessica, and Jeffrey Stamps. *The Teamnet Factor: Bringing the Power of Boundry Crossing into the Heart of Your Business.* Essex Junction, VT: Oliver Wight, 1993.

Maynard, Herman Bryant, Jr., and Susan E. Mehrtens. *The Fourth Wave: Business in the 21st Century.* San Francisco: Berrett-Koehler, 1993.

Miller, James B., with Paul B. Brown. *The Corporate Coach: How to Build a Team of Loyal Customers and Happy Employees.* New York: St. Martin's, 1993.

Mintzberg, Henry. *The Rise and Fall of Strategic Planning.* New York: Free Press, 1993.

Moody, Patricia E. *Breakthrough Partnering: Creating a Collective Enterprise Advantage.* Essex Junction, VT: Oliver Wight, 1993.

Morris, Daniel C., and Joel S. Brandon. *Reengineering Your Business.* New York: McGraw-Hill, 1993.

Neusch, Donna R., and Alan F. Siebenaler. *The High Performance Enterprise: Reinventing the People Side of Your Business.* Essex Junction, VT: Oliver Wight, 1993.

Pasmore, William A. *Creating Strategic Change: Designing the Flexible, High-Performance Organization.* New York: Wiley, 1994.

Pinchot, Gifford, and Elizabeth Pinchot. *The End of Bureaucracy and the Rise of the Intelligent Organization.* San Francisco: Berrett-Koehler, 1993.

Poirier, Charles C., and William F. Houser. *Business Partnering for Continuous Improvement: Make the Drive for Quality, Productivity and Profit Improvement a Permanent Feature of Your Company.* San Francisco: Berrett-Koehler, 1993.

Rayner, Steven R. *Recreating the Workplace: The Pathway to High Performance Work Systems.* Essex Junction, VT: Oliver Wight, 1993.

Rifkin, Jeremy. *The End of Work: The Decline of the Global Labor Force and the Dawn of the Post-Market Era.* New York: Jeremy Tarcher, 1995.

Roberts, Harry V., and Bernard F. Sergesketter. *Quality Is Personal: A Foundation for Total Quality Management.* New York: Free Press, 1993.

Schorr, John E. *Purchasing in the 21st Century: A Guide to State-of-the-Art Techniques and Strategies.* Essex Junction, VT: Wight, 1992.

Schumann, Paul, Donna Prestwood, Alvin Tong, and John Vanston. *Innovate! Straight Path to Quality, Customer Delight, and Competitive Advantage.* New York: McGraw-Hill, 1994.

Silver, A. David. *Strategic Partnering: How to Join Forces With Other Companies.* New York: McGraw-Hill, 1993.

Spendolini, Michael J. *The Benchmarking Book.* New York: AMACOM, 1992.

Szakonyi, Robert, ed. *Technology Management: Volume 1.* Boston: Auerbach, 1992.

_____. *Technology Management: Volume 2.* Boston: Auerbach, 1993.

Thomas, Dan. *Business Sense: Exercising Management's Five Freedoms.* New York: Free Press, 1993.

Toffler, Alvin. *The Third Wave.* New York: William Morrow, 1980.

_____. *Power Shift.* New York: Bantam Books, 1990.

_____. *Future Shock.* New York: Bantam Books, 1971.

Tomasko, Robert M. *Rethinking the Corporation: The Architecture of Change.* New York: AMACOM, 1993.

Webster, Frederick E., Jr. *Market-Driven Management: Using the New Marketing Concept to Create a Customer-Oriented Company.* New York: Wiley, 1994.

Whiteside, John. *The Phoenix Agenda: Power to Transform Your Workplace.* Essex Junction, VT: Oliver Wight, 1993.

Winslow, Charles D., and William L. Bramer. *Future Work: Putting Knowledge to Work in the Knowledge Economy.* New York: Free Press, 1994.

Zey, Michael G. *Seizing the Future: How the Coming Revolution in Science, Technology, and Industry Will Expand the Frontiers of Human Potential and Reshape the Planet.* New York: Simon & Schuster, 1994.

II. Manufacturing

Abegglen, James C. *Sea Change: Pacific Asia as the New World Industrial Center.* New York: Free Press, 1994.

Alexander, David C., and Babur Mustafa Pulat, eds. *Industrial Ergonomics: Case Studies.* New York: McGraw-Hill, 1991.

Bakerjian, R., ed. *Tool and Manufacturing Engineer's Handbook: Volume 7, Continuous Improvement.* Dearborn, MI: Society of Manufacturing Engineers, 1993.

Bhote, Keki R. *Strategic Supply Management: A Blueprint for Revitalizing the Manufacturer-Supplier Partnership.* New York: AMACOM, 1989.

Bidanda, Bopaya, David I. Cleland, and Shriram R. Dharwadkar. *Shared Manufacturing: A Global Perspective.* New York: McGraw-Hill, 1993.

Bidanda, Bopaya, and David I. Cleland, eds. *The Automated Factory Handbook: Technology and Management.* Blue Ridge Summit, PA: Tab Professional and Reference Books, 1990.

Bockerstette, Joseph A., and Richard Shell. *Time Based Manufacturing.* New York: McGraw-Hill, 1993.

Boothroyd, Geoffrey. *Assembly Automation and Product Design.* New York: Marcel Dekker, 1992.

Brooks, Roger B., and Larry W. Wilson. *Inventory Record Accuracy: Unleashing the Power of Cycle Counting.* Essex Junction, VT: Oliver Wight, 1993.

Burns, Marshall. *Automated Fabrication: Improving Productivity in Manufacturing.* New York: Prentice Hall, 1993.

Cali, James E. *TQM for Purchasing Management.* New York: Mcgraw-Hill, 1993.

Carroll, Paul. *Big Blues: The Unmaking of IBM.* New York: Crown Publishers, 1993.

Cedarleaf, Jay. *Plant Layout and Flow Improvement.* New York: McGraw-Hill, 1994.

Chow, Wee-Min. *Assembly Line Design: Methodology and Applications.* New York: Marcel Dekker, 1993.

Clement, Jerry, Andy Coldrick, and John Sari. *Manufacturing Data Structures: Building Foundations for Excellence with Bills of Material and Process Information.* Essex Junction, VT: Oliver Wight, 1992.

Correll, James G. *Gaining Control: Capacity Management and Scheduling.* Essex Junction, VT: Oliver Wight, 1990.

Dauch, Richard E., with Jack Troyanovich. *Passion for Manufacturing: Real World Advice from Dick Dauch—The Man Who Engineered the Manufacturing Renaissance at Chrysler.* Dearborn, MI: Society of Manufacturing Engineers, 1993.

Davidow, William H., and Michael S. Malone. *The Virtual Corporation: Structuring and Revitalizing the Corporation for the 21st Century.* New York: Harper Business, 1992.

Drexler, K. Eric, and Chris Peterson with Gayle Pergamit. *Unbounding the Future: The Nanotechnology Revolution.* New York: Morrow, 1991.

Erhorn, Craig, and John Stark. *Competing by Design: Creating Value and Market Advantage in New Product Development.* Essex Junction, VT: Oliver Wight, 1994.

Frangos, Stephen J., with Steven J. Bennett. *Team Zebra: How 1500 Partners Revitalized Eastman Kodak's Black and White Film-Making Flow.* Essex Junction, VT: Oliver Wight, 1993.

Galsworth, Gwen. *Smart, Simple Design: A Guide to Variety Effectiveness Planning.* Essex Junction, VT: Oliver Wight, 1994.

George, Stephen. *The Baldrige Quality System: The Do-It-Yourself Way to Transform Your Business.* New York: Wiley, 1992.

Gevirtz, Charles. *Developing New Products with TQM.* New York: McGraw-Hill, 1994.

Goddard, Walter E., and Richard C. Ling. *Orchestrating Success: Improve Control of the Business with Sales and Operations Planning.* Essex Junction, VT: Oliver Wight, 1988.

Greene, James H., ed. *Production and Inventory Control Handbook, Second Edition.* New York: McGraw-Hill, 1987.

Gunn, Thomas G. *In the Age of the Real-Time Enterprise: Managing for Winning Business Performance with Enterprise Logistics Management.* Essex Junction, VT: Oliver Wight, 1994.

Harmon, Roy L., and Peterson, Leroy D. *Reinventing the Factory: Productivity Breakthroughs in Manufacturing Today.* New York: Free Press, 1990.

_____. *Une Usine Pour Gagner: Techniques Pratiques D'Organisation Industrielle.* Paris: InterEditions, 1991.

_____. *Reinventar la Fabrica: Como Introducir Mejoras Sensibles en la Produccion Industrial.* Madrid: CDN (Ciencias de la Direccion), 1990.

_____. *Reinventando a Fabrica: Conceitos Modernas de Produtividade Aplicadas na Pratica.* Rio de Janeiro: Editora Campus, 1991.

_____. *Die Neue Fabrik: Einfacher, Flexibler, Produktiver-Hundert Fälle Erfolgreicher Veränderung.* Frankfurt: Campus Verlag, 1990.

_____. *Reinventare La Fabbrica.* Milan: ISEDI, 1991.

_____. *Rinnovare La Fabbrica: La Produzione Snella Dal Modello Alla Realta.* Milan: II Sole 24 Ore, 1994.

Harmon, Roy L., with Foreword by Leroy D. Peterson. *Reinventing the Factory II: Managing the World Class Factory.* New York: Free Press, 1992.

_____. *Das Management der Neuen Fabrik: Lean Production in der Praxis.* Frankfurt: Campus Verlag, 1993.

_____. *Reinventando a Fabrica II: Conceitos Modernos de Productividade na Practica.* Rio de Janeiro: Editora Campus, 1993.

Heaton, James E., ed. *The Expanding Role of Personal Computers in Manufacturing.* Dearborn, MI: Society of Manufacturing Engineers, 1986.

Hellebust, Karsten G., and Joseph C. Krallinger. *Strategic Planning Workbook,* second edition. New York: Wiley, 1993.

Hudson, William J. *Executive Economics: Forecasting and Planning for the Real World of Business.* New York: Wiley, 1993.

Hunt, V. Daniel. *Reengineering: Leveraging the Power of Integrated Product Development.* Essex Junction, VT: Oliver Wight, 1993.

Hutchins, Greg. *ISO 9000: A Comprehensive Guide to Registration, Audit Guidelines and Successful Certification.* Essex Junction, VT: Oliver Wight, 1993.

Juran, J. M. *Juran on Quality by Design: The New Steps for Planning Quality into Goods and Services.* New York: Free Press, 1992.

Karwowski, Waldemar, and Gavriel Salvendy, eds. *Organization and Management of Advanced Manufacturing.* New York: Wiley, 1994.

Keller, Maryann. *Collision: GM, Toyota, Volkswagen and the Race to Own the 21st Century.* New York: Doubleday, 1993.

Kraar, Louis, and Selichi Takikawa. *Japanese Maverick: Success Secrets of Canon's God of Sales.* New York: Wiley, 1994.

Krugman, Paul. *Peddling Prosperity: Economic Sense and Nonsense in the Age of Diminished Expectations.* New York: W. W. Norton, 1994.

Landvater, Darryl V. *World Class Production and Inventory Management.* Essex Junction, VT: Oliver Wight, 1993.

Martino, Joseph P. *Technological Forecasting for Decision Making.* New York: McGraw-Hill, 1993.

McGee, James V., and Laurence Prusak, with Philip J. Pyburn. *Managing Information Strategically.* New York: Wiley, 1993.

Meyer, Christopher. *Fast Cycle Time: How to Align Purpose, Strategy, and Structure for Speed.* New York: Free Press, 1993.

Miller, Jeffrey G., Arnoud DeMeyer, and Jinichiro Nakane. *Benchmarking Global Manufacturing: Understanding International Suppliers, Customers, and Competitors.* Homewood, IL: Business One Irwin, 1992.

Miller, L. *Concurrent Engineering Design: Integrating the Best Practices for Process Management.* Dearborn, MI: Society of Manufacturing Engineers, 1993.

Miller, Richard K. *Automated Guided Vehicles and Automated Manufacturing.* Dearborn, MI: Society of Manufacturing Engineers, 1987.

Muglia, V.O., ed. *Enterprise Information Exchange: A Roadmap for Electronic Data Interchange for the Manufacturing Company.* Dearborn, MI: Society of Manufacturing Engineers, 1993.

Nyman, Lee R. *Making Manufacturing Cells Work.* Dearborn, MI: Society of Manufacturing Engineers, 1992.

Palmatier, George E., and Joseph S. Shull. *The Marketing Edge: The New Leadership Role of Sales & Marketing in Manufacturing.* Essex Junction, VT: Oliver Wight, 1989.

Proud, John F. *Master Scheduling: A Practical Guide to Competitive Manufacturing.* Essex Junction, VT: Oliver Wight, 1994.

Ross, Alastair. *Dynamic Factory Automation: Creating Flexible Systems for Competitive Manufacturing.* New York: McGraw-Hill, 1992.

Rouse, William B. *Strategies for Innovation: Creating Successful Products, Systems and Organizations.* New York: Wiley, 1992.

Savage, Charles M. *Fifth Generation Management: Integrating Enterprises Through Human Networking.* Burlington, MA: Digital Press, 1990.

Schonberger, Richard J., and Edward M. Knod, Jr. *Synchro Service! The Innovative Way to Build a Dynasty of Customers.* Burr Ridge, IL: Irwin, 1994.

Shank, John K., and Vijay Govindarajan. *Strategic Cost Management: The New Tool for Competitive Advantage.* New York: Free Press, 1993.

Shunk, Dan L. *Integrated Process Design and Development.* Homewood, IL: Business One Irwin, 1992.

Sletten, Eric. *How to Succeed in Exporting and Doing Business Internationally.* New York: Wiley, 1994.

Spencer, Lyle M., Jr., and Signe M. Spencer. *Competence at Work: Models for Superior Performance.* New York: Wiley, 1993.

Suzaki, Kiyoshi. *The New Shop Floor Management: Empowering People for Continuous Improvement.* New York: Free Press, 1993.

Tincher, Michael G. *Top Management's Guide to World Class Manufacturing.* Kansas City: Lowell Press, 1993.

Tobin, Daniel R. *Re-Educating the Corporation: Foundations for the Learning Organization.* Essex Junction, VT: Oliver Wight, 1993.

Vanderspek, Peter G. *Planning for Factory Automation: A Management Guide to World-Class Manufacturing.* New York: McGraw-Hill, 1993.

Wallace, Thomas F. *Customer Driven Strategy: Winning Through Operational Excellence.* Essex Junction, VT: Oliver Wight, 1992.

_____. *MRP II: Making it Happen (Second Edition).* Essex Junction, VT: Oliver Wight, 1992.

Wallace, Thomas F., and Steven J. Bennett, eds. *Instant Access Guide: World Class Manufacturing.* Essex Junction, VT: Oliver Wight, 1994.

Walton, Mary. *The Deming Management Method.* New York: Putnam, 1986.

_____. *Deming Management at Work.* New York: Putnam, 1990.

Watson, Gregory H. *Strategic Benchmarking: How to Rate Your Company's Performance Against the World's Best.* New York: Wiley, 1993.

III. Information Processing

Barry, John A. *Technobabble.* Cambridge, MA: MIT Press, 1991.

Davenport, Tom. *Process Innovation: Re-engineering Work Through Information Technology.* Boston: Harvard Business School, 1993.

Feigenbaum, Edward, Pamela McCorduck, and H. Penny Nii. *The Rise of the Expert Company: How Visionary Companies Are Using Artificial Intellegence to Achieve Higher Productivity and Profits.* New York: Vintage Books, 1988.

Gorman, Michael M. *Enterprise Database in a Client/Server Database.* New York: Wiley, 1994.

Harmon, Paul, and Curtis Hall. *Intelligent Software Systems Development: An IS Manager's Guide.* New York: Wiley, 1993.

Renaud, Paul E. *Introduction to Client/Server Systems: A Practical Guide for Systems Professionals.* New York: Wiley, 1993.

Rheingold, Howard. *The Virtual Community: Homesteading on the Electronic Frontier.* New York: Addison-Wesley, 1993.

Schur, Stephen G. *The Database Factory: Active Database for Enterprise Computing.* New York: Wiley, 1994.

Watkins, Paul R., and Lance B. Eliot, eds. *Expert Systems in Business and Finance: Issues and Applications.* New York: Wiley, 1993.

IV. Logistics

Andersen Consulting. *Wholesale Food Distribution: Today and Tomorrow.* Falls Church, VA: National-American Wholesale Grocers' Association, 1993, pp. 29–31.

Bresticker, Robert B. *American Manufacturing and Logistics in the Year 2001.* Hoffman Estates, IL: Brigadoon Bay Books, 1992.

Harmon, Roy L. *Reinventing the Warehouse: World Class Distribution Logistics.* New York: Free Press, 1993.

_____. *Reinventando A Distribuicao: Logistica de Distribuicao Classe Mundial.* Rio de Janeiro: Editora Campus, 1994.

Harper, Rose. *Mailing List Strategies: A Guide to Direct Mail Success.* New York: McGraw-Hill, 1986.

Mulcahy, David E. *Warehouse Distribution and Operations Handbook.* New York: McGraw-Hill, 1994.

Robeson, James F., and William C. Copacino, eds. *The Logistics Handbook.* New York: Free Press, 1994.

Tompkins, James A., and Dale Harmelink, eds. *The Distribution Handbook.* New York: McGraw-Hill, 1994.

V. Health Care

Barge, Bruce N., and John G. Carlson. *Controlling Health Care and Disability Costs: Strategy Based Solutions.* New York: Wiley, 1993.

Cattalini, David, Karen M. Chin, Jack S. Partridge, and Brett Kirstein. *Ambulatory Surgery Best Practices.* Chicago: Andersen Consulting, 1992.

Ginsberg, Eli. *Health Reform: What Happened and What Needs to Happen.* New York: Free Press, 1993.

Ginsberg, Eli, with Miriam Ostow. *The Road to Reform: The Future of Health Care in America.* New York: Free Press, 1994.

Mechanic, David. *From Advocacy to Allocation: The Evolving American Health Care System.* New York: Free Press, 1986.

_____, ed. *Handbook of Health, Health Care and the Health Professions.* New York: Free Press, 1982.

Starr, Paul. *The Social Transformation of American Medicine: The Rise of a Sovereign Profession and the Making of a Vast Industry.* New York: Basic Books, 1982.

_____. *The Logic of Health Care Reform: Transforming American Medicine for the Better.* New York: Grand Rounds, 1992.

VI. Utilities

Flavin, Christopher, and Nicholas Lenssen. *Beyond the Petroleum Age: Designing a Solar Economy.* Washington, DC: Worldwatch, 1990.
_____. *Powering the Future: Blueprint for a Sustainable Electricity Industry.* Washington, DC: Worldwatch, 1994.

VIII. Government

Abrahamson, Jeffrey. *We, the Jury: The Jury System and the Ideal of Democracy.* New York: Basic Books, 1994.
Alston, Frank M., Margaret M. Worthington, and Louis P. Goldman. *Contracting with the Federal Government: Third Edition.* New York: Wiley, 1992.
_____. *Contracting with the Federal Government: Third Edition 1994 Cumulative Supplement.* New York: Wiley, 1994.
Chance, Edward W. *Visionary Leadership in Schools: Successful Strategies for Developing and Implementing an Educational Vision.* Springfield, IL: Charles C. Thomas, 1992.
Cornish, Edward, ed. *Habitats Tomorrow: Homes and Communities in an Exciting New Era.* Bethesda, MD: World Future Society, 1984.
Gaebler, Ted, and David Osborne. *Reinventing Government: How the Entrepreneurial Spirit Is Transforming the Public Sector.* New York: Plume, 1993.
Garreau, Joel. *Edge City: Life on the Frontier.* New York: Doubleday, 1991.
Hanushek, Eric A., et al. *Making Schools Work: Improving Performance and Controlling Costs.* Washington, DC: Brookings Institution, 1994.
Hickock, Eugene W., and Gary L. McDowell. *Justice vs Law: Courts and Politics in American Society.* New York: Free Press, 1993.
Kotler, Philip, Donald Haider, and Irving Rein. *Marketing Places: Building a Future for Cities, States, and Nations.* New York: Free Press, 1993.
Perelman, Lewis J. *School's Out: Hyperlearning, the New Technology, and the End of Education.* New York: Avon, 1992.
Trattner, Walter I. *From Poor Law to Welfare State: A History of Social Welfare in America.* New York: Free Press, 1994.

IX. Telecommunication

Cornerstone Distance Learning (Product Service Information). Triangle Park, NC: Northern Telecom, 1995.
Heldman, Robert K. *Future Telecommunications: Information, Applications, Services and Infrastructure.* New York: McGraw-Hill, 1993.
Huber, Peter. *1994 and After.* New York: Free Press, 1993.
Maki, Ken. *The AT&T EO Travel Guide: Your Complete Guide to Mobile Computing.* New York: Wiley, 1993.

X. Financial Services

Auriemma, Michael J., and Robert S. Coley. *Bankcard Business.* Washington, DC: American Bankers Association, 1992.

Compton, Eric N. *Principles of Banking: Fourth Edition.* Washington, DC: American Bankers Association, 1991.

Droms, William G. *Finance and Accounting for Nonfinancial Managers: Third Edition.* Reading, MA: Addison-Wesley, 1990.

Friedman, David H. *Money and Banking: Third Edition.* Washington, DC: American Bankers Association, 1993.

Niemira, Michael P., and Philip A. Klein. *Forecasting Financial and Economic Cycles.* New York: Wiley, 1994.

Oppenheim, Peter K. *International Banking: Sixth Edition.* Washington, DC: American Bankers Association, 1991.

Ruth, George E. *Commercial Lending: Second Edition.* Washington, DC: American Bankers Association, 1992.

Seifried, Edmond J. *Economics for Bankers: Second Edition.* Washington, DC: American Bankers Association, 1990.

Steiner, Thomas D., and Diogo B. Teixeira. *Technology in Banking: Creating Value and Destroying Profits.* Homewood, IL: Irwin One, 1990.

Thamara, Thomas. *Banker's Guide to New Growth Opportunities.* Engelwood Cliffs, NJ: Prentice Hall, 1988.

XI. Retailing

Feather, Frank. *The Future Consumer.* Los Angeles: Warwick, 1994.

Snider, Jim, and Terra Ziporyn. *Future Shop: How New Technologies Will Change the Way We Shop and What We Buy.* New York: St. Martin's, 1992.

Stone, Kenneth E. *Competing With the Retail Giants: How to Survive in the New Retail Landscape.* New York: Wiley, 1995.

XII. Transportation

Lowe, Marcia D. *Alternatives to the Automobile: Transport for Livable Cities.* Washington, DC: Worldwatch, 1990.

_____. *Back on Track: The Global Rail Revival.* Washington, DC: Worldwatch, 1994.

Vranich, Joseph. *Supertrains: Solutions to America's Transportation Gridlock.* New York: St. Martins, 1991.

ARTICLES

I. General

Arenberg, Thomas. "Communication: Key to Change." *Milwaukee Sentinel,* January 27, 1992.

_____. "Management Pay for Performance Is a Hot Issue." *Milwaukee Sentinel,* March 23, 1992.

_____. "Right Customer Service Is Competitive Edge." *Milwaukee Sentinel,* April 20, 1992.

_____. "Re-engineering May Improve Your Business." *Milwaukee Sentinel,* June 15, 1992.

_____. "Focused Cells Now Improve Service Industries." *Milwaukee Sentinel,* August 10, 1992.

_____. "Firms Trying New Ways to Increase Productivity." *Milwaukee Sentinel,* October 5, 1992.

_____. "Improvement Fatigue is Curable." *Milwaukee Sentinel,* November 30, 1992.

_____. "How to Help Your Company Survive Beyond This Year." *Milwaukee Sentinel,* February 1, 1993.

_____. "Build Better Bonds Between Business, Suppliers." *Milwaukee Sentinel,* March 29, 1993.

_____. "To Succeed, Avoid Comfort Trap, Take Risks." *Milwaukee Sentinel,* May 24, 1993.

_____. "Look Around; You Can Do Better." *Milwaukee Sentinel,* July 26, 1993.

_____. "Combine Opposing Strategies of Past to Succeed." *Milwaukee Sentinel,* August 30, 1993.

_____. "No Easy Fix." *Information Week,* September 20, 1993.

_____. "Management Most Often Cause for Failure of TQM Programs." *Milwaukee Sentinel,* October 18, 1993.

Aronson, Robert B. "Machine Tool 101: Machine Tools of the Future." *Manufacturing Engineering,* July 1994, pp. 39–45.

Bader, Nancy. "It's About Time, It's About Space." *CFO,* September, 1994, pp. 89–94.

Church, George J. "America's Frightening New World of Work: Jobs in an Age of Insecurity." *Time,* November 22, 1993, pp. 34–39.

Hammer, Michael. "Reengineering Work: Don't Automate, Obliterate." *Harvard Business Review,* July-August 1990, pp. 104–112.

Howard, T.J. "The Office Shapes Up: Future Workspaces Will Be Open, Friendly— Even with the Boss in the Middle." *Chicago Tribune,* August 22, 1993.

Krugman, Paul. "Competitiveness: Does It Matter?" *Fortune,* March 7, 1994, pp. 109–115.

Landro, Laura, David P. Hamilton, and Michael Williams. "Sony Finally Admits Billion-Dollar Mistake: Its Messed-Up Studio." *Wall Street Journal,* November 18, 1994.

Marsh, Barbara. "Chance of Getting Hurt is Generally Far Higher at Smaller Companies." *Wall Street Journal,* February 3, 1994.

Murray, Chuck. "U.S. Focused on the Wrong Vision," *Chicago Tribune,* October 19, 1993.

Narisetti, Raju. "Executive Suites' Walls Come Tumbling Down." *Wall Street Journal,* June 29, 1994.

Pastore, Richard. "The Classless Society: . . . Newer, Sexier Ways to Educate End Users." *CIO Magazine,* September 15, 1992, pp. 42–46.

Selz, Michael. "For Business Survival, Bigger Isn't Necessarily Better." *Wall Street Journal,* October 21, 1994.

Spiker, Barry K. "How to Manage Change." *Power Transmission Design,* October 1992.

Templin, Neal. "Wanted: Six Bedrooms, Seven Baths for Empty Nesters." *Wall Street Journal,* October 17, 1994.

Van, Jon. "Next Cost to Be Cut: The Office." *Chicago Tribune,* February 13, 1994.

II. Manufacturing

Alder, Alan L. "Ford's Dash(ing) Idea." *Chicago Tribune,* October 16, 1994.

Aliga, Alfonso A. "Forging Ahead with Quality Management." *The Business Star* (Manila), February 16, 1993.

_____. "Benchmarking: An Effective Tool for Improving Results." *The Business Star* (Manila), May 18, 1993.

_____. "The Triangle of Productivity." *The Business Star* (Manila), May 25, 1993.

Birchard, R. "Restructuring for Growth." *Enterprise,* Winter 1991, pp. 11–19.

Choy, Audrey. "VW's Flexible-Hours Plan Could Boost German Competitiveness— If It Works." *Wall Street Journal,* October 27, 1994.

Faltermayer, Edmund, with Wilton Woods. "Invest or Die." *Fortune,* February 22, 1993.

Franklin, Stephen. "Union vs. Tiremakers: Wearing Battle Gets Down to Rules of Road for Both." *Chicago Tribune,* October 23, 1994.

Heinzl, Mark. "Inco Moves to Take Miners Out of Mining." *Wall Street Journal,* July 6, 1994.

Mateja, Jim. "A Big Gap Among Makers of Auto Parts, Study Finds." *Chicago Tribune,* November 4, 1994.

Randle, Wilma. "Re-engineering Helps Firms Rethink Future." *Chicago Tribune,* February 28, 1993.

Taylor, Alex, with Sally Solo. "How Toyota Copes With Hard Times." *Fortune,* January 25, 1993.

"The Manufacturing Myth." *The Economist,* March 19, 1994, pp. 91–92.

Williams, Michael. "Back to the Past: Some Plants Tear Out Long Assembly Lines, Switch to Craft Work." *Wall Street Journal,* October 24, 1994.

Yates, Ronald E. "Detroit's Windshield of Opportunity Shrinks." *Chicago Tribune,* October 24, 1994.

III. Information Processing

Barber, Norman F. "EDI: Making it Finally Happen." *P & IM Review,* June 1991, pp. 35–40, 49.

Blades, John. "Books on Disk: An Idea Whose Time Has Come." *Chicago Tribune,* July 12, 1994.

Bulkeley, William M. "Speech Recognition Gets Cheaper and Smarter." *Wall Street Journal,* June 6, 1994.

Christian, Sue Ellen. "For Office on Wheels, Superhighway Is Here." *Chicago Tribune,* July 12, 1994.

Coates, James. "Key Part in Pocket PC? The Keyboard, Stupid." *Chicago Tribune,* June 5, 1994.

_____. "IBM Gives Windows Hearing." *Chicago Tribune,* November 9, 1994.

_____. "Promiscuous Path: Britannica Sheds Loyalty to Ink on Paper." *Chicago Tribune,* December 12, 1994.

de Lama, George. "Citizens Plugging Into Computer Government." *Chicago Tribune,* November 14, 1993.

Elliott, Stephen A., and David A. Stadler. "Remake Your Business." *Inform,* February 1992.

Falchero, Alessandro. "Le Flessibilita Strategiche Dei Nuovi Sistemi Informatici." *L' Impresa,* issue 2 (1993), pp. 30–34.

Grant, Linda. "Green Light for Growth: Xerox Bets on a New Generation of Digital Office Equipment." *U.S. News & World Report,* August 15, 1994.

Jackson, Ted. "The Human Touch: Computer Programs That Think Like People Put Some Money Managers on Cutting Edge." *Chicago Tribune,* November 29, 1994.

Pope, Ken. "The European Software Market: Hard Times Ahead for New Software Vendors." *The Journal of European Business,* May/June 1992, pp. 37–39.

Seigel, Jessica. "Many Booksellers Say They See the Interactive Handwriting on the Wall." *Chicago Tribune,* June 1, 1994.

Sussman, Vic. "News of the Wired: The Perils and Promise of Electronic Newspapering." *U.S. News & World Report,* May 16, 1994, pp. 60–62.

IV. Logistics

Copacino, William C. "Promoting the Logistics Function." *Traffic Management,* October 1989, pp. 35–36.

_____. "Tackling Unproductive Inventories." *Traffic Management,* November 1989, pp. 35–36.

Henkoff, Ronald. "Delivering the Goods." *Fortune,* November 28, 1994, pp. 64–78.

Maeda, Kenzo. "Reinventing Logistics." *Nikkei Logistics,* May 10, 1993, pp. 53–56.

Young, David. "Middlemen Caught in Evolving Market." *Chicago Tribune,* November 29, 1993.

V. Health Care

Beaubien, Greg. "Why Get Old." *Chicago Tribune,* October 20, 1994.

Cattalini, David. "Best Practices in Ambulatory Surgery." *Healthcare Forum Journal,* January/February 1993, pp. 28–29.

_____. "How Top Performers Manage Materials in Ambulatory Surgery." *Materials Management,* December 1992, pp. 16–17.

Emmel, Robert S. "Hospital Environments: The Future Lies With Business Recovery Planning." *Contingency Journal,* May/June 1991, pp. 8–10.

Luebke, Cathy. "Re-engineering Accounting Office Paves Way for New Mainframe." *The Business Journal* (Phoenix), June 19, 1992, pp. 23, 29.

Miller, Kurt, and Francine Gomberg. "Focused Care Centers, Decentralization, Cross Training, and Care Paths Define World Class Healthcare at Florida's Lee Memorial." *Strategies for Healthcare Excellence* (Santa Barbara), March 1992, pp. 1–7.

Miller, Kurt, and William Johnson. "Lee Memorial Hospital Records Positive Early Results for First of Several Focused Care Centers, Foundation of Hospitalwide Conversion." *Strategies for Healthcare Excellence* (Santa Barbara), October 1992, pp. 1–8.

Morris, Steven. "Health Providers Plan Electronic Network." *Chicago Tribune,* November 21, 1994.

Naj, Amal Kumar. "Big Medical-Equipment Makers Try Ultrasound Market." *Wall Street Journal,* November 30, 1993.

Nemes, Judith. "Overhaul Was Only First Step at Phoenix Facility." *Modern Healthcare,* February 15, 1993.

O'Leary, Meghan. "Reinventing the Heal." *CIO.* February 1993, pp. 32–40.

Scism, Leslie. "New York Finds Fewer People Have Health Insurance a Year After Reform." *Wall Street Journal,* May 27, 1994.

VI. Utilities

Associated Press. "New Light Bulb Seen as Future Energy Saver." *Chicago Tribune,* October 22, 1994.

Dellios, Hugh. "Brewer Fights to 'Stand Clear' of Recycled Water." *Chicago Tribune,* November 23, 1994.

"Energy: The New Prize." *The Economist,* June 18, 1994, pp. 3–18.

Linden, Eugene. "A Sunny Forecast: Always Cleaner Than Fossil Fuels, Renewable Power Sources May Soon Be Just as Cheap." *Time,* November 7, 1994, pp. 66–67.

VII. Gas and Oil

Gibbs, Everett S. "U.S. Independents Face New Age For Gas Under FERC Order 636," *Oil & Gas Journal,* October 19, 1992, pp. 49–54.

VIII. Government

Anderson, Jon. "The Global Classroom: New Technology May Mean Never Needing to Go to School." *Chicago Tribune,* October 25, 1994.

Associated Press. "U.S. Prison Population Near 1 Million." *Chicago Tribune,* June 2, 1994.

——. "Nation's Prison Population Now Exceeds Million." *Chicago Tribune,* October 28, 1994.

——. "U.S. Planning to Streamline Social Security: Private Business May Do Some Work." *Chicago Tribune,* April 10, 1995.

Barrett, Katherine, and Richard Greene. "No One Runs the Place: The Sorry Mismanagement of America's Colleges and Universities." *FW,* March 15, 1994, pp. 38–46.

Beck, Joan. "Practicing Stupid Jury Tricks: Picking 12 People Who Are a Cross-Section of the Population Is a Legal Nightmare." *Chicago Tribune,* December 15, 1993.

Becker, Robert. "Big Savings Found for Cities That Privatize." *Chicago Tribune,* March 15, 1994.

Benjamin, Daniel. "Giant Under Stress: With Unemployment Climbing in Germany, So Are Social Tensions." *Wall Street Journal,* November 4, 1993.

Bidinotto, Robert James. "Must Our Prisons Be Resorts?" *Reader's Digest,* November 1994, pp. 65–70.

Cohen, Laurence D. "Privatizing Public Schools Works." *Chicago Tribune,* November 25, 1994.

Christian, Sue Ellen. "Leaving City, Cook Behind: Inner Suburbs See Own Losses." *Chicago Tribune,* November 18, 1994.

"Computer Catch-up." *FW Financial World,* March 15, 1994.

"Education in Germany: The Next Generation." *The Economist,* August 20, 1994, p. 44.

Gratteau, Hanke, and Sarah Talalay. "Delivering Changes: Sweeping Reform Sought in Mail 'Culture'." *Chicago Tribune,* May 31, 1994.

Grossman, Ron. "SATs Get Dumber: New Scores Will Be Higher, but Standards Lower." *Chicago Tribune,* April 9, 1995.

Hall, Jon D., Ratu Kamlani, and Suneel Ratan. "Social Security: The Numbers Don't Add Up—and the Politicians Won't Own Up." *Time,* March 20, 1995, pp. 24–32.

Klein, Joe. "If Chile Can Do It . . . Couldn't (North) America Privatize Its Social-Security System?" *Time,* December 12, 1994, p. 50.

Knight Ridder. "Computer Technology May Someday Predict Which Patients Live, Die." *Chicago Tribune,* November 25, 1994.

Lapidus, June, and Deborah M. Figart. "Cut Welfare by Pay-Equity Reform." *Chicago Tribune,* July 26, 1994.

Lubman, Sarah. "Tests to Gauge Student Ability Create a Furor." *Wall Street Journal,* May 31, 1994.

McGinley, Laurie. "Flexing Muscles: Clinton's Regulators Zero In on Companies With Renewed Fervor." *Wall Street Journal,* October 19, 1994.

Nelson, Julie F. "GIS as Change Agent—Friend or Foe," *Geo Information Systems,* July/August, 1991.

Reardon, Patrick T. "More Chicagoans Find It Isn't Their Kind of Town." *Chicago Tribune,* November 28, 1993.

Reuters. "In 2050, Computer May Be Collegian's 'Campus'." *Chicago Tribune,* November 7, 1994.

Ricks, Thomas E. "Pentagon, in Streamlining Effort, Plans to Revamp Its Purchasing Procedures." *Wall Street Journal,* June 30, 1994.

Snow, Tony. "Isn't It Time to Get This House in Order?" *Chicago Tribune,* July 25, 1994.

Taylor, Marianne. "IRS Boss Looks to Compute a Higher Collection Rate." *Chicago Tribune,* November 7, 1994.

"Truely Digital." *The Economist,* May 21, 1994, p. 94.

Van, Jon. "Fingerprint Scans Pose Uses, Abuses." *Chicago Tribune,* June 6, 1994.

Warsh, David. "Study: More Choice—Not Spending More—Is Answer for Better Schools." *Chicago Tribune,* November 27, 1994.

Wildavsky, Rachel. "What's Behind Success in School?" *Reader's Digest,* October, 1994, pp. 49–55.

IX. Telecommunication

Carlton, Jim, and Don Clark. "Video Conferencing Takes Center Stage." *Wall Street Journal,* November 11, 1994.

Hass, Nancy. "Bound to the Printed Word: The Info Highway: Should the Nation's Newspapers Stick to the Business They Know Best?" *Newsweek,* June 20,1994, pp. 52–53.

Jones, Tim. "Time Pinch Controls How Americans Use Media." *Chicago Tribune,* November 7, 1994.

Reuters. "FAA Navigates New Uses for Satellite Technology." *Chicago Tribune,* November 20, 1994.

Richards, Bill. "Many Rural Regions Are Growing Again; A Reason: Technology." *Wall Street Journal,* November 21, 1994.

Van, Jon. "Ameritech Eyes Home Shopping." *Chicago Tribune,* June 2, 1994.

_____. "Interactive TV May Get Muted Reception." *Chicago Tribune,* June 13, 1994.

_____. "Voice-activated Phoning in Pipeline for Callers Wary About 11-digit Dialing." *Chicago Tribune,* February 20, 1995.

Yong-bom, Kim. "Korea Launches 1st Stage of Info Super Highway Project." *The Korea Times* (Seoul), April 23, 1994.

Ziegler, Bart. "Video Conference Calls Change Business," *Wall Street Journal,* October 12, 1994.

X. Financial Services

Associated Press. "Gap Still Broad: Twice as Many Blacks as Whites Are Rejected." *Chicago Tribune,* October 27, 1994.

"Bankers Trust's 2020 Vision." *The Economist,* March 26, 1994.

Baumgarten, Nancy. "Insuring Victory: USAA Uses Technology to Improve Customer Service." *Outlook,* Chicago: Andersen Consulting, 1993, pp. 32–33.

Berton, Lee. "New Form Seeks More Data from Business Borrowers: Banks May Require Additional Information to Help Cut Number of Bad Loans." *Wall Street Journal,* December 16, 1993.

Bleakley, Fred R. "Fast Money: Electronic Payments Now Supplant Checks at More Large Firms." *Wall Street Journal,* April 13, 1994.

_____. "How They Bounce! Bad-Check Toll Rises as It Becomes Easier to Pull Off Such Fraud." *Wall Street Journal,* December 2, 1993.

Bryan, Lowell, and Diana Farrell. "The Savings Surge." *Wall Street Journal,* November 7, 1994.

Coates, James, and Jan Crawford Greenburg. "Microsoft Case Enters New Realm." *Chicago Tribune,* April 30, 1995.

Coleman, Brian. "Central Europe Finds Future Is Plastic as Banks Rush to Promote Credit Cards." *Wall Street Journal,* April 22, 1994.

Crawford, William B., Jr. "First Chicago Trust Opens Gates: Internet to Provide Stockholders Electronic Access to Companies." *Chicago Tribune,* December 13, 1994.

Flaherty, Francis. "The Direct Approach: No-Load Stocks to Let Investors Bypass Brokers." *Chicago Tribune,* February 20, 1995.

Handley, John. "Computer Loans a Laptop Away." *Chicago Tribune,* October 30, 1994.

Jackson, William. "TRIUMPH Charges Forward: Giving Credit Where Credit Is Due." *Outlook,* Chicago: Andersen Consulting, 1993, pp. 23–24.

Leckey, Andrew. "Electronic Banking Hits Home." *Chicago Tribune,* November 3, 1994.

Lohse, Deborah. "Log On: You May as Well Get Used to It: High-tech Portfolio Management Is Coming." *Wall Street Journal,* December 9, 1994.

Marpe, James. "Image Technology in Banking: Enhancing Your Image," *Bank Management,* October 1990.

McCarroll, Thomas. "No Checks. No Cash. No Fuss?" *Time,* May 9, 1994, pp. 60–62.

Murray, Matt. "Banc One to Cut Work Force by 4,300 and Shut Down 100 Bank Branches." *Wall Street Journal,* November 22, 1994.

Paré, Terence P., with Patty de Llosa. "The New Merger Boom: New Combinations Are Reshaping America's Largest Industries, with Consequences for All. Shareholders Could Be the Big Losers." *Fortune,* November 28, 1994, pp. 95–106.

Pihl, Waino H., and Michael L. Wambay. "Matching Customer Segments with Products and Delivery Channels to Improve Profitability," in *Retail Distribution Strategies 2000.* Washington, DC: American Bankers Association, 1992, pp. 1–16.

Rudolph, Barbara. "Some Like Them Hot: A Global Lust for Dollars and Advanced Imaging Techniques Have Produced a Wave of Counterfeiting." *Time,* November 19, 1994, p. 76.

Schmeltzer, John. "Tack On $3 for That Trip to the Bank." *Chicago Tribune,* April 26, 1995.

_____. "Banking by Wire to Touch Nerves?" *Chicago Tribune,* May 24, 1995.

Schodolski, Vincent J. "No Cash, Plastic: Soon We'll Ship Out Smart Cards to Upload, Download Money." *Wall Street Journal,* June 19, 1994.

"Share Dispensers." *The Economist,* September 3, 1994, p. 73.

Springsteel, Ian. "The Best Road Traveled." *CFO Magazine,* September, 1994, pp. 103–106.

Stangenes, Sharon. "Banks Plan Computer Payment System for Business Clients." *Chicago Tribune,* March 14, 1994.

_____. "Plastic Advances To Compete with Travelers Checks in Test." *Chicago Tribune,* December 13, 1994.

Storts, William E., and Waino H. Pihl. "Assignment for Survival: Reinvent the Bank," *American Banker,* May 19, 1992.

"The Smart Card Cashes In." *The Economist,* January 29, 1994, pp. 73–74.

Van, Jon. "Interactive Service Will Turn Home Telephones into ATMs." *Chicago Tribune,* November 10, 1993.

Washburn, Gary. "CTA Card May Open a New Era: High-tech Fare Method on Way." *Chicago Tribune,* April 6, 1994.

XI. Retailing

Blumenthal, Karen. "Stores Tinker with the Hours They Stay Open." *Wall Street Journal,* October 28, 1994.

Brent, Paul. "Store Chains Put the Squeeze on Suppliers: Pressure to Adopt New Technology, Accept Concessions Puts Heat on Small Suppliers." *The Financial Post* (Toronto), November 26, 1994.

Clark, Don. "Microsoft, Visa to Jointly Develop PC Electronic-Shopping Software." *Chicago Tribune,* November 9, 1994.

De Lisser, Eleena. "Fast-Food Drive-Throughs Lose Speed." *Wall Street Journal,* October 27, 1994.

Greenberg, Daniel S. "Economic Villians: Overloaded Closets Help to Hurt the Economy." *Chicago Tribune,* November 4, 1994.

Ono, Yumiko. "Contacts by Mail Change Industry's Look." *Wall Street Journal,* October 11, 1994.

Ryan, Nancy. "Dominick's Takes Stab at Takeout," *Chicago Tribune,* November 14, 1993.

Schmeltzer, John. "Saturday Night Fever." *Chicago Tribune,* November 7, 1994.

Schoolman, Judith. "Big Savings Are In the Bag at These Food Stores." *Chicago Tribune,* November 7, 1994.

"The Interactive Bazaar Opens." *The Economist,* August 20, 1994, pp. 49–51.

Young, David. "Beef on the Comeback Trail; Restaurant Steak Sales Sizzle." *Chicago Tribune,* July 6, 1994.

XII. Transportation

Arndt, Michael. "Rail Workers Feeling Efficiency's Sting." *Chicago Tribune,* February 27, 1994.

Dahl, Jonathan. "Airlines Try Ticketless Systems, Giving Passengers New Gripes." *Wall Street Journal,* November 30, 1994.

Goering, Laurie. "High Tech Is Fertile Ground for Farmers: Satellite, Computer Control Join the Tractor." *Chicago Tribune,* November 7, 1993.

Hirsch, James S. "Add 'No Place to Park' to Flier's Airport Laments." *Wall Street Journal,* November 30, 1994.

_____. "The Paperless Society Takes a Leap Forward with a Ticketless Airline." *Chicago Tribune,* October 22, 1993.

Maclean, John M. "Rail Equipment Company Learns ABCs of Success: With Doom Barreling Down, Management, Workers Switch Tracks." *Chicago Tribune,* November 6, 1994.

Moseley, Ray. "Channel Tunnel Train Flies into the Future." *Chicago Tribune,* November 20, 1994.

Pearl, Daniel. "Railroads Are Being Pushed by the U.S. to Hasten Installation of Safety Systems." *Wall Street Journal,* July 13, 1994.

Robichaux, Mark. "TV Shopping Losing Its Shine for Retailers." *Wall Street Journal,* November 22, 1994.

Tagliabue, John. "Fiat Out to Tip Amtrak in Its Favor." *Chicago Tribune,* November 27, 1994.

Washburn, Gary. "Expressways Are Doomed, a Mayor Says." *Chicago Tribune,* June 13, 1994.

Ziemba, Stanley. "Train from Spain fit for Plains." *Chicago Tribune,* November 27, 1994.

INDEX

ABOUT THE AUTHOR

ROY L. HARMON founded Andersen Consulting's manufacturing productivity practice and provides advice to 1,000 clients throughout the world. He is co-author of *Reinventing the Factory,* and author of *Reinventing the Factory II* and *Reinventing the Warehouse,* all published by The Free Press.